The Management of Information Systems

the MANAGEMENT of INFORMATION SYSTEMS

KENNETH L. KRAEMER

WILLIAM H. DUTTON

ALANA NORTHROP

COLUMBIA UNIVERSITY PRESS

New York   1981

Library of Congress Cataloging in Publication Data

Kraemer, Kenneth L.
The management of information systems.

Bibliography: p.
Includes index.
1. Municipal government—United States—Data processing.
I. Dutton, William H., 1947–   joint author.
II. Northrop, Alana, 1949–   joint author. III. Title.
JS344.E4K72   352′.00028′54   80-12862
ISBN 0-231-04886-6

Columbia University Press
New York   Guildford, Surrey

This book is dedicated to collaborative research,
which can add to knowledge of the world
and make close and lasting friends.

Contents

Preface

THE RESULTS of this study challenge currently prevailing theories about the impacts of computing in organizations. Generally, promoters of computing, such as computer manufacturers and software vendors, claim that computing will improve the productivity, decision making, and work environment of people within organizations. Our initial concern, shared by many critics of the technology, was that the claims of these promoters were grossly exaggerated. And it was our initial assumption that even if the promoter's benefit claims were basically correct, the benefits would be offset by problems with computing. Thus, in our intensive study of 42 American cities, we sought to examine whether the benefit claims for computing were valid.

Broadly, we have found that, *when well-managed*, computers have real payoffs for government operations. Unfortunately, computer technology is not well managed in most cities. As a consequence, we have found that computers generate problems that, while not extreme, are often pervasive. Moreover, many of the payoffs have fallen far short of expectations.

However, the experience of a few cities, which have successfully managed the technology, indicates that the expected payoffs can be reasonably well achieved. The key to the computer's successful management lies in the policies used for the implementation of computing. Our study concludes that the single most important policy influencing the successful implementation of computing is a commitment to advanced technology. Specifically, we found that the more advanced the technology, the greater the payoffs from the computer's application. Other policies, such as user involvement and decentralization of computing, are important too, but currently they appear to have secondary importance in comparison with the state of the technology.

These results were surprising to us and undoubtedly will be

satisfying to some people, while disconcerting to others. Of course, promoters of computing will conclude that our study has only confirmed what they have known all along, and what their customers have known, as evidenced by their continuing investments in computer technology. However, the benefits of advanced technology are far less dramatic than suggested by the promoters. And the necessity for advanced technology places cities in a real dilemma. In order to approximate the potential benefits of the technology, cities must invest heavily in advanced technology. Yet most cities are not technologically advanced today, and they cannot bridge the gap between where they are and the leading edge of the technology, let alone keep up with the technology. The current era of tax limitations and inflation only exacerbates the problem. Therefore, in the foreseeable future, many cities will not achieve the benefits expected from the technology.

The critics of the growing trend toward computer automation in organizations might be concerned that our results oversimplify the very complex impacts of computing, and that they inadequately account for many subtle and indirect effects of this technology on issues ranging from the invasion of personal privacy to the cultural impacts of an increasingly computerized society. However, we think it is extremely important to note that this book presents the first systematic, empirical analysis of the actual organizational impacts from computing in local governments. And while there are, of course, impacts that we could not consider in the scope of our analysis, we believe that our analysis will withstand critical review. Moreover, we hope that it will stimulate focused and sharpened debate about the impacts of computers and the policies needed for successful management of computing in all organizations.

Most importantly, we hope that this book communicates our concern that many critics and promoters of computer technology ignore the contingent nature of computer impacts. We have found that computer impacts vary considerably, given the nature of the tasks to which they are applied, the character of the organizations that use them, and the management policies that govern the implementation of computer-based systems. Computers are not politically neutral, but neither do they have a systematic bias that uniformly benefits a particular interest. Rather, computers are a politically malleable technology, which can be shaped to serve a variety of interests if we gain a better understanding of these contingencies.

The plan of this book is as follows: Part 1 presents our research problem and describes our theoretical and methodological approach. Chapter 1 places issues concerning the management of information systems in the context of broader issues regarding the implementation of technology-as-an-administrative-reform in American local governments. It then turns to a discussion of our theoretical framework for exploring alternative approaches to the management of information systems. Chapter 2 presents our methodological approach to analyzing the impacts of alternative policies for the management of information systems.

Part 2 presents our research findings. Chapter 3 demonstrates the need for research aimed at improving the performance of computer-based information systems by showing how computing has become a major problem for urban managers. Chapters 4 to 8 focus on different kinds of information-processing tasks in local government and follow a common organization. Each chapter describes a specific information-processing task (e.g., budget control) in terms of its generic attributes, the rationale for its automation, and the alternative strategies for its implementation. The chapter then shows how this task has been automated, explores the impacts of automation, and looks at the relative success of alternative strategies for the implementation of computer-based systems for the task. Chapters 4 to 8 assess the following information-processing tasks: traffic-ticket processing, detective investigative support, patrol-officer support, police-manpower allocation, budget control, and policy analysis.

Part 3 summarizes our research by comparing findings across our six information-processing tasks. This comparative analysis yields a set of practical policy recommendations for the management of information systems. These should be considered in light of the more specific policy recommendations found at the conclusion of each chapter in Part 2.

We recommend that our readers follow the organization of the book. However, urban managers, data-processing specialists, and other practitioners might wish to begin with chapter 9 to obtain an overview of our findings and policy recommendations and also to determine which preceding chapters might be of particular value to concerns in their organization. Scholars will be especially interested in chapter 1, for this chapter integrates this study with a broad array of literature in public and business administration, organization theory, political science, and computer science.

About the URBIS Project

This book is a product of the Urban Information Systems (URBIS) Project, carried out during 1973–1978 by the URBIS Research Group of the Public Policy Research Organization (PPRO) at the University of California, Irvine. The project was supported by a grant from the National Science Foundation (NSF). The purpose of this project was to assess the state-of-the-art in local government computing, to evaluate its impact on government services and management decision-making, and to develop recommendations that local managers and officials could implement to make better use of information technology.

The project was conducted in two phases. The first phase was an extensive study of computing in over 700 U.S. cities and counties. This phase documented the kinds of data-processing activities ongoing, the extensiveness of computing use, the impacts of computing and the problems with computing as perceived by mayors, city managers, county administrators, county-board chairmen, and other chief executive officers in local governments. Results of this phase have been published in numerous articles appearing in practitioner and academic journals and in several books.

During the second phase, members of the project collected information in 42 cities for assessing the impact of specific policies for the management of computing in cities. Using this information, the study team assessed under what conditions it is advantageous, for example, to centralize computing services under one department, as opposed to allowing several departments to have their own computing. The second phase of the project has resulted in this book, which presents the findings about policies and impacts of computing in cities, and which can serve as a guide to officials concerned with the management of computing.

We began writing this book in the summer of 1977—a process that lasted over two years. However, books based on large-scale, multi-disciplinary research projects like URBIS are products of a larger team effort than suggested by the authorship of individual project publications. Through the life of the URBIS project, we have become indebted to the critical and unique contributions of many people who should share whatever credit this book deserves. Therefore, we would like to acknowledge the contributions of other members of the URBIS project to this book.

First, we thank our co-principal investigators on the URBIS project, whose scholarly contributions to the project and this book go far beyond our direct citations. Alexander Mood—the project's mathematician, statistician, and guru—was the key to shaping the overall "future cities" research design of the URBIS project. Rob Kling—the project's computer scientist, sociologist, and humanist—has been a continuing source of insights regarding the social role and impacts of computer technology. And, James Danziger—political scientist and master of communication—has driven us to question continually the litany of benefits often attributed to computing and has focused our attention on the political role of technical experts in the policy process.

Many other participants in the URBIS project made important contributions to the ideas presented in this book. Robert Emrey, Henry Fagin, James Jewett, Fred Tonge, and Enzo Valenzi participated in the design of the URBIS project during the summer of 1973. The importance of their early work is not forgotten.

Debora Dunkle, John Leslie King, Joseph R. Matthews, Linda Hackathorn, and David Schetter were invaluable to the URBIS project. Dr. Dunkle's talents in the art of social-science data analysis were critical to the substantive interpretations and methodological rigor of this book. Dr. King has been a critical intellectual resource for the project through his involvement in the field research and group discussions, and his insightful comments on the evolving drafts of this book. Joseph Matthews postponed a successful consulting career while involved with URBIS. His constant attention to the needs of practitioners is responsible for much of the project's value to local government officials. Linda Hackathorn assumed the staggering burden of managing the census-survey field operations and data reduction activities. Her competence is largely responsible for the quality of the URBIS data. David Schetter has been such a talented research administrator that we have often forgotten the difficulty of administering a multidisciplinary project in a complex bureaucratic environment of university and governmental agencies, procedures, regulations, and accounting systems.

In emphasizing the unique contributions of project participants, we do not wish to neglect their common contribution.

Throughout the project, we all learned from one another and so thoroughly integrated one another's perspectives that we frequently found it difficult to adequately acknowledge a single individual's contribution. Nowhere is this more true than in this book. Although the analysis and the writing were the product of the authors, we benefited immensely from the interactions with all of our colleagues during the entire project and wish to acknowledge their substantial indirect contribution.

We also acknowledge the support of others outside the URBIS Project. Lawrence Williams of the National League of Cities, Mark Keene and Stanley Wolfson of the International City Management Association, John Thomas and Bernard Hillenbrand of the National Association of Counties, and Robert Havlick and James Bohnsack of Public Technology, Incorporated, gave us the benefit of their knowledge about local governments, helped us to gain the support of specific cities and counties for our research, and helped to disseminate our research findings to their membership. The URBIS National Advisory Committee—Ruth Davis, National Bureau of Standards; Edward Hearle of Booz, Allen, and Hamilton; Gerald Fox of Wichita Falls; Robert Goldman of the Association of Bay Area Governments; Peter McCloskey of the Computer and Business Equipment Manufacturers Association; Ralph Young of Fairfax County; Robert Crain of the Rand Corporation; Donald Luria of the Bureau of Census; and Daniel McGraw of the State of Minnesota—provided critical review of our work at several stages of the project and lent us their considerable expertise. Our NSF Program Managers—Vaughn Blankenship, Richard Mason, and Frank Scioli—kept us continually aware of the need to address the policy issues as well as the intellectual issues of the research. Moreover, they helped us in a very practical way by bringing such experts as E. S. Savas, Bert Swanson, and Merrill Shanks to critique both the substance and the methods of the project at major junctures.

Many academic and professional colleagues contributed their comments and criticisms to early drafts of this book: Henry C. Lucas, John Kaiser, AnnaBelle Sartore, Tug Tumaru, John Van Maanen, Myron Weiner, and Paul Whisenand. Additional thanks are due to Deborah Silverman for her editing ability, which could turn some stiff academic passages into clearer-flowing English.

The PPRO professional staff rendered essential support throughout the project, and deserve special mention for their patience and competence. Doris McBride and Shirley Hoberman kept the project moving and on target. The PPRO secretarial staff, Nancy Brock, Elizabeth Kelly, Georgine Webster, Helen Sandoz, and Sherry Merryman typed, retyped, and always improved the torrent of manuscripts that flowed from the project.

Despite the many contributions to this study, any errors or omissions are the responsibility of the authors. And the order of authorship is random to denote equal contribution of the authors.

Kenneth L. Kraemer, *University of California, Irvine*
William H. Dutton, *University of Southern California*
Alana Northrop, *California State University, Fullerton*

All three authors are also affiliated with the
Public Policy Research Organization,
University of California, Irvine.

Part One

CHAPTER ONE
The Management
of Computer Technology

THE PERFORMANCE of organizations is bounded by the quality of their planning, management, and operational decisions. In turn, the quality of organizational decisions, from the most routine day-to-day operational decisions to the most novel planning decisions, is bounded by the availability of timely, accurate, and relevant information. Thus many efforts to improve organizational performance have been aimed at improving the sources, nature, selection, and utilization of information about the internal and external organizational environment.

Since the 1950s, organizations have been computerizing the storage, retrieval, and processing of huge amounts of data as a technological approach to improving the content and flow of information within organizations and between organizations and the broader society. However, such informational improvements have not always followed from the development of computer-based information systems. And computerization has often created new problems for organizations. In short, the introduction of computers and related telecommunications technologies may have created a "technological revolution" for modern organizations, but an "information revolution" has not clearly materialized. For these reasons, modern organizations are becoming increasingly concerned with how to manage computer-based information systems more successfully.

Until now, our knowledge of the most successful policies for the management of information systems has been based on a handful of case studies and anecdotal evidence. Little or no systematic empirical evidence has been available on the organizational impacts of computer-based information systems, or on the effects of alternative policies for the management of such systems.

In order to provide such evidence, this book concentrates on the management of computer-based information systems in American cities. We wanted to find out how computer-based information systems affect the performance of such local government information-processing tasks as traffic-ticket processing, detective investigative support, and policy analysis, and why computing affects performance as it does. We then asked how local government officials could implement computer-based information systems in ways that would improve the performance of such information-processing tasks.

In answering these questions, this book provides the first systematic, empirical assessment of the organizational impacts of computer technology and the consequences of alternative management policies for the implementation of computer-based information systems. In addition, we provide an innovative framework for understanding the various theoretical assumptions underlying different approaches to the management of such systems as well as other communication technologies in organizations. We arrive at a set of findings that are likely to be generalizable beyond the local government setting. But before we address these issues, it is important to show how the development of computer-based information systems is a recent manifestation of a much broader history in the development of public technologies designed to reform the administration of American local governments.

Technology and the Reform of Local Government

Improving the planning, management, and delivery of public services is an old problem for local governments. As far back as the 1920s, reformers were concerned with transforming local governments into "businesslike" organizations in which services could be efficiently provided without favoritism.

The earliest efforts to accomplish this transformation were aimed at intragovernmental, structural change. City planning departments were introduced during this period to create a formal planning capacity in government. In addition, the council-manager plan with nonpartisan ballots and at-large elections was introduced to improve the management capabilities of government.

At mid-century, however, emphasis shifted to intergovernmental reforms (Campbell and Bahl 1976). Metropolitan government, area planning councils, and citizen participation were structural reforms introduced to create an area-wide planning and coordinating capacity and to make government more efficient and more responsive in the provision of public services. These later reforms were aimed at bringing about a better fit "between economically and socially interrelated areas (called metropolitan) and the governmental jursidictions overlying them" (Campbell and Birkhead 1976:7), as well as the redistribution of resources to populations in greatest need.

Emphasis was to shift once again in the 1960s. World War II had prompted the development of public technologies such as management science techniques. The introduction of computers and advanced telecommunications techniques in the postwar years further altered the broader technology (the collection of specialists, apparatus, and techniques) available to policy-makers and -implementers.[1]

Americans, who had long tended to have an abiding faith in technology, translated this faith into a positive orientation toward the extension of technology into the management and operation of government affairs. Contemporary reform began to be aimed at developing technologies which would enhance productivity in the government sector in much the same way that the development of mass-production techniques revolutionized productivity in the private manufacturing sector. Just as technology "would send us to the moon," it was thought, technology might also solve the formerly intractable problems of government planning, management, and service delivery.

LaPorte and Metlay have observed that technological reforms based on this premise were at first met with relatively unalloyed enthusiasm by the educated public both in and out of government. But as the United States has experienced rapid technological development, and as the impacts of that development have become apparent, the public has become wary (LaPorte and Metlay 1975).

Also, an increasing number of authors have pointed out the limitations of technological reform (Nelson 1974; Rettig and Wirt 1976). The "moon shot" metaphor, which argues that if technology could accomplish the moon shot, it could also solve any number of problems in the public sector, is a common object of criticism, because it disregards both economic and market constraints on the development of technologies for the public sector. Most technological development must be incremental in relation to existing technology, because the development costs and marketing potentials of nonincremental breakthrough technologies are too great a risk to the private sector. In contrast, the breakthrough technology of the moon shot was comprehensive development, requiring extremely large commitments from the governmental sector. Similar commitments are not realistic for the broad array of public technologies involved in the everyday management and operation of urban services.

Another distinction frequently cited is that the socially based government problems which public technologies address might well be somewhat harder to solve than the engineering problems which space technologies overcame to reach the moon. At least, it is increasingly clear that the beneficial impacts of public technology are often less dramatic than anticipated. For example, several studies suggest that such administrative and management-science techniques as planning, programming, and budgeting systems (PPBS), zero-based budgeting (ZBB), and urban-development models have been implemented with little or no perceptible change in the quality of governmental budgeting or planning processes (Lee 1973; Shick 1971).

Even in areas where it is possible to use technology, there is an increasing awareness that technology is not only a solution to problems but also a source of new and unanticipated problems. As Emmanuel Mesthene has noted: "New technology creates new opportunities for men and societies, and it also generates new problems for them. It has both positive and negative effects, and it usually has the two *at the same time and in virtue of each other*" (1972:130).

More specifically, technology is a source of both managerial and political concern. Managerial concern stems from the growing awareness that unless the adoption and implementation of public technologies are properly managed, the expected benefits will not be achieved. Political concern stems from the expectation that the increasing reliance on sophisticated public technologies might well alter the power relationships among elected officials, bureaucrats, technicians, and citizens.

For example, some theorists fear that technological development might improve the productivity of urban bureaucracies but, at the same time, lessen their responsiveness to the public. Theodore Lowi (1968) has suggested that local governments tend to be well managed

Table 1.1
A Typology of Local Government Administrations

Productivity: Bureaucratic Efficiency and Effectiveness	Responsiveness to the Public	
	Low	High
High	The bureaucratic machine	The representative bureaucracy
Low	The unmanaged bureaucracy	The political machine

but poorly governed. He suggests that the growth of urban bureaucracies has increased their autonomy in relation to both elected officials and the general public. As a result, urban bureaucracies are now the new "machines," replacing the political machines of an earlier era (Table 1.1). Technological reform of local government, from this perspective, might further increase the size of urban bureaucracies and their monopoly of expertise, thus further decreasing their responsiveness to the community.

However, the advocates of technological development view technology as a means for increasing both the productivity and responsiveness of local governments. These advocates perceive local governments as being not only poorly governed but also poorly managed. Thus, they view technology as a tool for moving toward a more representative bureaucracy instead of a tool for increasing the power of the new bureaucratic machines (Table 1.1).

In short, concern is now focused on whether the intended functions of technological change are being achieved, to what extent, and with what unintended costs. As a result, the reform question has become a management question: How can technology be implemented more effectively to achieve its intended consequences? And the reform question has also become a political question: Who is served by technological reform?

The Computing Issue

One of the areas in which the impact of the trend toward technological reform has been most substantial is the area of computing. Computers are no longer limited to use by large cities; the adoption of computing has become widespread among local governments. By the mid-1970s, more than 90 percent of U.S. cities with populations greater than 50,000 utilized computers in their government operations (Kraemer, Dutton, and Matthews 1975). There is a similar proportion of computer users among county governments serving populations greater than 100,000 (Matthews, Dutton, and Kraemer 1976). Only among the very smallest city and county governments (those which serve less than 50,000 people) are computers used by less than half of the governments.

Not only is computing widespread, but its use is steadily increasing. Already, computing is utilized for an average of over 30 applications in each local government. These uses span such activities as monitoring departmental expenditures, paying employees, monitoring employee sick leave, sending utility bills, analyzing community demographic data, locating fire stations, allocating manpower, and forecasting the fiscal impacts of urban development. In short, computing increasingly is becoming a general-purpose tool within local government; in light of the 1975 plans of data-processing departments, the use of computing might double by 1980.

The rapid diffusion and development of computer technology is not surprising in light of early predictions made about the beneficial impacts of computers in organizations (Hoos 1960; Leavitt and Whisler 1958; Meyers 1967; Simon 1965). Like other technologies, the computer was viewed as a *deus ex machina* that would revolutionize the management and performance of organizations, as early factory automation had changed the production line. Computing was expected to accomplish this through a variety of organizational improvements (Fig. 1.1).

First, computers were expected to offer improved information for decision-making. Various theorists predicted that computers would create an "information nirvana" in organizations, leading to improved management decisions (Leavitt and Whisler 1958; Meyers 1967; Pendleton 1971; Simon 1965). Computers would provide more accurate and timely information, a wider range of information, more easily obtainable information, and decision aids, such as models and simulations, for analyzing the information. These technical improvements in information would increase the "means-ends rationality" of decision processes and therefore the quality of choices.

Second, improvements were expected in management control.

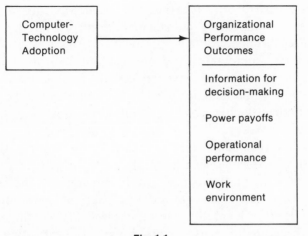

Fig. 1.1.
Expected outcomes of computer-technology adoption.

Although most of the early theorists treated the impacts of computing as largely apolitical, some predicted that computing might have power payoffs in addition to the more technical benefits (Downs 1967; Leavitt and Whisler 1958; Meyers 1967). In particular, power shifts were predicted to occur as a result of the information contained in computerized systems. Computers would extend superiors' control over the decision processes and performance of subordinates by quantifying more output information and making it readily available. And, generally, the power shifts would redound to the benefit of higher-level managers and support staff vis-a-vis elected officials, department heads, and lower-level staff.

Third, improvements were anticipated in operational performance. The phrase "office automation" was used early on to characterize the computer's expected impact on administrative operations (Hoos 1960; Simon 1965). Computers would increase the efficiency of operations by reducing staff, reducing costs, and increasing the speed and ease of performing various operations.

Computers also were expected to improve operational performance by increasing the effectiveness of operations along with cost savings. For example, they would help deter parking and traffic violations through improvements of traffic-ticket processing in the courts, help solve crimes through the improvement of information support to detectives and patrol officers in the field, and help ameliorate the urban fiscal crisis by improving management control over departmental expenditures throughout the government.

In addition, computers were expected to improve operational performance by providing new services not feasible manually. For example, they would facilitate sending informational and delinquent payment notices to citizens and generate many new kinds of reports and analyses.

Fourth, improvements were expected in the work environment (Blauner 1964; Greenberger 1966). The early theorists predicted that certain environmental changes would accompany the foregoing changes in the management and operation of government. For example, along with speeding up service delivery, computers would increase the need for consistency, accuracy, coordination and co-operation among departments in the handling of information. As a result, jobs in computerized offices would become more challenging and less routine, as dull and repetitive tasks were taken over by the computer.

Despite these optimistic predictions, some users have discovered that computer technology, like other technologies, is a two-edged sword (see Table 1.2). For example, computers initially were intro-duced in order to reduce the costs of government operations. But computers have themselves generated spiraling costs. Changes in the technology, such as the change from second to third generation, brought about such second-order changes as the need for expensive conversion of programs, hiring of new kinds of computer staff and

Table 1.2
The Reform and Post-reform Approaches

Perspective	Approach	
	Reform	Post-Reform
Technological development	Advanced technology	Appropriate technology
Structural arrangements	Classical structures	Participatory structures
Socio-technical design	Task efficiency	Human relations
Organizational context	Professional administration	Political administration

extensive retraining of both computer staff and users. Similarly, computers were supposed to enhance people's jobs, but many users have seen their jobs become like those in automated factories. They have experienced shift work, more rigid schedules and work measurement, and have felt depersonalization, a loss of autonomy, and dissatisfaction with their work. The impact has sometimes extended to middle managers. In fact, some early theorists believed the jobs of middle managers would undergo the greatest change of all (Hoos 1960; Leavitt and Whisler 1958). Furthermore, some have argued that the increasing size and complexity of computing operations in organizations have made it more difficult for managers and lay policy officials to control the technical experts who provide computing services (Danziger 1979). Derivatively, surveys have shown that public managers increasingly have come to recognize that computing-technology adoption, use, and development can be a problem beyond cost considerations (Danziger 1977; Dutton and Kraemer 1977).

These problems seem to suggest a general underpinning, namely that the benefits of automation have been far fewer than anticipated and the costs far greater. In particular:

1. Many of the anticipated benefits of computing have been realized only partially or have yet to be realized.
2. The life-cycle costs of computing have exceeded the initial costs considerably.
3. Unanticipated problems with the technology often have outweighed the benefits received.
4. The problems associated with computing have not been confined to service delivery; there have been unexpected political consequences as well.

The following newspaper story is typical of the experiences of an increasing number of local governments which illustrate how the computer as problem solver can turn into a problem generator. This abridged story is fact, not fiction. It is based on an experience of a large, sophisticated Western city with 20 years of experience in computers and data processing.

DREAM OF UTOPIAN COMPUTER REGIME TURNS INTO NIGHTMARE

BAY CITY. Back in the late '60s, when the story was just beginning, everybody knew that computers would someday provide the answer to all of mankind's woes. It was only a matter of time.

Anxious to be the first to show the

Given this perspective, numerous studies suggest that computer technology has been unsuccessfully implemented in many public and private organizations (Kling 1978; Kraemer and King 1976; Laudon 1974; Lucas 1973). As a consequence, our attention is focused on the reform of current policies for the implementation of computing. By changing the way that computing is implemented within organizations, it might be possible to achieve better the intended benefits.

Below, we present the major competing approaches to the implementation of computing in organizations. We begin by describing the approaches in general terms and deriving from them a set of alternative hypotheses concerning the implementation of computer technologies. We then describe the broader theoretical framework we use in the following chapters to assess both the hypotheses and the approaches themselves.

Competing Approaches: Reform versus Post-Reform

Research suggests that the value of computing to an organization is likely to vary with the kinds of tasks for which computing is used (Kraemer, Dutton, and Matthews 1975). Computers might perform better for routine tasks than for nonroutine tasks, as bookkeepers rather than as decision aids. What this suggests is that the performance quality of computing is contingent on the tasks for which it is used. Therefore, failures of the technology might simply indicate that it was applied inappropriately.

Beyond being affected by the match between a given task and available technology, the performance of computing technology is likely to be contingent upon the policy used to implement it. For example, a technology can be designed to be centralized or decentralized, or to be responsive or unresponsive to the needs of its users or the needs of the public it serves.

Broadly, approaches to computing implementation can be classified under two main headings: reform and post-reform (Table 1.2). The reform approach advocates the adoption of advanced technological developments, which are managed by hierarchical, classical structures so as to maximize the efficiency of the tasks for which the technology is applied. A professional administrative context is thought to be the most congenial to such an implementation process. In contrast, the post-reform approach advocates the adoption of appropriate (more conventional) technologies, which are managed by more fragmented, participatory structures so as to improve the human relations environment of the organization. The post-reform approach also suggests that the best organizational context for such implementation is a political administration, which is thought to improve performance by stressing responsiveness to the expressed needs of its own employees and of the public rather than reponsiveness to abstract principles of professional management.

The reform approach is clearly a descendant of the municipal reform movement of the early 1900s, with its stress on the goals of economy and efficiency. Furthermore, its primary orientation is toward administering public organizations in ways that will most efficiently serve the public. In contrast, the post-reform approach is largely a reaction to, and criticism of, the municipal reform movement. The post-reform approach developed in universities in response to issues raised by the labor-union movement following World War II. Since that time, it has characterized new approaches to organizational theory in public administration, political science, and sociology. The post-reform approach stresses the quality of life within organizations and the responsiveness of organizations to their clientele. The argument is that because people spend most of their lives in, and receive most of their services from, organizations, these organizations should be administered in ways that will be sensitive to the needs of their members and clientele.

We offer the reform/post-reform dichotomy as our attempt to create some order out of the seemingly disjointed debates in the literature and among practitioners. Today, the reform approach is most clearly articulated by the managers of local government data-processing departments and their technical staff. Very simply put, these managers generally advocate leading-edge technologies such as on-line computing and database management systems, centralized control such as through an independent electronic data-processing (EDP) department, the most efficient rather than the most user-oriented systems designs, and a professional administration that isolates computing from "political" pressures. Of course, many managers have advocated the opposite on occasions when it was either politically, administratively, or technically more practical, given the characteristics of their local government. For example, many managers have carried the banner of user-centered designs in cities where computing was under fire from user department heads.

In contrast, the post-reform approach is most clearly advocated by the nontechnical users of computing. Such users often wish to limit technological change in order to limit changes in their tasks, roles, and status within the organization. And users are most likely to advocate decentralization of control through mechanisms ranging from user committees to oversee the computing department to the location of computing facilities within their own department, a rather common plea with the advent of minicomputers. Likewise, users are the major advocates of user-centered designs, such as the use of interactive systems and the adoption of higher-level programming languages and generalized statistical packages that require less technical expertise to operate. Finally, users are often opposed to professional administration, as it generally means greater top-management control and less departmental (user) autonomy. Again, however, there is a variation in users' views, based as they are on the specific organizational context and individual differences in attitudes toward computing. For example, some of the most avowed advocates of leading-edge technologies are found among users.

A multitude of more specific computing policies can be derived from these two approaches. These in turn can be usefully classified according to four perspectives which suggest their underlying rationale. Three of these perspectives focus on the manner in which the technology is implemented: the development of the technology, the arrangement of bureaucratic-administrative structures, and the nature of the socio-technical design; the fourth perspective is the organizational context in which the technology is implemented.

Technological Perspectives

The performance of computing often is viewed as highly dependent upon the state of technological development (Gibson and Nolan 1974; Pendleton 1971). In fact, the most common approach of technical experts to local government problems is to pursue a technological solution. Even problems with computing are often approached by advocating the further development of the technology. A common claim is that "the payoffs are just around the corner"; once computer technology is developed to its full capacity, the benefits of the technology will be realized to their greatest extent, and the problems attendant on the technology will be minimized. Thus it is held that local governments must keep up with the state-of-the-art and maintain a highly sophisticated computing capability.

The reform approach to technological development follows the scientific-management school flowing from the work of Frederick Taylor (1916). The reform approach is advanced technology. Advanced technology is endorsed by an extensive literature on modernization, development, and routinization. The major thesis of this approach is that a technology goes through predictable stages of development. As an organization's technology continues through the development process, it is increasingly adapted to organizational needs and demands. While such an orientation is sometimes accused of reflecting a naive belief that development is synonymous with qualitative improvement, much of the literature in this area is careful in avoiding this linkage. This perspective is quite central to the literature on computing in organizations, especially that of Nolan (1973) and Pendleton (1971). The major thesis of the computing literature is that the value of an automated information system to an organization is dependent upon the developmental state of computer technology. The computer package–hardware, software, and personnel—should approach the most advanced technological stage appropriate for a given purpose. In effect, the literature suggests that the payoffs of computing must await advanced technological development. Complementary recommendations for policy-makers would include the following:

1. Automate information-processing tasks which are amenable to mechanization.
2. Automate all components of a discrete information-processing task.
3. Adopt computing at an early date.
4. Use sophisticated, modern computers.
5. Use existing capabilities of on-line, real-time processing, and data-base management.
6. Hire sophisticated computer experts.

The post-reform approach flows from contemporary criticisms of our increasingly technological society.[3] The critics of technological development advocate alternative, intermediate, or "appropriate," technology. This approach expresses a concern for the dysfunctions and spillovers of technological development. Freeways, nuclear power plants, herbicides, and computers are said often to be technological solutions to problems which could be solved in other ways with less dangerous or less costly side effects. In addition to the spillover effects, the critics of advanced technology suggest that sophisticated developments are often wasteful and unnecessary. Such critics ask whether it is really all that important to shave minutes off the processing of a traffic ticket, eliminate one clerk from the treasurer's office, and so on. In short, the use of advanced technology to increase the efficiency of organizations might be inappropriate. More generally, the claim is that advanced technology is often not the appropriate technological response.

Complementary recommendations for policy-makers would include the following:

1. Do not automate information-processing tasks that can be satisfactorily handled using manual operations.
2. Automate only those parts of an information-processing task that are a problem to the manual operation.
3. Move slowly in automating. Respond to actual problems rather than anticipated (and possibly never realized) needs.
4. Adopt computers sophisticated enough to do the job, no more.
5. Hesitate to use such sophisticated capabilities as on-line processing, real-time processing, and database management. These capabilities are more costly, create greater dependence on computing, and are more difficult to implement and maintain.
6. Gear the technology to the caliber of available personnel. Local governments generally cannot hire sophisticated computer experts, given the insufficient pool of experts, salary constraints of government, and competition from the private sector.

Structural Perspectives

Another perspective suggests that performance of the technology is dependent on the structural arrangements which govern its use. Reorganization is therefore a basic response to problems with the use of a technology. Common to structural remedies are departmental reorganizations, the decentralization or centralization of computing, or alterations in the reporting and control relationships among departmental units. This perspective assumes that problems with technology stem largely from organizational arrangements affecting the locus of control over computing resources. Reorganization might then create better conditions for managing the technology and thus for performance benefits.

The reform approach to the structural arrangements for implementation of technology follows the traditional school of public administration, flowing from the work of Max Weber (1947) and suggested in Taylor's (1911) work on the "principles of scientific management." Ostrom's (1973) and Golembiewski's (1977a) critiques of this classical school note that it is characterized by a top-down bias, favoritism for a single, dominant center or unitary hierarchy under a single chief executive, and support for the development of a core of well-trained, politically neutral professionals.

As McGregor (1960) notes, the classical strategy is based on a conservative view of work and the motivation of people in organizations. Work is viewed as generally distasteful, with individuals seldom

's for greater responsibility or
ecause they have to. And on the
cted within jobs that are rather
ig to Golembiewski (1977b), this
issical structures to recommend
vell-defined chain of command;
divisions of labor; functional
notion; and formal, impersonal
s and clients.
can be applied to a variety of
ippropriate structural arrange-
nputing. The classical strategy

of computing operations.
as of responsibility for services.
a computing decisions.
rgovernmental sharing, consoli-
d of computing resources.
s for computing.

ely to promote a clear chain of
)rocedures that are consistent

throughout the organization, as well as conforming with the principles of functional specialization and a clear division of labor. Limited involvement of users in computing decisions is consistent with a top-down vertical chain of command within the organization. Interdepartmental and intergovernmental data sharing and integration reinforce the effort to centralize computing operations, while charging for services provides a mechanism for enforcing the priorities of central policy-makers. Finally, organizational stability permits a more well-defined chain of command, as well as more stable, well-defined standard operating procedures.

The post-reform approach, in contrast, advocates participatory structural arrangements. The participatory strategy is like the classical in focusing on the structure of the organization. However, it is unlike the classical strategy in its prescriptions. The participatory strategy follows the "new public administration" and conforms to the concept of "democratic administration" developed most comprehensively by Ostrom (1973, 1977). Democratic administration has a "bottom-up" as opposed to a "top-down" bias. As suggested by Golembiewski (1977a) and Ostrom (1977), the bottom-up bias favors a heterogeneous organizational structure, characteristic of American federalism, rather than a unitary hierarchy. Democratic administration, according to Ostrom, draws its intellectual foundation more from the work of Alexander Hamilton and James Madison on federalism and constitutional rule than from the work of Max Weber on monocratic bureaucracy (Ostrom 1977:1509).

The participatory strategy is based on a more liberal, as well as a more complex, view of people in organizations: liberal, because it assumes that people are often likely to enjoy work and desire opportunties for greater responsibility and creativity in performing their jobs; more complex, because it assumes that a large variety of motives are operative in determining how people behave in organizations and that, therefore, the task of managing people is far more complex than issuing directives. Consequently, those who subscribe to the participatory strategy are far less supportive of the classic principles of administration. Some argue that such principles fail to describe real organizations. Others argue that the principles should not be used to describe real organizations because they are based on an inappropriate view of human nature (Golembiewski 1977b).

The logic of the participatory strategy also can be applied to the implementation of computing in local government. The participatory strategy would lead policy-makers to:

1. Decentralize the provision and control of computing operations.
2. Create fragmented, overlapping areas of responsibility for services.
3. Maximize the involvement of users in computing decisions.

Such policies are said to reflect more accurately what really happens in organizations, as well as to create structures that increase the flexibility and creativeness of members throughout the organization in performing their jobs.

Socio-technical Design Perspectives

Another factor that might shape the performance of computing is the way in which the technology has been integrated into the organization. It has been suggested that the successful implementation of computing might be contingent on the users within the organization and how they relate to the technology. For example, how much do they support technology's use? Are they motivated to use the technology? Are they skilled enough to utilize the technology? This perspective suggests that computing problems might best be addressed by training, or by changing the way in which users relate with the technology. But computing problems also may be addressed by changing the interactions of data-processing staffs with the users. Thus, computing can be integrated into the work environment by changing the attitudes and behaviors of the providers, as well as users, of data-processing services.

The reform approach stresses task efficiency in the socio-technical design of systems and, therefore, has much in common with the classical strategy regarding structural arrangements. That is, a technology should be designed in ways which maximize the efficiency of users in performing their tasks. The task-efficiency strategy is closely linked to the rational school of organizational theory. According to Golembiewski (1977b:62), such rationalists as Herbert Simon have

tended to emphasize technical analysis and quantitative methods, as in (1) Scientific Management, as manifested in time-and-methods, work and micro-motion analysis; (2) mathematical and statistical technologies for decision-making or problem solving; and (3) systems analysis associated with PPBS, as in cost-benefit analysis, and so forth.

From the task-efficiency strategy, the design of socio-technical systems tends to be a problem of arriving at the most rational (efficient) use of a technology within the organizational setting.

In contrast, the post-reform approach stresses human relations in the socio-technical design of systems. The human-relations strategy has much in common with the bottom-up bias of the participatory strategy regarding structural arrangements. However, the human-relations strategy goes beyond a concern for structure to encompass a broad concern for human relations over bureaucratic rules and technical efficiency. As Charles Perow observes (1972:106), the productivity of the organization, according to the human relationist, will be more dependent upon the attitudes and motivations of the employees than on bureaucratic rules, procedures, and lines of authority. In sum, organizational climate is more important to productivity than organizational structure. In this respect, the human-relations strategy or humanist school of organizational theory, has

tended to emphasize social integration and behavioral methods, as in (1) the Organizational Behavior literature which, in general, establishes the importance of meeting human developmental needs at work; and (2) the Organizational Development literature which, in general, proposes a set of learning designs to facilitate the development of organizational arrangements that will be growthful for humans by meeting their developmental needs. (Golembiewski 1970a:62–63)

Human relations and task efficiency are not necessarily incompatible, but these alternative strategies imply different priorities in the design of organizations and are a frequent source of debate in public administration and organizational theory.[4]

Notwithstanding a large number of conditions and qualifications, the human-relations strategy would lead policy-makers to design technology with a sensitivity to its impact on the quality of human relations within the organization. In terms of computing, such policy-makers would try to:

1. Help their personnel develop attitudes that support the use of computing and support the computing staff.
2. Design systems that have a positive impact on the work environment of people within the organization.
3. Train computing management and staff to communicate with and be responsive to users.

Organizational-Context Perspectives

One additional factor that is likely to affect the performance of technology is the character of the organization which adopts the technology. The successful implementation of computing might be contingent on the professionalism and reform orientation of the adopting organization. Professionalized and reform-oriented organizations might be more congenial to the use of high technologies.

The reform approach suggests that a professional administration is most likely to implement and use technology successfully. First, technology has often been viewed as a tool of the professional administrator, and several empirical studies suggest that professional administrators are among the primary beneficiaries of urban technology (Dutton and Kraemer 1977; Kraemer and Dutton 1979; Kraemer forthcoming; Laudon 1974). Because professional administrators tend to be more influential in the more reformed city-manager cities, as well as in cities with professional management practices, these cities might be most congenial to the implementation of urban technology.

The post-reform approach suggests that a political administration is more likely to implement technology successfully. According to the post-reformers, technology must be consistent with, and not harmful to, the interests of those who manage and use it. In contrast to professional administrators, political administrators—who are more prominent in cities with partisan elections, a mayor-council form of government, and few professional management practices—are likely to be sensitive to the variety of needs, demands, and interests of various people within the organization. Thus, political administration might well be more congenial to successful implementation.

Theoretical Framework for
the Analysis

Both the reform and post-reform approaches assume that the alteration of implementation policies (technology, structure, and socio-technical design) and their organizational context improve an organization by increasing its efficiency, effectiveness, even-handedness, and responsiveness. In essence, an organization can be shaped meaningfully by intelligent administration. But there is another perspective which questions the efficacy of either the reform or post-reform approaches to managing organizations. This latter perspective suggests that the performance of public agencies is shaped by the community and extra-community environment.

The community environment refers to the socioeconomic characteristics of the urban community in which the local government is situated. Relevant community socioeconomic factors include the size of the community, its social complexity, and its social status.

The extra-community environment refers to political and administrative factors outside the local government system. Such factors include state and federal policies affecting computing (e.g., external funding, privacy legislation), and state and federal reporting requirements, which might create demands for computing. Also, the activity of computer-technology suppliers and regional and national communication networks might be relevant to the diffusion of the technology.

According to this environmental perspective, the reform and post-reform approaches are merely administrative tinkering. In essence, meaningful change requires alterations far more fundamental than management policies.

The model adopted for the analysis in this book (Fig. 1.2) incorporates this additional set of variables as well as the management-policy variables in the conceptual model outlined above.

In our assessment of implementation outcomes, we focus on the organizational performance outcomes only, rather than on both organizational and community outcomes. This must be the initial focus, because managers must first know whether technology can improve the performance of organizations before they ever need to address the issue of technological impacts on the community outcomes. If technology can improve organizational performance, the second thing managers must know is how to make their organization's use of technology a positive tool of performance. Finally, with these currently unknown facts presumably in the managers' hands, they then can turn to the question of whether organizational performance improvements are compatible with continued or improved responsiveness and productivity in relation to the community. At that point, perhaps another large-scale study will be necessary to help managers integrate their own assessments of community needs with the ability of technology to respond to those needs. This study only indirectly

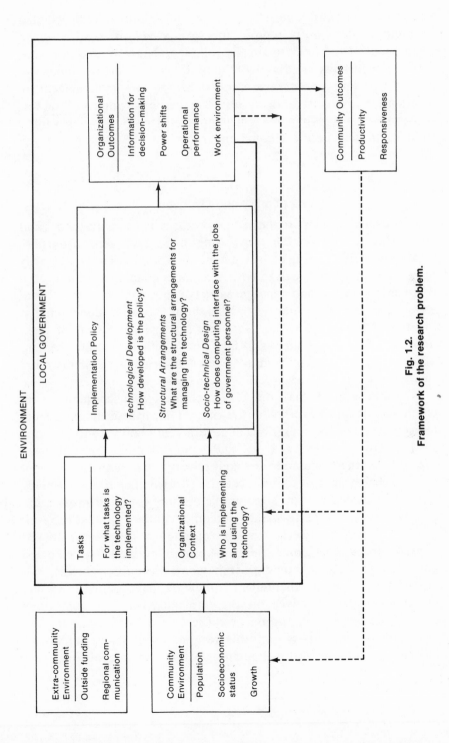

Fig. 1.2.
Framework of the research problem.

addresses this third question through our discussion of whether technology causes shifts in power among city-hall officials.

The goal of the analyses in the following chapters, based on the framework just discussed, is twofold: to test empirically the validity of the reform and post-reform approaches to the management of information systems; and to test whether environmental factors constrain the success of management policies. These tests will permit us to develop our policy recommendations for the management of information systems.

Summary and Overview

Public technologies are the primary reform instruments today, and computing is one of the most widespread and general-purpose technologies. But having an instrument of reform does not necessarily mean that reform will lead to positive change. Evidence has indicated that computing has had negative as well as positive impacts on local governments' service delivery. This book aims at developing a theoretical framework which supports systematic analysis of these impacts in order to understand how and whether local government officials can implement computer-based information systems more successfully.

We have argued that the potential performance outcomes of computing within government are many and diverse, ranging from improvements in the operations of government to power shifts among elected officials, top managers, and technical staff. Our approach suggests that these outcomes are likely to vary in part with the nature of the task being computerized, according to whether it is routine or nonroutine, whether it involves simple or more complex information processing. Not all performance outcomes can be expected to result from all tasks. But whether the appropriate outcomes are achieved depends upon management policy—how computing is implemented and the organizational context within which it is implemented.

We have presented a theoretical framework that organizes a variety of competing perspectives on the implementation of computing around two conflicting approaches. These approaches—reform and post-reform—encompass opposing technological, structural, socio-technical, and organizational perspectives on implementation. From each of these perspectives, we have derived a series of more concrete hypotheses and policy recommendations. In the following chapters, these hypotheses and derived policy recommendations are examined empirically, using the findings of the second phase of an extensive study of the state-of-the-art in local government computing. The study, called "Evaluation of Information Technology in Local Governments," was carried out from 1975 to 1979 by the Urban Information Systems (URBIS) research group of the Public Policy Research Organization (PPRO). During this phase, members of the project collected information in 42 cities for assessing the impacts of specific policies for the management of computing.[5] The final chapter presents a summary of findings and recommendations for successful management approaches to the implementation of computer-based information systems.

NOTES

1. Technology refers to the totality of rational methods employed in human activity (Ellul 1964; Winner 1977). "Public technology" is used generally to refer to the efforts of public organizations to bring technology to bear on public problems. It is used particularly to refer to the efforts of federal agencies to stimulate the dissemination, adoption, and implementation of new knowledge, hardware, systems, or techniques by state and local governments. Examples of federal government interest in helping to apply public technology to state and local government problems include "the R & D programs of federal domestic agencies, technical assistance programs, technical information clearinghouses, and dissemination programs" (Roessner 1976:205).

A series of government-related publications have promoted the application of science and technology to government problems. These include publications of the Federal Council for Science and Technology (1972), *Action Now* (1972), the Urban Institute (1971), and the Council of State Government (1972). A summary of the issues raised by these publications is presented by Roessner (1976).

2. Most studies of organizational innovation have based their assessments of technological change on comparing the performance of organizations which have adopted the innovation with organizations which have not. Yet, the simple adoption of

computing or other technologies does not always spell success (Brewer 1974; Yin et al. 1976). A technological innovation could work well in laboratory conditions but could be poorly used or underutilized in the real world. Therefore, an innovation might fail to serve the purposes for which it was adopted. Studies which focus simply on adoption tend, as a result, to be unsuccessful in assessing the impacts of technological as well as other kinds of organizational reforms. In fact, Campbell and Birkhead (1976:12) note that "despite all the efforts for reform and all the debate about it, the basic question 'What difference does it make?' remains unanswered."

3. An excellent review of these criticisms is provided by Winner (1977).

4. This debate is most clearly exemplified by two major articles (Argyris 1973; Simon 1973).

5. This study might be called a "policy-oriented technology assessment" (White et al. 1976:1–2), for we attempt to determine the consequences of various patterns and levels of computer utilization by government. We then provide several policy recommendations, based on our analysis, that suggest how certain desirable consequences can be encouraged and certain undesirable consequences can be discouraged or mitigated. But this study differs from a technology assessment (TA) in several aspects. First, we limit our consideration of consequences to a fairly well defined set of consequences posited in the literature on computing in organizations. Consequently, this study contributes to a full-scale TA but does not attempt to be such a full-scale study. The second and related difference is that our methodology differs from most examples of TA. We limit our analysis to those consequences which can be subjected to systematic empirical investigation within the practical limits of a single study. We do not attempt to identify and assess the full range of costs and benefits associated with all feasible policies. But we have chosen costs and benefits that range over various areas.

A useful discussion of TA is provided by Arnstein and Christakis (1975).

REFERENCES

Ackoff, Russell. 1967. "Management Information Systems." *Management Science,* 14(4):B147–56.

Action Now. 1972. Resolutions of the National Action Conference of Intergovernmental Science and Technology Policy. Harrisburg, Pa.

Argyris, Chris. 1970. "Resistance to Rational Management Systems." *Innovation,* 10:28–35.

——. 1971. "Management Information Systems: The Challenge to Rationality and Emotionality." *Management Science,* 17(6):B275–92.

——. 1973. "Some Limits of Rational Man Organizational Theory." *Public Administration Review*, 33(4):253–67.

Arnstein, Sherry R. and Alexander N. Christakis. 1975. *Perspectives on Technology Assessment*. Columbus: Academy for Contemporary Problems.

Blauner, Robert. 1964. *Alienation and Freedom: The Factory Worker and His Industry*. Chicago: University of Chicago Press.

Brewer, Gary. 1974. *Politicians, Bureaucrats and Consultants*. New York: Basic Books.

Campbell, Alan K. and Roy W. Bahl, eds. 1976. *State and Local Government: The Political Economy of Reform*. New York: Free Press.

Campbell, Alan K. and Guthrie S. Birkhead. 1976. "Municipal Reform Revisited: The 1970s Compared with the 1920s." In Alan Campbell and Roy Bahl, eds., *State and Local Government: The Political Economy of Reform*, pp. 1–15. New York: Free Press.

Council of State Governments. 1972. *Power to the States—Mobilizing Public Technology*. Lexington, Ky.: Council of State Governments.

Danziger, James N. 1977. "Computers and the Frustrated Chief Executive." *MIS Quarterly*, 1(2):43–53.

——. 1979. "The Skill Bureaucracy and Intra-organizational Control: The Case of the Data Processing Unit." *Sociology of Work and Occupations*, 6(2):204–26.

Danziger, James N. and William H. Dutton. 1977. "Technological Innovation in Local Government: The Case of Computing." *Policy and Politics*, 6(1):27–49.

Downs, Anthony. 1967. "A Realistic Look at the Final Payoffs from Urban Data Systems." *Public Administration Review*, 27(3):204–10.

Dutton, William H. and Kenneth L. Kraemer. 1977. "Technology and Urban Management: The Power Payoffs of Computing." *Administration and Society*, 9(3):305–40.

Ellul, Jacques. 1964. *The Technological Society*. Transl. by J. Wilkinson. New York: Random House, Vintage Books.

Federal Council for Science and Technology. 1972. *Public Technology: A Tool for Solving National Problems*. Washington, D.C.: U.S. Government Printing Office.

Gibson, Cyrus F. and Richard L. Nolan. 1974. "Managing the Four Stages of EDP Growth." *Harvard Business Review*, 52(1):76–88.

Golembiewski, Robert T. 1977a. "A Critique of 'Democratic Administration' and Its Supporting Ideation." *American Political Science Review*, 61(4):1488–1507.

——. 1977b. *Public Administration as a Developing Discipline, Part 1: Perspectives in the Past and Present*. New York: Marcel Dekker.

Greenberger, Martin. 1966. "The Priority Problems and Computer Time Sharing." *Management Science*, 12(11):888–1612.

Hoos, Ida R. 1960. "When the Computer Takes Over the Office." *Harvard Business Review*, 38(4):102–12.

Kling, Rob. 1978. "Automated Welfare Client-Tracking and Service Integration: The Political Economy of Computing." *Communications of the ACM*, 21(6):484–93.

Kraemer, Kenneth L. Forthcoming. "Computers, Information and Power in Local

Government." In A. Mowshowitz, ed., *Human Choice and Computers.* Amsterdam: North-Holland.

Kraemer, Kenneth L. and William H. Dutton. 1975. "Municipal Computers." *Urban Data Service Reports.* Washington, D.C.: International City Management Association.

——. 1979. "The Interests Served by Technological Reform: The Case of Computing." *Administration and Society,* 11(1):80–106.

Kraemer, Kenneth L., William H. Dutton, and Joseph Matthews. 1975. "Municipal Computers." *Urban Data Services Report,* 8(2):1–15.

Kraemer, Kenneth L. and John Leslie King. 1976. *Computers, Power and Urban Management.* Beverly Hills, Calif.: Sage Publications.

La Porte, Todd and Daniel Metlay. 1975. "Public Attitudes towards Present and Future Technologies: Satisfactions and Apprehensions." *Social Studies of Science,* 5:373–98.

Laudon, Kenneth C. 1974. *Computers and Bureaucratic Reform.* New York: Wiley.

Leavitt, Harold J. and Thomas L. Whisler. 1958. "Management in the 1980's." *Harvard Business Review,* 36(6):41–48.

Lee, Douglas B. 1973. "Requiem for Large Scale Planning Models." *Journal of the American Institute of Planners,* 39(3): 163–78.

Lowi, Theodore J. 1968. "Foreword." In Harold Gosnell, *Machine Politics: Chicago Model.* Chicago: University of Chicago Press.

Lucas, Henry C. 1973. *Why Information Systems Fail.* New York: Columbia University Press.

——. 1974. *Toward Creative Systems Design.* New York: Columbia University Press.

Matthews, Joseph R.; William H. Dutton; and Kenneth L. Kraemer. 1976. "County Computers: Growth, Usage and Management." *Urban Data Service Report,* 8(2).

McGraegor, Douglas. 1960. *The Human Side of Enterprise.* New York: McGraw-Hill.

Mesthene, Emmanuel G. 1972. "The Role of Technology in Society." In Albert H. Teich, ed., *Technology and Man's Future,* 1st ed., pp. 127–50. New York: St. Martin's Press.

Meyers, Charles A. 1967. *The Impact of Computers on Management.* Cambridge, Mass: MIT Press.

Nelson, Richard R. 1974. "Intellectualizing about the Moon-Ghetto Metaphor: A Study of the Current Malaise of Rational Analysis of Social Problems." *Policy Sciences,* 5(4):375–414.

Nolan, Richard L. 1973. "Managing the Computer Resource: A Stage Hypothesis," *Communications of the ACM,* 16(7):339–405.

Ostrom, Vincent. 1973. *The Intellectual Crisis in American Public Administration.* University, Ala.: University of Alabama Press.

——. 1977. "Some Problems in Doing Political Theory; a Response to Golembiewski's 'Critique.'" *American Political Science Review,* 61(4):1508–25.

Pendleton, J. C. 1971. "Integrated Information Systems." In *AFIPS Conference Proceedings,* 1971 Fall Joint Computer Conference, pp. 491–500. Montvale, N.J.: American Federation of Information Processing Societies Press.

Perrow, Charles. 1972. *Complex Organizations.* Palo Alto, Calif.: Scott, Foresman.

Pressman, Jeffrey L. and Aaron B. Wildavsky. 1973. *Implementation*. Berkeley, Calif.: University of California Press.

Rettig, Richard A. and John G. Wirt. 1976. "On Escaping the 'Moon Shot' Metaphor." *Policy Studies Journal,* 5(2): 168–71.

Roessner, J. David. 1976. "Research and Development: Making and Managing Policies." *Policy Studies Journal,* 5(2):205–11.

Shick, Alan. 1971. *Budget Innovation in the States.* Washington, D.C.: Brookings Institution.

Simon, Herbert A. 1965. *The Shape of Automation for Man and Management.* New York: Harper and Row.

——. 1973. "Applying Information Technology to Organizational Design." *Public Administration Review,* 33(3):268–78.

Taylor, Frederick W. 1911. *Principles of Scientific Management.* New York: Harper.

——. 1916. "Government Efficiency," *Bulletin of the Taylor Society,* 2:7–13.

Urban Institute. 1971. *The Struggle to Bring Technology to Cities.* Washington, D.C.: Urban Institute.

Weber, Max. 1947. *The Theory of Social and Economic Oganization.* Transl. by A. M. Henderson and Talcott Parsons. New York: Oxford University Press.

Westin, Alan and Michael Baker. 1972. *Databanks in a Free Society.* New York: Quadrangle Books.

White, Irvin L. et al. 1976. *First Year Work Plan for a Technology Assessment of Western Energy Resource Development.* Prepared for the Office of Research and Development, U.S. Environmental Protection Agency. Springfield, Va.: National Technical Information Service.

Winner, Langdon. 1977. *Autonomous Technology.* Cambridge, Mass.: MIT Press.

Yin, Robert K. and Suzanne K. Quick. 1977. "Routinization I: Thinking about Routinization." Santa Monica, Calif.: Rand Corporation (mimeographed).

Yin, Robert K.; Karen A. Hearld; Mary E. Vogel; Patricia D. Fleischauer; and Bruce C.Vladeck. 1976. *A Review of Case Studies of Technological Innovations in State and Local Governments.* Santa Monica, Calif.: Rand Corporation.

CHAPTER TWO
Research Methodology

THE AIM of our study was to find out which management policies improve the performance of automated applications in local government. The major weakness of prior studies was their research methodologies. For example, even such outstanding studies as Laudon's *Computers and Bureaucratic Reform* (1974) tended to be case studies of a handful of organizations, chosen on the basis of access, convenience, or interest (for example, because they had exceptionally good, or bad, reputations). Initially, we knew we wanted to draw a nationwide probability sample of comparable organizations, U.S. cities, for much the same reason that Gallup draws a nationwide probability sample of U.S. adults. We also wanted to draw a large enough sample to make meaningful generalizations, while keeping the sample small enough to conduct intensive research. Yet we did not want just to describe the management policies of U.S. cities. Instead, we knew that any useful policy advice to come from our study would have to describe what would happen if cities adopted a particular policy which the vast majority of cities are not now following. This latter objective could not be accomplished by using conventional probability sampling methods, because such methods are geared to describing the present population of cities and their policies and not what we desired to describe, which were "future" cities with optimal policies. Hence, we had to design a rather unconventional probability sampling method, one we were not even sure would work.

After months of design meetings and consultations, we felt we had developed a research design that utilized an innovative sampling design. Basically, our design is a variation on disproportionate stratified sampling technique, which is described later in this chapter. Forty-two cities would be sampled, based on their score on six different management-policy scales. The resulting sample of 42 cities displays a great deal more variation in the policies of interest to us than would a random sample of this size.

Now that we had a sampling method, we sought to overcome a second methodological weakness in prior studies. Such studies have generally described the success of computing in terms of a whole organization, yet organizations use computing for a variety of purposes with mixed levels of success. In cities, for example, the police department may manage its automated applications one way, finance another, and planning still another. If one looks just at management policies for computing in the city as a whole, one misses the variation in management policies, and thereby the variations in performance effects, across different automated applications. To overcome this problem, our study focuses on specific information-processing tasks that vary in their routineness and sophistication: (1) traffic-ticket processing, (2) patrol-officer support, (3) detective investigative support, (4) police-manpower-allocation support, (5) budget control, and (6) policy analysis. For each of these tasks in each city, we collected information about the community environment, organizational context, policies for managing computer-based information systems, and the performance of computing in five general areas: (1) *information for decision-making,* the quality of information for decision-making; (2) *management control,* improvements in the upward flow of information about the activities of subordinates; (3) *operational performance,* increases in efficiency, speed, and accuracy of government operations; (4) *work environment,* improvements in the work environment of those using computers or computer-based information; and (5) *power shifts.* In general, we collected that information necessary to explore our theoretical framework (Fig. 1.2) for the study of information systems in organizations. All the specific indicators used in this study are operationally defined in the Appendix.

The rationale and strategy of our research design is explained in detail elsewhere (Kraemer et al. 1976). In the following pages, we briefly outline the research design, how we collected our data, and how we present our study's findings in the later chapters.

Research Design

Rationale for the Design

Our research purpose has been to prescribe policies for "future cities," rather than simply to describe policy impacts in present cities.

We wanted to answer what would happen if cities did x (where x is a policy to decentralize computing, or to automate more, and so forth). Answering this type of question required us to make the best possible estimates of the effects of management policies, as well as environmental characteristics of the cities, such as city size and growth.

Two conventional approaches to deriving such answers have not been chosen. The most conventional approach is an experimental design in which conditions are controlled such that only the policy variables are manipulated to examine how they affect the policy-outcome variables (Campbell and Stanley 1963; Suchman 1967; Campbell 1969). This means that the experimenter has control (preferably by random assignment) of the policy variables. However, the natural settings of the governments do not allow for such control, and so we chose not to await the occurrence of natural experimental conditions.

A second conventional approach is to sample cities randomly and control statistically for other policies and city characteristics to determine the impact of a given policy on a given variable (Kerlinger 1964; Leege and Francis 1974). Such a design would be useful if the sample were quite large, if the policies of interest would be adequately represented in a random sample, and if the effects of each policy were easily distinguishable. However, resources limited us to sampling about 40 cities; many policies of interest are rare and therefore would be underrepresented in a random sample; and policy outcomes are expected to be quite difficult to discern, given the large number of other variables (noise) affecting the same outcomes. Consequently, the random sample approach would be fruitless, for we would be unable to answer our research questions.

Description of the Design

Our major problem, then, was to fashion a research design, based on a small sample, which incorporated variation on the major policy variables and which maximized the likelihood of discerning any policy outcomes. Our response was a fusion of research methods that constitutes a modest design innovation. By drawing a highly stratified sample of 40 cities (stratifying simultaneously on six policy variables), we ensured adequate variation of important policies and substantial statistical independence among these policies, such that their independent effects could be assessed. And by selecting half of the cities on each policy variable from the rare policy extreme, we increased the chances that any policy outcomes would be distinguishable.

Our approach is clarified best by first describing the initial phase of this research, which was designed for selection of the second-phase sites. Phase I consisted of a nationwide census survey of the 403 U.S. cities with populations over 50,000. This survey was conducted in early 1975 and consisted of three self-administered questionnaires. One was mailed to the chief executives, and two were mailed to the data-processing managers in the cities. The chief-executive questionnaire was returned from 82 percent of the officials surveyed. The other two questionnaires were returned from 81 percent of the cities using computers (Hackathorn 1975).

These questionnaires were designed to gather data about the cities and their computer use to discover in which cities the major policy questions could be examined most fruitfully. On the basis of returned questionnaires, indices were constructed for each of six major policy variables. Each city was scored by its degree of automation, degree of sophistication of data processing, degree of data integration, degree of decentralization of computing resources, and degree to which users are charged for computing services.

With the use of U.S. Census data available for all cities, regression analysis was performed for estimating prediction equations for each policy variable on the basis of the city's demographic characteristics. These prediction equations were then used to estimate the scores on each policy variable for those cities which did not respond to the questionnaires (close to 20 percent of the population), but for which we had obtained the relevant demographic data. In this manner, real or estimated scores on all policy variables were obtained for all 403 cities.

From this population of cities, 93 cities that reported having, or were estimated to have, a negligible degree of automation were dropped from the larger population for determining the Phase II cities. The remaining population of 310 cities was then partitioned in $2^6 = 64$ strata by making each policy variable dichotomous. That was done by treating all scores of each policy variable below the third quartile as low, and all scores above the third quartile as high. Thus, on any variable, the population of cities was split into two groups; the six splits define the 64 strata.

The third quartile was chosen as the cutting point from inspection of the distribution of cities on each (policy) stratification variable. Figure 2.1 illustrates the kind of skewed distribution each policy variable tended to approximate. Thus, dichotomization tended to group cities on each index into those with common policies and those with relatively rare policy extremes—those which were highly automated, decentralized, integrated, sophisticated, involving users, and charging for services.

To select our 40 Phase II cities from the 64 strata, we first randomly selected a balanced set of 40 strata from all possible balanced sets. This ensured that there would be 20 cities on the high side and 20 on the low side of each of the six policy variables. However, nine of the 40 selected

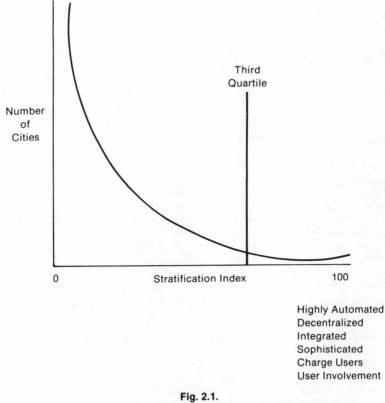

Highly Automated
Decentralized
Integrated
Sophisticated
Charge Users
User Involvement

Fig. 2.1.
Illustration of distribution approximated by site-selection index.

strata had no cities within them. Each empty stratum was filled by the city in the closest stratum. From this point, we randomly chose one site from each of the 40 strata. Two additional cities were added to compensate for city refusals and missing data. (In two cities, the police departments refused to cooperate.) These 42 cities are listed along with their populations in Table 2.1.

Our research design meant that our cities would not be representative of all the cities in the initial survey. For example, the Phase II cities tend to have larger populations but do not reflect any regional bias (Table 2.2). Table 2.3 compares the Phase II cities with the Phase I cities in terms of technological and structural policies. As the table indicates, the two samples have similar ranges in the policies. But the Phase II cities are clearly more highly automated, sophisticated, decentralized, and integrated, and they involve users more and charge more often for computer use. Hence, by selecting half of the cities on

Table 2.1
Cities Visited in Phase II Study[a]

	Population		Population
Albany, N.Y.	115,876	Milwaukee, Wis.	717,124
Atlanta, Ga.	497,024	Montgomery, Ala.	183,471
Baltimore, Md.	905,759	New Orleans, La.	593,471
Brockton, Mass.	89,040	New Rochelle, N.Y.	75,385
Burbank, Calif.	88,580	Newton, Mass.	91,073
Chesapeake, Va.	89,580	Oshkosh, Wis.	53,155
Cleveland, Ohio	751,046	Paterson, N.J.	144,830
Costa Mesa, Calif.	72,729	Philadelphia, Pa.	1,948,609
Evansville, Ind.	138,690	Portsmouth, Va.	110,963
Fort Lauderdale, Fla.	139,543	Quincy, Mass.	87,966
Florissant, Mo.	66,006	Riverside, Calif.	139,269
Grand Rapids, Mich.	197,534	Sacramento, Calif.	254,362
Hampton, Va.	120,779	San Francisco, Calif.	715,674
Kansas City, Mo.	507,242	San Jose, Calif.	446,504
Lancaster, Pa.	57,589	Seattle, Wash.	530,890
Las Vegas, Nev.	125,641	Spokane, Wash.	170,516
Lincoln, Neb.	149,518	St. Louis, Mo.	622,236
Little Rock, Ark.	132,482	Stockton, Calif.	107,459
Long Beach, Calif.	358,673	Tampa, Fla.	277,736
Louisville, Ky.	361,453	Tulsa, Okl.	331,800
Miami, Beach, Fla.	86,974	Warren, Mich.	179,234

[a] This listing gives the names and 1970 Census populations of the municipalities visited. They were selected according to a stratified sampling process to assure a wide diversity of data-processing environments.

Table 2.2
Phase II Cities Compared with Phase I Cities by
Population and Region

	Phase II Cities (N = 42) %	Phase I Cities (N = 403) %
Population		
50,000–100,000	26	61
100,000–250,000	36	25
250,000–500,000	17	8
Over 500,000	21	6
Region		
Northwest	19	21
North Central	24	27
West	26	24
South	31	26
Puerto Rico	0	2

each of six policy variables from the rare policy extreme, we increased our chances that any policy outcomes would be distinguishable.

Information-Processing Tasks

People tend to speak generally about the impacts of computers and computer-based information systems. However, we found that an empirical assessment of computer impacts is sooner or later driven to

Table 2.3
Phase II Cities Compared with Phase I Cities in Terms of
Technological and Structural Policies

Technological and Structural Policies	Phase II Cities (N = 42)		Phase I Cities (N = 403)	
	Mean	S.D.	Mean	S.D.
Degree of automation (total applications operational)	47.4	26.3	31.3	22.7
Degree of sophistication of data processing	5.2	7.7	1.5	8.8
Degree of decentralization of computing resources	2.3	8.7	.3	7.6
Degree of integration	38.0	29.1	23.3	24.9
Degree of user involvement in design	.5	.2	.4	.2
Charging policy	.5	.5	.2	.4

focus on the specific tasks that computers perform. For example, statements that computers "save time" are more easily and more objectively assessed by focusing on specific computerized tasks; that is, do computers save time in processing traffic tickets, balancing the city's expenditure and revenue figures, and/or searching for a want or warrant on a criminal suspect? For this reason, primarily, the second phase uses the information-processing task as a focal point for selecting respondents, gathering data, and assessing policy outcomes.

"Information-processing task" is a term used to signify an activity that has a specific objective, explicitly involves information process-ing, and *might* be automated (Kraemer et al. 1976). For example, most cities regularly issue a payroll, which involves translating records of hours worked, pay rates, and payroll deductions into a payroll check. Thus "payroll processing" can be designated an information-process-ing task (IPT). Similarly, the searching of a file of utility customers for unpaid bills is an IPT, "utility-customer inquiry."

The IPT is an attractive unit of analysis, for it permits more objective and quantifiable observations of computer impacts. However, there are 300 such IPTs covering the full range of services provided by most city governments, although the IPTs do cluster in functional areas. Therefore, to be able to generalize beyond any specific IPT and also to investigate IPTs in a systematic and empirical fashion, which demands an in-depth analysis, we needed a small sample of IPTs.

IPTs were sampled on the basis of two criteria. First, we wished to generalize beyond any specific type of activity which an IPT involves; therefore we sampled IPTs from each of six generic types, which we label record-keeping, calculating/printing, record-searching, record-restructuring, sophisticated analytics, and process control. Each type is shown in Table 2.4 in terms of its general characteristics and the specific IPT(s) studied. As the table illustrates, each IPT varies most importantly by the degree of sophistication in the information pro-cessing involved.

Second, project resources limited us to investigating only a few IPTs, but we wanted to generalize beyond any single functional area of government services. Hence, we chose six IPTs within four functional areas:

Police
  1. Police-Manpower-Allocation Support

Table 2.4
Types of Information-Processing Tasks and Associated Applications

Type	Characterization	Applications Chosen
1. Record-keeping	Activities which primarily involve the *entry, updating, and storage of data*, with a secondary need for access; the computer facilitates manageable storage and easy up-dating for nearly unlimited amounts of information.	Traffic-ticket processing
2. Calculating/printing	Activities which primarily involve *sorting, calculating, and printing of stored data* to produce specific operational output; utilizes the computer's capabilities as a high-speed data processor.	Budget control (reporting)
3. Record searching	Activities where *access to and search of data files* is of primary importance; by defining parameters, relevant cases can be retrieved from a file with speed and comprehensiveness; on-line capability of computer is particularly useful.	Detective investigative support Patrol officer support
4. Record restructuring	Activities which involve *reorganization, reaggregation, and/or analysis of data*; the computer is used to link data from diverse sources or to summarize large volumes of data as management and planning information.	Policy analysis
5. Sophisticated analytics	Activities which *utilize sophisticated visual, mathematical, simulation, or other analytical methods to examine data*; the special capabilities of computers make possible the manipulation of data about complex, interdependent phenomena.	Patrol manpower allocation
6. Process control	Activities which approximate a cybernetic system; *data about the state of a system is continually monitored and fedback to a human or automatic controller* which steers the system toward a performance standard; the computer's capability for real-time monitoring and direction of activities is utilized.	Budget control (monitoring)

2. Detective Investigative Support
3. Patrol-Officer Support
Courts
4. Traffic-Ticket Processing
Finance
5. Budget Control
Planning and Management
6. Policy Analysis

Thus, by focusing on six specific IPTs within six generic types of tasks and four functional areas, we could generalize beyond any particular IPT or functional area and also collect objective indicators of policy outcomes.

Data Collection

Fieldwork

Each city selected for Phase II was visited. Six investigators, including the authors, spent an average of three person-weeks in each of eight or more sites as part of a larger project team. These site visits were used to gather three kinds of data.

First, 50–100 self-administered questionnaires entitled "National Study of Computers in Cities" were completed by the users of computer services in each site. Respondents were selected on the basis of their roles in city government and their relationships to our six IPTs. Table 2.5 shows each kind of respondent, the number of questionnaires distributed to respondents of each role, and the percentage of returned questionnaires. Each role yielded a high response rate, the average being 82 percent, because the investigators collected most questionnaires while in the city and made extensive follow-ups by mail and phone. These questionnaires covered users' perceptions of computing impacts, problems, and benefits. The analysis of these questionnaires is a major data source throughout this study, because it provides comparative assessments of perceived computer impacts within relatively well-defined roles in each city.

Second, about 40 personal interviews were conducted with elected officials and municipal personnel involved with each of the six IPTs studied in each city. These interviews were semi-structured. That is,

Table 2.5
Survey Respondents and Response Rates

Kind of Respondent	Number of Questionnaires Distributed	Number Returned	Response Rate, %
Mayor & mayor's staff	79	58	73
Council & council staff	266	117	44
Manager (chief appointed official) and staff	97	81	84
Urban databank custodians[a]	106	93	88
User department and division heads	544	494	91
User department administrative assistants	161	120	75
User department accountants	96	81	84
Budget reporting and monitoring heads	75	65	87
Budget analysts	83	70	84
Accountants	87	77	89
Traffic ticket directors	42	35	83
Traffic ticket supervisors	70	55	79
Traffic ticket clerks	175	149	85
Police manpower-allocation supervisor	40	40	100
Police manpower-allocation analysts	57	48	84
Police records division clerks	67	62	93
Police EDP specialists	6	6	100
Detective supervisors	90	81	90
Detectives	533	435	82
Patrol officers	548	468	85
All Respondents	3,222	2,636	82

[a] Includes planning staff and specially identified databank custodians.

investigators used cross-examination, department records, their own judgment, and a general investigative approach in order to code each city on the basis of a structured set of items. For example, an investigator might speak with a police chief, several police captains and lieutenants, detectives, and the city manager, as well as search police-department documents to determine who were minor and major participants in decisions over the adoption of computer applications to support detective investigation activities. We refer to this strategy as "structured field coding" to indicate the central feature: coding cities in a structured way, but coding in the field rather than on the basis of schemes developed to combine various sources and items of data long after the investigator has visited the city. This field coding was structured by six IPT questionnaires:

Questionnaire Title	*Information-Processing Task*
Management Oriented Computing	—Policy analysis: urban databanks and operational databanks
Budget Monitoring and Reporting	—Budget control
Detective Investigative Support	—Detective investigation
(Self-Administered Questionnaire)	—Patrol-officer support
Police Patrol Allocation	—Patrol manpower allocation
Traffic-Ticket Processing	—Traffic-ticket processing

Each IPT questionnaire corresponds to one of the six information-processing tasks, with one exception. "Patrol-officer support" was covered entirely by a section of the self-administered questionnaire completed only by patrol officers.

One additional questionnaire, entitled "Local Government Data Processing Installations 1976," was completed by the data-processing manager(s) and staff of each computer installation in each city visited. These included independent EDP departments, subunits of the finance department, police units, utility- and planning-department installations, as well as joint city and county installations, and so forth. Private service bureaus sometimes provide computing services to cities but were not surveyed.

Finally, we made extensive use of case studies, which were written up after each site visit. References to these cases are found in the text, but our reliance on them for insights is far more extensive than these references indicate.

Respondent Selection

The methods used for selecting respondents were specifically tailored to each information-processing task. The general strategy was to identify those roles most important to each information-processing task and purposively sample people performing those roles. Roles such as mayor, manager, and head of the budget reporting unit define specific respondents. In these cases, each specific respondent was contacted. If that respondent could not be interviewed or given a self-administered questionnaire, the investigator then went to the next most appropriate respondent, often to such people as Acting Mayor, Assistant City Manager, and Deputy Finance Director. Roles such as council member, detective, or traffic-ticket clerk define large groups of respondents. In these cases, we approximated a random sample of these groups to the degree feasible at each site. Sometimes this was impossible, but most of the time it was reasonably well accomplished.

Presentation of Findings

Once the data were collected, we constructed our indicators of organizational outcomes (information for decision-making, management control, operational performance, and work environment), and of implementation policies (technological development, structural arrangements, socio-technical design, and organizational context). The construction of the dependent variables was unique for each IPT studied, because the performance of, for example, manpower-allocation programs must be judged by different criteria than, say, the performance of traffic-ticket processing. The construction of the independent variables also tended to be unique for each IPT because the computer installation servicing the police department may not have been the same installation as that servicing the finance department in a given city. Moreover, each of our six IPTs has its own specialized computer applications and must be evaluated in terms of their number, sophistication, and routinization.

In Part 2 of this study, Chapter 3 presents some overall findings about the impacts of computing. All of the "IPT" chapters (4–8) have a similar organization. Each begins with an introduction to what is involved in the information-processing task in question, and what are the expected benefits to be realized from automation. Next we assess the performance impacts of computing operations by comparing automated with unautomated cities. We then describe the degree to which cities have moved away from the traditional manual systems and have implemented computing along the lines of a reform or post-reform approach. But because impacts vary among automated cities, we turn finally to an assessment of alternative approaches to the implementation of computing in order to discover those policies which might improve the performance of computing operations.

A correlational design is used to assess the degree of statistical association between each implementation strategy and its hypothesized consequences—the performance of the technology. Then, multivariate methods are employed to estimate the independent and combined effects of each strategy on its associated impacts. In this way, the analysis first builds an understanding of the independent effects of each strategy (or policy approach) and then an understanding of the combined effects of different policies. Throughout, multivariate techniques are used also to assess whether the observed relationships between policies and impacts can be explained or statistically accounted for by nonpolicy variables in our analysis, such as city size or growth.

Multivariate analyses are subject to numerous problems of measurement and interpretation involving such issues as multi-collinearity, measurement error, the treatment of missing data, and so on. As a consequence, the analyses that support the arguments of this book are the end product of months of index construction and computer analyses, and numerous refinements of our analysis strategy. For example, concerns for multi-collinearity led us to develop a number of composite indices that combine measures of similar attributes (such as technological sophistication) which are highly correlated among themselves. In addition, we tested for multi-collinearity in the regression equations. More generally, we have attempted to be sensitive to such issues throughout all stages of data analysis and interpretation.

For economy and clarity of expression, we often deviate from strict statistical terminology and discuss the various relationships in *causal* terms. It is important to note that our "one point in time" correlational design does not strictly permit such causal interpretations. We can rule out (disconfirm) a large number of plausible alternative hypotheses by using a sophisticated array of multivariate techniques. But we cannot assert that the findings of our study *confirm* a specific set of causal statements. Notwithstanding this classic limitation, when we presume, and have some evidence to suggest, causal relationships among our variables, we use causal language. Our confidence in making causal statements is enhanced by the research design on which this study is based. While our observations are constrained to only one point in time and to only 42 cities, the research design maximizes our ability to discern any policy–outcome relationships under these constraints.

In each IPT chapter, we also present comparative rankings of our cities on the various performance indicators. Such rankings will allow readers to find their own cities or to find a comparable city. The rankings may on occasion be outdated, but the listing of specific cities and their rankings should, we hope, bring more concreteness to the evaluation of information systems in organizations.

In sum, this study is an attempt to describe the effects which various computer-implementation policies have on the organizational performance of future cities. Consequently, managers can read each IPT chapter and find the answers to questions such as, What will happen if a city does "*x*," where "*x*" is a policy to decentralize computing, to automate more government functions, or to involve users in design of computer applications?

REFERENCES

Campbell, Donald T. 1969. "Reforms as Experiments." *American Psychologist*, 24(4): 409–29.

Campbell, Donald T. and Julian C. Stanley. *Experimental and Quasi-Experimental Designs for Research*. Chicago: Rand-McNally.

Hackathorn, Linda. 1975. "The URBIS Census Survey: A Description and Evaluation of Data Collection Procedures and Response Patterns." Irvine: Public Policy Research Organization, University of California.

Kraemer, Kenneth L.; James N. Danziger; William H. Dutton; Alexander Mood; and Rob Kling. 1976. "A Future Cities Survey Research Design for Policy Analysis." *Socio-Economic Planning Sciences*, 10(5):199–211.

Laudon, Kenneth C. 1974. *Computers and Bureaucratic Reform*. New York: Wiley.

Leege, David C. and Wayne L. Francis. 1974. *Political Research*. New York: Basic Books.

Kerlinger, Fred N. 1964. *Foundations of Behavioral Research*. New York: Holt, Rinehart and Winston.

Suchman, Edward A. 1967. *Evaluation Research*. New York: Russell Sage Foundation.

Part Two

Part Two

CHAPTER THREE
The Impacts of Computing

THE EARLY LITERATURE[1] on the impacts of computing in organizations is extensive and suggests that computing is likely to have many dysfunctional side effects as well as positive benefits for organizations (Kraemer and King 1977; Westin and Baker 1972). For example, concern has been expressed over the potential threats to privacy from computer-based files ever since the proposals for a national databank in the late sixties. However, the prominence of speculative works and the lack of empirical descriptions of actual dysfunctional impacts have lessened the effect of such concerns.[2] And the anticipated benefits of computing have had a correspondingly greater effect on the decisions of organizations seeking ways to improve the quality of their information systems.

Benefits of Computing

Among the major benefits that had been anticipated from computing were improvements in the information for planning and management decision-making, in administrative control, in the operational performance of departments, and in the work environment of employees (Hearle and Mason 1963; Kraemer et al. 1974). It was also anticipated that these benefits would greatly exceed, or at least equal, the direct costs of computing (Mitchel 1968; Weiner 1969). This anticipation led to the early adoption and use of computing in local governments and to its subsequent widespread expansion throughout government departments and agencies (Kraemer, Dutton, and Matthews 1975; Matthews, Dutton, and Kraemer 1976). But to what extent have the benefits been achieved? This chapter explores each of these dimensions, using the perceptions of top managers (chief executives, department heads, division heads), and occasionally of lower-level department staff in our 42 cities.

Better Information for Decision-Making

Computers were expected to increase the quality of information in the government, the availability of information for decision-making, the use of information, and the contribution of information to planning and management decisions (Downs 1967; International City Management Association 1971; Leavitt and Whisler 1958; Simon 1960, 1965). Generally, it appears that, in our cities, computers have increased the technical quality of information and that the information is used by government officials. But the information is only somewhat helpful in making decisions, and much of the information needed for government decision-making still is not available.

Computing clearly has increased the technical quality of information and its accessibility. This improvement has been fostered by the demands of computers for consistent data and by the capabilities of computers for automatic error-checking, immediate correction, and rapid access to large data files. Consequently, it is not surprising that most top managers in most of our cities feel that computer data are as accurate as manual data. Nor is it surprising that the managers feel that computing has increased the correctability and currency of information, and the speed with which it can be retrieved (Table 3.1).

Computer-based information also is used with increasing frequency by government officials. When computers first were installed in government, they were used mainly by lower-level staff for routine tasks such as accounting, billing, and record-keeping. As computer use has been extended, many of these automated routine tasks have been found to contain information useful to top managers; therefore, computers have been used to restructure this information into management reports (Dutton and Kraemer 1977, 1978). As might be expected, then, top managers in our cities currently are occasional-to-frequent users of computer-based information, typically in the form of routine reports from the departments, or in the form of responses to special inquiries. Most top managers never use a computer terminal themselves, and they request others to get information from a computerized file only several times a year on the average. However, they receive reports based on computer data a few times a month.[3]

Despite the better technical quality and the greater use of computer-based information, at least half of the managers in our study feel that computing has not increased the ease of access to information or the

Table 3.1
Technical Quality and Availability of Information
(N = 42 cities[a])

Item	Index of Agreement[b]
Technical Quality of Information	
Computerized data is as accurate as data in manual records and files	84
It does not take too long to get the information I need from the computer	73
Information is not difficult to change or correct once it has been put on a computerized file	67
The computer provides me with more up-to-date information than that previously available	53
Availability of Information	
Computers have made it easier for me to get the information I need	54
Computers save me time in looking for information	50
The computer makes new information available to me which was not previously available	45

[a]Respondents for each city include the mayor, city manager, or chief administrative officer and department and division heads.

[b]The index of agreement is the mean of the mean response within each city across all respondents, where individuals' reponses were scored as: 0, disagree; 33, somewhat disagree; 67, somewhat agree; 100, agree.

availability of new information in the government (Table 3.1). It also appears that computer-based systems currently are only "somewhat useful" to management decision-making and government planning. From the standpoint of management decisions, this result occurs primarily because few automated applications have been designed specifically to serve the management needs of local officials outside of the finance area. This is illustrated by the fact that top managers see computer-based information as more useful for decisions involving financial matters—salary negotiation, budget making, expenditure control—than for management decisions involving manpower allocation or goal setting for subordinate units and individuals; even so, they feel that the computer-based financial information is only "somewhat useful" (Table 3.2).

The situation for planning decisions is similar to that for management decisions. Top managers in our cities see computer-based information as only "somewhat useful" for monitoring community

Table 3.2
Computer Impacts on Management and Planning Decisions
(N = 42 Cities)

Item	Index of Usefulness[a]
Management Decisions	
How useful to you has computer-based information been during the annual budget cycle?	62
How useful to you has computer-based information been for day-to-day expenditure decisions?	51
How useful to you has computer-based information been for salary questions and negotiations?	46
How useful to you has computer-based information been in allocating manpower?	29
Has computer-based information aided you in setting realistic goals for the units or individuals you supervise?	31[b]
Planning Decisions	
How useful to you has computer-based information been in providing indicators of community conditions, such as employment, housing, age or income of residents?	39
How useful to you has computer-based information been in identifying city problems?	35
How useful to you has computer-based information been in determining solutions to city problems?	39

[a] This index of usefulness is the mean of the mean response within each city across all top-manager respondents, where individuals' responses were scored as: 0, no computer-based information; 25, not at all useful; 50, somewhat useful; 75, useful; 100, very useful.

[b] This item was scored somewhat differently. Responses were scored: 0, no computer-based information; 25, not at all; 50, yes, in a few cases; 75, yes, in many cases; 100, yes, in nearly all cases.

conditions, identifying city problems, and determining solutions to these problems (Table 3.2). Many planning decisions require broad-based data about community conditions (e.g., housing supply, occupancy, ownership, or condition), whereas most automated processes focus narrowly on a few limited features, e.g., condition of rental housing for the processing of a housing occupancy certificate. Because most such processes are automated independently, the data they contain are unrelatable and cannot be used to form a consolidated picture. Consequently, current automation in cities seldom serves planning directly, and when planning is not served directly, it is served poorly.

Taken together, these facts about the quality, use, availability, and contribution of computer-based information indicate that the anticipated decision-making benefits from computing generally have been achieved in limited areas and with limited success.

Greater Management Control

Computers also were expected to improve the ability of top managers to control subordinate departments and individuals through increased information about the quantity and quality of performance, through more frequent reporting of such information, and through the elimination of "filtering" of information by lower-level staff (Argyris 1970; Simon 1971; Whisler and Meyer 1967). Within our cities, some improvement has been achieved in the area of fiscal control (Table 3.2), but computing has not improved the general ability of top managers for monitoring and control.

Most control-oriented uses of computing are a by-product of operational automation and consist of simple listings and comparisons of inputs (effort, dollars) to government activities rather than the outputs/outcomes of these activities. Therefore, the use of such information for control is likely to be limited. This is borne out by the opinions of top managers in our cities. Top managers tend to feel that computers have had little effect on their ability to control units under their responsibility, to identify problems, abuses, or inefficiencies in these units, or to monitor the performance of individual subordinates in these units (Fig. 3.1). Consequently, it appears that administrative control benefits have yet to be achieved to any substantial degree.

Productivity in Operational Performance

Computers were supposed to have their greatest impacts on the operational performance of government departments, particularly on efficiency and to a lesser extent on effectiveness (Hearle and Mason 1963; International City Management Association 1971; Kraemer et al. 1974; Weiner 1969). With regard to operational *efficiency*, the computer's vast capabilities for storing, retrieving, and processing information were expected to pare down rapidly the "army of clerks" in city and county halls, thereby reducing costs without a loss in service effectiveness. However, it has been apparent for some time that staff

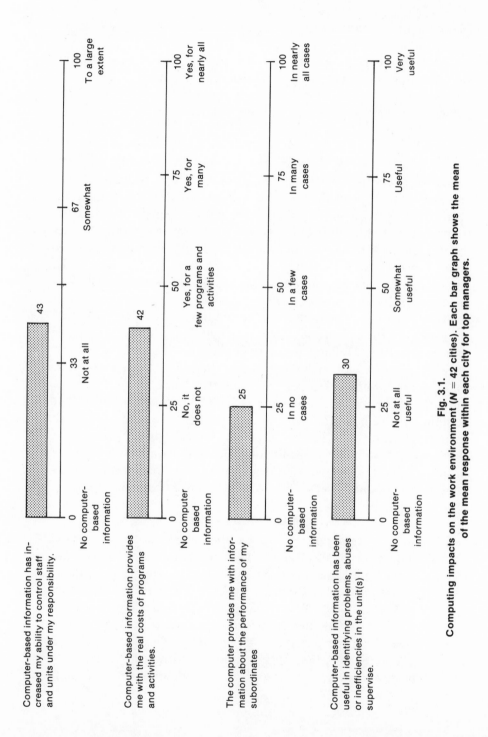

Fig. 3.1.

Computing impacts on the work environment (N = 42 cities). Each bar graph shows the mean of the mean response within each city for top managers.

and cost savings from automation occur mainly in large-volume, highly repetitive information-processing tasks such as tax, utility, and other billing operations. Since most city functions involve many varied, small-volume information-processing tasks, the overall efficiency benefits from computing have been considerably less than expected (Danziger 1975; Quinn 1976). This fact is reflected in the perceptions of our top managers, who are extremely divided over whether computers currently produce staff and cost savings (Table 3.3).

The dashed hopes for large cost savings from most municipal automation have been replaced by hopes for future cost avoidance.

Table 3.3
Computer Impacts on Efficiency of Operational Performance and the Effectiveness of Public Service
(*N* = 42 Cities[a])

Item	Index of Agreement[b]
Efficiency of Operational Performance	
Cost Savings:	
Where they have been applied, computers have reduced the number of people necessary to perform tasks in my department	42
Where they have been applied, computers have reduced the cost of department operations	53
Cost Avoidance:	
Computers allow departments to handle a greater volume of service without corresponding increases in cost	69
Effectiveness of Public Service	
Computers have increased the effectiveness of my department in serving the public	60
Computers have made it easier to handle routine citizen requests for information	60
Computers seldom make things hard for citizens because mistakes in computer records take a long time to correct	46
Citizen complaints about this department seldom are related to foul-ups or problems we have with the computer	67

[a] Respondents for each city include the mayor, city manager, or chief administrative officer and department and division heads.
[b] The index of agreement is the mean of the response within each city across all respondents, where individuals' responses were scored: 0, disagree; 33, somewhat disagree; 67, somewhat agree; 100, agree.

There is the expectation that as population grows—and therefore municipal service demands rise—computers might allow departments to handle the larger volume of services without increased cost, thereby justifying the early computing investment by long-term cost savings (Mitchel 1968; Weiner 1969; Wright 1972). This expectation might be realized in cities with rapid population growth, but not in cities with static or declining populations. Interestingly, though, most top managers in most cities in our study feel that cost avoidance does occur (Table 3.3).

With regard to operational *effectiveness*, the computer's overall impact has been marginal, almost imperceptible. Computers were supposed to free city professional/technical staff from routine operations so they could give more attention to service delivery to citizens (Weiner 1969; Wright 1972). But while the computer has made some tasks easier for city staff, like handling routine citizen requests for information, it has also increased the number of tasks the staff must perform. In addition, the computer has created difficulties for citizens, including the deciphering of bills, notices, and other computerized documents and the detection and correction of errors in these records. Therefore, it is not surprising that the top managers in our cities are mixed in their opinions about whether computers have increased the effectiveness of departments in service to citizens (Table 3.3).

The computer's overall impact on operational performance appears marginal. Improvements in the efficiency of operations are perplexing. Staff and cost savings are doubtful, although cost avoidance seems more probable; however, cost avoidance depends upon high-growth situations. Improvements in the effectiveness of operations also are perplexing because computers appear to make tasks easier for the government bureaucracy but they create difficulties for citizens.

Improved Work Environment

Computers were supposed to improve the work environment of government officials by making work more varied and interesting, by relieving day-to-day work pressures, by providing easy access to information they need, and by increasing their influence over others (Leavit and Whisler 1958; Weiner 1969). While impacts have occurred in these areas, their overall effect is problematic in regard to top managers. Top managers are in moderate agreement that computers have increased the number of different things they do in their job, but

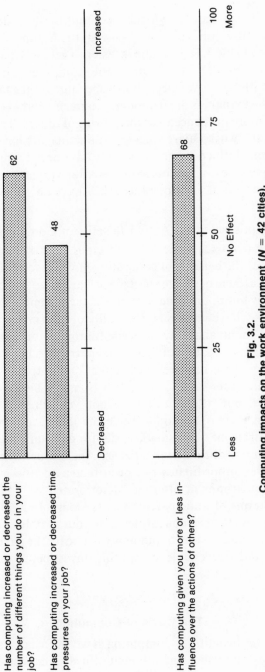

Fig. 3.2.
Computing impacts on the work environment (*N* = 42 cities).
Each bar graph represents the mean of the mean response within
each city for top managers.

they are divided about whether computing has decreased time pressures in the job (Fig. 3.2), saved them time in looking for information (Table 3.1), or made it easier to get information they need (Table 3.1). On the other hand, the computer's impact on the managers' influence over peers and subordinates has been uniformly positive—the managers are in moderate agreement that computing has given them more influence over the actions of others. Thus computing impacts on the work environment of top managers have been mixed. The managers' influence and job variety have been increased, whereas their time pressures and access to information vary; for some managers these have increased and for others they have decreased.

Anticipated vs. Actual Benefits of Computing

It is clear from the experience of cities and the opinions of top managers that the benefits of computing have yet to be achieved, have turned out differently than expected, or have been mixed—occurring in some cities but not in others. Whereas the technical quality and use of information have increased, the utility of information for decision-making and the availability of needed information are problematic. Although slightly greater management control has been achieved over fiscal matters, there has been little effect on control of subunits and individuals in other areas. Future costs might be avoided in high-growth cities, but most cities have not yet achieved staff or cost reductions in their operations. While the interface between government and citizens has been made easier for city staff, the interface has been made more difficult for citizens. And though the influence of managers over subordinates has been increased, the managers' personal work environment often has deteriorated.

Thus, in terms of anticipated benefits, computing appears to be a mixed blessing. It also constitutes a serious problem for managers because it raises a question about how to increase the payoffs, given the substantial and irreversible computing investments made by local governments.

The Costs of Computing

Whereas the benefits of computing have been far less than those anticipated by many local government officials, the costs have been far more than anticipated. The reason is that the computing budget inadequately reflects the total annual costs or the life-cycle costs of computing in local governments.

The Computing Budget

At first glance, the computing budget represents a relatively small proportion of the total annual operating budget in most cities— around 1 percent on the average. The range of expenditures for computing is from 0.5 percent in the smaller cities to 6 percent in the largest cities (Kraemer, Dutton, and Matthews 1975). However, it is becoming increasingly clear that the budgeted expenditures for computing sometimes represent only about one-third to one-half of the real expenditures for computing in cities.[4] Thus, the average annual expenditures for computing might be more like 2 to 3 percent of the city's annual operating expenditures; the range is from 1 to 12 percent.

This clouding of the real expenditures for computing stems from several budgeting and accounting practices, as well as from efforts by computing managers to shift certain costs back to the user departments. First, many computing-equipment expenditures, such as those for remote terminals and other equipment in the user departments, sometimes are included in the budgets of the user departments rather than in the budget of the computing unit. Second, expenditures for new systems development sometimes are included in the budget of the user departments, in contracts let by the user departments, or in federal and state project grants to the user departments, rather than in the budget of the computing unit. Third, expenditures for systems analysts and programmers located permanently in the user departments are included in department budgets rather than in the computer budget. Fourth, in recent years, computing units have begun to return the responsibility for inputing data, checking data for errors, and correcting the errors to the departments through the use of on-line remote data-entry procedures. This practice shifts real costs to the user departments for personnel and equipment—often without corresponding decreases in the computing budget.

The net effect of the foregoing practices is that the computing unit's budget rarely reflects the real expenditures for computing.[5] Therefore many public officials seriously underestimate those expenditures.

Life-Cycle Costs of Computing

The systematic underestimation of computing expenditures might be unimportant if computing budgets were remaining stable or decreasing. But like the local government budget as a whole, they are not.[6] In the case of computing, several factors generate continually increasing costs. First, while the unit costs of computing equipment are decreasing, the equipment being used is increasing rapidly in terms of the number of units used, their size, and their sophistication—all of which increase costs. Second, the cost of keeping up with advances in computing technology means that equipment and programs sometimes must be scrapped before their useful life is ended. Sometimes the pressure to keep up is forced upon the computing staff by manufacturers who discontinue (or threaten to discontinue) equipment or software support; sometimes the pressure also might be self-induced by the desire of computing staff to have the best and the latest technology. Regardless of the source of the inducement, the effect is to increase the costs not only of the technology, but also of training the computer staff to work with it, of converting application programs to run on it, and of training people in the departments to use it. While the costs to the computing department show up clearly as computing costs in its budget, the costs to the user departments do not show up as computing costs. Rather, they appear as increased costs of operations, or decreased effectiveness, or both.

Third, computer applications have a limited useful life, just as computing equipment does. In the life cycle of computer applications, there are costs for development, implementation, operation and maintenance, and eventually for redevelopment. The useful life cycle of computer applications is decreasing rapidly in cities, owing to frequent changes in federal and state legislation, reporting and auditing requirements, and administrative procedures governing local governments. When combined with locally induced changes from the user departments, the effect is to require that computer applications be redeveloped more frequently. Each change in requirements, and each change in computing technology, results in the applications becoming increasingly complex, and as the complexity of applications increases, the demand for additional sophisticated staff increases proportionately. The rising costs of sophisticated, experienced staff lead to considerably increased costs for the applications. In fact, expenditures for development and maintenance now exceed those for computing equipment and will consume an increasing proportion of total computing expenditures in the future (Goldberg 1973).

Fourth, the foregoing elements of cost interact with one another, creating a cost spiral. Each change in computing technology introduces additional costs into the system's life cycle of computer applications. Each requirement for change in computer applications generated by federal, state, or local officials creates additional staff costs, and sometimes equipment (e.g., storage) costs. Eventually, the accumulation of these changes generates a demand for increased, and possibly more sophisticated, computing technology.

Apparent vs. Real Costs of Computing

The costs of computing in local governments are deceptive. This is because they are intertwined with department costs of handling information and because computing technology is a complex, interrelated package, whose costs are very large and only partially visible in

Table 3.4
Perceived Computing Problems
(N = 42 Cities)

Item	Problem Index [a]
Information problems	
Difficulties in accessing computer-based data gathered or held by other departments and agencies	38
Slow response of data processing to requests for information	36
Computer-based data not available for the analysis of specific questions or problems	27
Operational problems	
High cost of computer use	47
Difficulty in getting priority in using the computer	34
Foul-ups in day-to-day computer operations	33
Frequent technical and organizational changes in data-processing services	22

[a] The problem index is the mean of the mean response within each city across all top managers, where individuals' reponses were scored as: 0, not a problem; 33, at times a problem; 67, often a problem; 100, very often a problem.

the computing budget. The costs of computing, both visible and invisible, also are increasing and will continue to increase as more government activities become automated and as the complexity of the computing package grows. All of this suggests that computing currently consumes considerably more of the city's budget dollar than most local officials believe, and that computing will consume even more in the future. The normal underestimation of cost is especially significant given that "the high cost of computer use" is the number one operational problem with computing as perceived by top managers (Table 3.4).

Overall, it is unclear whether the dollar costs of computing exceed the benefits, because the benefits are mixed and the dollar costs are unclear. It is apparent, however, that the benefits of computing do not now clearly outweigh the costs, and therefore the costs of computing are, and will continue to be, a problem for top managers in cities.

Unanticipated Problems with Computing

Technical and managerial problems with the computer's use have generated indirect costs, including organizational costs, in addition to the direct dollar costs. Most of these problems were unanticipated by managers, users, or computing staff when computing was originally introduced into local government. These problems may have become commonplace to computing staffs since that time, but even today they remain novel and disconcerting to managers and users.

Most problems with computing center around difficulties in getting information that top managers need and around difficulties in day-to-day operations with computing (Bostrom and Heinen 1977; Dutton 1975; Kraemer and King 1979). Informational problems seem especially severe. While there is a mass of computerized data in city hall, top managers find that the data they need for analysis of specific questions or problems frequently are not available in the automated systems of the government. Even when the data are available, the managers have difficulties in retrieving computerized data gathered by the operating departments, because the data are organized for other purposes. As a result, the computer staff often takes a long time to respond to the managers' requests for information and the response arrives too late to be useful.

Typically, top managers in cities experience these informational problems only to a moderate degree (Table 3.4). But the fact that they experience them at all is serious, especially when the claims of computing promoters about decision-making benefits are contrasted with the computer's limited impact to date (Table 3.2).

Operational problems with computing include difficulties in getting priority access to the computer, foul-ups in daily operations, and frequent changes in technical features or administrative procedures for computing services. Whereas the informational problems discussed above are felt directly by top managers, the operational problems are felt directly by department staff. However, since managers typically report that moderate operational problems exist (Table 3.4), they undoubtedly hear about them from their staffs, and the fact that managers hear about them indicates that the problems are substantial. Consequently, these problems generate indirect costs not only from delays and mistakes in operations but also from the need for managerial attention.

The Distribution of Benefits and Costs

In addition to the problematic nature of the benefits and costs of computing, it appears that the distribution of benefits and costs within the municipal bureaucracy might be different than anticipated and might have political consequences (Downs 1967; Kraemer and King 1976). When computing was first adopted, many local officials assumed that the impacts would be distributed evenly—no one department, group, or individual in the government would necessarily have a greater share of the benefits or a greater burden of the costs. Or, if some gained greater benefits, it was assumed they would also bear proportionately greater costs.

The experience with computing in cities has in fact shown, though, that the benefits and costs are not distributed equally or proportionately. Those who own and control the technology benefit more than those who do not (Dutton and Kraemer 1977; Kraemer and Dutton 1979; Kraemer forthcoming). Higher-level managers enjoy information benefits at the expense of lower-level operating units, which must collect the data these managers need. Staff units, such as finance and planning, benefit when they are able to gain access to data collected by other units without having to pay for the cost of collection. In sum, individuals and staff groups who know how to use automated information gain at the expense of those who do not. Thus computer technology appears to have subtle and unexpected effects on the distribution of information in the government, and on the distribution of the costs for collecting and maintaining that information. To the extent that some local government actors are able to use information to influence policy outcomes toward ones they prefer, computing also might produce power shifts among various actors in local government.

These political impacts can be illustrated by briefly examining the distribution of information benefits, work impacts, and computing problems within the municipal hierarchy.

Although computing has not greatly improved decision-making and control in government (Table 3.2), where improvements have occurred, they have primarily benefited top managers and staff rather than department managers, support staff, and professional staff (Table 3.5). Ironically, departmental staff frequently must generate and maintain the very information used by top managers to supervise the departments.

The impacts of computing on the municipal work environment also are differentially distributed among top managers and department staff. Although computing increases work and time pressure for everyone, lower-level managers and staff report such increases more often than do higher-level managers and staff (Table 3.6). And lower-

Table 3.5
**Usefulness[a] of Computer-Based Information for Decision Making,
by Level of Hierarchy**

		Computer-Based Information Has Been Useful in:				
Level of Municipal Hierarchy	N	Annual Budget Cycle	Daily Expenditure Decisions	Salary Questions	Allocating Manpower	Setting Goals for Lower Units
Chief executive	31	84[a]	66	68	38	40
Top staff	33	67	53	49	30	34
Department heads	42	58	48	40	29	30
Support staff	34	64	58	46	28	31
Professional staff	38	56	44	34	29	31

[a] The "usefulness" for each class of respondents is an average score over all responding cities. Respondents were asked to indicate for each decision whether computer-based information was: 0, not available; 25, not at all useful; 50, somewhat useful; 75, useful; 100, very useful.

Table 3.6
Percentage of Cities Reporting Changes in Work and Job Pressure,
by Hierarchical Level of Staff

Level of Staff in Municipal Hierarchy	N	Computing Has Affected:					
		Number of tasks in the Job			Time Pressure in Work		
		Increased	No Change	Decreased	Increased	No Change	Decreased
Chief executive	27	16	76	8	0	68	32
Top staff	31	34	57	9	13	65	22
Department heads	42	43	57	0	7	72	21
Support staff	39	74	26	0	33	62	5
Professional staff	42	69	31	0	5	50	45
Clerical staff	40	46	42	12	35	50	15

level staff feel these work impacts more directly than top staff. They tend to come in direct contact with computing, use it daily, and use it more in their jobs. Consequently, they are more dependent upon computing and are more pressured by its regimen.

Finally, problems with computing are experienced more often by department managers, support staff, and professional staff than by either top managers and staff or clerical staff. The problems that particularly plague these middle-level staff include lack of data needed for analysis, slow response of data processing to information requests, foul-ups in daily operations, difficulty in getting priority for computer use, and frequent technical and organizational changes in computing services (Table 3.7). Of course, clerical personnel experience these problems more often than top managers, but not as often as the middle-level staff.

Computing, Managers, and Implementation Policy

Despite the marginal performance of computing in most cities, the potential performance is great, given that some cities have already achieved substantial benefits. Every manager knows of at least one city that has achieved information benefits, better control, improved operations, and work enhancement from computer usage. These cities demonstrate that the costs, problems, and distribution effects of computing can be controlled to maximize the performance outcomes.

One of the major reasons why so many cities have not achieved good

Table 3.7

Percentage of Cities Reporting Computing Problems[a] by Type of Problem and by Hierarchical Level of Staff

Level of Staff in Municipal Hierarchy	N	Computer Data Not Available for Analysis	Slow Response of Data Processing to Information Requests	Foul-Ups in Daily Operations	Difficulty in Getting Priority for Computer Use	Frequent Technical and Organizational Changes in Computing Services	Difficulty in Getting Access to Other Departments' Computer Data	High Cost of Computer Use
Chief executive	30	37	18	15	15	11	32	26
Top staff	42	58	50	17	42	13	40	57
Department heads	42	74	50	29	64	26	45	45
Support staff	42	62	64	44	54	23	33	35
Professional staff	42	90	81	81	24	40	36	50
Clerical staff	42	50	45	48	33	28	21	50

a Includes all those cities which indicated that these issues are "at times a problem."

performance from computing, and have experienced problems with it, is that most managers shy away from computing, preferring to leave the management of this critical government resource to someone else—usually the data-processing manager. In contrast, cities that have achieved success with computing without great problems have had managers who took an active role in determining strategies and policies for the implementation of computing.

Implementation policy is the instrument by which local government managers might turn around their computing operations and achieve marked improvements in performance, and marked reductions in problems with computing. In order to achieve these improvements, managers must know the effects of different strategies and policies for the implementation of computing. In the following chapters we look more closely at the impacts of different policies on specific "information-processing tasks."

NOTES

1. Within the text of this chapter, we refer only to some of the most prominent and influential works on computer impacts within local government. Moreover, the literature specifically dealing with computer impacts in local governments is very limited in comparison to that dealing with business. For a comprehensive review of the literature on computer impacts within business and government, see Kraemer and King (1977).

2. Of course there are some important exceptions to this generalization. Notable among them are Rule (1974) and Westin and Baker (1972).

3. These tendencies are based on the average response of top managers in our 42 cities to a series of questions on computer utilization. These data are reported in Kraemer, Dutton, and Northrop (1979).

4. For example, see the recent PPRO (1979) study of computing expenditures in Orange County, California.

5. This is not to say that the reverse doesn't also happen. When computing is provided free to all departments in the city, a portion of each department's

expenditures is reflected in the computing budget where previously it was reflected in the department budgets. This situation further complicates the problem of determining real expenditures for computing.

6. During the 1960s and 1970s, local government revenues and expenditures have been escalating rapidly for such reasons as expanding scope of, and demand for, public services in an era of inflation. And it may well be that the costs of computing and other communication technologies have increased at a slower pace than other services.

REFERENCES

Argyris, Chris. 1970. "Resistance to Rational Management Systems." *Innovation*, 10: 28–35.

Bostrum, R. and J. Heinen. 1977. "MIS Problems and Failures: A Socio-technical Perspective." *MIS Quarterly*, 1(3): 17–32.

Danziger, James N. 1975. "EDP's Diverse Impacts on Local Governments." *Nation's Cities*, 13(10): 24–27.

——. 1977. "Computers and the Frustrated Chief Executive." *MIS Quarterly*, 1(2): 43–53.

——. Forthcoming. "The Skill Bureaucracy and Intra-organizational Control: The Case of the Data Processing Unit." *Sociology of Work and Occupation*, 6(2): 204–26.

Dial, O. E. 1968. *Urban Information Systems: A Bibliographic Essay*. Cambridge, Mass.: Urban Systems Laboratory, Massachusetts Institute of Technology.

Downs, Anthony. 1967. "A Realistic Look at the Final Payoffs from Urban Data Systems." *Public Administration Review*, 27(3): 204–10.

Dutton, William H. 1975. "Major Policy Concerns Facing Chief Executives" and "Executives Cite Common Data System Problems." *Nation's Cities*, 13(10): 28–30 and 33–36.

Dutton, William H. and Kenneth L. Kraemer. 1977. Technology and Urban Management: The Power Payoffs of Computing." *Administration and Society*, 9(3): 305–40.

——. 1978. "Management Utilization of Computers in American Local Governments." *Communications of the ACM*, 21(3): 206–18.

Goldberg, J., ed. 1973. *Proceedings of a Symposium on the High Cost of Software*. Palo Alto, Calif.: Stanford Research Project 3272.

Greenberger, M.; M. A. Crenson; and B. L. Crissy. 1976. *Models in the Policy Process*. New York: Russell Sage Foundation.

Hearle, E. F. R. and R. J. Mason. 1963. *A Data Processing System for State and Local Governments*. Englewood Cliffs, N.J.: Prentice-Hall.

International City Management Association (ICMA). 1971. "Managing data for decisions." *Public Management*, 53(10): 2-26.

———. 1977. "The Computer Boom." *Public Management*, 59(12): 2-18.

Kraemer, Kenneth L. 1964. "The Evolution of Information Systems for Urban Administration." *Public Administration Review*, 29(4): 389-402.

———. Forthcoming. "Computers, Information and Power: A Stage Theory." In A. Mowshowitz, ed., *Human Choice and Computers*. Amsterdam: North-Holland Publishing Co.

Kraemer, Kenneth L. and William H. Dutton. 1979. "The Interests Served by Technological Reform: The Case of Computing." *Administration and Society* 11(3): 80-106.

Kraemer, Kenneth L.; William H. Dutton; and Joseph Matthews. 1975. "Municipal Computers: Growth, Usage and Management." *Urban Data Service*, 8(2): 1-15.

Kraemer, Kenneth L.; William H. Dutton; and Alana Northrop. 1979. *The Management of Urban Information Systems, URBIS Final Report, Vol 1*. Washington, D.C.: National Technical Information Service.

Kraemer, Kenneth L. and John Leslie King. 1976. *Computers, Power and Urban Management: What Every Local Executive Should Know*. Beverly Hills, Calif.: Sage Publications.

———. 1977. *Computers and Local Government*, Vol. 2: *A Review of Research*. New York: Praeger.

———. 1979. "Comparative Study of Computer Impacts and Policies in Cities." Irvine, Calif.: Public Policy Research Organization.

Kraemer, Kenneth L.; William H. Mitchel; Myron E. Weiner; and O. E. Dial. 1974. *Integrated Municipal Information Systems*. New York: Praeger.

Leavitt, Harold J. and Thomas L. Whisler. 1958. "Management in the 1980's." *Harvard Business Review*, 36(6): 41-48.

Lucas, Henry C. 1975. *Why Information Systems Fail*. New York: Columbia University Press.

Mitchel, William H. 1968. "An Approach to the Use of Digital Computers in Municipal Governments." Ph.D. dissertation, University of Southern California, School of Public Administration.

Public Policy Research Organization (PPRO). 1979. "Facilities Management in Orange County: An Assessment." Irvine, Calif.: PPRO.

Quinn, Robert. 1976. "The Impacts of a Computerized Information System on the Integration and Coordination of Human Services." *Public Administration Review*, 36(2): 166-174.

Rule, James. 1974. *Private Lives and Public Surveillance*. New York: Schocken Books.

Simon, Herbert A. 1960. *The New Science of Management Decision*. New York: Harper and Row.

———. 1965. *The Shape of Automation*. New York: Harper and Row.

———. 1971. "Designing Organizations for an Information Rich World." In Martin

Greenberger, ed., *Computers, Communications, and the Public Interest.* Baltimore: Johns Hopkins Press.

Weiner, Myron E. 1969. *Service: The Objective of Municipal Information Systems.* Storrs: Institute of Public Service, University of Connecticut.

Westin, Alan and Michael Baker. 1972. *Databanks in a Free Society.* New York: Quadrangle Books.

Whisler, Thomas L., and Henry Meyer. 1967. *The Impact of EDP on Life Company Organization.* New York: Life Office Management Association.

Wright, J. Ward. 1972. "Information Systems: The Search for a New Approach." *Nation's Cities,* 10(1): 13–40.

CHAPTER FOUR
A Replacement for the Clerical Army: Traffic-Ticket Processing

CLERICAL TASKS were the first targets of computer automation in city hall. City officials hoped that automation would reduce the "army of clerks" in city hall and prevent future increases in the number of clerks required to handle the volumes of records accompanying city growth. Not only would automation allow the same number of clerks to process a greater volume of records, but it would allow them to process each record more accurately and consistently. Furthermore, the automation of clerical activities would, they hoped, provide benefits beyond clerical efficiency by capturing new and better information for citizens, clerks, and managers (Marenco 1965, 1966; Mumford and Banks 1967; Laudon 1974).

Automation of Traffic-Ticket Processing

Traffic-ticket processing is a classic clerical task much like utility billing, payroll processing, and tax billing. As with these other tasks, when the processing volumes increased, the work pressure felt by traffic clerks and supervisors also increased and so did the difficulty of keeping up with the work load.[1] The volume of traffic tickets in cities has not only been increasing annually but has always varied seasonally (with Christmas shopping and summer vacations). Consequently, some traffic agencies have found themselves so swamped with ticket backlogs that they have had to forgive parking tickets by the tens of thousands. This not only reduced city revenues from fines but also discouraged citizen compliance with parking laws. It also allowed citizen scofflaws and the "fixing" of tickets by government officials. Moreover, in some cases it seemed that the courts only added to the problem by siding with the worst offenders. A story taken from our site visits illustrates this point:

Last year the Public Prosecutor himself had over 100 outstanding parking tickets and a warrant was issued for his arrest. He fought it in court and a judge agreed with him that the statute of limitations for parking tickets ought to be only six months rather than two years. This action wiped out approximately 50 to 100 thousand parking tickets that had been outstanding—all because the City of Cleveland had not been able to process outstanding parking tickets. (URBIS Case Report, Cleveland)

In sum, traffic ticket automation has been aimed at speeding up ticket processing and eliminating the abuses that have crept in. Specifically, automation was expected to improve the information available to traffic clerks by providing capabilities for automatic identification of citizens with multiple unpaid tickets, automatic issuance of delinquent notices to citizens, easy identification of tickets by individual or vehicle (for answering queries by police officers in the field, for helping citizens who lost their tickets, or for internal processing), and gathering statistics on recovery of fines and disposition of tickets. Automation also has been expected to reduce the work pressure and perhaps even improve the work environment of traffic clerks. Lastly, it has been expected to help enforce compliance with traffic laws, ensure fair and equal treatment of offenders, and eliminate ticket fixing (Fig. 4.1).

However, the experience of some cities suggests that these expectations are based on inadequate assessments of potential implementation problems. For example, automation is expected to improve the information available to traffic clerks by providing record-keeping capabilities of the computer to keep track of the current status of tickets and by providing record-searching capabilities to identify unpaid tickets quickly. Yet automation is frequently blamed for incredible errors as a result of poor information. Nearly every city's local newspapers have carried horror stories about innocent citizens who were victimized by automatic "notice to pay," "notice to appear," or "notice that license tags would not be renewed," because their license numbers were entered by mistake on computerized traffic files. Automation also might result in problems and failures with electronic or mechanical equipment. Consider the case of Little Rock:

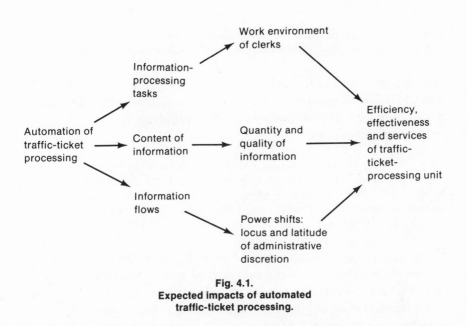

Fig. 4.1.
Expected impacts of automated
traffic-ticket processing.

The system was to use a mark sense card reader to completely automate the input of data from stamped parking tickets to the recording and sending of delinquent notices and warrants. However, the initial try of the complete system resulted in parking tickets stacking up for two months. Apparently the marks on parking tickets were a fraction of an inch off and were not read by the mark sense card reader. The city auditor found out about this, told a council member, and the council member made a significant public issue of it, calling for putting the new city manager on probation. (URBIS Case Report, Little Rock)

Problems can also arise with the expectation that automation will improve the clerical work environment by eliminating dull, repetitive manual tasks and providing new capabilities. Poorly designed systems have the opposite effect. For example, the early batch-oriented systems actually disrupted ticket-processing work flow, provided out-of-date information, and increased the work load of traffic clerks. Modern, on-line systems also can have their problems:

Personnel are highly supervised in the unit. They seem to have a fairly rigid work environment, and they are evaluated through the use of computer printouts. The printouts show the number of entries (cash collection, data update, query, retrieval) made at each terminal and by each operator. As a result, the traffic supervisor has been able to locate operators that have a low number of entries and has moved them to other windows or moved them out of the traffic division. (URBIS Case Report, Kansas City)

And finally, consider the expectation that automation will reduce the amount of administrative discretion in handling tickets by better accounting for every citation. No longer should a patrol officer, clerk, or other municipal official be able to "lose" a ticket:

There is an interesting capability in this system in that it lists all parking ticket numbers which are missing. If a particular parking ticket officer fails to issue a certain number ticket or a certain set of tickets, these are listed on a computer printout. It is thus possible for the police supervisors to see who has failed to turn in what tickets. (URBIS Case Report, Baltimore)

Consequently, everyone is assured more equal treatment and fixing tickets is minimized. Yet the case can be made that more, not less, administrative discretion is needed to permit flexible, sensitive, and fair administration of public services. Wilson (1968) argues that equal treatment is not always the fair, wise, and evenhanded thing to do in the administration of justice.

Computer-based systems, therefore, might or might not be potential tools for improved ticket processing. Their success can be heavily influenced by the approach used in implementing these systems. While some research has been conducted into the determinants of traffic-ticket practices (Gardiner 1969), research has been lacking on the impacts of computerization, and the impacts of computer-implementation strategies, on the performance of traffic-ticket-processing agencies.

This chapter describes traffic-ticket processing in local government, explores the impacts of automation, looks at implementation strategies, and evaluates the success of alternative strategies. Based on these findings, the chapter concludes with a set of policy prescriptions about how best to implement computer-based traffic-ticket processing.

Traffic-Ticket Processing in Local Governments

Most cities process several hundred thousand traffic tickets per year[2] through their traffic agency—usually an agency of the city or county court, although sometimes within the police department. Most of the tickets are their own, but cities might receive one-fourth of their total from other law-enforcement agencies.

Each ticket requires a series of actions on the part of the traffic agency. Typically, after a ticket is written and edited by the police department, several copies of the ticket are transferred to the traffic agency. The ticket is then checked against a transmittal sheet from the police and reviewed for errors such as an inappropriate ordinance number. Corrections normally require permission of the prosecutor's office—another transaction. Once the ticket is reviewed and edited, a search is made of motor-vehicle license and operator's license records (locally and through the state) to determine whether the automobile or driver has previous convictions, outstanding tickets, or an expired license. If such a search is positive, this information is appended to the ticket and the citizen is given a mandatory court appearance, increased fine, or normal fine depending on the nature of the offense. This information must be easily and quickly retrievable to aid clerks in subsequently handling the payment of fines, for example, so that payment of the initial fine is not accepted when a court appearance or increased fine or bail is required because of the citizen's previous driving record.

Once this information is gathered on the individual ticket, the information must be stored, sent to other agencies, and retrieved when payment is made or is overdue. If it is overdue, a delinquent notice might be sent out. At a later date, nonpayment might result either in an arrest warrant being issued, or in the state department of motor vehicles being notified so that the license holder cannot renew his/her driver's license until the original fine plus an additional fine for late payment have been paid. All these steps in processing a traffic ticket may be done by one clerk, as in a craft shop. Or, as in some agencies, a different clerk may perform each step—more like a production-line operation.

Finally, a series of reports is likely to be generated on the basis of tickets processed. These reports might summarize for the traffic-ticket director such factors as the volume of tickets processed, fines collected, and number of delinquent tickets, as well as tickets by location or intersection for the traffic engineer, or tickets by type of offense for the police planners and analysts. In all, the processing of traffic tickets requires a large number of precise transactions, which involve record-keeping, record-searching, record-routing, and printing.

The Impact of Traffic-Ticket Automation

Obviously, when cities decide to automate their traffic-ticket operations, they expect to improve the efficiency and effectiveness of services, and they expect to be able to offer new services. For example, when Chicago automated its operations in the mid-1970s, the city fathers hoped to curb the nonpayment of tickets. And in the minds of many citizens, that decision to automate signaled the end of stuffing parking tickets under their cars' front seats. But are the expected benefits of automating realized?

Performance Payoffs

Let us begin by considering whether automation increases the number of citations paid. The rationale for traffic tickets is enforcement of the law, and cities have learned that charging a fine discourages illegal parking and other violations. Yet the collection of traffic-ticket fines has become an end in itself, because it is an important source of revenue for a city. Consequently, no American city has emphasized law enforcement as an end over revenue generation to the extent done by one foreign country, where it has been found that "letting air out of tires" is a better deterrent to parking violations than are fines (Italy, reported on "60 Minutes"). Instead, in American cities, the "bottom line" in traffic-ticket processing is the revenue received (measured by dollar volume of citations which are paid). This is nicely illustrated by a newspaper article on the City of Long Beach:

CITY'S TICKET TO $1 MILLION PAID ILLEGAL PARKING FINES

"By this time we were totally frustrated with the city," he recalled.

"They had shoeboxes full of tickets," said City Auditor Robert Fronke, who shook his head in disbelief.

Auditors from Fronke's office visited the municipal courts in late 1977 on a routine check. They discovered the city had been losing about $1 million a year since the street sweeper tickets began in 1975.

"We asked the courts and city management for cooperation and they both put considerable resources into developing a new system as soon as possible," Fronke said.

TABLE 4.1.
Perceived Impacts of Computing in Automated
Traffic-Ticket-Processing Agencies

Has the use of computers and automated files in this department increased, decreased, or had no effect on the number of citations paid?

	Parking Viola-tions		Moving Viola-tions	
	%	N	%	N
Evidence it has decreased the number of fines paid	0	0	0	0
Believe it has decreased the number of fines paid	0	0	0	0
No effect	28	7	39	9
Believe it has increased the number of fines paid	28	7	35	8
Evidence it has increased the number of fines paid	44	11	26	6

When you consider the total staff involved in your operation, has the use of computer and automated citation files in this department altered the size of your staff relative to your working load?

	%	N
Evidence staff has increased (relative to work load)	6	2
Believe staff has increased	6	2
No difference	28	9
Believe staff has decreased	16	5
Evidence staff has decreased (relative to work load)	44	14

Allowing for inflation and salary increases, has the use of computers and automated citation files in this department altered your costs relative to your work load?

	%	N
Evidence costs have increased (relative to work load)	16	5
Believe costs have increased	16	5
No difference	26	8
Believe costs have decreased	29	9
Evidence costs have decreased (relative to work load)	13	4

Has the use of computers and automated files in this department led to any new services to citizens?

	%	N
No	53	17
Yes	47	15

Has the use of automation in traffic ticket processing had any effect on the ease or difficulty of "fixing" traffic tickets?

	%	N
Made it easier	0	0
No effect	45	13
Made it more difficult	55	16

Table 4.2
A Comparison of Operational Performance in Automated and
Unautomated Traffic-Ticket-Processing Operations

Operational Performance Characteristics	Automated		Un- automated		Partial Cor- relation, Con- trolling for City Size
	%	N	%	N	
Percentage of moving violations paid in 1975					
Less than 76 percent	37	7	25	1	−.12
From 76 percent to 94 percent	32	6	50	2	
Over 94 percent paid	32	6	25	1	
Percentage of parking violations paid in 1975					
Less than 62 percent	35	7	29	2	−.21
From 62 percent to 80.5 percent	25	5	57	4	
Over 80.5 percent paid	40	8	14	1	
Percentage of tickets paid within 30 days					
Moving	61	21	70	6	−.11
Parking	49	21	41	7	.18
Total personnel per 100,000 tickets					
Less than 8.2	35	9	25	1	−.13
From 8.2 to 17	35	9	25	1	
Over 17 personnel	30	8	50	2	
Total clerical personnel per 100,000 tickets					
Less than 6.6	38	10	0	0	−.30*
From 6.6 to 13	31	8	50	2	
Over 13 personnel	31	8	50	2	

"It had become common knowledge that you could throw away a parking ticket and nothing would happen," said Ronald Long, city computer project manager.

"If you didn't want to, you didn't have to pay," Long said, adding with satisfaction, "but you can't do that any longer."

"The payment rate already has gone up," Weaver said. "This system looks promising."

"The parking ticket system, including terminals and programs cost about $100,000," Long said. "It is expected to bring in $1 million in 1978–79," he said. "And that's a conservative estimate." (*Los Angeles Times,* October 1, 1978, pp. 1, 6)

It is often argued that computing can improve the revenue-collection success of traffic-ticket operations by keeping better track of tickets issued, thereby enabling the agency to follow up on those not paid, and

Table 4.2 (continued)

Operational Performance Characteristics	Automated		Un-automated		Partial Correlation, Controlling for City Size
	Mean	N	Mean	N	
Number of ticket-processing errors in last month					
Moving	7	27	3	7	.11
Parking	24	31	25	9	.06
Hours from ticket arrival to entry in all operations—manual and automated					
Moving	52	28	49	6	.06
Parking	35	30	35	9	−.02
Average number of days after date for payment or court appearance before action is taken					
Moving violations					
First delinquent notice mailed to offender	7	21	24	6	−.30
Bail increased	11	22	13	5	−.13
Warrant issued for arrest of offender	25	27	37	7	−.31*
Parking violations					
Registered owner of vehicle identified	16	26	41	6	−.39*
First delinquent notice mailed to offender	27	26	53	6	−.31*
Bail increased	32	26	53	6	−.12
Warrant issued for arrest of offender	79	24	78	6	−.02

*$P < .05$.

by changing the likelihood that an unpaid ticket will disappear (which, in turn, should alter the motorist's decision not to pay a traffic violation).

In each of our cities, we asked for evidence in the traffic agencies of the effect of computer use on the number of citations paid. Our resultant coding for each automated site showed that parking violations were indeed perceived as more likely to be paid (Table 4.1). And while moving violations are generally more severe and less likely to get lost even with manual systems, 35 percent of the agencies believed that computing had increased the number of moving violations paid, and an additional 26 percent provided some evidence to that effect.

However, the records show no significant difference when auto-mated and unautomated cities are compared in terms of the per-centage of tickets paid in 1975 (Table 4.2). And there is no significant difference if we compare the percentage of tickets paid within 30 days (Table 4.2). In both cases, we controlled for city size, since large cities tend to be automated and face a larger problem of visitors receiving traffic tickets and not paying them.

It is important to point out, however, that while agency records are often a more objective indicator of performance than interviews, a surprisingly large number of traffic agencies do not keep records from which it is possible to obtain a reasonably accurate estimate of the number of tickets issued, processed, or paid. Consequently, our findings are inconclusive as to whether automation leads to an increase in paid traffic violations or not.

Another major justification for the automation of clerical opera-tions is improvement of the efficiency of operations. In this respect, traffic-agency supervisors tend to perceive a reduction in staff relative to their work load and, to a lesser extent, a reduction in costs relative to work load even with allowances for inflation and salary increases (Table 4.1). Agency records also suggest that automated operations tend to have significantly smaller clerical staffs than do unautomated operations (Table 4.2).

In addition, an improvement in the efficiency and effectiveness of traffic-ticket processing was expected to enable a city to offer new services or new "levels" of service. In both these respects automation has lived up to its expectations.

To begin with, 47 percent of the traffic-ticket-processing agencies can cite additional services provided since automation (Table 4.1). The most common examples are the sending of delinquent notices and, in a few cases, reminder notices to citizens. Several traffic-ticket agencies have automated court scheduling and docketing as well as case tracking systems as an aid to the court and prosecutor. Other examples include the generation of data and statistics for the police department and traffic engineer, such as reports listing traffic tickets by type of offense, by location of offense, and by the time of day. The large number of cities offering new services is especially important because automated cities are offering these new services while also experiencing reductions in personnel needed to process tickets.

Another new, but normally unintended, service or function of computing in traffic-ticket processing has been an increase in the difficulty of fixing traffic tickets (Table 4.1). The very process of automation requires that sequenced tickets be accounted for and that the multiple records of each ticket correspond. Therefore, no longer can a traffic ticket be torn up by a traffic officer or clerk. Now it takes several, technically sophisticated actions by more than one person to eliminate the record from both manual and computerized files.

Furthermore, computing has speeded up aspects of ticket processing. Compared with unautomated sites, the automated sites take significantly fewer days to issue warrants for moving violations (Table 4.2). The automated sites also take significantly fewer days to identify the owners of vehicles and to mail delinquent notices for parking violations (Table 4.2). In fact, the major benefit of automating traffic-ticket processing might be the ability of the agency to meet scheduled dates more closely, maintain less of a backlog, and therefore conform more closely to the legally prescribed time periods for ticket-processing activities. For example, in one city:

Automation seems to help meet strict deadlines. A number of clerks indicated that there is just no question about getting things done according to set-up deadlines for tickets. Also the ease of finding tickets and processing tickets was emphasized by a lot of the clerks. (URBIS Case Report, Kansas City)

In contrast, automation has not led to increased efficiency and effectiveness in every area of traffic-ticket processing. Specifically, not all normal services are done at high levels of efficiency with the aid of computers. For example, as many ticket-processing errors tend to occur in automated as in unautomated sites (Table 4.2). And both automated and unautomated cities take the same amount of time to enter tickets in all relevant files (Table 4.2); this situation could be due to the fact that many cities must maintain manual as well as automated files.

Finally, computing has had a major impact on the nature of information in the traffic-ticket agency. Most traffic-ticket supervisors and clerks believe that computing improves the information available to them by providing them new, more up-to-date information that is more easily and quickly received (Table 4.3). Even their complaints sometimes highlighted subtle information benefits from automation:

Accuracy seemed to be one of the only complaints. Traffic clerks were always concerned with their inability to correctly read the license numbers on tickets because

Table 4.3
Traffic Personnel's Perceptions of Computer Impacts and
Views Toward Data Processing

	Percentage of Cities Agreeing (N = 28)	Average Score[a]
Computer impacts		
Computer makes new information available	61	56
Computer provides more up-to-date information than manual files	71	65
Computers make it easier to get information	84	73
Computers save time in looking for information	74	70
Computer data are less accurate than manual records	4	19

[a]Average scores are the mean of individual responses within each city, scored 0 to 100. Each variable was dichotomized to represent the percentage of cities with scores greater than 50, indicating "frequently true" and "nearly always true."

of poor writing by traffic officers. However, accuracy was greatly enhanced by their ability to use the police department's computerized alias name file. According to one respondent, a frequent problem is that when you look for a John Smith who should be in the warrant file, you go to the computer and 10-to-1 he's got a bunch of aliases. Without the computer there would be nothing to go on and there would be no record of previous citations for the individual. These performance impacts are fairly well summed up by the comment of one traffic clerk who said "When the computer is down, we're lost." (URBIS Case Report, Kansas City)

The importance of the information benefits provided by computing is reinforced by our interviews with the clerical personnel and supervisors within the traffic-ticketing agency. The "availability of information" is one of the most commonly mentioned positive aspects of computing in traffic-ticket processing. Other information and efficiency benefits are also commonly mentioned (Table 4.4). The only dislikes stem from technical failures to keep the computer functioning in an increasingly computer-dependent department, and failures to keep the data "clean," since inaccuracies are often more apparent than when an operation was manual (Table 4.4).

In sum, automation of the ticket-processing task has resulted in increased efficiency, effectiveness, and the provision of new services, as well as improved service levels. These performance payoffs run the gamut from more accurate data to personnel savings to mailing out delinquency notices.

Implementation Strategies

Local governments vary extensively in the ways they have implemented computer-based systems for traffic-ticket processing. Generally, however, automated cities in our sample have tended to follow appropriate technology, classical structure, and human-relations implementation strategy.

Technological Development

There are two strategies to the technological development of ticket processing. The first, advanced technology, is advocated by reformers who advise traffic agencies to automate early, develop a large number of applications, encourage high levels of computer use, develop the capacity for generating a variety of reports, and accept the attendant high levels of technological instability (Nolan 1973). In contrast to this approach is the much more limited and incremental approach to technological development, advocated by post-reformers, that most of our cities have taken—appropriate technology. Advocates of this strategy suggest that cities hold back on automation until there is a clear and demonstrated need, concentrate resources by developing a

TABLE 4.4
The Likes and Dislikes of Computing Users in
Traffic Ticket Processing

Likes	Percentage of Cities (N = 31)	Dislikes	Percentage of Cities (N = 31)
Availability of information	45	Technical problems (down, overloaded, broken hardware)	36
Improves information, more accurate, complete, up-to-date, easier to read	39	Information not accurate, incomplete, hard to read, inaccurate entry loses information	26
Can process citations faster	39	Not flexible enough	13
Less paperwork, filing	29	Slower than manual systems	7
Makes job easier	23	Difficult to use, complicated to query	3
Better able to answer citizen inquiries	19	Runs cost too much, EDP expensive, money should go elsewhere	3
Enjoyable, interesting activity	3		

small number of applications, focus on quality rather than quantity or sophisitication of reports, and hold development to a rate consistent with maintaining enough stability in the technology to avoid the inefficiencies involved in continually learning new systems and procedures.

The appropriate-technology strategy is evident from the pace, degree, use, and sophistication of automation for traffic-ticket processing. The pace of automation has been slow and incremental. As late as 1975, only about 40 percent of American cities over 50,000 in population had automated some traffic-ticket-processing application.[3] Within our 42 cities, about three-fourths (32 cities) use computers for some traffic task; however, 87 percent of our cities use computers for budget tasks, and 100 percent use computers for police tasks.[4] Fully half of our automated traffic sites are late adopters of computing, having adopted computing in the 1970s.[5]

Most automated cities have automated only a small proportion of their traffic-ticket-processing tasks. Most commonly, computing is a record-keeper, maintaining records of all citations (Table 4.5). For example, computing is used often as a high-speed printer, printing delinquent notices and arrest warrants, and as a record searcher,

TABLE 4.5
Operations Which are Automated for Traffic Ticket Processing

	Percentage of Automated Sites Which Automate This Operation For:	
Operations	Parking Violations (N = 32)	Moving Violations (N = 32)
Maintaining records of all citations	69	66
Searching records to answer inquiries from citizens	48	39
Searching for previous citations of person, vehicle	55	65
Determining, calculating, proper bail, fines	41	21
Printing of delinquent notice(s)	68	42
Printing of arrest warrants	48	58
Other operations	45	60
Mean number of operations automated	3	3

searching for previous citations (Table 4.5). No single operation predominates, however. In effect, most ticket agencies have automated only parts of their processing tasks and somewhat different parts at that. Our average city has automated only three out of seven applications for the processing of parking or moving violations (Table 4.5).

Given this moderate degree of automation, automated traffic-ticket-processing agencies fall far short of early images of the automated office. Computing seldom pervades the office environment. First, a small percentage of traffic personnel is involved in the use of computing files. In a third of the automated cities, over 80 percent of traffic personnel use computer files; but in 41 percent of our cities, less than 20 percent of the personnel use computer files. Second, computing is infrequently used. Fully a third of the automated cities use the computer only weekly or even less frequently. Given the daily issuance and payment of tickets, nearly one-third of the automated cities have to be running the main processing of tickets as a manual operation.

Thus, traffic-ticket processing is best understood as a computer application of recent vintage, which most cities appear to be implementing piecemeal and at a moderate pace of development. Some cities, though, are highly automated and did take the advanced approach to technological development. For example, Kansas City has an extensively automated and sophisticated traffic-ticket-processing operation.

The Kansas City Police Department made an early commitment to extensive automation and initiated the automation of traffic-ticket processing as part of that commitment. After traffic-ticket data are entered on computer files by clerks in the police department, the traffic clerks in the municipal court pick up the physical tickets. Court clerks then check each ticket against a computerized transmittal sheet which lists all tickets. When ordinance changes are required on the tickets, the clerks obtain approval from the city prosecutors. The clerks also use a teletype connection with Jefferson City, the state capital, to search for previous conviction records (by license number and by name when available) and attach information on previous convictions to the ticket. The clerks then code all computerized entries as either positive or negative, indicating whether or not the citizen has previous convictions or an expired license.

When a traffic violator comes to pay a ticket, the cashier enters the ticket number on the cash register, triggering an on-line search of the computerized record. The cashier is then signaled if the citizen is not allowed to pay the ticket and must have a court appearance. If the citizen does not have previous convictions or an expired license, then the citizen pays the cashier and the ticket is automatically cleared. In addition to the on-line cash registers, there are on-line terminals at each service window so the traffic clerks can handle direct or telephone inquiries.

Computing is also used by management to monitor the work of traffic-ticket clerks in Kansas City. Clerks are evaluated informally through the use of computer printouts that show the number and kinds of entries and searches made at each terminal by each clerk. Supervisors have located clerks with exceptionally few entries or searches and have occasionally moved them to busier stations. In all, Kansas City uses computing for 12 tasks beyond those listed in Table 4.5. Some of these tasks are: weighted case-load scheduling, checking cash balances with cashier balances, updating court journals and court disposition records, identifying defendants with aliases, and printing reminder as well as delinquent notices. But Kansas City clearly is an exception.

Structural Arrangements

There are two approaches to structural arrangements for automated traffic-ticket processing. The reform, or classical, approach that most of our cities have taken suggests that one should centralize the major decision-making about system design in the director of the traffic-ticket agency and the EDP unit. One should also centralize resources outside the agency. In this way, centralized control is maintained and the automation of ticket processing is integrated into the priorities and organizational constraints of the city government. In contrast, the post-reform, or participatory, approach suggests that one should decentralize design decisions by involving clerks and supervisors in system design. One should also decentralize computing resources by giving the agency its own computer facility and by linking it to multiple computing facilities. In this way automated ticket processing would be controlled by those who are closest to the needs and problems of the information-processing task. Generally, cities have heeded the classical message, as evidenced by low levels of user involvement, centralized sources for computing services, and charges for computer time.

Users' involvement in the design of traffic-ticket-processing operations is low; the central EDP staff and traffic agency directors have a clearly dominant role in the design of applications. For example, a variety of users can have a say in the design of traffic-ticket-processing operations; however, there are degrees of involvement ranging from membership on the design team, to consulting, to no role at all. The traffic agency's director and the central EDP staff have been on the design team in over half of our cities. In terms of having either a consultant or design-team role, the traffic agency's director has taken part in 87 percent of our cities, the central EDP unit has taken part in 71 percent, the computer specialist in the agency has taken part in 40 percent, and the supervisors in the traffic division have taken part in 59 percent. In contrast, clerical personnel, the most direct users, have been consulted in the design of ticket applications in only 16 percent of the cities. They have not participated on design teams.

The centralized provision of computing to traffic agencies is underscored by the fact that none of the 32 automated traffic agencies has its own computer system. Two-thirds (66 percent) use a single, centralized computing facility, but the other third are dependent on multiple computing facilities of the city, county, region, or state.[6] Most agencies (66 percent) use the city's facility; 50 percent use a county or regional facility, and 30 percent use the state's.[7]

A classical approach is suggested also by the charging policies of cities. Fully 56 percent of our cities charge traffic agencies for their actual amount of computer use. A major reason that the traffic agency is charged for its computer time more often than other departments (for example, only 38 percent of finance departments are charged even a flat fee for computer time) is that traffic is a revenue-generating department, similar to a utility department. The imposition of charging schemes by city management is based more often on the revenue-generating capacity of an agency than on the notion of regulating computer use.[8] Despite the intent, charging for computer time performs a regulatory function by encouraging departments to limit the development and use of computer systems.

Socio-technical Design

There is a reform, as well as a post-reform, approach to the design of computer systems. Reformers stress task efficiency—the design of computer systems so as to maximize the efficiency of information-processing tasks. The post-reformers stress human relations—the design of information systems so as to improve the quality of work within the organization. Our cities have heeded the human-relations message of the post-reformers in their design of traffic-ticket-processing systems. Equally important, there have been several improvements in task efficiency, and these improvements have not lowered the quality of work.

Computing has altered the work environment of traffic clerks by changing the task work flow from a craft shop, where all clerical staff tend to perform the different operations of the agency, to a production line, in which each member of the clerical staff specializes in a smaller part of the total operation. During our field research, we classified each traffic-ticket agency by whether it most closely approximated a production line, craft shop, or mixed (production line–craft shop) work-flow organization. While only 11 percent of the nine unautomated sites were classified as production line, fully 53 percent of the 32 automated traffic agencies were classified as production line. Likewise, 67 percent of the unautomated sites were classified as craft shop, compared to only 28 percent of the automated sites. The remaining unautomated and automated sites were representative more of a mixed work flow: 22 and 19 percent, respectively.

Assessment of Implementation
Strategies

While most of our automated cities are in an early development stage, they are nonetheless receiving increased efficiency, effectiveness, and service benefits from the use of computer systems. Yet not all traffic agencies have attained the same degree of benefits from automation. Clearly, some automated agencies perform better than others. Differences in approaches used in the implementation of computing might offer the explanation for these variations in benefits. Thus, the issue we wish to address here is whether the appropriate or advanced technology, participatory or classical structural arrangements, and human-relations or task-efficiency design, increase the performance of traffic-ticket agencies. We also consider the degree to which the community's environment and organizational context imposes constraints on the performance of automated traffic-ticket-processing operations.[9]

Surprisingly, however, the move to a production-line work environment has not brought about the more routine, more pressured, and more supervised work environment feared by many. In fact, when field-researcher ratings of automated and unautomated sites are compared, there are no important differences between automated and unautomated sites in the degree to which personnel can determine task order, in the pressure imposed on staff to keep up with the work load, or in the capability of supervisors to trace errors to the individual responsible for them. These findings are largely a consequence of the routineness and small scale of most automated and unautomated operations. Traffic-ticket-processing operations are so routine that even craft-shop operations offer little flexibility. There are only so many ways to process a traffic ticket. And traffic-ticket operations are of such a small scale that computing is not necessary for close supervision of the activities of clerical personnel. When supervisors can look over the shoulders of clerical personnel, automated reports are likely to increase neither the degree of work pressure nor the level of supervision.

In fact, a positive perspective on automation's effect on time pressures was gained by asking clerks whether they believe computing has changed the time pressures on their job. While clerks in 19 percent of our cities said computing increased time pressures, clerks in 39 percent of the cities answered that computing decreased time pressures (Table 4.6). Since there is no difference between automated and unautomated sites in terms of pressure to keep up with the work load, cities that automated must formerly have had greater work pressures, which may be a major reason behind their automation. Because automation might decrease time pressures on clerks, it should thereby have positive effects on the job satisfaction of traffic ticket clerks. In fact, in 57 percent of our cities, clerks said that computing had raised their sense of accomplishment (Table 4.6). And since automation has had no effect on the degree to which their work is supervised, or on their opportunities to work with people (Table 4.6), computing can be

TABLE 4.6
Traffic Personnel's Perceptions of Changes in
the Work Environment Caused by Computers[a]

Work Impacts	Traffic Clerks, % Indicating: (N = 28)
Has computing changed the number of things you do?	
(0) Decreased	11
(50) Not affected	46
(100) Increased	43
Average score	(61)
Has computing changed time pressures on your job?	
(0) Decreased	39
(50) Not affected	43
(100) Increased	18
Average score	(47)
Has computing changed your sense of accomplishment?	
(0) Lowered	7
(50) Not affected	36
(100) Raised	57
Average score	(70)
Has computing changed your opportunities to work with people?	
(0) Decreased	4
(50) Not affected	78
(100) Increased	18
Average score	(52)
Has computing changed the degree your work is supervised?	
(0) Decreased	11
(50) Not affected	85
(100) Increased	4
Average score	(49)

[a] Average scores are the mean of individual responses within each city, scored from 0 to 100. Each variable was trichotomized to represent the percentage of cities with scores less than 33.3, between 33.3 and 66.7, and greater than 66.7.

said to have had mainly positive effects on the work environments of traffic ticket clerks.

This positive work environment created by automation is probably a major factor accounting for our finding that clerks want to use computers and data processing more in fully 75 percent of our cities. Moreover, four-fifths of the traffic-agency directors and clerks also believe that computers will greatly improve the way their jobs are done in the next five years. And the positive effects of computing are not limited to the work environment of clerks. Traffic directors and clerks in about three-fourths of our cities believe that computing has increased the effectiveness, and improved the image, of the traffic-ticket agency. Consequently, automation may be viewed positively by traffic personnel because it is perceived to have both positive work-environment impacts and positive job-performance impacts.

In sum, those cities which have automated some part of the ticket-processing task have managed to build a receptive climate among their personnel. It appears that the human-relations approach was the prevalent implementation strategy. Automation has had positive impacts on the work environment, with the net result being an extremely positive attitude toward computing on the part of the traffic personnel.

The research strategy involves inter-correlating measures of these implementation strategies with a summary performance index. These correlations provide the initial description of patterns of relationships between implementation approaches and performance. However, to isolate those policies that are most important in explaining traffic-ticket-process outcomes, a multiple stepwise regression analysis is performed.[10]

Performance Index

The automation of traffic-ticket processing is intended to increase the efficiency and effectiveness of this processing task, and to allow for new services. In all, we have seven indicators of performance: three each for efficiency and effectiveness and one for new services.[11] The efficiency of current staffing levels is measured by the total number of clerical personnel in the traffic agency for every 100,000 tickets processed in 1975. Cost savings relative to work load and staff savings relative to work load are two measures based on interviews with traffic supervisors and directors in each city.

The effectiveness of the agency in revenue collection is measured by the percentage of parking and moving-violation tickets paid during the 1975 reporting year. The other measure of effectiveness is based on a factor analysis that included measures coded by investigators on the basis of whether or not automation increased the number of parking and moving violations paid. The "increased payment scale" is derived from the first factor and is defined by those agencies experiencing an increase in ticket payment due to automation. "New services" is a measure of whether or not computing has allowed the traffic agency to provide new services to citizens.

TABLE 4.7
Traffic-Ticket-Processing Performance Index
($N = 32$)

City	Performance Index Scale	City	Performance Index Scale
Very High		**Medium** (*cont.*)	
Baltimore, Md.	.91	Philadelphia, Pa.	−.07
High		Atlanta, Ga.	−.08
Las Vegas, Nev.	.66	Lancaster, Pa.	−.11
Paterson, N.J.	.66	Burbank, Calif.	−.14
Riverside, Calif.	.49	Montgomery, Ala.	−.19
Seattle, Wash.	.46	Spokane, Wash.	−.24
New Orleans, La.	.45	**Low**	
Kansas City, Mo.	.43	Portsmouth, Va.	−.28
Stockton, Calif.	.40	Tampa, Fla.	−.42
New Rochelle, N.Y.	.39	Oshkosh, Wis.	−.42
Lincoln, Nebr.	.35	Sacramento, Calif.	−.48
Brockton, Mass.	.30	Cleveland, Ohio	−.56
Warren, Mich.	.27	Louisville, Ky.	−.60
Medium		St. Louis, Mo.	−.66
Tulsa, Okla.	.22	**Very Low**	
Costa Mesa, Calif.	.21	Grand Rapids, Mich.	−.82
Milwaukee, Wis.	.18		
San Francisco, Calif.	.17	Mean	.05
Little Rock, Ark.	.10	Standard Deviation	.43
Long Beach, Calif.	.07		

Each of these indicators was standardized so that city scores had a mean of zero and standard deviation of one, with higher scores representing increased efficiency, effectiveness, or service. The average score for a city over all seven indicators is used as our summary index of automated traffic-ticket-processing performance. Table 4.7 shows the distribution of automated traffic agencies on this performance index.

The distribution of cities on the performance index reflects two tendencies. First, many cities scoring high on some performance indicators score low on others. Thus, few cities have very high or very low summary scores. Second, a number of high-performance cities, such as Baltimore and Kansas City, have taken a relatively advanced approach to technological development, which includes on-line applications to support traffic-ticket processing.

Independent Variables

Implementation measures have been divided into three general categories: technology, structure, and socio-technical design. Measures have been developed to assess the impact of the community environment and organizational context as well. Technological characteristics refer to the technological development of automated ticket processing. Indicators of technological development include measures of the degree of automation, including the number of operational computer applications supporting ticket processing (total, parking subtotal, and moving violations subtotal), the number of applications automated by the city, and the percentage of statistical reports that are computer generated. The degree of sophistication is measured by a sophistication-factor score for the city installation serving traffic; a measure of the degree to which computer terminals are used to answer information queries; and the number of on-line applications automated by the city. Utilization is measured by the frequency of automated system use reported by respondents. Routinization is measured by the first year in which the city automated a traffic ticket application. Other measures of technology include the degree of technological instability and the frequency of processing errors. Technological instability is the number of technological changes—such as change in the generation of machines, programming languages, and so forth—made in the traffic agency's computer installation within the preceding year. Ticket processing errors is a factor score that reflects the number of parking and moving-violation errors in processing tickets over a typical month.

Operational indicators of structural characteristics include measures of user involvement, decentralization, charging policy, organizational instability, and integration. "User involvement in design" measures the degree to which a variety of traffic personnel participated in the design of ticket-processing applications, and there is also a measure of installation user involvement, which is based on the degree of user participation in the city's overall data-processing operations. "Multiple computing sources" measures the degree of decentralization by the number of computing installations that serve each traffic agency. High scores for user involvement and multiple sources of computing suggest conditions of relative decentralization and fragmentation of computing services and control.

Other structural variables include "charging," which measures whether or not the traffic agency is charged for computer use. "Structural instability" is a measure of organizational change, which indicates the number of personnel and structural changes, as opposed to technological changes, made in the last year at the computing installation serving the traffic agency. Integration is measured by whether or not computerized files are shared by departments within the city. This indicator is therefore a measure of both the potential and the propensity for integration of departmental operations.

Two operational indicators of the socio-technical design are derived from a factor analysis of five items that measured the attitudes and opinions of traffic personnel about computing, computing personnel, and the impacts of computing on their job. "Amount of work" is a scale that indicates the degree to which traffic personnel perceive computing to have increased their number of tasks and work pressures. This measure also indicates a negative attitude toward computing. The "positive work scale" indicates the degree to which personnel (1) perceive computing to have increased their sense of accomplishment, (2) perceive computing personnel in a positive light, and (3) believe computing has lessened their job pressures. A third work-environment measure indicates the amount of pressure on clerks to keep up with their work load. And "craft shop" measures the degree to which the agency operates in a craft-shop versus production-line mode.

Indicators of the organizational context are: whether or not a city has slack financial resources (surplus funds that can be devoted to new or expanded tasks), council-manager government, and professional management practices, and the number of statistical reports produced.

Finally, a selection of community environment characteristics is included. Indicators of the community environment include total population in 1975, population growth from 1970 to 1975, and the influence and activity of political parties in the community.

Findings

Table 4.8 presents the relationships between each implementation strategy or environmental variable and our index of ticket-processing performance. A positive association between a strategy and the performance index indicates that the strategy is conducive to improved performance. Conversely, a negative relationship indicates that the implementation strategy in question tends to be associated with relatively low levels of performance in ticket processing. For example, the total number of automated traffic applications has a positive .42 association with the performance index. This finding indicates that cities with more automated applications supporting ticket processing tend to score higher on the performance index. Hence, the more that traffic-ticket processing tasks are automated, the more the computing can improve the performance of traffic-ticket-processing operations by keeping better track of tickets issued, enabling the agency to follow up on those not paid, and changing the likelihood that an unpaid ticket will disappear.

Overall, Table 4.8 suggests that ticket-processing agencies with higher levels of performance tend to be more technologically advanced and more classical in structural arrangements, and to be in growing cities with slack financial resources (Table 4.8). Advanced technology is suggested by high performance being associated with a higher degree of automation (although not necessarily local automation) and a higher level of sophistication. However, performance is unrelated to other measures of technological development and to measures of utilization and routinization.

Classical structural arrangements are suggested in that higher performing agencies have lower levels of user involvement and more centralized rather than multiple sources of computing (Table 4.8). Socio-technical design is neither consistently nor strongly associated with performance.

The community and organizational environment are also associated with the performance of automated traffic-ticket-processing agencies. Specifically, growing cities with slack financial resources tend to have higher levels of performance (Table 4.8). On the one hand, such cities might have fewer traffic problems and fewer parking and other traffic violators who are nonresidents. On the other hand, the fiscally healthy cities might be more automated and more classical in management and thereby achieve higher levels of performance. In fact, our analysis reveals this to be the case.

The independent contributions of advanced technology, classical structure, community environment, and organizational constraints

TABLE 4.8
Pearson Correlations between Traffic-Ticket-Processing
Performance and Implementation

	Traffic Performance	
Implementation Policy	r	N
Technological development		
Degree of automation		
Number of automated operations	.42*	32
Number of automated parking operations	.36*	32
Number of automated moving operations	.13	32
Number of automated applications	−.16	32
Percent of EDP generated statistical reports	.14	32
Degree of sophistication		
Sophistication of installation	.13	27
Degree of terminal queries	.24	30
Number of applications on-line at city level	.21	26
Utilization		
Degree of computer utilization	.11	28
Routinization		
First year of automation	−.01	25
Other		
Technological instability	.10	28
Ticket-processing errors	.02	32
User involvement		
User involvement in design	−.19	32
Installation user involvement	−.25	27
Centralization-decentralization		
Multiple computing source	−.25	32
Other structural arrangements		
Charging for computer use	−.25	27
Structural instability	−.05	28
Interdepartmental data sharing	−.14	28
Socio-technical design		
Sensitivity to work environment		
Amount of work scale	−.18	28
Positive work scale	.07	28
Pressure to keep up with work load	−.05	32
Sensitivity to work flow		
Craft shop	−.14	32
Organizational Context		
Slack financial resources	.41*	32
Council-manager government	−.05	32
Professional management practice	.09	32
Number of statistical reports	−.15	32
Community Environment		
Total 1975 population	−.02	32
Population growth 1970–75	.36*	32
Partisan environment	−.04	32

*$P < .05$.

can be estimated through the use of multiple regression. Table 4.9 presents the results of a stepwise multiple regression of the independent variables.

Regression analysis further supports advanced technology and classical structural arrangements as successful strategies for the implementation of traffic-ticket-processing operations independent of environmental and organizational constraints. Only two variables, the number of automated applications and the use of multiple computing sources, have statistically significant independent associations with performance. Together, they explain about one-third (31 percent) of the variation in performance among cities (Table 4.9). The high-performance agencies are the most automated and are dependent on fewer sources for computing resources.

Once these technological and structural variables are accounted for, community and organizational variables fail to explain an important component of the remaining variations among cities. In other words, traffic agencies with higher levels of performance tend to have more traffic-ticket applications automated and tend to be served by only one computing facility. Hence, the automation of ticket-processing tasks allows an agency to handle parking and moving violations more efficiently and effectively along with providing new services. To the extent that the computing is provided by only one facility, the city's ticket-processing task is also more integrated and better designed to service the agency's needs. As the advocates of classical structure

TABLE 4.9
Correlations and Path Coefficients for Traffic-Ticket-Processing Performance, T (Dependent Variable)

Independent Variables	Zero-Order Correlation	Path Coefficient	Variance Explained (%)
Number of automated operations: X_1	.42	.52	18
Multiple computing sources: X_2	−.25	−.38	13

$R = .56$ Total variance explained = 31%
$T^* = -.15 + .13X_1 - .25X_2$
    (.05)   (.13)

*Regression coefficients unstandardized; standard errors in parentheses.

argue, integration and centralization lead to more efficient and effective information processing.

To summarize, our findings tend to support a reform approach to the implementation of computer technology. The reform approach is suggested by the importance of advanced technology, represented by the degree of automation, and classical structural arrangements, represented by the centralization of computing resources, to improved performance. The approaches of cities toward socio-technical design appear to be unimportant to traffic-ticket-processing performance. However, this is probably because automation is a uniformly positive force in the traffic-ticket-processing work environment. The automation of such highly routine, repetitive clerical tasks might be a basic improvement of the work environment, irrespective of variations among cities in the way computing is implemented. Thus, while a task-efficiency approach of the reformers is not directly supported, our evidence does not show this approach as detrimental either. Finally, it is clear that implementation policies can make a difference; performance is not predetermined by the community environment.

Policy Recommendations

Policy recommendations flow directly from our findings concerning the conventional practices of traffic-ticket-processing agencies and the determinants of the successful implementation of computing. Many traffic-ticket-processing agencies are unautomated. However, among the automated agencies, computing has been implemented in ways that are consistent with appropriate technology, classical structure, and human relations. That is, cities have tended to follow a post-reform approach to the implementation of traffic-ticket-processing applications.

In contrast to conventional practice, our findings support the wisdom of a reform approach to implementation. Automation pays off for traffic-ticket processing and possibly other routine, repetitive clerical tasks. In addition, advanced technology buys more benefits, especially when implemented on the basis of classical structural principles. On the basis of these findings, it is possible to prescribe several implementation policies for information-processing tasks which are like those involved with traffic-ticket processing.

Technological Development

The advanced-technology approach should be used, in that cities should do the following.

1. *Automate.* Automation appears to provide information benefits, increased efficiency and effectiveness, and new services. Furthermore, these performance payoffs are accompanied by improvements in the work environment of traffic clerks.

2. *Automate a large proportion of clerical operations.* Computing could be used to automate one or more of the following tasks: recordkeeping, record-searching, calculating, and printing. Cities that have automated a large proportion of these tasks tend to perform significantly better than cities that have automated a smaller proportion of them. Possibly, the automation of a small segment of a clerical operation speeds only one part of an integrated and sequential process, and thereby the total task is not appreciably affected. In fact, the automation of segments may create bottlenecks out of manual operations. Thus, the comprehensiveness of automation, not the number of applications, is important.

3. *Develop more sophisticated applications, especially on-line inquiry capabilities.* On-line processing provides more up-to-date and easily retrieved information for handling citizen inquiries and ticket payment. Similar systems, such as utilities customer service and citizen complaint processing, in which the currency and availability of information is crucial to the service, might also benefit from sophisticated computing.

4. *Do not be concerned with the utilization or routinization of computer applications.* When automation is a necessary component of a routine clerical operation, utilization and routinization become minor issues. Since computing will be utilized whenever it is necessary in performing a task, more computer use cannot buy more payoffs. Computing is necessarily routinized whether introduced early or late, except when it is optional to performing a task.

Structural Arrangements

The classical approach to structural arrangements should be used. Specifically, cities should do the following.

1. *Centralize computing operations.* Relying on multiple sources of

computing might appear to increase an agency's flexibility. However, it is more likely that the agency is highly dependent on each of the multiple sources for different transactions and information, which increases the agency's difficulty in coordinating and processing information.

2. *Limit user involvement.* Manual agencies develop standard operating procedures, which often tend to approximate a craft shop. Yet the efficient automation of ticket processing might necessitate relatively major changes in those standard operating procedures. Thus, including users in the design of major changes in the system might increase the difficulty of instituting the innovations, because clerks and supervisors will have an interest in maintaining a stable, familiar work environment. This situation should be avoided, since emulating manual operations is not using the greatest potential of computer technology.

Socio-Technical Design

Post-reformers are concerned that the automation of clerical tasks will be dehumanizing by creating more tedious, repetitive, assembly-line jobs. Thus, the post-reformers stress a human-relations approach to socio-technical design. Our findings do not support the post-reform concern for the impact of automation on clerical tasks. Traffic clerks are nearly uniform in their positive evaluation of computing. Automated clerical operations improve the work environment, and differences among cities in their approach to socio-technical design do not have appreciable effects on these improvements. Thus, the use of computing, whether task-efficiency or human-relations oriented, has a positive impact on the work environment.

Organizational Context

Neither the reform nor post-reform approach to organizational context affects successful implementation. Perhaps such routine operations are less subject to the problems which may be generated by a political administrative context.

Summary

Automation of traffic-ticket processing does result in more effective processing and efficient operations, and allows agencies to provide new services. But the strategies an agency chooses to follow in implementing an automated system affect the degree to which it receives improved performance payoffs. Earlier in this chapter, we argued that most traffic agencies have chosen appropriate technology, classical structure, and human relations approaches to implementation. Then we presented data indicating that an advanced development and classical structure approach leads to more performance benefits.

Cities might have chosen the appropriate versus the advanced approach, not because they were ignorant of which strategy contributes to the best performance outcomes, but rather because of the organizational constraints on local government decision-making. Historically, public agencies have adopted policies and innovations incrementally (Lindbloom 1973). Only in exceptional cases have American governments taken the comprehensive non-incremental approach to policy-making or to technical innovation. There are many reasons for this pattern, a major one being that incremental change is less risky. If a policy or technology proves to be a failure or poorly conceived, the resulting costs are kept to a minimum and the system is salvageable. However, in terms of automating traffic-ticket processing, cities that comprehensively change their processing operations need not fear failure. Instead, they are likely to improve their operations through advanced technological development.

NOTES

1. See chapter 1 for a review of this literature.
2. A more general description of traffic-law-enforcement practices is provided by Gardiner (1969) for Massachusetts. However, there are important state and local variations.
3. Based on the 1975 URBIS census survey of U.S. cities over 50,000 in population.

4. It is surprising that traffic-ticket tasks are not among the most commonly automated information-processing tasks, given that clerks were generally early targets for automation. In fact, in a 1960s survey of 251 police departments, the most commonly automated applications were traffic citations (Whisenand and Hodges 1969). Apparently, subsequent traffic-ticket automation has not kept pace with early trends in police computing.

5. In part, the lower than expected, and more recent, automation of traffic-ticket processing might be due to this task's connection with the court system, which is by its very nature slow to adopt new technologies and operating procedures (Hartje 1975).

For example, one ticket-agency's director noted that it took a great deal of persuasion and a lot of time to convince the judges and most of the lawyers within the court system that something could be produced on less than legal size paper and still be usable! It is not just the orientation of lawyers regarding EDP, but also the fragmentation and decentralization of authority within the court system, that impedes the adoption of technological and managerial innovations. However, since the report of the President's Commission on Law Enforcement and Administration of Justice (Haloran 1967; McKee 1973), criminal-justice administrators have begun to turn increasingly to the use of modern management technology, automated information systems, and related computer technologies. See, for example: Adams (1971, 1972), Anderson (1972), Blaine (1970), Hartje (1975), Kleps (1970), Polansky (1973), and Winters (1971). Serious reservations have been raised about these developments by Hartje (1975), Holt (1972), Reich (1973), Tribe (1972), and Whitebread (1970).

Adoption might have been slowed also by the inter-organizational nature of traffic-ticket-processing agencies, which often necessitates agreement among state, county, city, police, and court administrators and executives before adoption or implementation decisions can be made.

6. Traffic agencies tend to use multiple computing facilities, given the nature of this processing task. For example, a search is made of motor-vehicle license and operator files (locally and through the state) to determine whether the automobile or driver has previous convictions, outstanding tickets, or an expired license.

7. These percentages total to more than 100 percent owing to the use of multiple facilities.

8. Earlier research (Dial et al. 1970) indicates that municipal agencies which generate independent revenues—such as water, gas, or electric utilities—traditionally have been charged for computing services, whereas general-fund departments have not been charged.

9. Of course, a large number of other factors might explain the performance of traffic-ticket-processing operations. Such factors as the enforcement policies of the police, practices of the state department of motor vehicles, the severity of fines, and the quality of personnel provide alternative explanations that are beyond the scope of this study. While this analysis cannot rule out such alternative explanations of performance, it can establish the presence of a relationship between implementation strategies and performance.

10. The method employed is to allow, initially, all measures of implementation strategies to enter the equation, but to report only those measures of implementation

strategies that satisfy the criteria of achieving at least a .05 significance level. The correlation and regression analysis provide the basis for statements concerning the most important implementation policies.

11. Several performance indicators were not used owing to the large proportion of unavailable data, such as the dollar amount of tickets issued and paid. Also, some data were rounded into less precise categories for analysis because the accuracy of the data did not justify higher levels of precision. For example, we trichotomized our measures of the percentages of traffic and parking tickets paid rather than using the exact percentage reported.

REFERENCES

Adams, Eldridge. 1971. "The Move toward Modern Data Management in the Courts." *University of Florida Law Review,* 23(2):250–60.

——. 1972. *Courts and Computers.* Chicago: American Judicature Society.

Anderson, Charles. 1972. Opening comments as panelist for symposium, "Courts of Tomorrow." *Jurimetrics Journal,* 12(4):195–97.

Blaine, Gerald S. 1970. "Computer-based Information Systems Can Help Solve Urban Court Problems." *Judicature,* 54(4):149–53.

Blauner, Robert. 1964. *Alienation and Freedom: The Factory Worker and His Industry.* Chicago: University of Chicago Press.

Crossman, E. R. F. W. and S. Laner. 1969. *The Impact of Technological Change on Manpower and Skill Demand: Case Study and Policy Implications.* Berkeley: University of California, Department of Industrial Engineering and Operations Research.

Dial, Oliver E.; Kenneth L. Kraemer; William H. Mitchel; and Myron E. Weiner. 1970. *Integrated Municipal Information Systems.* New York: Praeger.

Gardiner, John A. 1969. *Traffic and the Police: Variations in Law Enforcement Policy.* Cambridge, Mass.: Harvard University Press.

Greenberger, Martin. 1966. "The Priority Problems and Computer Time Sharing." *Management Science,* 12(11):888–1612.

Halloran, Norbert A. 1967. "Modernized Court Administration." In President's Commission on Law Enforcement and Administration of Justice, *Task Force Report: The Courts.* Washington, D.C.: Department of Justice.

Hartje, John. 1975. Comments, "The Systems Approach to Criminal Justice Administration." *Buffalo Law Review,* 25(1):303–56.

Hearle, Edward F. R. and R. O. Mason. 1963. *A Data Processing System for State and Local Governments.* Englewood Cliffs, N.J.: Prentice-Hall.

Holt, Don. 1972. *The Justice Machine: The People vs. Donald Payne.* Boston: Ballantine Books.

Kleps, Ralph N. 1970. "Computers and Court Management." *Judicature,* 53(8):322–25.

Kraemer, Kenneth L. and John Leslie King, 1977. *Computers and Local Government:* Vol. 1: *A Manager's Guide.* New York: Praeger.

Laudon, Kenneth C. 1974. *Computers and Bureaucratic Reform.* New York: Wiley.

Lindblom, Charles E. 1968. *The Policy-Making Process.* Englewood Cliffs, N.J.: Prentice-Hall.

Marenco, Claudine. 1965. "Gradualism, Apathy and Suspicion in a French Bank." In W. H. Scott, ed., *Office Automation: Administrative and Human Problems.* Paris: Organization for Economic Cooperation and Development.

——. 1966. "The Effects of Rationalization of Clerical Work on the Attitudes and Behavior of Employees." In J. Stieber, ed., *Employment Problems of Automation and Advanced Technology.* Conference Proceedings of International Institute for Labor Studies, Geneva, 1964. New York: St. Martin's Press.

McKee, William S. 1973. "Computers and the Courts—Recommendations Made to the Courts Task Force." *Rutgers Journal of Computers and Law,* 3(1):134–51.

Mumford, Enid and Oliver Banks. 1967. *The Computer and the Clerk.* London: Routledge and Kegan Paul.

Nolan, Richard. 1973. "Managing the Computer Resource: A Stage Hypothesis." *Communications of the ACM,* 16(7):399–405.

Polansky, Larry P. 1973. "Contemporary Automation in the Courts." *Law and Computer Technology,* 6(6):122–40.

Reich, Robert B. 1973. "Operations Research and Criminal Justice," *Journal of Public Law,* 22:357–87.

Sartore, Anna Belle and Kenneth L. Kraemer. 1977. In Kenneth L. Kraemer and John Leslie King, eds., *Computers and Local Government* Vol. 2: *A Review of Research.* New York: Praeger.

Schumacher, B. G. 1967. *Computer Dynamics in Public Administration.* Washington, D.C.: Spartan Books.

Tribe, Laurence H. 1972. "Policy Science: Analysis or Ideology?" *Philosophy and Public Affairs,* 2(1):66–110.

URBIS Research Group. 1976. "Little Rock Case Study." Mimeographed. Irvine: Public Policy Research Organization, University of California, Irvine.

Whisenand, Paul T. and John D. Hodges. 1969. "Automated Police Information Systems: A Survey," *Datamation,* 15(5):91–97.

Whitebread, Charles H., ed. 1970 *Mass Production Justice and the Constitutional Ideal.* Charlottesville: University of Virginia Press.

Wilson, James Q., ed. 1968. *City Politics and Public Policy.* New York: Wiley.

Winters, Glenn R. 1971. "Innovations in Court Administration." *Judicature,* 55(5): 194–97.

CHAPTER FIVE
Intergovernmental Intelligence Systems and Police Investigation

FEDERAL, STATE, and local governments collect information about individuals, or intelligence files,[1] in order to administer taxes, distribute welfare payments, issue licenses, and enforce laws. Given the multitude of overlapping federal, state, and local jurisdictions, several government jurisdictions need much of the same information about many of the same individuals. Moreover, many government agencies increasingly feel the need to relate data in one set of files with those in another set of files, in order to check the accuracy of information and to obtain a more complete picture of an individual's status or activity. For example, in an attempt to reduce fraud and catch welfare cheaters, the Carter administration has recently proposed the development of a National Recipient System. When the system is fully operational in 1983, it is expected that the system will

collect and store confidential financial information on 15 million welfare recipients in all 50 states plus U.S. territories.

The system will be limited to those who receive cash assistance under the Aid to Families with Dependent Children program, almost 90 percent of whom are women and children. . . . The system's computers will check the names and social security numbers of AFDC applicants and recipients in each state and territory against various federal files, such as those for military pensioners and civil service and disability insurance beneficiaries. (*Los Angeles Times,* May 6, 1979, pp. 1, 23)

This trend toward interagency and intergovernmental intelligence systems is in marked contrast to the traditional tendency for each governmental agency and jurisdiction to collect its own information in order to ensure bureaucratic control over the accuracy, precision, content, and use of information (Intergovernmental Task Force on Information Flows 1968). This new trend has been stimulated by the

demonstrated potential of computers for overcoming technical ob-
stacles in the development of large, intergovernmental computer
networks. It has also been fueled by the potential of computers for
mitigating certain bureaucratic constraints on the sharing and consolidation of data by different governmental units (Westin and Baker
1972; Laudon 1974). That is, computing might help to overcome the
structural fragmentation of government by supporting intelligence
systems that centralize the storage of information but decentralize the
entry, retrieval, and use of information about individuals collected
from a multitude of agencies representing a multitude of governmental
jurisdictions.[2]

Examples of currently operational computerized intelligence systems include court-case tracking systems, which track individuals
through court, prosecution, and law-enforcement agencies that span
jurisdictional boundaries; and social-service information and referral
systems, which track individuals through city, county, and private
social-service agencies.[3] But the most inclusive, well-established, and
highly sophisticated intergovernmental intelligence systems serve the
criminal-investigation activities of local police agencies.[4] These systems have evolved over more than a decade of development by federal,
state, and local law-enforcement agencies.

Early on, the Federal Bureau of Investigation perceived an ad-
vantage in gaining centralized control over information collected by
state and local law-enforcement agencies on the criminal histories and
status of known offenders and wanted persons, and created a National
Crime Information Center (NCIC). NCIC centralized the storage of
information about persons wanted for serious offenses. But the FBI
goals were compromised by state and local jurisdictions, which refused
to relinquish control over their own criminal information systems. As a
result, NCIC evolved into a set of linkages between the national center
and comparable centers within each state and within many local police
agencies.

Beyond the NCIC type of information, local police agencies
maintain a great variety of intelligence information, and some agencies
have chosen to automate much of it. Consequently, today there is an
extensive nationwide network of local, regional, state, and national
computer-based files, which share and integrate information on tens of
thousands of persons for whom outstanding wants (orders to pick up

for police questioning) and warrants have been issued for all kinds of offenses, along with an assortment of other crime information, such as criminal histories, stolen property, stolen vehicles, and traffic offenses. For example, consider the case of Little Rock, Arkansas:

The police applications in Little Rock are quite recent and automation is relatively extensive. The only completely local applications are field interrogation reports and parking violations. However, the police have access through Little Rock and through state and federal files to wants and warrants, stolen vehicles, alias names, a parole file and a state detention file, as well as the normal NCIC data files. Finally, through other agencies, they have access on-line to stolen property files, motor vehicle registrations and criminal history files. (URBIS Case Report, Little Rock)

As a result of these automated files, the police officers in a number of cities can radio or "key" in (on a portable computer terminal located within the police car) a suspect's name and birth date or license number and know within moments whether the individual is wanted for even minor traffic offenses at the local level, for more major offenses anywhere in the state, or for major (Type I) crimes anywhere in the nation.

Thus, local governments not only can use the NCIC files but also can develop their own intelligence files, which might increase the effectiveness of local agencies in dealing with local offenses, including such minor offenses as traffic and parking violations. Therefore, a major issue for local government officials is whether to adopt, at the local level, computer applications that support police investigations.

Successful Automation of Police Investigative Support

The benefits of automated investigative-support systems are expected to be considerable, and to stem from improvements in information processing, content, and flows (Fig. 5.1). The automation of criminal and investigative records is expected to facilitate greatly the day-to-day work of detectives and patrol officers in completing forms, conducting searches, following leads, and handling field investigations. To the extent that automation is facilitative, it is expected to improve the work environment; that is, to reduce time pressures and the work load of menial tasks and to increase the job satisfaction and personal influence of detectives and patrol officers.

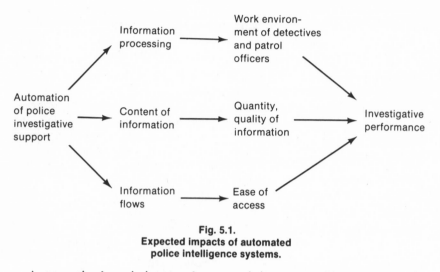

Fig. 5.1.
Expected impacts of automated
police intelligence systems.

Automation's main impact, however, is its expected improvement in the content of information available to detectives and patrol officers. Automation is expected to ensure greater attention to the accuracy, timeliness, and relevance of data, and to provide for the consolidation and integration of data from multiple police records. These improvements in the quantity and quality of available information are expected, in turn, to improve the investigative performance of the police by enabling them to develop more "workable" cases and more cleared cases in terms of solving crimes, and improved court cases in terms of supporting criminal prosecution.

The automated linkage of selected criminal files among local law-enforcement agencies and with state and federal agencies is expected to improve the flow of information throughout the law-enforcement system. Criminal activities, and criminals, frequently cross legal-jurisdictional boundaries, and the creation of automated linkages is expected to facilitate access to nonlocal criminal files for local law-enforcement agencies.

Collectively, these improvements in the quantity and quality of available information, the work environment of police investigators, and the ease of access to intergovernmental crime files, are expected to improve not only investigative performance but, ultimately, the ability of police departments to apprehend wanted or dangerous persons, solve serious crimes, support criminal prosecution and discern criminal patterns (Colton 1978; Murphy 1975; Whisenand and Tamaru 1970).

Given the potential payoffs from successful automation, it is important to assess the actual impacts of these systems on the performance of police investigative agencies. It is also important to assess which management strategies are most successful for implementing police systems, and to assess the effects that environmental variables may have on implementation. Therefore, this chapter (1) describes police investigative support in local government, (2) examines the impact of locally automating this task, (3) shows the way this task has been implemented at the local level, and (4) assesses alternative approaches to implementing computing for police investigative support at the local level.

Police Investigative Support in Local Government

Police investigative work is conducted by both detectives and patrol officers in local governments. Automated criminal-intelligence systems support both groups, but each makes somewhat different uses of these systems. In general, detectives engage in many nonroutine searches of multiple files, using multiple-search criteria and looking for relationships, whereas patrol officers engage in standard searches of a few files looking for specific facts.

Detective Support

Detectives spend a great deal of time not only searching through police-department files, but also completing forms, writing reports, and occasionally sitting in front of a computer terminal asking how to enter a suspect's name to obtain his criminal history. Computing is one device among many designed to support detectives in their investigative activities by making selected information easier to locate and retrieve. To illustrate this, let us "walk through" the various files that a crime investigator might utilize.

A crime is likely to result in an initial crime report being written by the police officer who was dispatched to the scene. In the case of a serious and "workable" offense, a detective would be assigned to the case.[5] The detective might begin the investigation by determining the identities and criminal histories of all those listed on the crime report as suspects, victims, and witnesses. By searching wants and warrants, criminal history, and alias name files, the detective obtains a background check on each suspect and each person likely to be interviewed.

With additional information from the crime report or interviews, the detective might also search through field interrogation reports that patrol officers completed on suspicious persons interviewed within the particular neighborhood at approximately the same time as the crime. Or perhaps a parking or traffic ticket was issued near that location, introducing another suspect. The crime report might also describe certain identifying characteristics of the crime, such as a burglary in which the entry was made through the kitchen window with a knife. In this case, the detective might wish to search through other burglary cases with a similar modus operandi (MO). Possibly, a license number was taken, justifying a search of motor-vehicle license files; or maybe a firearm was found, warranting a search for its registered owner. The search can also go on through fingerprint files, photograph files, records of property sold to pawn shops, lists of stolen vehicles, files of known members of organized crime, and records of the physical descriptions of known offenders.

Once a suspect is in custody, another series of record searches can ensue to corroborate or determine the validity of the suspect's testimony or statements to the police. Did the suspect receive any parking or traffic tickets during the period of time he claims to have been out of town?

In short, detective investigation involves many record searches for a large variety of reasons and circumstances.

Also contributing to the number of record searches is the fact that a detective would want information not only from the city police department but also from the county, surrounding cities, the state police, and possibly one or more federal law-enforcement agencies. Thus, not only does detective investigation involve a large number of searches, but each search involves the records of a large number of other police agencies and jurisdictions. As a consequence, detectives either constrain their search activity, spend all their time with search activity, or integrate the information of the multiple police jurisdictions in such a way that it can be easily and rapidly retrieved. The integrated storage, search, and retrieval of criminal information is the task of automated computer applications that support detective investigation.

Patrol Support

Patrol-officer support is more routine and specialized than detective investigative support. When stopping a motorist, spotting an abandoned car, or conducting a field interrogation, patrol officers usually begin with a driver's license, a license plate, or an individual's name. Normally, they are concerned with whether the individual has any outstanding wants or warrants, ranging from unpaid parking violations to major criminal offenses. While the patrol-officer's information search is more structured than the detective's, it is still massive unless the officer constrains his search activity, spends his day with the first motorist he stops, or integrates the information collected by multiple jurisdictions in such a way that it can be easily and rapidly retrieved. Again, the integrated storage, search, and retrieval of criminal information is the task of computer applications designed to support patrol officers; these are, importantly, a subset of the computer applications designed to support detectives.

The Impacts of Investigative Automation

If there is one area of local government operations in which the public, as well as administrators, believes computing has truly made a difference, it has to be police investigation.

Computers were introduced into police operations in order to provide quicker access to more up-to-date, more extensive, and more accurate information. Of course, the final payoff from computing was said to be more effective police departments. For example, with information assistance from computing, detectives would be able to handle a higher case load, while making more arrests and, in turn, clearing more cases. Similarly, patrol officers would be able to identify and apprehend more wanted persons, because they could quickly check on their cars' consoles whether a person had an outstanding want or warrant, or whether the car in question was stolen. In sum, computing appeared to many to be the great panacea in the "war" against crime in America. But have the expected benefits been achieved? In particular, has local automation produced greater benefits than computerized systems available to police departments through state and national linkups?

Information Benefits

Information benefits were the key payoffs expected from computing, and detectives and patrol officers do believe computing improves the quality of their investigative information. In three-fourths, or more, of our cities, detectives generally agreed that computers make it easier for them to get information, save them time in looking for information, and provide them with more up-to-date information (Table 5.1). Las Vegas illustrates both the benefits and the current limitations of information support for police investigative activities:

Table 5.1
**Respondents' Perceptions of Computer Impacts and Views
toward Data Processing by Role**
(N = 41)

	Detective Units		Patrol Units	
Computer Impacts[a]	*Percent Agreeing*	*Average Score*	*Percent Agreeing*	*Average Score*
Computer makes new information available	66	57	78	58
Computer provides more up-to-date information than manual files	73	62	90	66
Computers make it easier to get information	88	70	100	73
Computers save time in looking for information	83	67	92	69
Computer increases the amount of information I must review and analyze	17	39	10	39
Automated information is difficult to change or correct	10	35	8	36
Computer data is *less* accurate than manual records	2	24	0	22
It takes too long to get the computerized information I need	7	26	2	24

[a] Percentage of cities in which the average score for detectives suggested *agreement* with the statement. Agreement equaled an average score greater than 50 on a scale of 0 disagree; 33 somewhat disagree; 67 somewhat agree; 100 agree.

Most of the detectives agree that they have more information available or at least that it's in an easier form. Basically, it [the computer] provides helpful information which saves them time, and, in some cases, makes information available which otherwise they might not have been able to get or simply wouldn't have had the energy to get. It doesn't allow rich combinatorial possibilities. It doesn't really tell them much about other forms of tracing criminal activity besides the use of names since there is no MO file, no alias file, and none of the sorts of restructuring capabilities that might be useful for a full detective investigative support system. (URBIS Case Report, Las Vegas)

Still, in over half of the cities, detectives generally agreed that computers make new information available. Furthermore, detectives in less than 10 percent of the cities are critical about computerized information in terms of accuracy or even length of time to receipt. Patrol officers are even more positive about the informational impacts of computing (Table 5.1).

Performance Payoffs

Interviews with detectives suggest that many of the performance payoffs of computing are achieved whether or not the city has local investigative applications. In over 90 percent of the detective units, at least some detectives believe that computing results in more workable and more cleared cases (Table 5.2). These responses reflect the belief that computing provides more leads out of what otherwise would be unproductive information. For example, before automated searches of vehicle license plates, the police seldom followed up on a license-plate number as a lead in minor offenses; what is now conventionally perceived as a "workable lead" was an unworkable lead for minor offenses without the use of computing. A specific example of such operational payoffs is provided by Little Rock:

The detectives most emphatic about the operational impacts of computing were in the Stolen Property Division. Their basic [computer-related] job consists of getting records from pawn shops which list all the property pawned as well as identification numbers attached to that property and the names of individuals pawning the property. Then, the detectives routinely sit down at the terminal, punch in the property identification numbers and try to find a hit against the stolen property files. The detectives regard the time-saving and amount of stolen property located as substantial due to this process. (URBIS Case Report, Little Rock)

Table 5.2
Perceived Impacts of Computing in Automated Detective Investigative Support[a]

	Percentage of Cities Where:[b]				
	No detective Perceives Outcome	Few Perceive Outcome	Most Perceive Outcome	All Perceive Outcome	N
More workable cases—all cities	8	35	39	18	40
Not locally automated	8	42	25	25	12
Locally automated	7	32	47	14	28
More cleared cases	10	42	40	8	40
Not locally automated	8	34	50	8	12
Locally automated	11	46	36	7	28
Improved court cases	25	48	22	5	40
Not locally automated	17	50	25	8	12
Locally automated	29	46	21	4	28
Time savings—allow detectives to work adequately on more cases	18	32	32	18	40
Not locally automated	17	41	25	17	12
Locally automated	18	29	35	18	28
Hinder investigations at times	22	61	15	2	40
Not locally automated	42	33	25	0	12
Locally automated	14	71	11	4	28

[a] Based on interviews with detectives and detective supervisors in each city.
[b] Rows total 100 percent across.

And in another city:

While I was watching them operate [burglary division detectives] there was one case which came up which linked up in a search chain some stolen property, a person who was the receiver of the property, a person who was living with the receiver who later reported the same property stolen again, and another person who was a well-known "fence" in the area. It was clear that there was some sort of scam going on, or that there was no honor among thieves. (URBIS Case Report, Las Vegas)

Computers are less frequently perceived to improve court cases; in only one-fourth of the sites do most, or all, of the detectives believe that the use of computerized information improves their court cases (Table 5.2). Computerized information can affect cases in court allowing for more thorough investigations, which then can contribute to fewer dismissals (Greenwood et al. 1975). At the same time, such information as criminal histories is often inadmissible as evidence, although it may be important to establishing a case against the suspect. Another way that computerized information can improve a court case is through improving the credibility of detectives in the eyes of juries. By mentioning that he used computer technology in the investigation, the detective enhances his image as a professional and scientific investigator.

Since both those effects are indirect, it is not altogether surprising that improved court cases are not one of the biggest benefits from computing. In contrast, time savings are perceived by most detectives in over half of the cities (Table 5.2). Typical responses from the detectives included such things as:

"It's a quick way to search files that would otherwise take hours and hours to complete." "Time is the biggest thing." "It's the convenience of it." "You get a result a lot faster from the computer. Before, you had to send teletypes, or telephone the state offices, and they got to it when they could." (URBIS Case Report, Tampa)

As an illustration of the computer's time-saving benefits, one detective recounted an episode in which he decided to search the manual vehicle-registration files, looking for a particular license number:

I went down to the local state motor vehicle office where manual records are kept. This was at a time when the state's computer systems weren't working, and I had to search the tag files by hand. They were sorted by name and all I had was a license number. I did it only once; never again! I like the quickly accessed information provided by the computer. (URBIS Case Report, Tulsa)

In addition, detectives believe that computing allows them to work adequately on more cases than they could otherwise. Those who say that they cannot work more cases often claim that they can free more time for other activities, such as field interviewing. Thus, our findings might even underestimate the degree to which computing saves time.

Consistent with these positive views, most detectives believe that computing does not hinder investigations. In only one-fifth of the detective units did most or all of the detectives feel that computing sometimes hindered investigations. Normally, this is claimed to be the case because of inaccurate information that causes a delay in the search process. Duplication is another complaint. The same person might appear in the criminal history file under his real name and two different aliases. Such repetition delays, sometimes confuses—and always irritates—the investigator.

Detective Performance and Local Automation

Whether or not to have local automation is the primary issue facing municipal officials concerned with the automation of police applications. The performance of detectives in units with and without locally automated detective applications can be compared to assess the value of local automation. Of the 41 detective units investigated, 13 (31 percent) have no application automated at the local level (Table 5.3). These "locally unautomated" sites depend on automated files at the state and national levels, which are likely to be reached via one or more teletype terminals.

Police performance was assessed through self-administered questionnaires provided to detectives and patrol officers, and through archival data on clearances, arrests, and staffing. The questionnaires asked police officers a series of specific questions regarding their use of automated files. Table 5.3 displays the mean responses of detectives for those sites with, and without, local police applications that support detective investigation. These scores for both types of cities, along with correlations, provide a basis for estimating the impact of local automation on computer use, case load, leads, clearances, and arrests.

Detective Use of Automated Data

Detectives use computer files for about half of the cases that they actively investigate, although manual files are more frequently used for investigation than are computer files (Table 5.3a, b). Detectives in locally automated cities use both manual and computer files as frequently as detectives in locally unautomated cities.

Detective Case Loads

Local automation affects neither the case loads that detectives can actively handle nor the number of cases assigned to a detective. Generally, detectives are assigned about 43 cases per month and actively investigate about 32 (Table 5.3c, d).

Leads

Local automation does not tend to make more cases "workable." There is little difference between locally automated and unautomated sites in terms of how many cases would have been "unworkable"

Table 5.3

Detective Performance in Automated and Unautomated Sites Based on Questionnaire Responses of Detectives

Performance Characteristic	Locally Unautomated (N = 13)	Locally Automated (N = 28)	Overall Average (N = 41)	Pearson's Correlation Coefficient	Controlling for City Size
a. Number of the last 10 actively investigated cases where computer files were used in the investigation	5.10	5.76	5.55	.11	.03
b. Number of the last 10 actively investigated cases where manual files were used in the investigation	7.12	6.84	6.93	-.07	-.07
c. Average number of cases assigned in last month	45.40	41.72	42.88	-.07	-.01
d. Number of cases actively investigated over the past month	30.96	32.34	31.90	.04	.14
e. Number of the last 10 actively investigated cases which would have been *unworkable* without use of computer files	2.07	1.77	1.87	-.11	-.15
f. Number of the last 10 arrests which were assisted by computing	3.44	3.42	3.43	-.01	-.11
g. Number of the last 10 arrests which *probably* would not have been made without the use of computerized information	1.74	2.18	2.04	.18	.19
h. Number of the last 10 cases cleared by arrest or by investigation of in-custodies which were assisted by computing	3.83	4.09	4.00	.06	-.07
i. Number of arrests which the detective was credited with	5.63	8.52	7.61	.33*	.31*
j. Number of last 10 cleared cases which probably would not have been cleared without the use of computerized information	1.64	1.37	1.46	-.14	-.23
k. Number of the last 5 in-custodies which were linked to uncleared cases through computerized information	1.14	1.42	1.33	.19	.12

*$p < .05$.

without the use of computing. In general, detectives believe that one or two cases out of every ten would have been "unworkable" without computing (Table 5.3e).

Arrests and Clearances

The final payoff of computing in the detective unit is increasing the number of arrests and cleared cases. Overall, the detective performance data suggests that computing aids in making arrests and clearing cases.

These patterns can be illustrated first with arrests. Detectives say that at least three out of ten arrests are aided by computing (Table 5.3f), that about two out of ten arrests would probably not have been made without the use of computing (Table 5.3g), and that about four of ten cases cleared by arrest or by the investigation of in-custody cases were assisted by computing (Table 5.3h). While computing seems to be instrumental to the arrests made by detectives, it does not at first seem to be more instrumental in the sites with locally automated detective applications than in locally unautomated sites. An interesting contrast is that detectives with locally automated applications tend clearly to make more arrests (Table 5.3i). Since detectives with locally automated applications tend not to be assigned more cases or to actively work more cases than detectives with non-locally-automated applications, one would not expect the former to make more arrests, especially when they say computing was no more instrumental to them. Given this contradictory situation, our sense is that detectives get more critical information from their locally automated applications then they perceive. Our data tend to support this interpretation (Table 5.3j).

Clearances follow the same basic patterns. Detectives indicate that at least one of ten cases probably would not have been cleared without the use of computing (Table 5.3j). Also, detectives indicate that computing is important to about one out of five in-custody cases which they link to uncleared cases (Table 5.3k). But locally automated sites are not more successful.

In sum, detectives in automated departments do not tend to perform better due to their use of locally automated files. At the same time, detectives in locally automated departments do make significantly more arrests. Therefore, the performance indicators in Table 5.3 are merely suggestive that local automation does not aid performance overall. Yet there are great variations among automated departments in terms of computer-assisted arrests, clearances, and case loads. As a result, whether locally automated departments receive better performance from their detectives may depend on how well the departments implemented their local applications, in technological or structural terms.

One point should be emphasized, based on the findings in Table 5.3: automation *per se* pays off in better performance for investigative units. For example, over one case in ten was cleared through the use of computerized information, and more than one out of five in-custody cases was linked to uncleared cases through computerized information.

Patrol Performance and Local Automation

Because patrol officers use a more specialized group of computer applications, the use of computing and *local* wants/warrants and stolen vehicle files are expected to enhance the performance of patrol officers, just as it is argued in the literature that computing enhances the performance of detectives. Computing is thought to increase the likelihood of patrol officers' locating stolen vehicles and people with outstanding wants and warrants by making the information more easily and quickly available, and by pooling information from a larger array of local, state, and national police agencies. Automation of such files at the local level is believed to enhance the effectiveness of these systems by incorporating many local offenses—such as traffic and parking violations—not included on state and national files, which are restricted by the severity of the offense and the likelihood of extradition. But does local automation increase use of computers and accuracy in patrol performance? Moreover, does it increase the number of "hits" (e.g., the match of a name with an outstanding want or warrant, or the match of a license number of a stopped vehicle with that of a stolen vehicle)?

Computer use

Local automation tends to increase the number of searches of wants and warrants by patrol officers. In locally automated sites, they search for outstanding wants or warrants on 14 of every 20 people they stop,

Table 5.4

A Comparison of Operational Performance in Locally Automated and Unautomated Sites for Patrol Officer Support Applications

Patrol-Officer Performance	Officers in Locally Un-automated Sites (N = 18)	Officers in Locally Automated Sites (N = 22)	Overall Average (N = 40)	Pearson's Correlation Coefficient	Controlling for City Size
a. For how many of the last 20 persons stopped by you for traffic violations (or other violations, suspicious behavior) did you request a search of outstanding wants and warrants?					
Average number of wants, warrants, searches	11.46	13.50[a]	12.49	.31*	.30*
b. For how many of the last 20 stopped or inspected vehicles did you request a search of a stolen-vehicles file?					
Average number of stolen-vehicle searches	11.50	11.69[b]	11.60	.02	–.02
c. For how many of the last 20 persons on whom you have requested a search of wants and warrants did you discover an outstanding want or warrant?					
Average number of outstanding wants, warrants discovered	2.31	3.24[a]	2.78	.30*	.24
d. For how many of the last 20 searches which you have made of a stolen-vehicles files have you discovered a stolen vehicle?					
Average number of stolen vehicles discovered	.78	1.24[b]	1.01	.19	.16
e. How many times during the last year has the use of computerized police files led you to detain a person who should not have been detained?					
Average number of mistaken detentions	1.56	2.52[a+b]	2.09	.23	.10
f. How many times during the last year has the use of computerized police files led you to arrest a person who should not have been arrested?					
Average number of mistaken arrests	.35	.73[a+b]	.56	.29*	.23

[a] Wants and warrants are automated locally as well as by the state and national levels.
[b] Stolen-vehicle files are automated locally as well as by the state and national levels.
*P < .05, difference between locally automated and unautomated sites.

while elsewhere patrol officers search for outstanding wants or warrants on only about 11 of every 20 people they stop (Table 5.4a). The same pattern does not hold, though, for requesting searches of stolen-vehicles files (Table 5.4b). Of the last 20 stopped or inspected vehicles, patrol officers in sites with a local stolen-vehicles file made an average of 12 searches as did officers in sites without a locally automated file. In part, this search rate could be due to stolen vehicles being listed in most state files, thus making it unnecessary duplication to have local stolen-vehicles files.

Patrol Officer "Hits"

There may be as great as a 5 percent increase in the number of hits made on outstanding wants and warrants due to local wants and warrants files (Table 5.4c), while local automation does not appear to increase appreciably the number of hits made on stolen-vehicle searches (Table 5.4d). Of special interest is the sizeable number of hits made on both wants and warrants and stolen-vehicles files. As many as 15 percent of the wants and warrants searches yield a hit, while about 5 percent of all stolen-vehicle searches yield a hit.[6]

Accuracy

When automating wants and warrants and stolen-vehicles files at the local level, each department runs a calculated risk of making false arrests or falsely detaining people owing to incorrect or outdated data. Although manual files may be no more up-to-date or accurate, patrol officers in locally automated sites search the files more frequently, thus increasing the possibility of mistaken arrests.

Nonetheless, the responses of patrol officers suggest that mistaken detentions and false arrests are rarely caused by the use of computing; the average is less than three mistakes per patrol officer per year (Table 5.4e). While this rate is high from the perspective of those detained or arrested, it is clearly an exceptional event in police work. Furthermore, there are few clear differences between cities with and without computerized local police systems in their rates of false detentions (Table 5.4e). But patrol officers in locally automated sites say they average one more false arrest per year due to computer files than do other patrol officers (Table 5.4f).

Unlike our previous findings with detectives, local automation means that patrol officers not only use computerized systems more but also get more hits. Local automation pays off in better patrol-officer performance, but the degree to which a police department receives that payoff still may depend upon which implementation strategies are chosen.

Department Performance and Local Automation

The individual performance of detectives and patrol officers is important and suggestive of the performance outcomes of computing for the whole police force. However, it is also important to consider the performance of the department as a whole. If computing improves the performance of both detectives and patrol officers, then one would expect city police departments with local computer applications to perform better than city police departments without such applications. To compare departmental performance, we use traditional indicators based upon the most widely available crime statistics. These are collected from the various local departments by the Federal Bureau of Investigation.[7] The weaknesses of such measures have been documented elsewhere.[8] Here, these measures are used as one among several sets of measures, each with its own particular weakness.

The efficiency of the department in terms of how large a staff it maintains, given its crime work-load, is judged by dividing the number of crimes reported in 1975 by the number of personnel (Table 5.5). This measure standardizes the number of personnel by a rough measure of work-load variations across cities. Local automation fails to be associated with staff efficiencies. Locally automated departments do not have fewer sworn officers, fewer civilian employees, fewer detectives, fewer civilians in the detective unit, or fewer personnel in the records division per 1,000 crimes reported.

The effectiveness of the department is represented by four different measures. In each city investigators collected an estimate of the percentage of stolen property recovered by the police in 1975. While such estimates are certainly less than precise, they are relatively common estimates made by most departments by reasonably common procedures. A more standard measure of effectiveness is the clearance rate within the city. We have collected the clearance rates of all Type I crimes (the most serious level of crimes, e.g., murder, armed robbery, rape), as a group and for individual categories. From the clearance rates of 1975 and 1971, we have also calculated a measure of change in

Table 5.5
A Comparison of Operational Performance in Locally Automated and Unautomated Investigative Support Applications[a]

Operational Performance Characteristic	Locally Unautomated (N = 13)	Locally Automated (N = 28)	All Cities (N = 41)	Pearson's Correlation Coefficient
Personnel per 1,000 crimes reported:				
Sworn officers	38.30	41.24	40.30	.03
Civilian employees	8.43	7.86	8.04	−.04
Sworn officers in detective division	5.48	5.67	5.61	.01
Civilian employees in detective division	.34	.48	.43	.15
Personnel in records division	2.40	3.18	2.93	.08
Percentage of stolen property recovered	29	33	32	.17
Clearance rates[b]				
Total crime index (all Types I)	20	20	20	−.02
Rape	44	50	48	.15
Robbery	35	32	33	−.11
Assault	62	60	61	−.06
Burglary	15	17	17	.11
Larceny	20	18	19	−.10
Auto theft	17	16	17	−.04
Change in clearances 1971–1975[c]				
Total crime index	1.55	3.76	3.06	.03
Rape	−27.84	−12.05	−17.17	.23
Robbery	11.18	15.67	14.21	.05
Assault	− 1.68	− 3.33	− 2.80	−.02
Burglary	3.48	13.14	10.01	.06
Larceny	− 4.47	18.33	11.17	.21
Auto theft	27.46	30.57	29.56	.01
Reported crime per 100,000 population				
Total crime index	6,328	9,875	8,750	.21
Rape	21*	63	50	.28*
Robbery	163*	626	479	.28*
Assault	170*	452	363	.34*
Burglary	3,773	2,786	3,099	−.10
Larceny	3,616	4,802	4,026	.15
Auto theft	644	1,017	898	.15

[a] All data are for the 1975 reporting year unless otherwise noted. Source for reported crimes and clearances is the Federal Bureau of Investigation, Crime in the United States 1975 (Washington, D.C.: FBI, 1975). In general, the average clearance rates for the 41 sample cities are quite similar to national averages, which supports the representativeness of the URBIS sample.
[b] Number cleared by arrest divided by total crimes reported.
[c] Clearance rate in 1975 minus the clearance rate in 1971, divided by the clearance rate in 1971.
*$P < .05$, difference between locally automated and unautomated sites.

clearances over time. Presumably, departments that have been locally automated would make greater progress than locally unautomated departments in increasing their clearance rates over time. Finally, we have also collected statistics on the number of Type I crimes reported to the police, which we have standardized by population.

In general, locally automated police departments show higher levels of performance. They tend to recover a larger percentage of stolen property, to show greater increases in their rape and larceny clearance rates over time, and to show greater increases in their total clearance rates—and robbery, burglary, and auto-theft clearances—over time, although none of these differences is statistically significant. Yet the FBI data show no difference in 1975 clearance rates for locally automated and unautomated sites. Therefore, the trend suggests that local automation of investigative applications does not clearly lead to improvements in departmental effectiveness. However, if we take into account the fact that locally automated cities have significantly more rapes, robberies, and assaults per 100,000 population, then locally automated cities are more efficient, because they have the same clearance rates and staff size as unautomated cities but a larger crime rate. This finding puts into perspective the apparent lack of performance differences between locally automated and unautomated cities.

In conclusion, detectives and patrol officers perceive large information and performance benefits from automated police systems. Local automation, though, does not clearly contribute to detective performance but does contribute to better patrol-officer performance. And in terms of departmental-level performance, local automation allows police departments to maintain the same clearance rates as locally unautomated departments, with the same number of personnel per 1,000 crimes, but within the constraints of a larger crime rate. Since implementation strategies for computing may affect the degree to which an agency gets performance payoffs, we now discuss which technological, structural, and socio-technical policies lead to more efficient and effective law enforcement.

Implementation Strategies

Local governments generally, and our 41 cities in particular, vary in the ways they have implemented investigative support applications. Some cities have no local computer applications, relying totally on the automated files of federal and state law-enforcement agencies. Yet many cities have developed a wide array of computer-based files that can be queried from computer terminals located in the records divisions and investigator offices—as well as in patrol cars of some city police departments, such as Cleveland's. And while some city police departments utilize a central city or regional data-processing facility, many departments now operate their own computing facilities. Likewise, some cities have instituted strict standard operating procedures (SOPs) and rigid guidelines on use to ensure the efficient use of computing resources. In contrast, many cities have developed very flexible procedures and guidelines to accommodate the individual styles of officers, and have developed user-oriented software to enable users lacking technical training to have access to and to query computer-based files more easily.

These variations in the implementation strategies of local governments can be roughly classified by whether they involve primarily a reform or a post-reform approach to implementation, and can be viewed from three perspectives: technological development, structural arrangement, and socio-technical design. On this basis, our cities have primarily followed the implementation strategies of advanced technology, a mix of structural arrangements, and a human-relations approach to socio-technical design.

These variations in the implementation strategies of local governments clearly are important, because they dramatically affect the size and composition of police budgets. But do they affect the performance of detectives and patrol officers? Here we describe these strategies. In the next section, we evaluate their impact on performance.

Technological Development

Advocates of advanced technology argue that police departments should automate early and extensively, develop a high level of computing sophistication, and accept the costs of technological instability which accompany advanced development. The appropriate technology advocates suggest that police departments do just the opposite. For example, departments should concentrate their resources by developing a small number of local applications, hold back on automation until there is a clear and demonstrated need, and hold development to a rate consistent with maintaining enough stability in the technology to avoid the inefficiencies of continually learning new systems and procedures.

In general, U.S. cities that have automated locally have followed the reform or advanced technology approach to technological development. Similarly, the 28 of our 41 cities (one police department refused to be studied) that have automated locally have tended to take this course. That is, police agencies tend to have automated early, developed a large number of local applications, encouraged high levels of computer use, developed the capacity for flexible searches, and had on-line access.

The Pace and Degree of Automation

Police departments automated their information systems early on. The local development of automated police applications began in the 1950s with crime reporting applications, and peaked in the late 1960s and early 1970s with investigative, dispatch, and resource allocation applications. By the middle 1970s, about 80 percent of U.S. cities with populations over 50,000 had adopted computer applications in the area of police protection (Kraemer, Dutton, and Matthews 1975). Most (68 percent) of the 41 cities in our sample have adopted at least one of the major applications that support patrol and detective investigation (Table 5.6).

Encouraged both by public concern for better law enforcement and by large financial support from the Law Enforcement Assistance Administration (Colton 1978), development has been extensive. Already, no police department or detective unit is completely unautomated. All departments have some level of access to some state and national automated criminal information. But the cities vary in terms of the variety of automated information available, its mode of access, and its location. Locally, cities have automated an average of about seven computer applications supporting detective and patrol investigations. The most common local police applications are local wants/warrants and stolen-vehicles files (Table 5.6). A one-fourth to one-half of the sample sites have also adopted applications focused on detective investigation, such as criminal offense, alias, stolen property, criminal history, known offenders, and field-interrogation-report files. Intelligence compilations sometimes are automated, but the existence of such files is commonly denied. The least common and most difficult-

Table 5.6
Operational Computer Applications in Local-Government Installations
Which Support Police Investigation
(N = 41)

Kind of Application	Percentage of Cities Where Operational	Mean Year Automated	Percentage of Operational Applications On-Line
Wants/warrants file[a]	49	1971	80
Stolen-vehicles file[a]	49	1971	80
Criminal-offense file	44	1972	39
Alias name file	39	1973	67
Stolen-property file	32	1972	62
Field-interrogation-report file	24	1972	70
Known-offenders file	24	1973	50
Criminal-history file	24	1972	67
Intelligence compilations	7	1974	67
Modus operandi (criminal-patterns file)	10	1973	50
Fingerprint file	12	1971	80
One or more of the above	68		

[a]These are the major files used for patrol support.

to-automate applications are modus operandi and fingerprint files. In general, *local development has been designed to build upon and enhance the value of state and national systems (NCIC) to which it is linked.*

The kinds of data files that have been automated to support detective investigation and police patrol are shown in Table 5.7, along with the percentage of cities with access to this information in only manual form, or in automated form through either batch processing or on-line terminals. Automated wants and warrants files, which are available to all departments through NCIC, are not listed. The next most commonly available automated data are the registered owners of motor vehicles and the identities of stolen motor vehicles. More than 90 percent of the cities have automated access to this information, nearly always by teletype or terminal. The wide availability of vehicle information is due to automation by the state departments of motor vehicles, which update the information continuously through renewals and which make this information accessible to state and local law-enforcement agencies. Such information is especially useful to patrol officers in the field, but it also is used by detectives following leads (for

Table 5.7

Kinds and Location of Computer-Based Data Available for Police Investigation, in Percentages

(N = 41)

Kinds of Data Files	Not Available	Availability[a] — Cities Where:			Location[a] — Cities Where Access Is:		
		Only Manual Files	Batch Access	On-Line Search[b]	Only through Other Access	Only This Agency	Both this Agency and Others
Field-interrogation-report (FI) cards	12	68	5	15	12	88	0
Known offenders	10	52	15	23	33	54	13
Intelligence compilations	10	49	2	39	82	12	6
Persons or crimes committed with particular M.O.	43	40	10	7	28	58	14
Persons passing bad checks, check forgery, bad credit cards, other "worthless" documents	17	58	10	15	30	20	50
Criminal history of individual	0	32	7	61	53	18	29
Index to photograph of individual	5	70	5	20	10	70	20
Fingerprints of individual	2	81	0	17	28	44	28
Owner of motor vehicle	0	2	2	96	100	0	0
Stolen motor vehicles	0	7	7	86	76	3	21
Owner of registered firearm	22	44	2	32	86	7	7
Owner of stolen property	5	24	10	61	79	14	7
Pawn file, persons pawning property	20	53	7	20	55	27	18
Traffic-, parking-violations files	17	42	17	24	29	65	6

[a] Rows under "Availability" total 100 percent across, as do rows under "Location".
[b] On-line searches include directly using a terminal and phoning or asking a terminal operator (whether local or at outside agency) to do so.

example, full or partial license-plate numbers can be used as leads). Also, automated criminal-history files are available to most (68 percent) of the cities and are normally on-line (Table 5.7). These files sometimes contain a large assortment of information in addition to criminal histories, such as physical descriptions, aliases, and places of residence. In many cities, criminal-history files are among the most important files in detective investigation.[9]

Other detective applications tend to be components of criminal history and NCIC networks, or specialized information files. Automated files of the owners of stolen property are available to most cities (71 percent) and are used for the return and identification of the few stolen items for which owners can report property identification numbers. Automated intelligence compilations on members of organized crime are available to special units of many police departments (41 percent), which have formed a separate national computer network. Automated files with listings of owners of registered firearms are available to many departments (at least 34 percent) through the NCIC network, as is some information on stolen property. Automated traffic- and parking-violation files are available to nearly half (41 percent) of the units but are rarely used in detective investigation. Still, they have been used on occasion with headline-grabbing success—such as in aiding the identification of "Son of Sam" in New York City. Automated known-offender files are often simplified versions of a criminal-history file and are available to about 38 percent of the cities. These files allow investigators to keep track of persons with criminal records who reside in the area. Automated pawn files are available in about one-fourth (27 percent) of the cities, and are used in the investigation of pawn-shop sales to identify the sellers of stolen property.

Criminal-history files and NCIC files often contain an index of the existence and location of fingerprint records and photographs for an individual. But only in rare instances is this information directly accessible through an automated application (17 percent and 25 percent, respectively).[10] Also less frequently automated are files of persons passing bad checks (25 percent), which are used more as a record-keeping system than as an investigative tool.

Finally, field interrogation (FI) reports and modus operandi (MO) are rarely put on automated files but are areas of new development and wide potential use in detective investigation. Field interrogation cards are completed by patrol officers during the routine questioning of suspicious persons. Automated FI files are only available to about 20 percent of the cities and are used to identify potential witnesses and suspects who may have been near the location of a crime.[11] Modus operandi files are automated by development of an elaborate code, which describes the distinguishing characteristics of a crime pattern, such that new cases can be linked with older cases possibly committed by the same person(s). In this way, leads from separate crimes can be combined to develop a more complete and more workable case for investigation. Automated MO files are available to about 17 percent of the detective units.

In summary, not only the rapid pace of automation, but also the extensiveness of automation and the variety of automated files within local police agencies, indicate that cities are following an advanced approach to police intelligence automation. However, our findings do not indicate that cities have reached an advanced stage of development. Even though some police departments began to automate early, most of the local law-enforcement applications have been adopted since the 1970s (Table 5.1). Consequently, these applications are neither well routinized nor totally integrated into detective and patrol operations. This is because most computer applications require several years to design and redesign before they satisfy users' needs and are technically reliable. In this regard, less than half (41 percent) of our automated cities have completed two or more revisions, updates, or reconceptualizations of the majority of their police applications. And even if these applications were well designed and maintained from the beginning, they might take several years to affect standard operating procedures. Consequently, it is not surprising that most detective units do not depend only on automated information but still rely heavily on manual files. In fact, in only one of our cities are detectives and patrol officers dependent on computing for some tasks (Kansas City).

The Sophistication of Investigative Applications

The advanced sophistication of computing for police investigations is reflected in two general features of the technology: "on-lineness" and search flexibility. A high proportion of locally automated applications in the police function are on-line (Tables 5.1 and 5.2), even though on-line computer applications compose a minority of local-government computer applications as a whole (Kraemer, Dutton and Matthews 1975; Matthews, Dutton and Kraemer 1976). On-line applications permit detectives in one-third of the cities to have direct personal access to computer files from their normal work area, although only eight percent of the detective units make all queries in this way.[12] Still, most detective units use multiple means of access to computer files.

Typically, detectives phone or hand inquiries to a terminal operator in the records division of police departments.[13] But detectives also search through computer printouts and mail written requests for automated information. Computer printouts are routinely generated by most police installations, which list such things as outstanding stolen vehicles. Many questions can therefore be answered by thumbing through a printout at the back of the office. And in some major offenses when a broad search is made of, for example, "all 1975 two-door green-and-white Chevys," then a rather large listing is generated which results in a detective spending a great deal of time with computer printouts. Seldom is a written request used for a computer inquiry, unless it would require an unusually large output, such as a search of partial license plates.

Many automated applications for detectives also facilitate sophisticated search procedures, such as permitting detectives to search files with incomplete or incorrect information. More specifically, detectives can make an initial inquiry with an incomplete or misspelled name in 58 percent of the locally automated sites, with a physical description of a person in 50 percent, with a motor-vehicle description in 44 percent, with an MO description in 27 percent, and with a description of stolen property in 26 percent of the locally automated sites. The proportions of locally *un-automated* sites which can make such initial inquiries are somewhat smaller: 54, 36, 27, 22, and 18 percent, respectively.

By doing repeated searches with somewhat inaccurate and partial information, a detective is sometimes able to work a case which otherwise would have been unworkable. However, the leads provided to detectives are often too vague for these expanded searches. Furthermore, broader searches of files for partial license plates or motor-vehicle descriptions often result in such large numbers of "hits" that extensive manual searches of lengthy printouts are required. Thus, detectives often limit expanded searches to major crimes.

The Use of Automated Files by Detectives

The frequency of computer use is another indicator of the advanced technological development of automated investigative applications. Specifically, detectives tend to use automated files in most of their cases (Table 5.8). In only one city with access to computer-based files do most detectives tend to use computing merely as a last resort.[14] By contrast, detectives in ten cities routinely run all possible queries at the start of each case. Interestingly, the frequency of computer use is similar in locally automated and locally unautomated sites.

Structural Arrangements

Advocates of classical structure recommend low levels of user involvement, the use of a citywide data-processing installation, the centralization of access to computing through skilled operators, and a charging scheme for computer use. In contrast, the participatory structure advocates recommend high levels of user involvement, a decentralized police installation, multiple sources of computing rather than greater reliance on only local files, and no charging. The police departments in our cities have followed a mixed approach to the implementation of police investigative support automation, reflecting some aspects of both classical and participatory structures.

TABLE 5.8
Detective Utilization of Automated Files

General Pattern of Computer Use By Detectives	Percentage of Automated Cities			
	Non-locally Automated		Locally Automated	
	%	N	%	N
Never use	0	0	0	0
Use as a last resort	0	0	4	1
Use when they believe computer will provide needed information—do *not* use in most cases	17	2	21	6
Use when they believe computer will provide needed information—use in *most* cases	58	7	50	14
Routinely run all possible queries at start of each case	25	3	25	7
Total	100	12	100	28

[a]At least three detectives in each site were asked: How frequently do you query computer files? When? What about other detectives?
[b]Cities where detectives have access to computer-based files.

TABLE 5.9
User Involvement in Design of Local Police Applications
(N = 25)

Category of Officials	Percentage of Locally Automated Cities[a] in Which Official Had:		
	No Role in Design	Consultant Role	Membership on Design Team
Chief appointed official and staff	96	4	0
Chief elected official and staff	100	0	0
Police chief, commissioners, and top department managers	32	52	16
Departmental computer specialist	12	4	84
Middle management—captains, lieutenants	24	40	36
Detectives	44	40	16
Outside police agency	68	4	28
Outside consultant or service bureau	56	4	40
Central EDP unit	40	4	56

[a] Rows total 100 percent across.

User Involvement in Design

A mixed approach is evident from the strategies cities have used for design of police applications. Investigative applications tend to be designed by a computer specialist within the police department working with the central data-processing department (Table 5.9). If police personnel are directly involved in design, they tend to be middle managers, such as captains and lieutenants of the various patrol and investigative divisions. Working detectives and police chiefs participate infrequently in the design of investigative applications. But if we consider a consultant role along with a design-team role, then our cities have extensively decentralized design decisions. Police computer specialists in 87 percent of our cities, captains and lieutenants in 76 percent, police chiefs in 68 percent, and detectives in 56 percent have taken part in some phase of application design.

Centralization-Decentralization

When it comes to the policy of centralization or decentralization of computing facilities, police departments have put themselves in a peculiar centralized-decentralized position. For example, 29 percent of the police departments in our 28 automated cities use their own police installation as well as others, while 72 percent use only a nonpolice computer installation. The bureaucratic autonomy of police agencies within local governments promotes decentralized control of automation—giving police departments somewhat more control than other operating departments. Yet, at the same time, the military structure of police agencies promotes centralized, hierarchical control of computing decisions within the department.

Other Structural Arrangements

Local police departments are following a number of other strategies that reflect a mixed approach. First, charging users for computer time is a control mechanism—one means of limiting computer use to necessary and important file searches. Nearly half of our cities (42 percent) have chosen the classical structural arrangement of charging police departments for computer time, and the others (58 percent) have chosen the participatory arrangement of not charging. A second way of limiting use is to require prior approval before a detective (or a patrol officer) can search a file. Yet in 71 percent of our locally automated cities (and in 75 percent of our nonlocally automated cities), approval is never needed. And while about one-fourth of the detective units do require approval, this is only for special kinds of computer inquiries, such as those that generate costly batch searches. Likewise, most locally automated departments (72 percent) facilitate computer use by providing a skilled operator to assist the officers and often to handle their search requests. Only 3 percent of the detective units were not provided access to a skilled terminal operator to assist them with their queries. Finally, police departments tend to eschew the classical approach to training. In fact, only 10 percent of the detective units were trained in the use of computing by a person with prior detective experience. Most departments tend to rely on skilled operators and "learning by doing." Detectives learn by making their own inquiries with the help of their fellow detectives, skilled operators, and user manuals. Consequently, the structural arrangements that shape detective access to automated files are a combination of participatory and classical arrangements.

Socio-technical Design

Human-relations advocates are most concerned with the manner in which computing is integrated with the police work environment. The human relationists suggest that computing be implemented in ways that reduce job pressure, create more variety, lead to a greater sense of accomplishment, and develop support for computing and computer staff. Advocates of the task-efficiency strategy stress that one should be more concerned with the most efficient way to implement automated applications, since the "happiest" workers are not necessarily the most productive. Although most organizational behavior literature does show that the happiest workers are not always the most productive ones, it is hard to overlook the impact of computing on the work environment as a factor that will shape its performance as an investigative tool. One means for assessing the work impact of automation is to examine the responses of detectives who were asked to discuss what they most liked, and then what they least liked, about the use of computing in their jobs.

Computers and the Work Environment

The most frequently mentioned benefits of computing focus on time savings (Table 5.10). Investigators, especially in locally automated sites, feel that computing saves them time in their investigations by reducing the time spent in record searches. Related to this notion is the relatively frequent comment that computing saves the investigator a significant amount of paper work (Table 5.10), although less so in locally automated sites. Consistent with a task-efficiency perspective is the frequently mentioned belief that computing improves the performance of the detective, especially in locally automated sites. Detectives in most of the units (65 percent) mention that computing increases leads and makes cases more workable.

Even more informative is what detectives like least about computing (Table 5.10). The most widespread complaint, especially in locally automated sites, is that technical problems sometimes frustrate their use of the technology. The next most common complaint concerns the accuracy of information. Thus, the dislikes of detectives underscore the fact that computing is viewed as a positive contribution to the job, but that problems with the technology—the hardware and data

TABLE 5.10
The Likes and Dislikes Mentioned by Computing Users in Detective Units,
in Percentages

	All Cities (N = 40)	Locally Un-automated (N = 12)	Locally Automated (N = 28)
Likes [a]			
Saves time in investigation	85	80	86
Increases leads and workable cases	65	58	68
Reduces paper work	35	42	32
Speeds arrest	35	33	36
Clears more cases	20	8	25
Enjoyable, interesting activity	12	0	18
Improves quality of court cases	10	17	7
Helps work in custodies	8	0	11
Improves office environment: saves space, looks nice, quiet	8	0	11
Dislikes [a]			
Technical problems (down, over-loaded, broken hardware)	90	83	93
Information not accurate, incomplete, hard to read, inaccurate entry loses information	55	33	64
Lack of flexibility in use	30	25	32
Detectives do not know how to use	28	0	39
Waste of time, less successful than other activities, not the way to do detective work	18	17	18
Difficult to use, complicated to query	15	0	21
Runs cost too much, EDP expensive, money should go elsewhere	2	0	4

[a]Mentioned or emphasized by detectives.

quality—are a source of irritation. Supporting this generalization is the fact that only about one in five detective units mentioned that computing is a waste of time or less successful than other detective activities.

This positive view toward computing is corroborated by detectives' perceiving other positive, or at least neutral, computer impacts on their job (Table 5.11). First, detectives and patrol officers in over 90 percent of the cities believe that computing has either decreased or not affected

TABLE 5.11
Respondents' Perceptions of Changes
in the Work Environment Caused by Computers[a]
(*N* = 41)

	Detective Units: Percent Indicating	Patrol Units: Percent Indicating
Has computing changed time pressures in your job?		
(0) Decreased	49	45
(50) Not affected	46	47
(100) Increased	5	8
Average score	(34)	(37)
Has computing changed your sense of accomplishment?		
(0) Lowered	2	0
(50) Not affected	32	22
(100) Raised	66	78
Average score	(69)	(74)
Has computing changed your opportunities to work with people?		
(0) Decreased	2	0
(50) Not affected	76	80
(100) Increased	22	20
Average score	(56)	(59)
Has computing changed your influence over the actions of others?		
(0) Less influence	0	0
(50) No change	83	52
(100) More influence	17	48
Average score	(57)	(67)
Has computing changed the number of things you do?		
(0) Decreased	0	0
(50) Not affected	46	20
(100) Increased	54	80
Average score	(68)	(75)
Has computing changed the degree your work is supervised?		
(0) Decreased	0	2
(50) Not affected	93	68
(100) Increased	7	30
Average score	(52)	(56)

[a]Average scores are the mean of individual responses within each city, scored from 0 to 100. Each variable was trichotomized to represent the percentage of cities with scores less than 33.3, between 33.3 and 66.7, and greater than 66.7.

their job pressures. Second, detectives and patrol officers in nearly every city believe that computing has raised or at least not affected their sense of accomplishment. Third, in nearly every city they believe that computing does not affect their opportunities to work with people. Also, computing seems to have no decisive impact on the level at which detectives are supervised or have influence over the actions of others. Yet a number of patrol officers believe that computing has increased their level of supervision,[15] as well as given them more influence over the actions of others.

Taken together, detectives and patrol officers tend to view computing from a positive perspective. This is not to say that all police in all departments like and use computing. Many have intense negative opinions about the impact of computing on police work. However, most detectives and patrol officers in most departments believe that computing increases the efficiency of their search activity and aids the effectiveness of their job performance along with improving the work environment. It appears that the automation of police information systems has followed a post-reform, human-relations strategy, resulting in the dual payoff of perceived performance benefits and improved quality of working life.

Organizational Context

Another perspective places more importance on the nature of the organizational context than on the way in which a particular technology is implemented by the organization. Advocates of professional administration—the reformers—believe that for computing to be well implemented, the organizational environment must be conducive to the efficient use of technological innovations. Specifically, administrationists believe that the more reformed, nonpartisan, and professionalized organizations will be better able to implement successfully and use computer technology. In contrast, advocates of political administration—the post-reformers—believe that the less reformed, more partisan, and less professional organizations will be more responsive to intra- and inter-organizational needs and demands, and hence more successful in the implementation process.

The organizational context of our cities varies widely and is in a transition period with an uncertain outcome. However, police departments have clearly been increasing their reformed, nonpartisan, professional character over the last 20 years. That is, the current trend among police departments is toward a more professional administration.

Assessment of Implementation Strategies

Computing tends to improve the performance and work environment of detectives and patrol officers. In addition, the *local* automation of police applications tends to marginally enhance these positive computer impacts. However, there is a great deal of variation in the efficiency, effectiveness, and work environments of detectives and patrol officers in locally automated cities. Systematic differences in the way computing was implemented at the local level could explain these variations in outcomes. This section explores these differences and derives prescriptive advice for local governments on the best strategies for implementing local government intelligence systems, such as that of the police.

Our research strategy is again to develop indicators of implementation policies which represent the technological, structural, design, and organizational-context strategies of the reform and post-reform advocates, along with indicators of the community setting. A correlational design is used to assess the statistical relationship between these implementation policies and an index of performance for both detectives and patrol officers. Multivariate regression techniques are used to sort out the variables that are most explanatory of the performance differences among locally automated police departments. Taken together, these correlations and regressions can be used to derive policy advice on the most effective strategies for implementing local police-intelligence systems.

Performance Variables

Two performance indices were developed—one for detective applications and another for patrol applications.[16] The detective performance index is composed of six scales. One scale is called "Improved performance," representing the degree to which detectives and field researchers believed that computing leads to more workable cases, more cleared cases, improved court cases, and higher case loads. "Computer-assisted clearances," the second scale, is based on the responses of detectives to questions concerning the number of arrests, clearances, and workable cases linked to the use of computer files. "Clearance rate" is based on departmental records of recovered property, crime clearances, and arrests. "Case load" is based on the responses of detectives to questions concerning the number of cases they are assigned and actively investigate. "Centrality of computing" is based on the responses of detectives to questions concerning the proportion of their cases, clearances, and arrests for which they used computing. "Clerical inefficiency" is based on departmental records of the number of clerical and civilian staff within the department per 1,000 Type I crimes committed in 1975. Each of these scales was standardized so that city scores had a mean of zero and standard deviation of one on each of the six scales. The average score for the city on all six scales is used as our detective performance index.

The patrol performance index is based on the responses of patrol officers to questions concerning the proportion of people and vehicles for which they conducted wants/warrants or stolen-vehicle checks as well as the number of hits they obtained. The responses of patrol officers to these items form a single factor. The standardized factor scores for cities are used as our patrol performance index. All performance indicators are operationally defined in the Appendix.

Tables 5.12 and 5.13 show the distribution of cities on the detective and patrol performance indices, respectively. Interestingly, cities are not necessarily high or low performers in both the detective and patrol areas. For example, Cleveland does not have a high performance score for detective applications but scores high for patrol applications. Cleveland recently placed remote terminals in police cars, which suggests a differential in technological development between their detective and patrol operations that might account for performance differentials. In addition, fewer cities have locally automated patrol-support applications than have locally automated detective-support applications. More generally, many high-scoring cities are sites of extensive police computing. Long Beach, Kansas City, New Orleans, and Little Rock have all had relatively advanced technological development of detective applications, and each scores relatively high on the detective performance index.[17] Yet, some cities with little advanced technological development, such as Patterson, also score high on this index.

TABLE 5.12
Detective-Investigation Performance Index

City	Investigation Performance	City	Investigation Performance
Very high		**Medium** (*cont.*)	
Paterson, N.J.	1.03	Cleveland, Ohio	−.06
		Montgomery, Ala.	−.07
High		Ft. Lauderdale, Fla.	−.07
Long Beach, Calif.	.72	San Francisco, Calif.	−.17
Little Rock, Ark.	.71		
Chesapeake, Va.	.56	**Low**	
Seattle, Wash.	.52	Burbank, Calif.	−.27
Kansas City, Mo.	.48	Portsmouth, Va.	−.35
New Orleans, La.	.45	Newton, Mass.	−.35
Riverside, Calif.	.32	Tulsa, Okla.	−.38
		Hampton, Va.	−.38
Medium		Lancaster, Pa.	−.60
Philadelphia, Pa.	.22	Louisville, Ky.	−.63
Las Vegas, Nev.	.20	Evansville, Ind.	−.64
Atlanta, Ga.	.18		
Baltimore, Md.	.10	**Very low**	
St. Louis, Mo.	.09	Lincoln, Nebr.	−.76
Sacramento, Calif.	−.05	Grand Rapids, Mich.	−.84

TABLE 5.13
Patrol Performance Index

City	Patrol Performance	City	Patrol Performance
Very high		**Medium** (*cont.*)	
Seattle, Wash.	2.45	New Orleans, La.	.02
San Francisco, Calif.	1.94	Philadelphia, Pa.	−.06
St. Louis, Mo.	1.63	Riverside, Calif.	−.13
Long Beach, Calif.	1.44	Little Rock, Ark.	−.15
		Lancaster, Pa.	−.22
High			
Cleveland, Ohio	1.33	**Low**	
Kansas City, Mo.	.84	Louisville, Ky.	−.42
Burbank, Calif.	.82	Chesapeake, Va.	−.68
Las Vegas, Nev.	.67	Grand Rapids, Mich.	−.74
Sacramento, Calif.	.32	**Very low**	
Medium		Atlanta, Ga.	−.86
Tulsa, Okla.	.13	Lincoln, Nebr.	−1.00
Paterson, N.J.	.10	Hampton, Va.	−1.33

Independent Variables

The implementation variables fall into five broad categories: technology, structure, socio-technical design, organizational context, and community environment. The technological variables represent differences among cities in features of the police computing technology. Indicators of computing technology include the amount of automated criminal information available, the number of locally automated applications, the number of on-line applications, the level of computing sophistication, the amount and centrality of computer use, the year in which the first investigative (patrol) applications were automated at the local level, the degree of technological instability, and the proportion of investigative applications that has been redesigned and reconceptualized over time.

The structural variables represent differences among cities in the organizational policies that govern the management of computing. Indicators include the degree of user involvement in design of computer applications; the amount that users are involved in decisions concerning the data-processing installation; the existence of a decentralized police computer installation; the decentralization of access to computerized information via terminals in the police department; the relative control over computing decisions exercised by elected officials, managers, and users; the degree to which police are charged for computing services; the amount of instability in the organizational policies governing computing; the number of sources available for computer-based information; the presence of a skilled terminal operator to assist officers; the use of technical training programs; and the degree of interdepartmental data sharing.

The socio-technical design variables represent differences in the way computing has been integrated into the detective's (or patrol officer's) work environment. Various measures of the relationship of computing to the detective's work environment are summarized by a single scale of the degree to which computing creates more job pressure, more tasks for detectives, less of a sense of accomplishment, and less support for the technology. Cities scoring high on this scale are likely to have been insensitive to the work environment of computer users when implementing computer applications. A comparable scale has been developed to reflect the work environment of patrol officers. In addition, a separate scale represents the degree to which patrol officers are supportive of computing.

Implementation Policy	Detective Performance	
	r	N
Technology		
Degree of automation		
Amount of automated criminal information	.45*	28
Degree of local automation	.64*	28
Degree of sophistication		
Number of on-line applications	.51	28
Level of sophistication	.07	28
Utilization		
Detective use	.23	28
Centrality of computing	.33	28
Routinization		
Year of detective automation	−.18	26
Other technical arrangements		
Technological instability	.10	28
Stage of redesign	−.04	22
Structure		
User involvement		
User involvement in design	.47*	28
User involvement at installation level	−.30	27
Centralization-decentralization		
Police installation	.30	28
Decentralized personal computing	.41*	28
Control of computing decisions		
Elected official control	−.21	27
Central management control	−.05	28
User control	.02	28
Other structural arrangements		
Charging for computer use	−.35	26
Structural instability	.11	28
Multiple sources of computing	.30	28
Skilled operator available	−.42*	25
Technical training provided	−.01	28
Interdepartmental data sharing	−.12	27
Socio-technical design		
Job pressure	−.45*	28
Community environment		
1970 to 1975 population	.21	28
Reported crimes per 1,000 population	.05	28
Population growth 1970–75	−.01	28
Organizational context		
Slack financial resources	.03	28
Council-manager government	.16	28
Professional management practices	−.01	28
Partisan environment	−.24	28
Number of patrol cars on duty	.21	28
Officers per crime	.27	28

*$P < .05$.

Indicators of the organizational context include the implementation of professional management practices in the city government, the influence and activity of political parties in the city, the number of patrol cars on duty over a 24-hour period, and the number of police officers per reported crime.

Finally, indicators of the community environment include total population in 1975, population growth from 1970 to 1975, and the crime rate.

All of the foregoing indicators are listed in Tables 5.14 and 5.16 and are operationally defined in the Appendix.

Findings

Detective Performance and Implementation Strategies

A mix of advanced technology, participatory structural arrangements, human relations, and professional-administration implementation strategies contribute toward better performance of computer applications for detectives. Among these strategies, advanced technological development is the most important for successful implementation (Tables 5.14 and 5.15), explaining about 40 percent of the variation in performance scores. More specifically, the most powerful independent predictors of high detective performance are the degree of local automation, the reduction of job pressures by computing, user involvement in design, and a nonpartisan political environment (Table 5.15). Together these variables explain over three-fourths of the variation in performance scores.

Advanced technology is implied by the fact that cities with the higher detective performance scores have a larger number of locally automated applications (Table 5.15). In addition, cities with higher performance scores are more likely to have a wider variety of automated criminal information, a larger number of on-line applications, and greater utilization of computer technology (Table 5.14). However, performance is not associated with several measures of technological development, including technological instability and stage of design.

Participatory, as opposed to classical, structural arrangements are suggested by the high levels of user involvement in the design of applications for the higher-performance cities (Table 5.15). Also, high performance is more characteristic of cities with decentralized and

TABLE 5.15
Correlations and Path Coefficients for Detective Performance, P
(Dependent Variable)

Independent Variables	Zero-Order Correlation	Path Coefficient	Variance Explained (%)
Degree of local automation: X_1	.64	.46	41
Job pressure: X_2	-.45	-.54	19
User involvement in design: X_3	.47	.35	9
Partisan environment: X_4	-.24	-.29	8

$R = .88$ Total variance explained = 77%.
$P^* = -.52 + .08X_1 - .32X_2 + .006X_3 - .004X_4$
         (.02)   (.08)   (.002)   (.002)

*Regression coefficients unstandardized; standard errors in parentheses.

more fragmented computing—cities where police have their own computing installations and with decentralized personal computing (Table 5.14). Furthermore, such classical structural arrangements as charging and provision of a skilled operator are associated with relatively poor performances (Table 5.14). While there is a tendency for high levels of user involvement within the data-processing installation to be linked with poor performance, the general pattern of relationships within police points toward participatory structures.

A human-relations strategy appears to be the best approach to socio-technical design of detective applications. In fact, our single measure of job pressure accounts for nearly 20 percent of the variation in performance scores (Table 5.15). Some cities have not designed applications in ways that clearly enhance the work environment of detectives. Apparently, such insensitivity to the work environment translates into lessened performance for detectives.

A professional administrative, rather than political administrative, approach to the organizational context is supported by our findings. Most importantly, a partisan political environment appears to detract from detective performance (Table 5.15). Consistent with this tendency is the finding that performance is higher in cities that utilize professional management practices (Table 5.14).

Interestingly, these implementation perspectives are better explanators of the performance of computing for detectives than are measures of the community environment (Table 5.14). In this respect, the success of computing is more dependent on implementation strategies than on the setting within which computing is implemented.

Patrol Performance and Implementation Strategies

A mix of advanced technology and professional-administration implementation strategies contributes toward better performance of computer applications for patrol officers. Among these strategies, advanced technology is clearly the most important for successful implementation. The highest performance scores for patrol applications are registered by cities with the earliest dates of adoption and the greatest utilization of professional management practices. Together, these two variables explain 62 percent of the variation in performance scores.

Advanced technology is indicated by the tendency for the more routinized sites (with the earliest dates of adoption) to have high scores (Table 5.17). In addition, several other indicators of advanced technology have some association with high performance, including a broader variety of automated criminal information, a greater number of on-line applications, higher utilization, and more technological instability (Table 5.16). Generally, the more routinized sites are those with a greater variety of automated information ($r = .47$) and a larger proportion of applications that have been redesigned ($r = .46$). However, the more routinized sites are not necessarily more sophisticated in their applications ($r = .10$).

The more routinized sites also tend to have different structural arrangements. The routinized patrol applications are in cities with a police installation ($r = .51$), decentralized personal computing terminals ($r = .49$), fees charged for computer use ($r = .58$), multiple sources of computing ($r = .45$), greater user control ($r = .41$) and less central management control ($r = .53$). Thus, routinization as measured by the date of adoption is only in part indicative of advanced technology. It also suggests a set of participatory structural arrangements which, except for charging policies, tend to control computing in routinized sites.

The participatory structures strategy is somewhat supported in that routinized sites tend to follow this approach and, indeed, most of the

TABLE 5.16
Pearson Correlations between Patrol Performance and Implementation Policies and Environments

Implementation Policies	Patrol Performance: Patrol Hits	
	r	N
Technology		
Degree of automation		
Amount of automated criminal information	.49*	22
Degree of local automation	.14	22
Degree of sophistication		
Level of sophistication	.16	22
Utilization		
Patrol officer use	.30	22
Routinization		
Year of patrol automation	−.65*	22
Other technological arrangements		
Technological instability	−.34	22
Stage of redesign	.20	18
Errors	.21	22
Structure		
User involvement		
User involvement design	.44*	22
User involvement at installation level	−.07	21
Centralization-decentralization		
Police installation	.33	22
Decentralized personal computing	.46*	27
Control of computing decisions		
Elected official control	.12	21
Central management control	−.29	22
User control	.40*	22
Other structural arrangements		
Charging for computer use	.43*	20
Structural instability	.07	22
Multiple sources of computing	.41*	22
Skilled operator available	.11	19
Technical training provided	.46*	22
Interdepartmental data sharing	.19	22
Socio-technical design		
Job pressure	−.20	22
Support for computing	−.10	22
Organizational context		
Slack financial resources	−.47*	22
Council-manager government	−.16	22
Professional management practices	.29	22
Partisan environment	.09	22
Number of patrol cars on duty	.27	22
Officers per crime	.22	22
Community environment		
Total 1975 population	.13	22
Population growth 1970–75	−.31	22
Reported crimes per 1,000 population	.46*	22

*$P < .05$.

structural associations with performance are considerably reduced once routinization is accounted for (Table 5.17). However, even with degree of routinization controlled, high police involvement in the design of applications and high police control of technical training are associated with high patrol performance.[18]

No socio-technical design variable has a direct statistical association with performance with (or without) controls for routinization (Tables 5.16 and 5.17).

A professional-administration orientation of the organizational context is suggested in that high patrol performance scores are characteristic of cities using professional management practices (Table 5.17). However, neither a council-manager form of government nor a nonpartisan political environment appears to explain patrol-officer performance.

The larger and more uncontrollable community environment is associated with patrol performance, but these associations appear to be spurious. Specifically, high-crime cities without slack financial resources have higher performance ratings (Table 5.16). This association can be explained by the fact that routinized cities tend to be those without slack financial resources ($r = .41$) and with high crime rates ($r = .48$). Once routinization is controlled for, these environmental associations vanish (Table 5.17).

To summarize, our findings tend to support a mixture of the reform and post-reform approaches to the implementation of computer

TABLE 5.17
Correlations and Path Coefficients for Patrol Performance, P
(Dependent Variable)

Independent Variables	Zero-Order Correlation	Path Coefficient	Variance Explained (%)
First year of automation: X_1	–.65	–.75	42
Professional management practices: X_2	.29	.46	20

$R = .79$ Total variance explained = 62%
$P^* = 20.27 - .29X_1 + .005X_2$
          (.07)   (.002)

*Regression coefficients unstandardized; standard errors in parentheses.

technology. The reform approach is suggested by the importance of advanced technology (represented by the degree of local automation) and professional administration (represented by the use of professional management practices) to improved performance of detectives and patrol officers. The post-reform approach is suggested by the importance of participatory structural arrangements (represented by the degree of user involvement) and human-relations approach to socio-technical design (represented by lessened job pressures) to the improved performance of detectives. Interestingly, the approaches of cities toward socio-technical design appear to be unimportant to improved performance of patrol officers. But participatory structural arrangements are positively, though not significantly, related to improved patrol performance. Finally, our findings indicate that these implementation policies really can make a difference to police investigation outcomes; performance is not predetermined by the community environment.

Policy Recommendations

Our policy recommendations flow directly from our findings concerning the conventional practices of police investigative agencies and the determinants of successful implementation of computing. Most police agencies have one or more automated applications serving detective and patrol functions. A substantial proportion are locally automated, as well as having access to state and federal automated files. Among the locally automated agencies, computing has been implemented most successfully when it has been consistent with advanced technology, participatory structural arrangements, human-relations and professional-administration strategies. Overall, cities should follow a mixed approach to implementation of police investigative applications. We prescribe several implementation policies for information-processing tasks, and for intelligence systems, which are like those involved with police investigative support.

Technological Development

The advanced technology approach should be used, in that cities should do the following.

1. *Automate.* Local automation appears to provide information benefits and improved performance for both detectives and patrol

officers. Furthermore, these performance payoffs are accompanied by improvements in the work environment of detectives and patrol officers.

2. *Automate early*. The routinization of automation, or the extent to which it has become an accepted, routine part of police investigative operations, importantly affects the performance of detectives and patrol officers. The longer the application has been around, the more likely it is to have the bugs worked out and to be commonly used.

3. *Automate a large proportion of available investigative support files*. The greater the number and variety of police records and operations automated, the greater the quantity and quality of information that detectives and patrol officers can utilize in their work. Also, the greater the amount of *local* (versus state and federal) automation, the more improved the performance of detectives, patrol officers, and the police department generally. In fact, greater local automation is one of the most highly explanatory variables of detective performance. Also, the sophistication of computing appears to be less important than the overall degree of automation.

4. *Automate rapidly*. Given that technological development is associated with improved performance and technological instability is not associated with performance, rapid development is likely to be more effective than a conservative, "go-slow" strategy. Some students of local government computing suggest that the havoc wrought by technological development may counteract the positive functions of development (Kling and Scacchi 1979). However, neither technological nor structural instability appears to affect the performance of computing operations. Possibly the benefits of development outweigh the inefficiencies caused by technical changes. Alternatively, perhaps the negative externalities of technological instability are borne by a small group of programmers and analysts who become the middlemen between the technology and the users.

5. *Develop on-line inquiry capabilities*. On-line processing is important to the ease and speed of access to automated criminal information.

Other technological variations in implementation policy are less likely to improve the performance of police computing operations. Surprisingly, the level of technological sophistication (apart from on-lineness) is not an important independent variable in the explanation of intercity variations in performance. Undoubtedly, it is important for the city to have a level of technological sophistication sufficient for it to automate a large number of local, on-line applications and provide reliable access to computerized information from multiple sources. Such levels of sophistication are formidable. Yet increasing the sophistication, independent of providing a greater degree of automated criminal information, does not appear to be an important means for increasing performance.

Structural Arrangements

Participatory structural arrangements should be used whenever possible in order to increase police control of computing, or at least to make computing highly responsive to the police. Specifically, cities should do the following.

1. *Involve users in design of applications.* The more closely users are involved in the design of computer applications, the more likely that the applications will meet their needs, be understood and accepted by the users, and be utilized. Extensive user involvement in design is especially important where record-searching activities are nonroutine, as in the case of detective investigation support, because the users are critically needed to specify the nature of search processes and information content. User involvement is less important for standard, routine record-searching, such as that needed by patrol officers.

2. *Decentralize computer access to facilitate personal computing.* The more direct the involvement of users with the technology, the greater their ability to mold it to their own specific needs, and to their changing needs. Decentralized access facilitates direct involvement of users with the technology.

Socio-technical Design

A human-relations approach to socio-technical design is recommended to ensure that computer applications improve the work environment of police officers. On the one hand, police guard their time carefully, and time wasted on the phone or computer terminal is particularly resented. On the other hand, where applications are designed in ways that reduce job and time pressures, police are likely to be appreciative and supportive users.

Organizational Context

A professional-administration approach, or an approach that develops an organizational environment that is conducive to professional management practices, is recommended. The professional-administration principles of reform—professional management and nonpartisanship—appear to be more conducive to the successful implementation of police computing than do the political principles of unreformed structures, more personal management, and partisan politics.

Summary

Cities are generally following a post-reform approach to the implementation of detective and patrol allocations. Whereas through the 1960s and early 1970s, advanced technology characterized technological development for the police, the late 1970s have brought technological development in line with the other post-reform strategies of participatory structures and human relations. The retreat from advanced to appropriate technology is mainly reflected in the decline of federal (particularly Law Enforcement Assistance Administration) funding for police computing. Technological-development strategies are the most important to realizing improved patrol allocation performance, and our policy recommendation lies in the advanced-technology approach to development. The recent retreat from advanced technology may be an unwise strategy in the police area. Our findings support the early development of extensive police automation if one's goal is to improve the payoffs of computer technology for the police.

Recent trends of police departments to follow participatory structural arrangements and human-relations strategies for the implementation of computing appear to be more in line with our findings, which support both of these post-reform approaches. And the long-term effort to reform and professionalize the management practices of local governments is likely to have positive spin-offs for police computing operations.

NOTES

1. Our concept of intelligence systems is a general one, referring to systems that handle data about an organization's environment (Wilensky 1967). It does not refer to

the specialized systems concerned with organized crime and police misconduct that serve the intelligence divisions of police agencies.

2. The third-generation computers of the mid-1960s provided the hardware for developing large, integrated information systems. Technological developments since that time, such as distributed computing networks, have been increasingly sophisticated in their capability for integrating the storage, search, and retrieval of information collected from a variety of sources and geographic locations.

3. Such systems are discussed in Hamilton and Work (1973), Kling (1978), and Quinn (1976).

4. See Laudon (1974).

5. Normally, when cases are referred to the detective division, one or more supervisors screen cases and assign only workable cases to detectives. This is the case in about 70 percent of the sample cities. No screening is used in about 17 percent of the cities, and the remaining cities have some mix of screening procedures.

6. These high percentages reflect the general tendency for police officers to request searches more often on "suspicious" persons, often failing to make searches on local and familiar people.

7. For a complete description of these measures, see Federal Bureau of Investigation (1975).

8. A recent treatment of the problems with these measures can be found in Greenwood et al. (1975).

9. One of the earliest cities to develop computing for detective investigation—Kansas City, Missouri—bases its investigative system on what is largely a criminal-history file. Detectives require either a name or an address to successfully search departmental computer files. They cannot search files only on the basis of an MO or physical description. However, if a name or address is available to the detective, the system yields the individual's physical description, aliases, criminal history, previous parking and traffic violations, and a measure of the fit between search criteria and recorded data. For example, if a search for a John Doe is entered along with a specific birth date, height, weight, race, and sex, then all records of individuals who fit that name and description for at least 55 percent of the parameters entered will be identified and listed.

10. In Evansville, Indiana, some fingerprints are coded on an automated file. Therefore, fingerprints taken at the scene of a crime can be coded and entered for an automated search of the department's fingerprint files. Hits with this system provide an entry to a microfilm copy of the individual's prints, photographs, and criminal history.

11. One consequence of using FI cards in this way is the greater likelihood of certain population groups—such as young black males—being linked with more crime incidents, because officers are more likely to stop such individuals for routine questioning.

12. Before automation, a detective would walk to the Dutch door of the records division and ask a clerk for the file on a particular person. Now a clerk is as likely to query a computer file as a manual name index.

13. The two major patrol-support files—wants/warrants and stolen vehicles—are on-line in most (80 percent) of the cities that have automated them. However, access to

these files by patrol officers in the field generally is over the phone to police dispatchers.

14. Although every city has one or more detectives who avoid the use of computing with a passion, every city also has one or more detectives who develop a reputation for being a computer enthusiast in an extreme. In fact, a concern expressed by some of the elder detectives is that young recruits often know how to use the computer but do not know how to conduct an interview—which, to many detectives, is the key to quality in detective investigation.

15. Although many performance data are computerized, the supervisors normally have a better knowledge of job performance than is contained in the records. Thus, while detectives believe that performance is weighed in their evaluation, it is logical that they do not feel that computing affects their performance evaluation.

16. The entire range of performance indicators presented in the previous section were reviewed as possible measures of the performance of computing in the police. Several variables were eliminated on the basis of their limited variation across police departments. Others were eliminated to avoid repetition. (Repetition can result in oversampling certain features of performance and therefore disproportionately influencing the results.)

17. See, for example, IBM (1973).

18. The partial correlation for "user involvement in design" is .40 and for "technical-training provided" is .42.

REFERENCES

Colton, Kent W. 1978. *Police and Computer Technology: Use, Implementation and Impact*. Lexington, Mass.: Lexington Books.

Dial, O. Eugene; Kenneth L. Kraemer; William H. Mitchel; and Myron E. Weiner. 1970. *Municipal Information Systems: The State of the Art in 1970*. Washington, D.C.: Department of Housing and Urban Development.

Federal Bureau of Investigation. 1975. *Crime in the United States*. Washington, D.C.: Federal Bureau of Investigation.

Greenwood, Royston; C. R. Hinings; and Stewart Ranson. 1975. "Contingency Theory and the Organization of Local Authorities: Part 1. Differentiation and Integration." *Public Administration*, 53: 1–23.

Hamilton, William A. and Charles R. Work. 1973. "The Prosecutor's Role in the Urban Court System: The Case for Management Consciousness." *Journal of Criminal Law and Criminology*, 64(2): 183–89.

IBM. 1973. Investigative Support at the City of Long Beach Police Department.

Intergovernmental Task Force on Information Flows. 1968. *The Dynamics of Information Flow*. Washington, D.C.: Intergovernmental Task Force on Information Flows.

Kling, Rob. 1978. "Automated Welfare Client Tracking and Service Integration: The Political Economy of Computing." *Communications of the ACM*, 21(6): 484–93.

Kling, Rob and Walt Scacchi. 1979. "Recurrent Dilemmas of Computer Use in Complex Organizations." In *AFIPS Conference Proceedings,* Vol. 48, pp. 107–15. Montvale, N.J.: AFIPS Press.

Kraemer, Kenneth L.; William H. Dutton; and Joseph Matthews. 1975. "Municipal Computers: Growth, Usage, and Management." *Urban Data Service Report,* 8(2): 1–15.

Kraemer, Kenneth L. and John King. 1977. "An Analytical Overview of Urban Information Systems in the United States." International Institute for Applied Systems Analysis (IIASA), Research Memorandum.

Laudon, Kenneth C. 1974. *Computers and Bureaucratic Reform.* New York: Wiley.

Matthews, Joseph R.; William H. Dutton; and Kenneth L. Kraemer. 1976. "County Computers: Growth, Usage and Management." *Urban Data Service Report,* 8(2): 1–10.

Mitchell, Grayson. 1979. "Computer to Aid Welfare Policing." *Los Angeles Times.* Sunday, May 6, pp. 1, 22, 23.

Murphy, John J. 1975. *Arrest by Police Computer.* Lexington, Mass.: Lexington Books.

Quinn, Robert. 1976. "The Impacts of a Computerized Information System on the Integration and Coordination of Human Services." *Public Administration Review,* 36(2): 166–74.

Schumacher, B. G. 1967. *Computer Dynamics in Public Administration.* Washington, D.C.: Spartan Books.

Westin, Alan and Michael Baker, 1972. *Databanks in a Free Society.* New York: Quadrangle Books.

Whisenand, Paul T. and Tug T. Tamaru. 1970. *Automated Police Information Systems.* New York: Wiley.

Wilensky, Harold. 1967. *Organizational Intelligence.* New York: Basic Books.

CHAPTER SIX
A Tool for Scientific Management: Computing and Police Manpower Allocation

MANAGEMENT-SCIENCE techniques have found increasing use since their development during World War II. Techniques such as linear programming, dynamic programming, queuing models, inventory models, and simulations are all approaches to optimizing the utilization of scarce resources.[1] The use of such techniques in state and local government has lagged behind their use in national-defense agencies and the industrial sector. Historically, response of state and local governments to the growing service demands has been to increase the number of public employees and the amount of public revenue. During the 1970s, however, state and local governments began to feel the pressure of tighter budgets in the face of continually increasing demands for service and higher wages, and increasing costs of such inflexible budget items as retirement and workman's compensation. These pressures forced public administrators to look for alternatives to personnel and revenue increases as a means of addressing public-service demands (Larson 1973; National Commission on Productivity 1974). In turn, many public agencies looked to management science as a tool for increasing the productivity of scarce public resources. Presumably, more technical-rational allocations of resources might allow public agencies to provide more services with the same, or less, money and personnel.

This chapter assesses the implementation of computerized management-science models by focusing on manpower allocation in city police departments.[2] Management use of computing in law enforcement has been encouraged by the President's Commission on Law Enforcement and the Administration of Justice (1967a,b), which called for the improvement of management information by using the huge stores of data that are routinely collected by police agencies. Additional impetus was provided by passage of the Law Enforcement Assistance Act in 1965. This Act created funding for state and local agencies through the Law Enforcement Assistance Administration (LEAA) for the purchase of police computers, the development of automated information systems, and the applications of management-science techniques such as police manpower-allocation models. In addition to federal encouragement and funding, automation has been spurred by the efforts of local police administrators to modernize and professionalize their management practices (Colton 1972).

Currently, manpower allocation is believed to be one of the most important uses of computing for nonroutine police operations.[3] Yet the implementation of computer-based manpower-allocation systems has had disappointing results. For example, Herbert and Colton conclude the following about manpower-allocation models in St. Louis, Boston, and Los Angeles:

These cases demonstrated the technology's difficulty in achieving clearcut, long-term acceptance. . . . In St. Louis, for instance, none of the district captains is currently requesting the computer-generated resource-allocation reports, and the board of commissioners and the command staff are doing little to encourage the system's use. In Boston the patrol force simulation model was abandoned several years ago, and serious questions have been raised regarding the less-complicated manual resource-allocation procedures implemented on an experimental basis in 1974.

In Los Angeles, however, the ADAM Historical Reporting System that was implemented in June 1975 is still in operation in 1977. . . . However, the LEMRAS/ADAM dynamic deployment model was dropped in 1974. Moreover, the current ADAM package no longer includes forecasts of future needs. Rather, the LAPD's deployment recommendations are based on manual calculations utilizing computer-generated reports of historical data. Technical benefits have been achieved from computerized reports in terms of reducing the manpower required to analyze workloads, but the service impacts are still unclear in terms of the influence the system has had on the response without delay to calls for service. Finally, one of the original service objectives of the LAPD's resource-allocation effort—to improve crime prevention—has essentially been abandoned. (Colton 1978, p. 139)

These and other experiences indicate that although sophisticated models have been implemented, they frequently have not been used, or have been misused, to such an extent that serious questions have been raised about the value of continued development and diffusion of such techniques (Brewer 1973; Colton 1978; Lee 1975). In this chapter, therefore, we address whether certain strategies for implementing police manpower-allocation systems can improve the performance and use of such systems.

Successful Automation of Manpower Allocation

Manpower-allocation systems are designed to improve the efficiency and effectiveness of services (Fig. 6.1). Specifically, police manpower-allocation systems are designed to improve police services, as evidenced by such indirect measures of performance as crime rates, response times, and clearance rates. Improvements in the technical rationality of decisions are expected to result from the greater utilization of information for decision-making. Greater information use is expected to result from improvements in the quantity and quality of available information. Computing is expected to increase the quantity and quality of information by improving the work environment of police analysts, by changing the content of information, and by increasing the centralization of information. However, the relationship between the implementation of patrol manpower-allocation systems and police services involves several important assumptions.

First, the use of computer-based information systems is expected to increase the technical-rational basis of allocation decisions. Research suggests that the delivery of many public services is influenced by the pulling and hauling of diverse community groups and interests, rather than by an explicit policy based on such criteria as need or equity (Jacob 1973). A computer-based information system might provide the police department with better information with which to make technical-rational decisions and resist interest-group pressures. However, some studies suggest that police allocation decisions already tend to be left to the discretion of police bureaucrats, who make decisions on the basis of technical-rational criteria (Mladenka and Hill 1978). Thus, the very need for computer-based information systems is a matter of debate.

Second, and implicit in the above debate, is the assumption that allocation decisions *should* be made on technical-rational criteria, rather than on criteria which are more sensitive to the unique problems

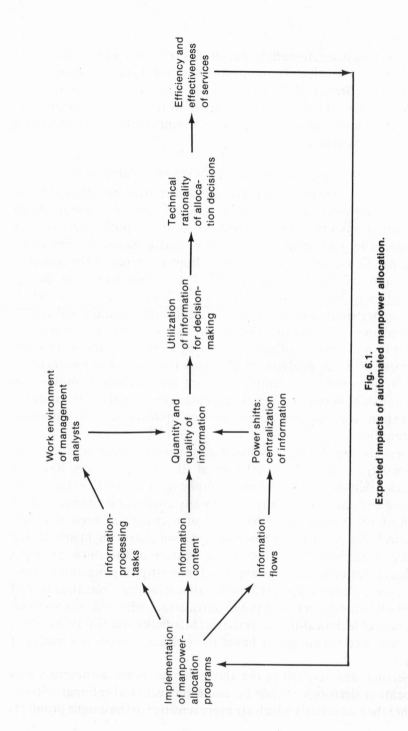

Fig. 6.1.
Expected impacts of automated manpower allocation.

of different population groups. Recent research suggests, however, that technical-rational criteria lead police forces to devote proportionately more resources to poor as opposed to wealthy areas, given the higher level and greater severity of street crimes in the former (Mladenka and Hill 1978). Thus, technical-rational criteria can be compatible with sensitivity to unique problems of population groups. Yet other research has suggested that technical-rational criteria have been used to justify oppressive levels of social control by the police in poor, black, and other minority-group neighborhoods, contributing to feelings of harassment and social injustice (Levy et al. 1974).

This chapter (1) describes police manpower-allocation decisions in local government, (2) explores the impacts of automation, (3) shows the way this task has been implemented, and (4) looks at the success of alternative strategies for the implementation of computer-based police manpower-allocation systems. Based on these findings, we conclude with a set of policy prescriptions stating how best to implement computer-based police manpower-allocation systems specifically, and management-science applications generally.

Patrol Manpower Allocation in Local Governments

As crime rises in importance as a public concern, it is not surprising that local police departments are facing a great deal of public dissatisfaction with both the adequacy and equity of police services (Aberbach and Walker 1970; Ostrom 1975), but because public concern over the cost of government services is so great, local government cannot simply respond to this dissatisfaction by increasing the size of police forces. Patrol-allocation decisions of police departments are therefore aimed at improving the adequacy of current police departments and ensuring the equity of police services—that is, ensuring that the allocation of police officers is based on some objective definition of need, as opposed to some arbitrary allocation permitting bias or favoritism toward special groups, neighborhoods, or interests.

Police manpower allocation is a complex matter, however. Allocation decisions are complex in the first instance because there are a large number of alternatives which might feasibly accomplish the same objectives. Departments can redraw the boundaries of police districts, change the manpower levels per district, change the length or phasing of patrol shifts, move special patrol units around, or change the activities of patrol officers. Also, these alternatives are politically sensitive, given public concerns for cost and equity, and police concerns about the desirability of any given change.

Police manpower-allocation decisions are further complicated by the uncertainty surrounding their outcomes. Most allocation schemes are based on an assumption that response times and manpower levels are associated with crime incidents. And, in fact, the bulk of research supports the notion that the faster the police response, and the higher the police manpower level in an area, the lower the crime rate (Press 1971; Wilson 1975). However, some research, such as the Kansas City patrol experiment (Kelling, et al. 1974), questions the relationship between faster response times and reduced crime. Also, there is a growing belief that redeployment of patrol officers from low-crime areas to high-crime areas only leads to a displacement of crime, rather than to a reduction of crime. Therefore, some police departments are moving toward relatively steady manpower levels with reallocations focusing on the "activities" of patrol officers. For example, since only about 10 percent of the police officer's time is spent in "law enforcement" as opposed to other activities (Wilson 1970), the officer's time allocated to different activities might be varied depending upon characteristics of an officer's patrol (e.g., crime incidents, calls for service, and population). Thus, "law enforcement" activity might be increased in high-crime areas, whereas "crime-prevention" activities might be increased in low-crime areas.

Finally, patrol allocation decisions are complicated by the difficulty of measuring service need and delivery. Calls for services, crime incidents, traffic accidents, population density, street miles, and so on, are among the best available indicators of a need for police services but are inadequate in themselves. Even more difficult to measure is the adequacy of police service delivery. Here most police departments are left with clearance rates, response times, and citizen complaints as crude indicators of service delivery (Hatry 1974; Lineberry 1975), yet only a small proportion of police calls for service require an immediate response, most are not for serious crimes, and most service delivery takes place after the police arrive at the scene.

In the face of these highly complex and politically sensitive issues, local police departments have traditionally followed a decentralized and incremental strategy. Much reliance has been placed on district commanders, who make their case to central management concerning the manpower required for their district. In turn, precinct commanders make their case to district commanders. Through this adjustment process, based on field experiences and the ad hoc use of service and crime statistics, a city's district boundaries, manpower levels, and other allocation policies evolve over time in an incremental fashion.

Although many departments might arrive at highly rational allocation decisions following traditional decision-making processes (Mladenka and Hill 1978), several factors threaten the rationality of the traditional process. First, patrol officers, precinct commanders, and district commanders have a stake in maintaining and enhancing the manpower levels within their patrols. Factors other than objective need can enter their decisions regarding manpower needs. Second, the final allocation decisions made by central management might be more heavily influenced by the negotiating style and skill of particular district commanders than by the objective needs of districts. Also, in the absence of clear decision criteria, police bureaucrats might be more prone to favoritism toward particular districts or patrols. In this context, computer-based manpower-allocation systems might offer the means for making more rational allocation decisions, because they use objective indicators of need and explicit decision criteria.

The Impacts of Manpower-Allocation Automation

Automated manpower-allocation models are expected to increase the efficiency and effectiveness of police services by improving the technical rationality of allocation decisions. The improved rationality of decision-making is based on the premise that automation will increase the quantity and quality of information. In turn, these improvements should lead to a greater use of information for decision-making, thereby increasing the rationality of allocation decisions. But do they?

Information Benefits

The automation of patrol manpower allocation is most directly aimed at improving the quantity and quality of information available to police analysts. In a majority of the automated sites, the analysts do

believe that computers provide easier and quicker access to more
timely and new information (Table 6.1). However, in about 40 percent
of the automated sites, computer applications are perceived as not
providing more timely or new information. Thus, the information
benefits of computing are debatable. Computing tends to improve the
quantity and quality of information in a majority, but not in an
overwhelming proportion, of automated sites.

San Francisco's experience illustrates why the information benefits
might be so open to question. On the one hand, the information
currently available to the police analysts is somewhat limited; on the
other hand, their experience with more sophisticated forms of
information has been disappointing. The following comment from the
URBIS fieldwork illustrates the problem:

The San Francisco Police Department currently has a reasonable array of data
available from computer files about field operations and crime incidents. However, it is
not extensive and is only kept in a very straightforward statistical summary fashion.
There are no analytic reports based on the available data. In fact, there are hardly any
reports that one would call analytic at all.

Table 6.1
Police Analysts' Perceptions of Computer Impacts on Information
$(N = 28)$

Computer Impacts on Information	Percentage Agreeing	Average Score[a]
Computers have made it easier for me to get the information I need	82	69.5
Computers save me time in looking for information	79	69.3
The computer provides me with more up-to-date information than that available in manual files	64	61.4
The computer makes new information available to me which was not previously available	57	60.7
The computer has increased the amount of information I must review and analyze in my job	43	52.9
Information is difficult to change or correct once it has been put on a computerized file	18	38.7
Computerized data are less accurate than data in manual records and files	11	22.7
It takes too long to get the information I need from the computer	11	31.5

[a]Average scores are the mean of individual responses within each city, scored 0 to 100. Each
variable was dichotomized to represent the percentage of cities with scores greater than 50,
indicating "frequently true" and "nearly always true."

It should be noted that in the early 1970's San Francisco did implement the LEMRAS manpower allocation system. However, it was rejected after several years. The explanation [for the rejection] was that the population and crime patterns in San Francisco are relatively stable; LEMRAS is supposedly useful only where there is fluctuation in crime patterns and dynamic population movement. It was felt that the costs of the system's maintenance in terms of data gathering and analysis were simply too high for the benefits received and thus, the system was eliminated. (URBIS Case Report, San Francisco)

Utilization of Information for Decision-Making

The utilization of automated information for decision-making is difficult to assess, given the many factors that might be taken into account in decisions. In our attempt to assess utilization, we focus on the overall frequency with which allocation analyses are conducted, the frequency of reallocations, and the perceived importance of automated information relative to other decision inputs.

Frequency of Allocation Analyses

Automated police departments more often analyze crime, service, or arrest data to evaluate current allocations of patrol officers, but differences between automated and unautomated departments are small (Table 6.2). Only about half of the automated sites evaluate their allocation decisions with these data as often as four times per year, compared to 40 percent of unautomated sites. About one-third of the automated sites (32 percent), and two-thirds of the unautomated sites (60 percent) have analyzed this allocation data less than once or twice in the last five years (Table 6.2). In sum, allocation analyses tend to be done very infrequently in many cities, whether automated or not.

Frequency of Reallocations

Automated sites tend to reallocate manpower somewhat more frequently than unautomated sites. However, this tendency is neither uniform nor statistically significant, and it masks a great deal of variation among the automated sites. Automated sites are somewhat more likely to have changed the manpower regularly scheduled per patrol shift, and the level of manpower allocated per district. In contrast, unautomated sites have more frequently changed the length or phasing of patrol shifts than have automated sites. And more unautomated than automated sites have made four or more changes in the level of manpower allocated per district during the last year. Of

Table 6.2
Frequency of Manpower Changes in Automated and Unautomated Sites

	Unautomated cities								Automated cities								Pearson's Correlation Coefficient	Partial Controlling City Size
	Never in Last 5 Yrs.		1-2 Times Last 5 Yrs.		1-2 Times a Year		4 Times or More		Never in Last 5 Yrs.		1-2 Times Last 5 Yrs.		1-2 Times a Year		4 Times or More			
	%	N	%	N	%	N	%	N	%	N	%	N	%	N	%	N		
Allocation analyses Analyzed service, crime incident or arrest data to evaluate current allocation of patrol	20	2	40	4	0	0	40	4	6	2	26	8	16	5	52	16	.18	.18
Kind of reallocation Changed manpower level regularly scheduled per shift	40	4	30	3	20	2	10	1	19	6	52	16	16	5	13	4	.10	.07
Changed manpower level regularly scheduled per district	33	3	11	1	11	1	44	4	20	6	43	13	16	5	20	6	-.15	-.17
Changed the boundaries of police districts or divisions	20	2	70	7	0	0	10	1	16	5	74	23	6	2	3	1	-.08	-.07
Changed police shifts (length or phase)	10	1	90	9	0	0	0	0	42	13	36	11	13	4	9	3	.06	.10

course, the frequency of reallocations is not equivalent to the rationality of allocation decisions. Reallocations could be unnecessary. Or reallocations could be more frequent where less information is available and uncertainty is greater. Furthermore, manpower needs could be addressed in ways other than by altering allocation policies, such as by the use of special preventive patrols. Consequently, automated allocation programs might not necessarily be ineffective just because reallocations have not been more frequent.

Factors Shaping Allocation Decisions

A more direct indication of relationships between automation and allocation decisions is revealed by interviews that addressed the major factors which shape the department's allocation decisions. Table 6.3 is consistent with other data in suggesting a rather disappointing picture. Only two automated sites (8 percent) mentioned an automated patrol-allocation model as one of the most important factors shaping allocation decisions in the police department (Table 6.3).[4] In part, this result reflects the primitive stage of technological development; that is, allocation analyses usually summarize service data but rarely provide prescriptive forecasts of manpower needs. While automated service data are among the most important factors shaping allocation decisions in nearly three-fourths (71 percent) of the automated sites, manually generated service data are among the most important in 80 percent of the manual sites. Furthermore, and of equal importance, factors such as personal experience, emergencies, and political considerations weigh heavily in allocation decisions in both automated and unautomated cities. The URBIS fieldwork indicates that political considerations are particularly important. For example, consider the experience of the following city:

Automated data has not entered into decisions about [manpower] allocation. As a good old country boy police department in the South, most of these decisions are seat-of-the-pants subjective appraisals by the police. This information is tempered by scanning very roughly certain summaries of the major crimes that have occurred in the previous night and in the previous month. Each shift lieutenant on the three shifts has authority to allocate one or two extra cars as needed. On the heaviest shift there are two extra cars available in theory. These essentially serve as back-up cars and there is no real allocation going on.

The last major reallocation decision occurred several years ago. The chief realized that there was a very uneven distribution of criminal activity in a sense of response to

Table 6.3

Most Important Factors Shaping Allocation Decisions between Automated and Unautomated Sites

| Factors | Percentage of Cities Noting Factor as One of the Most Important | | | | | Pearson's Correlation Coefficient | Partial Controlling City Size |
| | Unautomated (N =10) | | Automated (N = 31) | | | | |
	%	N	%	N			
Automated patrol-allocation model or program	0	0	8	2		.14	.07
Automated service data aggregated at district or precinct level	0	0	71	22		.48*	.45*
Manually generated service data	80	8	39	12		-.35*	-.33*
Personal experience, judgment	80	8	68	21		-.12	-.05
Emergencies, crime wave, i.e., massage parlor problem, slasher, etc.	30	3	32	10		.02	.01
Political considerations or pressures, i.e., council member asks for more service to district	20	2	32	10		.12	.14

*P < .05.

calls across the three shifts, being very heavy on the 4 p.m. to midnight shifts. Consequently, he reallocated cars more heavily towards that shift. When he did this reallocation, the city manager pressured him to return to even distribution of cars across shifts. The underlying rationale of the city manager was not rational in any allocation sense, but politically it was highly rational. If he would have maintained a system of unequal distribution it would have meant that during one or two of the shifts, some of the districts would have zero cars covering them. This was seen as politically unpalatable, even though a district might have very sparse population and virtually no calls for service during certain shifts. Under pressure from the city manager, the chief returned to equal distribution of officers and cars across shifts. (URBIS Case Report, Chesapeake)

The experience of Las Vegas shows the importance of even broader political considerations:

The politics of metropolitan reorganization swamp the decisions that might otherwise be made about officer allocation. Part of the arrangement that was made when the city and county merged was to try to even out patrol coverage. The county sheriff's department was substantially undermanned as far as patrol officers covering areas. What happened when the consolidation occurred was that the consolidated police officers were spread out so there would be better coverage in the county outlying areas. This means two things. One was that there was an absolute reduction in the extensiveness of coverage in the city, and secondly it meant that many cars that were previously two-person cars were converted to one-person cars. An additional factor involved was a political decision made through the police officers' union which was asking for more money and the city and county governments compromised by offering a 4-10 work structure—that is, four days at ten hours rather than the previous five day, eight hour work week. These factors explain the only major reallocations that have occurred in beat structure and officer manning over the past few years—that is, the consolidation of city and county into Metro involving a reallocation of officers and the change of the beat structure by going to a 4-10 system and the impacts that these have had. The commander in charge of allocation acknowledged that apart from these factors, there were no decisions made and no decisions pending or even considered in the reallocation of police manpower. (URBIS Case Report, Las Vegas)

When asked more precisely about the factors that caused the last major reallocation of manpower, automated cities are more likely to mention changes in available manpower or changes in city boundaries (Table 6.4). But automated sites are not more likely to have had a major reallocation due to increases in service calls, crime incidents, or arrest rates. These latter findings suggest that one reason why automated cities are not more likely to reallocate manpower is that

Table 6.4

Factors That Caused Last Major Manpower Allocation between Automated and Unautomated Sites

| | Percentage of Cities Mentioning Factor | | | | | |
| | Unautomated (N = 10) | | Automated (N = 31) | | Pearson's Correlation Coefficient | Partial Controlling City Size |
Factors	%	N	%	N		
Outcomes of manpower-allocation model	0	0	3	1	.09	.07
Change in service data, i.e., rise in number of calls	40	4	58	18	.16	.10
Change in crime or arrest rate	20	2	32	10	.12	.06
Change in available manpower	0	0	32	10	.32*	.32*
Change in patrol policies	30	3	29	9	-.01	.02
Change in city boundaries	0	0	29	9	.30*	.25
Apparent problems with response time	30	3	48	15	.16	.13

*$P < .05$.

these cities do not differ from unautomated cities in terms of crime-level response times or patrol policies, changes that cause a majority of reallocations.

Utilization for District-Level Decisions

So far we have been talking about central allocation decisions in terms of frequency and causes. Central allocation decisions may also be viewed in terms of utilization. For example, central management might use allocation analyses to control or centralize district-level decision-making. Yet this does not appear to be the case to an important extent. Central management in automated sites is somewhat more likely to set specific allocation guidelines, which district commanders are less likely to alter, but this tendency is weak and statistically insignificant (Table 6.5).

Similarly, central management in automated sites is not more likely to use service, crime, or arrest data to evaluate the quality of district or precinct commanders and supervisors (Table 6.6). Again, our data indicate that cities with an automated manpower-allocation appli-

Table 6.5
Extent to Which Central Allocation Decisions Affect the Way District Commanders and Supervisors Allocate Personnel within Their Operational Command[a]

	Unautomated cities		Automated cities	
	%	N	%	N
Central allocation just sets general rules and distributes personnel among districts. District commanders make day-to-day allocations.	37	3	30	9
Central allocation sets specific allocation guidelines, but district commanders have full authority to alter them.	37	3	33	10
Central allocation sets specific allocation guidelines, which district commanders rarely alter, and only in special circumstances.	25	2	37	11

[a]Pearson correlation between automation and centralization of decision making is .10, and the partial controlling for city size is .05. Neither relationship is statistically significant at the .05 level.

Table 6.6
Extent to Which Service Data, Crime-Incident Data,
or Patrol-Allocation Analyses Are Used to Evaluate the Quality of
District or Precinct Commanders and Supervisors

	Unautomated cities (N = 10)		Automated cities (N = 31)	
Frequency of Use[a]	%	N	%	N
Not used	67	6	52	16
Occasionally	22	2	19	6
Often	0	0	3	1
Regularly used	11	1	26	8

[a]The Pearson correlation between automation and frequency of use is .16, and the partial controlling for city size is .13. Neither relationship is statistically significant at the .05 level.

cation do not differ from unautomated cities in terms of their policy-making.

Analyses of service, crime, and arrest data can also be used to meet regular reporting requirements; put out press releases (listings of crimes committed); legitimize allocation decisions to the public and elected officials; justify budget allotments; and evaluate patrol practices, traffic engineering, and, most importantly, the day-by-day placement of preventive patrol cars. In fact, some of the most frequent and imaginative users of patrol-allocation studies are preventive patrol officers who try to anticipate short-term shifts in the need for police manpower.[5] Our study, though, does not evaluate automated allocation applications in terms of these more auxiliary uses.

Performance Payoffs

Finally, let us turn to the real test of police manpower-allocation applications: whether they improve the efficiency and effectiveness of police services. Given the early stage of manpower-allocation technology and our findings to this point, it is surprising that over three-fourths (77 percent) of the automated police departments have some evidence to suggest that automation led to improvements in performance (Table 6.7). One illustration of the operational performance benefits is provided by the Atlanta fieldwork:

There has been very definitely a high payoff in the use of the computer crime statistics [developed for manpower allocation analyses]. The man who is in charge told me that for the first time in the history of the Atlanta Police Department, they are able to make allocation decisions based on what they feel is best in terms of fighting crime, and there

Table 6.7
Effect of Computers on Police Manpower Allocation Performance[a]

	Automated sites	
Field-Investigator Rating of Performance Effect	%	N
No effect	22	6
Some effect, but vague impressionistic evidence	44	12
Some effect, and specific evidence provided	33	9

[a]Question: "Has use of computers to aid police manpower allocation led to any improvements in performance, such as lessening response times or increasing arrest rates?"

are two things which led to their ability to do this. One is the election of Maynard Jackson as mayor and the second is the implementation of the crime statistics on the computer. The election of Jackson as mayor for the first time made it possible for them to have a sympathetic ear in city administration who finally would hear that most of the crime does not occur out in the suburbs or out in the rich areas of town, but it occurs downtown around the poor and the blacks, and therefore, that is where the police force should be concentrated. The old mayor was interested in making sure that the needs of the rich, influential people in the community were met; whenever they wanted more police presence in their areas, they got it. The technical aspect, or the contribution of the computer, is that for the first time, they really have the statistics to show in unarguable fashion that crime is really happening down in the poor sections of town so now when a councilperson or some influential person starts to hassle the police department about putting more patrolmen out in their area, they are able to get out the statistics and say, "Where do you want me to take the men out of? Do you want a man out of an area with a crime index of 20 and put him in your area with a crime index of 6?" And since the person knows that the mayor won't force that to happen because he doesn't think it's right, there's really nothing he can do. So the computerized statistics have played a major role, together with the political change, in the ability of the department to allocate men in ways that they feel really fight crime. (URBIS Case Report, Atlanta)

Atlanta also illustrates some unanticipated operational benefits from the data used for manpower allocation:

The most important reason that the Deputy Director in Charge of Field Operations wants that information [on dispatches and responses to calls for service] is not so much so he can allocate the patrols. He wants it so he and his field lieutenants are able to "get on those men's asses and make sure they're doing their preventive patrolling and not screwing around." One of the biggest impacts the information has had so far is when they've got a high crime rate in an area, say a lot of burglaries in a district where a man's assigned, they call him and ask him "What's going on?" Always in the past he has been able to make the excuse, "Aw, I just get so many doggone calls all the time that I never get a chance to get out and do preventive patrol." With the information they are getting now, they're able to say, "Look, here—you got so many calls that day, there are so

Table 6.8

Selected Mean Response Times in Automated and Unautomated Sites[a] and Crime Clearance Rate

	Averages for:		Pearson's Correlation Coefficient	Partial Controlling City Size
	Unautomated cities (N = 10)	Automated cities (N = 30)		
Highest-priority dispatches				
Mean seconds from incoming call to dispatch	62.3	71.7	.06	.03
Mean minutes from dispatch to arrival	4.3	3.7	−.20	−.17
Second-priority dispatches				
Mean seconds from incoming call to dispatch	167.0	178.9	.03	−.01
Mean minutes from dispatch to arrival	6.0	7.4	.19	.16
Crime clearance rate[b]	−.09	.04	.08	.06

[a] No difference in means between locally automated and locally unautomated sites is statistically significant at the .05 level of confidence. Controlling for city size does not affect the strength of these relationships.

[b] This index is a measure of the degree of success in crime clearance. It is a factor score of three clearance measures: (1) percentage of stolen property recovered in 1975; (2) total 1975 Type I crime-clearance rate; and (3) percentage improvement in clearances for all Type I crimes from 1971 to 1975.

many calls on the average per day during the last month and that means at such and such minutes per call, you couldn't have had less than an average of five hours a day for preventive patrol time. So if you're really patrolling, how come the crime rate in your area is so doggone high compared to everybody else's." As he characterized it, "They can't say anything to me about that." I asked him [the Deputy Director of Field Operations] if this kind of information had made any difference in service delivery outcomes and he said, "Yes, definitely." But his reason wasn't the reason we normally expect from patrol allocation [more effective deployment of manpower]. His reason is that these guys get out there and do their job when they know that somebody is able to check up on them and hassle them if they are lazy, so it's definitely a case in which the top management and middle management in the department are using computer data to really ride herd on patrol officers. (URBIS Case Report, Atlanta)

Still, only about one-third of our cities had specific evidence rather than vague impressions. And in fact there is no statistically significant difference between automated and unautomated sites in terms of the more objective measures of performance: dispatch times and clearance rates (Table 6.8).

It might be, though, that automated sites have more calls for service per patrol officer. The relatively equal response times in automated and unautomated sites, then, could reflect positively on the automation of patrol manpower-allocation analyses. However, city size, which is associated with crime rate, does not explain the lack of performance differences between automated and unautomated cities.

In summary, the actual impacts from automation of patrol manpower allocation are nowhere near the expected impacts. Automated sites do tend to have more and better information than unautomated sites, but this information does not appear to be especially important in decision-making. Factors other than automated data or allocation models are stressed overwhelmingly. Perhaps, then, our automated cities have not seriously used their applications so that they could affect the efficiency and effectiveness of police services.

Implementation Strategies

Local police departments, especially in our 42 cities, vary in the ways they have implemented computerized models for patrol manpower allocation. A few departments have purchased sophisticated computer programs, but most rely on simple statistical reports of crime by area and time of day. In some cities, central management, elected officials, and computing staff are importantly involved in the adoption and design of manpower-allocation systems, while in most cities the police department is relatively autonomous of these officials outside the department. The design of some computer-based allocation systems stresses efficiency to the point that allocation analysts feel pressured, district commanders feel threatened, and patrol officers feel monitored. In one city, the Planning and Research Division of the police department was so efficient in monitoring calls, responses, and performance that it earned the title of "Snitch Squad." Yet, in most cities, manpower-allocation systems function as rather unobtrusive aids to decision-making.

These varied implementation strategies of police departments can be classified by whether they tend to follow a reform or post-reform approach to implementation, and can be viewed from three perspectives: technological development, structural arrangements, and socio-technical design. On this basis, our city police departments have tended to follow the implementation strategies of appropriate technology, participatory structural arrangements, and a human-relations approach to socio-technical design.

Are most police departments following the best implementation strategies? Do different strategies importantly affect the quality of allocation decisions? In the next two sections, we try to answer these questions.

Technological Development

The technological development of patrol manpower-allocation systems clearly is the most significant strategic choice facing police departments in terms of direct costs. Advocates of advanced technological development advise police departments to automate early, adopt sophisticated and standard allocation programs, and encourage frequent utilization by police management analysts. In contrast, advocates of appropriate technology suggest that advanced technology is too expensive, goes beyond the needs of local police departments, and creates hassles in keeping up with technological change without, in turn, delivering improved performance.

Advanced technological developments are aimed at providing management with an on-line, interactive computer simulation model for evaluating the service impacts of alternative allocation decisions. "Hyper-cube" (Larson 1972, 1973, 1978) is only one of the growing number of relatively sophisticated computer programs and routines designed to aid patrol allocation, including such intriguing techniques as PCAM (Patrol Car Allocation Methodology), developed by Rand, and LEMRAS (Law Enforcement Manpower Resources Allocation System), developed by IBM. These allocation programs forecast the consequences of alternative allocation decisions. They also improve on more standard "work load" and "hazard" formulas.[6]

Despite large public and private commitments to the development of sophisticated technology, models have not been very important to patrol manpower-allocation decisions in local police departments. Even when sophisticated and transferable packages such as LEMRAS and PCAM are adopted, they are underutilized in terms of their technical capabilities. In short, most cities have rejected advanced technological development in the implementation of patrol manpower-allocation systems.

Degree of Automation

The rejection of advanced technology is evident from the small proportion of all cities over 50,000 in population in 1975 that had adopted LEMRAS (6 percent) or another manpower-allocation program (18 percent). Most cities (60 percent) have automated some police service data, and generate reports from these data, but this typically defines the extent of computer technology supporting patrol manpower allocation (Colton 1977).

Our 40 cities are somewhat more sophisticated than the average American city, in that about 72 percent use some automated data for allocation decisions. Still, only 39 percent of our cities have an automated allocation program (Table 6.9). In most cities, management analysts use a completely manual operation, or they use computer-based reports on an ad hoc basis.

The low sophistication of police manpower computing also reflects the rejection of advanced technology. Only a small proportion of cities have adopted the packaged programs such as LEMRAS (Table 6.9). In addition, the use of computing is largely limited to the aggregation and statistical reporting of data, rather than the estimation of manpower needs or the implications of alternative allocation decisions. Only 2 of our 16 cities with allocation programs use computing for predictive purposes. Standard packages are potentially more sophisticated. However, the most frequent use of these packages is to generate routine

Table 6.9
Computer-Assisted Patrol-Officer Allocation[a]

	Percentage and Number of Cities	
	%	N
Completely manual operation	24	10
Ad hoc use of automated data[b]	37	15
Allocation program (developed in-house)	17	7
Allocation program (standard package such as LEMRAS)	12	5
Allocation program (modified standard package)	10	4
Total	100	41

[a]Question: "Does your department use a computer program to assist in patrol-officer allocation? Was this developed in-house or is it a standardized program transferred here?"

[b]One or more computer applications supply data used to support those involved with patrol-officer allocation decisions. However, no special program has been developed to serve this function.

police reports such as Uniform Crime Reports (UCR). Their primary purpose has not been to inform patrol manpower-allocation decisions.

The conventional use of computing is reflected in the computer-based allocation programs developed in-house to serve patrol-allocation decisions. In-house packages are generally report generators. These packages are used to aggregate raw data such as crime incidents, calls for service, accidents, and population characteristics in order to compute statistical data such as frequencies, averages, and percentages by police district, time of day, day of week, or other temporal and geo-based categories. Such programs have been developed by Costa Mesa, Fort Lauderdale, Grand Rapids (which has developed a Standard Police Allocation Resource Management Information System, called SPARMIS), St. Louis, Tampa, and Riverside.

Tampa's reporting system borrows features from St. Louis's system and illustrates the variety of reports that are generated for allocation purposes and reporting requirements. Reports of the Tampa Police Department include: (1) a monthly crime report by type of crime and location, the number of reported crimes, clearances, and arrests; (2) an age, sex, race printout on offenders; (3) a year-to-date report of Type I crimes for UCR reporting; (4) a National Safety Council summary of traffic accidents; (5) a citation and accident comparison report by geographic areas within the city; (6) about 10 maps that summarize different kinds of crime incidents within each geographical area; (7) an assignment record, which reports for each day and shift the number of police and administrative service calls recorded on dispatch records; (8) a 28-day summary of police services, which is generated from detective and juvenile-officer work sheets; (9) additional maps that summarize all accidents, fatal injuries, and citations for each geographical area and shift; and (10) a street intersection printout of traffic accidents. Only Tulsa has developed in-house programs which are more sophisticated and which provide predictions of allocation outcomes.

Still, automation tends to increase the sophistication of allocation analyses, in that automated cities have a greater variety of crime and service data available for analysis. And police departments with automated manpower-allocation programs tend to use a greater variety of data for determining manpower allocations (Table 6.10), although such cities also make extensive use of data from manual files. Automation tends to increase the likelihood that departments use response times, the distribution of calls across kinds of services, clearance and arrest rates, property loss, crime projections, and physical or social data (Table 6.10). Calls for service and crime incidents are the most commonly used statistics for allocating manpower in cities with or without automated manpower-allocation programs.

It is important that the data used for patrol allocation be easily aggregated at multiple levels of analysis to address allocation issues both among and within police districts. For example, if central-management analysts wish to guide or evaluate the allocation decisions of district commanders, then the analysts must have data at a level of detail finer than the district. However, automation is not strongly related to the detail of available aggregations. For example, more unautomated sites (45 percent) have data aggregated by subdivisions of patrol areas than do automated sites (35 percent). Yet this fine level of detail might be of little value without automation, given the tremendous time and effort that would be involved in manually reaggregating these data at different levels of analysis. Again, cities have implemented automated systems that fall far short of available advanced technology in this area.

The length and phasing of patrol shifts (such as moving from an 8- to a 10-hour shift) is a major allocation decision, which should be empirically assessed. For this purpose, a capability for aggregating allocation data over different time periods would broaden the range of

Table 6.10
Information Used in Department to Determine Police Patrol Allocation

| | Unautomated Cities (N = 10)[a] | | | | Automated Cities (N = 31)[a] | | | | | |
| | Not Used | | Used | | Not Used | | Manual-Data | | Automated Data | |
Kind of Data	%	N	%	N	%	N	%	N	%	N
Police service data										
Number of calls	20	2	80	8	10	3	19	6	71	22
Response time	60	6	40	4	42	13	10	3	48	15
Type of call	40	4	60	6	26	8	13	9	61	19
Crime-incidence data										
Crime rate	20	2	80	8	23	7	19	6	58	18
Traffic accidents and/or violations	50	5	50	5	39	12	6	2	55	17
Clearance and/or arrest rate	80	6	20	2	54	17	10	3	36	11
Property loss	100	10	0	0	81	25	3	1	16	5
Crime projections	100	10	0	0	68	21	16	5	16	5
Pysical, social data										
Total population	80	8	20	2	68	21	26	8	6	2
Population density	70	7	30	3	58	18	36	11	6	2
Street miles	90	9	10	1	81	25	16	5	3	1

[a]Rows under "Unautomated Cities" and under "Automated Cities" total 100 percent across.

allocation decisions that can be analyzed. Here, automated sites are far more likely than unautomated sites to have aggregated summary data by both patrol shifts and time of day. About three-fourths (73 percent) of the automated sites can aggregate police service, crime, or incident data by patrol shift, compared to less than half (44 percent) of the unautomated sites. Even more dramatically, 83 percent of the automated departments can aggregate by time of day, compared to only 38 percent of the unautomated departments. In summary, the automation of crime and service data increases the relative sophistication of allocation and analysis. At the same time, the absolute level of sophistication remains low.

The Orientation of Computing

Patrol-allocation analyses are normally a central-management function within police departments. Patrol-allocation analysts tend to be located under a commander or captain (or other officer immediately below the Chief of Police) in charge of patrol officers, divisions of planning and research, and preventive patrol sections. Although a few of the big-city police departments—like Los Angeles and San Francisco—have computing specialists, systems analysts, and modelers who conduct the analyses, most police departments assign this task to regular police officers. These officers learn about computing and data processing on the job. The lack of technical expertise in the role of patrol-allocation analyst reflects the fact that police departments have conventionally adopted appropriate technology for meeting reporting requirements, rather than adopting advanced technologies for patrol-allocation analyses.

The appropriate-technology strategy is also reflected in the style of computer use by allocation analysts. Patrol-allocation analysts in only about one-third (32 percent) of our automated cities use a computer terminal as often as a few times a month. In contrast, police-allocations analysts in two-thirds (67 percent) of our automated cities request others to obtain computerized information as often as a few times a month or more. And the most common use of computing by patrol-allocation analysts is simply the receipt of the regular computer-based reports (Table 6.11). In fact, analysts in 96 percent of the automated sites receive a computer-based report at least a few times a month.

Table 6.11
Utilization of Computing by Patrol Manpower Analysts
($N = 22$)

	Frequency of Use[a]					
	Less than Twice a Year		Several Times per Year		A Few Times A Month or More	
Kind of Use	%	N	%	N	%	N
Personally use a computer terminal	45	10	23	5	32	7
Request others to get information from a computerized file	4	1	27	6	69	15
Receive computer-based report	0	0	4	1	96	21
	Occasionally		Often		Very Often	
	%	N	%	N	%	N
In summary, during the course of the year, do you use computers or computer-based information in your job?	9	2	23	5	68	15

[a]Rows total 100 percent across.

While the analysts in 68 percent of the automated cities perceive themselves as "very often" using computer-based information, their use tends to be limited to the review of computer-generated reports.

Computer-based allocation analyses might be too recently adopted to be sophisticatedly and routinely used by police departments. Only one of our cities had automated some police service data by 1965. And the only city to have adopted LEMRAS as early as 1966 was the development site for the LEMRAS package. Generally, computer-based patrol-allocation programs were not adopted until the early 1970s. The average date of adoption for our cities was 1973.[7] Thus, at the time of this study, most cities had had only two to three years to acquire the expertise and other resources to apply these systems in a sophisticated and routine way. And, given that police computing technology continues to undergo a significant amount of change and redevelopment, the situation might change.[8]

Structural Arrangements

Information systems are more likely to be shaped by the goals and structure of an organization than vice versa (Laudon 1974). Thus, it is not surprising that the approach of police departments to the implementation of manpower-allocation systems mirrors two structural aspects of law-enforcement agencies in local government. First, the police department has considerable autonomy when compared to other local government operating departments. Second, police departments are modeled after military organizations. In comparison with most other operating departments, implementation structures follow a more hierarchical and centralized pattern within the police department. Overall, therefore, structural arrangements tend to be a mix of both participatory and classical strategies.

User Involvement in Adoption

Departmental autonomy and centralization are reflected in the kinds of officials involved in decisions to adopt patrol manpower-allocation applications. On the one hand, departmental autonomy (decentralization) is suggested by the lack of participation of either the chief appointed or elected official, and especially by the relatively low level of participation of the central computing unit in police-department adoption decisions. Police departments also appear to be relatively autonomous with respect to other local, state, and federal police agencies, in the sense that outside police agencies have played a nominal role in adoption decisions. On the other hand, departmental centralization is suggested by the lack of participation by patrol officers in adoption decisions. The major participants in adoption decisions are central managers within the police department (top and middle managers) and the departmental EDP specialists.[9]

User Involvement in Design

The design of patrol manpower-allocation programs is also decentralized in respect to the city and centralized within the police department. Manpower-allocation programs tend to be designed by computer specialists within the police department, rather than by the central computing unit. And police computer experts tend to be located within the unit responsible for the processing of the reports and statistics used for manpower-allocation decisions, whether that department is the records division or the planning and research division. However, central managers within the police department maintain an important role in the design of manpower-allocation programs, while city management—whether the top elected or appointed officials—is removed from design decisions (Table 6.12).

Centralization-Decentralization

The police department is one of the most decentralized computing operations within local government. Not only is user involvement in adoption and design more often concentrated within police departments, but also these departments are more likely to have a computer installation devoted to their own operations. About one-fourth (26 percent) of the cities with automated patrol manpower-allocation programs have a police computing installation. In addition, nearly three-fourths (71 percent) of the police departments with automated

Table 6.12
Participation in Designing Computer Applications to Support Patrol-Officer Allocation

	Level of Participation[a]						
	No Role in Design		Consulted but Not Formally on Design Team		Formally on Design Team		Total
Participants	%	N	%	N	%	N	N
Chief appointed official and staff	96	27	4	1	0	0	28
Chief elected official and staff	100	29	0	0	0	0	29
Department top managers (chief, commissioners)	50	15	37	11	13	4	30
Computer specialist in department	15	4	0	0	85	23	27
Middle management (captains, lieutenants)	17	5	33	10	50	15	30
Patrol officers	80	24	20	6	0	0	30
Outside police agency	87	25	10	3	3	1	29
Outside consultant or service bureau	53	16	10	3	37	11	40
Central EDP unit	44	13	3	1	53	16	40

[a]Rows total 100 percent across.

allocation applications have computer terminals located within the police departments.[10]

Charging

Participatory management is reflected in the charging policies of most police departments. Surprisingly few (23 percent) police departments charge for the actual amount of computing resources used by the police. And only another 10 percent charge a flat rate to the police departments. Most police departments (68 percent) have free computing, paid for from the general fund or from grant monies. Overall, then, manpower-allocation systems have been structurally implemented in a mixed fashion.

Socio-technical Design

Observers of police computing have suggested that systems are designed to reflect a concern more for task efficiency than for human relations (Whisenand and Tamaru 1970). However, we find that police computing does reflect a concern for human relations. Police analysts are favorable toward computing, view computing as a contribution to their work, and perceive data-processing specialists as helpful to their efforts. Only district commanders are likely to complain about the outcomes of manpower-allocation analyses. So, manpower-allocation applications have made a positive contribution to the work environment of users—department top managers and patrol-allocation analysts. However, the use of such analyses might well exacerbate tensions between department central managers and those they monitor—district officials and patrol officers.

Computers and the Work Environment

Manpower-allocation analysts are exceptionally positive about computer technology. All (100 percent) of the analysts surveyed want to use computers more in doing their job. Furthermore, nearly all the analysts surveyed are optimistic concerning the value of the technology. Analysts in 89 percent of the cities agree that, within the next five years, "computers will greatly improve the way my job is done" and that "computers will greatly improve the operations" of the city.

The high support for computing seems to reflect a belief that computing is highly instrumental to the work of the allocation analyst.

When asked what they like most about the use of patrol manpower-allocation techniques, the police officers involved with allocation decisions are likely to emphasize information benefits and increases in the ease with which they can do their jobs. (Table 6.13). Analysts in a sizable proportion of the cities also note the use of computing to support the legitimacy of allocation decisions. Surprisingly, police in less than one-fourth of the cities (22 percent) mention increased performance of patrols as a feature they like most about allocation applications. The features that police like least about allocation programs relate to their poor design and implementation. For example, technical problems are the most commonly mentioned negative aspect (Table 6.13).

Table 6.13
Likes and Dislikes Concerning Use of Computers to Aid
in Police Manpower Allocation

	Cities in Which Mentioned	
	%	N
Features which are most liked		
New or more information available	96	26
Can do more easily	56	15
Can do more often, allocations more timely	44	12
Provides legitimacy, support to desired or needed changes in allocation—to other police or city officials	37	10
Seems to increase performance of patrols	22	6
Features which are least liked		
Technical problems, bugs in programs	52	14
Difficult to use	44	12
Poor design of programs, i.e., assumes fixed districts, cannot consider variations in work shift	33	9
Inaccurate, incomplete information	33	9
Officers or analysts don't agree with results	22	6
Less successful than other means of information for determining reallocation	19	5
Costs too much to develop and use, money should go elsewhere	15	4
No evidence it improves performance of patrols (response time, arrest dates)	7	2
Poor allocation formula, inappropriate weighting of factors	4	1

Table 6.14
Analysts' Perceptions of Changes in the Work Environment Caused by Computers
($N = 28$)

Work Impacts	Percentage Indicating
Has computing increased or decreased the number of different things you do in your job?	
Decreased	7
Not affected	19
Increased	74
Average score[a]	(79.3)
Has computing increased or decreased time pressure in your job?	
Decreased	15
Not affected	44
Increased	41
Average score	(61.1)
Has computing raised or lowered your sense of accomplishment in your work?	
Lowered	0
Not affected	32
Raised	68
Average score	(80.7)
Has computing increased or decreased your opportunities to work with people?	
Decreased	0
Not affected	54
Increased	46
Average score	(69.5)
As a result of computing, is your work more or less closely supervised?	
Less closely supervised	25
No difference	64
More closely supervised	11
Average score	(43.8)
Has computing given you more or less influence over the actions of others?	
Less influence	0
No change	39
More influence	61
Average score	(76.3)

[a] Average scores are the mean of individual responses within each city, scored 0 to 100. Each variable was trichotomized to represent the percentage of cities with scores less than 33.3, between 33.3 and 66.7, and greater than 66.7.

Computing seems to have a positive effect on the work environment of allocation analysts. Specifically, analysts believe that computing has created more job variety, a greater sense of accomplishment, and a greater sense of personal efficacy or influence (Table 6.14). On the negative side, computing is sometimes viewed as increasing the time pressures on allocation analysts. However, this seems to be the only factor detracting from a generally positive view of the work-environment impacts of computing.

Consistent with these positive perceptions of computing, allocation analysts view the data-processing staffs favorably. In fact, analysts view data-processing staffs as being much less technocratic than do most other respondents. This positive view toward the data-processing staff characterizes allocation analysts in about 80 percent of the police departments with automated manpower-allocation applications. More specifically, analysts in about 80 percent of the departments believe that data-processing personnel promote the use and expansion of computer applications. Yet they also believe that the computing personnel respect their opinions, are concerned with their problems, and do not confuse their conversations with computerese or become so intrigued with new applications that they neglect the maintenance of current ones (Table 6.15).

Table 6.15
Allocations Analysts' Views toward Data Processing[a]
(N = 28)

Views toward Data Processing	Percentage Agreeing	Average Score
This city's data-processing unit promotes the expansion of computer use in our government operations	74	73.1
Computer personnel respect my opinions about our department's computing needs	87	78.7
Data-processing personnel are more intrigued with what the computer can do than with solving the problems of my department	22	29.8
Data-processing staff confuse our conversations with their technical language	22	36.5
Data-processing staff are more interested in working on new computer uses than in making improvements in ones we now use	17	31.8

[a]Average scores are the mean of individual responses within each city, scored 0 to 100. Each variable was dichotomized to represent the percentage of cities with scores greater than 50, indicating agreement.

The District Commanders' View:
A Nonuser Perspective

Whereas the automation of patrol manpower-allocation programs might contribute to the job of analysts, it might well detract from the job of district commanders. Such programs make more detailed information more readily available to central police managers. This information is expected to permit central management to reassess, and thereby more frequently change, the decisions of district commanders. While our earlier analysis suggested that automation has not appreciably increased the centralization of allocation decisions, district commanders might disagree. In cities with automated allocation programs, district commanders and supervisors are more likely to complain about the number of patrol officers allocated to their respective districts (Table 6.16). Thus, computing might be consistent with a human-relations strategy in respect to the primary users of the technology (allocations analysts) but not to district commanders.

In the view of some district commanders, computing is implemented from a concern for task efficiency rather than from a concern for human relations. Still, complaints are widespread among district commanders in only about one-fifth (22 percent) of the automated cities (Table 6.16). In fact, there are many cases where the use of more systematic data has satisfied the complaints of district commanders, who believed that previous allocations were not made on technical-rational criteria. Consequently, quantitative data can sometimes serve a legitimizing function in resolving conflicts among district commanders in the allocation of police manpower.

Overall, patrol allocation programs are not a major issue to the

Table 6.16
Complaints by District Commanders and Supervisors about the Number of Patrol Officers Allocated to Their Areas, in Automated and Unautomated Sites
(*N* = 27)

	Unautomated		Automated	
	%	N	%	N
None complain	40	2	21	6
Very few complain	20	1	39	11
Some complain	40	2	18	5
Many complain	0	0	11	3
Nearly all complain	0	0	11	3

police. They are perceived as providing an additional, and sometimes an improved, source of information for a variety of tasks, only one of which is patrol allocation. Moreover, the use of these applications is often discretionary. Those who like and trust the computer-based printouts will use them, while others will develop an alternative system, whether in consists of colored pins on a wall map or simple listings of crime reports.

Organizational Context

Our earlier characterization of the organizational climate of police departments (chapter 5) can be generalized to this function as well. However, police investigation is centered in the records division and detective units of police departments, but manpower-allocation analyses are centered in an analysis unit such as a Planning and Research Division. Typically, these divisions are staffed by younger police officers with more formal schooling than the majority of officers. Given the staffing of these divisions, they often represent the most professionalized sector of the department. In this respect, the organizational climate of patrol-allocation analysts is more characterized by professional administration than is the climate of investigative and patrol officers. However, patrol-allocation analysts are the providers and seldom the end users of analyses. And, in this respect, decision-makers in the police department tend to exist in a highly political environment. Thus, the organizational climate of manpower-allocation analyses is clearly mixed.

Assessment of Implementation Strategies

Cities in our sample that have implemented computer applications in support of patrol manpower allocation have tended to follow an appropriate-technology strategy of automating only the basic applications. Not only have they steered away from advanced technology, they have also steered toward other post-reform approaches to automation by following a human-relations strategy in the implementation of computing. Yet the success of patrol manpower applications is mixed and certainly disappointing, given the claims of promoters. Most automated sites tend to obtain improved information benefits and some improvements in performance. But these impacts are not being achieved in a significant proportion of the automated sites. Here we explore the determinants of successfully implementing patrol manpower-allocation applications, and assess whether there are systematic differences between the sites that have been more, and less, successful in achieving the benefits of automation. We then offer prescriptive advice on the best implementation strategies for manpower-allocation applications.

To accomplish these goals, we focus only on those cities with automated applications which support patrol-allocation analyses. For these automated sites, we first describe the pattern of relationships between measures of implementation policies and a summary index of automated patrol-officer allocation performance. Simple zero-order correlations provide an initial description of these relationships between implementation policies and performance. However, to identify those policies that best predict performance, a multiple stepwise regression analysis is used.

Performance Variables

The automation of patrol manpower-allocation programs is primarily designed to increase the efficiency and effectiveness of patrol operations. The performance of automated patrol-allocation analyses is measured by a summary index that combines the three following indicators: improved performance, time to arrival, and clearance rate. "Improved performance" is a single item which indicates the degree of evidence suggesting that the use of computers to aid police manpower allocation led to any improvements in performance, such as shortening response times (Table 6.17). "Time to arrival" is a factor score which reflects the amounts of time from the dispatch of highest and second highest priority calls for police service to the arrival of police at the scene (see Appendix). "Clearance rate" is a factor score which reflects the performance of the police department in clearing Type I crimes (see Appendix).

Each of these indicators was standardized so that city scores had a mean of zero and standard deviation of one on each of the three performance indicators. The average score for a city on all three items is used as our summary index of automated patrol-allocation performance. Table 6.17 shows the distribution of automated patrol-allocation sites on this performance index.

Table 6.17
Automated Patrol-Allocation Performance Index

City	Index Score	City	Index Score
Very High		Medium	
Philadelphia, Pa.	1.07	Hampton, Va.	.02
Paterson, N.J.	1.07	Chesapeake, Va.	−.06
Baltimore, Md.	.94	Las Vegas, Nev.	−.12
		Seattle, Wash.	−.22
High		Riverside, Calif.	−.22
Lancaster, Pa.	.72		
Portsmouth, Va.	.64	Low	
Miami Beach, Fla.	.63	Atlanta, Ga.	−.47
Evansville, Ind.	.51	St. Louis, Mo.	−.60
San Jose, Calif.	.48	Oshkosh, Wis.	−.64
Stockton, Calif.	.42	Very Low	
Tampa, Fla.	.40	Warren, Mich.	−.77
Newton, Mass.	.35	Sacramento, Calif.	−.78
Louisville, Ky.	.34	Fort Lauderdale, Fla.	−.81
Costa Mesa, Calif.	.33	Grand Rapids, Mich.	−.88
		San Francisco, Calif.	−.88
Medium		Long Beach, Calif.	−.88
New Orleans, La.	.17		
Kansas City, Mo.	.13		
Tulsa, Okla.	.05	Average Score	.03
Little Rock, Ark.	.04	Standard Deviation	.60

The rankings of cities on this index are interesting in two respects. First, the index scores are not widely distributed. Second, the rankings show no clear tendency to reflect regional, size, or technological patterns, with the somewhat surprising exception that cities with the highest index scores tend to be highly partisan cities (Table 6.17).

Independent Variables

Independent variables fall within four general categories represented by the technological-development, structural-arrangement, socio-technical-design and organizational-context perspectives, plus a fifth category, the community environment. Technological-development policies are measured by the following: number of automated patrol-allocation applications; whether or not the city uses a specialized computer-allocation program; the number of on-line applications; the variety of automated data; the sophistication or aggregation ability of data; the sophistication of the installation serving police; the frequency of computer use; the frequency of patrol-allocation analyses; and whether automated data are used for policy legitimation. Also included as technological policies are the first year in which the police department was automated and the first year that patrol allocation was automated. Finally, a measure of the instability of the technology has been included to assess its impacts on patrol allocation performance.

Structural policies include the following indicators of user involvement: the extent to which users were involved in the adoption or design of applications to support patrol allocation, and the extent to which middle management or a police computer specialist was involved in the application design. To indicate centralization or decentralization of computing, we use whether there is a police computer installation and how many computer terminals there are in the police department. Control of computing decisions involves another set of structural policies: the extent to which elected officials, users, or the city's central management exercise control over computing decisions that affect patrol allocation. Finally, charging policy and structural instability are two other structural policies that are looked at to determine their impact on patrol allocation performance.

Socio-technical design is represented by three variables. "Job enrichment" is a factor score that measures the degree to which patrol-allocation analysts perceive computing to have provided them more job variety and accomplishment. "Job pressure" is a factor score measuring the degree to which patrol allocation analysts feel more time pressures as a result of computing. The relationship of computing to the district commander's job is measured by the presence of "district-level complaints" (Table 6.18).

The organizational context is measured by the "context" variables, and the community environment by the "environmental" variables.

Findings

The success of automated patrol-allocation analyses is determined most importantly by structural strategies for implementation. Neither technological development nor socio-technical design strategies have a strong relationship to performance (Table 6.18).

Participatory structural arrangements that increase the autonomy of police computing contribute to better patrol-allocation performance. Specifically, performance is relatively higher in cities that limit the involvement of elected officials in data-processing decisions, provide

Table 6.18
Pearson Correlations between Automated Manpower-Allocation
Performance and Implementation Policies
($N = 31$)

Implementation and Environmental Variables	Patrol-Allocation Performance Index	
	r	N
Technological development		
Degree of automation		
Number of automated applications	.32*	31
Specialized computer package	−.17	31
Degree of sophistication		
Number of on-line applications	−.04	31
Variety of automated data	−.09	31
Data sophistication	.03	31
Sophistication of installation	−.49*	31
Orientation of computing		
Use of computing	−.13	27
Frequency of allocation analyses	−.02	31
Use of computing for policy legitimation	−.09	27
Routinization		
First year of police automation	.06	31
First year of patrol-allocation automation	−.14	26
Other technological arrangements		
Technological instability	.06	31
Structural arrangements		
User involvement		
User involvement in adoption	.07	31
User involvement in design	.25	31
Middle-management involvement in design	−.08	30
Police computer-specialist involvement in design	.32*	31
Centralization-decentralization		
Police installation	.15	31
Decentralized peripherals	−.10	31
Control of computing decisions		
Elected officials control	−.50*	30
Central-management control	−.04	31
User department-heads control	−.47*	31
Other structural arrangements		
Charging for computer use	−.50*	31
Structural instability	.07	31
Socio-technical design		
Job enrichment	−.14	28
Job pressure	−.11	28
District-level complaints	.02	28

Table 6.18 (*continued*)

Implementation and Environmental Variables	Patrol-Allocation Performance Index	
	r	*N*
Environment		
Total population 1975	.25	31
Population growth, 1970–1975	.06	31
Reported crimes per 1,000	−.33*	31
Context		
Slack financial resources	.25	31
Partisan politics	.26	31
Council-manager form	−.24	31
Professional management practices	−.15	31
Centralized allocation decisions	.07	30
Number of patrol cars on duty	.28	31
Officers per crime	−.07	31

*$P < .05$.

free computing to the police, and involve police computer experts in the design of allocation programs (Table 6.19).

Elected-official control of data processing limits the autonomy of allocation analyses by interjecting political, as opposed to technical-rational, criteria. Charging for computer use also limits autonomy by imposing constraints on the kinds and quantity of allocation analyses. And the design of allocation programs by people outside the police department limits the autonomy of allocation analysts to incorporate design criteria considered important by the local police department. Thus, our findings support prior studies that suggest that police departments do apply rational criteria in allocating manpower. To the extent that participatory structural arrangements are employed, the ability of the police department to apply rational criteria is increased, resulting in improved manpower-allocation performance.

Technological variables are less important in explaining successful patrol-allocation performance. There is a tendency for cities that do have a number of computer applications in this area to be more successful in patrol-allocation performance. However, the more sophisticated the computer installation in terms of hardware, software,

Table 6.19
Correlations and Path Coefficients for Automated Manpower-Allocation
Performance, P (Dependent Variable)

Independent Variables	Zero-Order Correlation	Path Coefficient	Variance Explained (%)
Elected official control of EDP decisions: X_1	−.50	−.41	25
Charging policy X_2	−.50	−.42	15
Police computer-specialist involvement in design X_3	.32	.33	11

$R = .72$ Total variance explained $= 51\%$
$P^* = .27 - .01X_1 - .006X_2 - + .22X_3$
          (.00)   (.002)   (.11)

*Regression coefficients unstandardized; standard errors in parentheses.

and personnel capabilities, the less successful the performance. A structural explanation could explain why sophisticated installations appear dysfunctional. Specifically, the most sophisticated installations tend to be located outside the police department. Such centralization limits the autonomy of the police department, which decreases the performance of manpower allocation.

Variations in socio-technical design fail to be associated with successful implementation. Possibly, this is because allocation analysts and district commanders are not the principal actors who determine the fate of allocation analyses. Managers in the police department and central administration are the end users of patrol-allocation analyses. To these users, variations in socio-technical design are of relatively little concern.

Finally, the organizational context and community environment figure little in successful implementation of patrol manpower allocation, except to the extent that fiscal conditions force cities to use a charge system for computing in spite of the problems it generates.

Policy Recommendations

Technological Development

Our recommendations in the area of technology are limited. For the most part, variations in technological capabilities among our 31 automated cities are not great, and while some cities do have package programs such as LEMRAS, most of these cities do not use these programs or have eliminated the predictive capabilities of the programs. Nonetheless, we recommend that cities do the following.

1. *Automate a number of applications to support manpower allocation.* While the benefits of automating manpower allocation per se are inconclusive and disappointing, among the automated cities in our sample we find that the greater the number of automated applications available in a given city, the higher the performance score of that city.

2. *Proceed incrementally in devising and adopting sophisticated manpower-allocation applications.* With the currently designed applications, an emphasis on sophisticated techniques may be counterproductive to patrol manpower performance. In our 31 cities, a sophisticated technological approach was negatively correlated with patrol manpower performance. Two aspects can be considered. First, a critical problem with "packaged programs" in their degree of flexibility in accounting for differences among cities. The tenor of interviews in our 31 automated cities indicated that for many of them the packaged programs were either unworkable or that such packages needed modifications to account for specific city problems. For example, of the 4 cities in our sample that had adopted LEMRAS, 2 of the cities no longer use it and 1 city has modified it to the extent that it is now simply a report generator. Only 1 of the 4 cities has continued to place some reliance on this package. Hence, 3 of the 4 cities rejected this method rather than improving on its capabilities. This leads to the second point; namely, the "state-of-the-art" in providing automated decision-making capabilities is yet in an infant stage. Each new packaged program has improved on the earlier methods. PCAM, for example, takes into account some of the problems encountered with LEMRAS. Yet, of the 3 cities that have rejected LEMRAS, none has moved to a newer packaged program. Rather, when LEMRAS proved unworkable for the city, the packaged program was shelved. Sophistication can lead to a backward step providing even less automated support for patrol manpower allocation if policy-makers proceed in an "all or nothing" approach in this area.

Structural Arrangements

Participatory structural arrangements are crucial to the automation of patrol manpower allocations. Specifically, cities should proceed as follows.

1. *Involve police users in the design of allocation programs.* It is necessary that computing decisions of this nature include all levels of the police department, and especially computer specialists within the department.

2. *Decentralize decisions about automation of patrol manpower allocation to the police.* When political considerations are included in decision-making, the technical rationality of manpower allocation is lessened. As a consequence, cities where elected officials are involved in computer decision-making tend to have lower clearance rates and slower response times.

3. *Do not charge for computer use.* Under conditions of fiscal problems within the city, charging for computer time and memory may appear to be a desirable solution. However, charging tends to limit the autonomy of allocation analysts. This effect is detrimental to successful patrol-allocation performance. Thus, while charging may be dictated by citywide fiscal problems, that policy is likely to hinder allocation performance.

Socio-technical Design

Ensure that computing neither increases job pressure nor detracts from the job. Automated patrol-allocation programs are already poorly and infrequently used. If computing has a detrimental effect on the analysts, all the money, time, and effort being put into automated applications can only continue to give little return.

Organizational Context

The organizational context within which manpower allocation is performed does not place any major constraints on the optimal performance of computing. Our research indicates that only the political context of the city is perhaps associated with more successful performance. This indication may be due to the fact that a political context creates a greater need for the reallocation of manpower on the basis of rational criteria (need for service), as opposed to political criteria. Also, the use of automated patrol-allocation analysis provides a means for professionals within the police department to overcome their political context by aiding them in the documentation and legitimation of their allocation decisions. Thus, the introduction of automated patrol-allocation analysis within a political context might well cause the greatest changes in allocations and performance. If this interpretation is accurate, then a city with a professional administrative context should not necessarily expect to implement manpower allocation programs less successfully than a city with a political context.

Summary

Cities have tended to follow a post-reform approach to the implementation of patrol-allocation analyses. They have avoided advanced technology, classical structural arrangements, and task efficiency in favor of the pragmatic use of appropriate technology (e.g., routine statistical reporting applications), mixed structural arrangements, and human-relations perspectives.

Structural policies are the most important to realizing improved patrol-allocation performance, and our policy recommendations lie in the participatory-structure perspective. It is clear that control should not be centralized to elected officials, where "politics" can work against rational-technical decisions. Instead, the complexity of patrol-allocation performance and its supporting computer application require a decentralized, police-oriented structure.

Current variations in technological development, except number and sophistication of applications, appear irrelevant to the success of implementation. However, this finding does not necessarily support the technology now used by police departments. In fact, advanced technology has never been implemented, at least in our sites. We argue instead that the current use of primitively automated patrol-allocation applications buys little for police departments, because we find almost negligible differences in the performance of automated and unautomated sites. Perhaps advanced technological development will achieve more in terms of patrol-allocation performance than the primitive systems now being used.

Furthermore, approaches to the socio-technical design of patrol-allocation applications appear irrelevant to successful implementation—but only as currently implemented. If police departments were to adopt an advanced-technology approach to patrol allocation, there would probably be higher levels of dissatisfaction on the part of district commanders and much more dependence on police computer specialists, rather than on police officers trained to read statistical reports.

That is, advanced technology might result in a move toward task efficiency, in contrast to the more common human-relations approach to socio-technical design.

Finally, the organizational context also appears irrelevant to successful implementation. Our data only suggest that a political context might be associated with more successful performance. To the extent that this indication reflects reality, we believe that a political context is not in itself more conducive to optimal performance. It is likely that automated patrol-allocation analysis is a means to overcome the political context by offering empirical legitimation of allocation decisions by professionals. This interpretation is reinforced by the finding that elected-official involvement is associated with lower levels of performance.

NOTES

1. At the operational level, a management-science model might provide a single course of action for utilizing a given resource under a set of realistic assumptions. At the strategic and policy levels, a management-science model might only be expected to provide some insight into, and understanding of, the implications of decisions which involve multiple actors with often conflicting objectives. Still, such models could answer many "what if" questions at the policy level and therefore lead to more rational action by decision-makers.

2. Police manpower allocation is a useful focus, given that (1) some of the earliest and most intensive efforts to apply computerized models in local government have been within the police department, (2) computer use for police manpower allocation is a high priority in most police departments (Colton 1978), (3) police services are similar to other public services in that service need and service delivery are extremely difficult to measure, and (4) police services and manpower are among the most costly items in the budgets of local governments.

3. Colton's 1972 and 1974 surveys show that police departments perceive resource-allocation activities as their most important computer applications (Colton 1972, 1974, 1978).

4. The following comment from an URBIS case report illustrates such a site:

The use of computer files for patrol allocation is not extremely sophisticated yet it is seriously and carefully done. The police department obtained a version of LEMRAS and has modified it somewhat for local use. By taking the current districts as they stand, the model aggregates geo-coded areas to provide an average response time for each district. In this manner the police analysts can see if particular districts in the city are having significantly lower or higher response times than others. They then redraw the districts, eye-balling the map to make sure that they adequately consider major thoroughfares, dead ends, cul-de-sacs, etc. They then rerun the program which provides new average response times for the new districts. By doing a series of iterations of this procedure, they are able to equalize response times among districts. Thus, the redistricting is a process of iterating redraws to equalize response times and using personal judgment in making the district boundaries reasonable from a patrol standpoint.

What was most interesting was the enthusiasm and seriousness with which the commanders and analysts involved in reallocation decisions used computer files. They were quite supportive of the whole effort. They were particularly pleased with their ability to use past response data to predict the effectiveness of redistricting. They also seemed to be quite excited in looking at the new printouts and generating this data. (URBIS Case Report, Little Rock)

5. Determining day-to-day allocations of activities to police officers is a developing area of police management that is being considered in Kansas City.

6. The work load and hazard formulas are based on differing assumptions concerning the most important factors to consider in the determination of manpower allocations. Such factors often include the crime rate, calls for service, and street miles. Weights are assigned to each factor. If the hazard formula is being utilized, then weights reflect the relative importance of each factor to crime prevention; if the work-load formula is being utilized, then weights reflect the relative number of man-hours required to handle each factor. The appropriate number of patrol units or officers per district is then calculated from the proportion of "hazard" or "work load" within the district, relative to the total hazard or work load for the city. These formulas are relatively simple, based upon the "informed subjective judgment" of officials of the city, and can be implemented on a manual or automated basis (Chaiken 1975; Chaiken, et al. 1975; Chelst 1975).

7. The first and average years of adoption for allocation systems vary somewhat by the kind of system, as illustrated below:

Kind of System	First Year Adopted	Average Year Adopted
Automated service data	1965	1973
LEMRAS	1966	1972
Other allocation package	1967	1974

8. Police computing installations that have automated patrol manpower-allocation applications show moderate levels of instability. For example, 29 percent have changed development priorities, 13 percent have changed to a later-generation machine, but only 10 percent have made a major change in programming languages over the last year. None has changed its major equipment vendor during the last year. Therefore, it seems that patrol-allocation applications are being implemented in a moderately unstable technological environment. This reflects neither "advanced" nor "appropriate" patterns of technological development.

9. One indicator of role in adoption is the percentage of our cities in which each type of actor was a major participant in adoption/ nonadoption decisions. In this respect, major participants were department top managers in 74 percent of our cities, department computer specialists in 61 percent, department middle managers (captains and lieutenants) in 45 percent, the central computing unit in 29 percent, the chief appointed city official and his staff in 10 percent, and the chief elected city official and his staff in 7 percent. Neither patrol officers nor an outside police agency was a major participant in any city's adoption decisions.

10. Of course, computing in police departments is continually going through structural change. Nearly one-fifth (16 percent) of the computer installations that have automated manpower-allocation applications have changed top computing management within the last year. An almost equal proportion of these installations (13 percent) have experienced a change in the relationship between computer installations, such as consolidation, division, or the establishment of new installations. A small proportion of installations have changed departmental location (6 percent) or physical location (6 percent) within the last year.

REFERENCES

Aberbach, Joel D. and Jack L. Walker. 1970. "The Attitudes of Blacks and Whites toward City Services." In John P. Crecine, ed., *Financing the Metropolis,* pp. 519–37. Beverly Hills, Calif: Sage Publications.

Brewer, Gary D. 1973. *Politicians, Bureaucrats and the Consultant.* New York: Basic Books.

Chaiken, Jan. M. 1975. *Patrol Allocation Methodology in Police Departments.* Santa Monica, Calif.: Rand Corporation.

Chaiken, Jan. M.; Thomas Conbill; Lee Holliday; David Jaquett; Michael Lawless; and Edward Quade. 1975. *Criminal Justice Models: An Overview.* Santa Monica, Calif.: Rand Corporation.

Chelst, Kenneth. 1975. *Implementing the Hypercube Queuing Model in the New Haven Department of Police Services: A Case Study in Technology Transfer.* Santa Monica, Calif.: Rand Corporation.

Colton, Kent W. 1972. "Uses of Computer by Police: Patterns of Success and Failure." *Urban Data Service Report,* 4(4). Washington, D.C.: International City Management Association.

——. 1977. "Computers and the Police: Police Departments and the New Information Technology," *Urban Data Service Report*, 6(11). Washington, DC: International City Management Association.

Colton, Kent W., ed. 1978. *Police and Computer Technology: Use, Implementation and Impact*. Lexington, Mass.: Lexington Books.

Danziger, James N. and William H. Dutton. 1977. "Technological Innovations in Local Governments: The Case of Computers," *Policy and Politics*, 6:27–49.

Downs, Anthony. 1967. *Inside Bureaucracy*. Boston, Mass.: Little, Brown.

——. 1976. "A Realistic Look at the Final Payoffs from Urban Data Systems." *Public Administration Review*, 27(3):204–10.

Hatry, Harry P. 1974. "Measuring the Quality of Public Service." In Willis H. Hawley and David Rogers, eds., *Improving the Quality of Urban Management*, pp. 39–63. Beverly Hills, Calif.: Sage Publications.

Jacob, Herbert. 1973. *Urban Justice: Law and Order in American Cities*. Englewood Cliffs, N.J.: Prentice-Hall.

Kelling, George L.; Toney Pate; Duane Dieckman; and Charles F. Brown. 1974. *The Kansas City Preventive Patrol Experiment: A Technical Report*. Washington, DC: Police Foundation.

Kraemer, Kenneth L. and John Leslie King. 1977. *Computers and Local Government*, Volume 1: *A Manager's Guide*. New York: Praeger.

Larson, Richard C. 1972. *Urban Police Patrol Analysis*. Cambridge, Mass.: MIT Press.

——. 1973. "Resource Allocation in Public Safety Services." Paper presented at the Symposium on Research Applied to National Needs, National Science Foundation, Washington, D.C., November 18–20.

——. 1978. *Police Deployment*. Lexington, Mass.: Lexington Books.

Laudon, Kenneth C. 1974. *Computers and Bureaucratic Reform*. New York: Wiley.

Lee Douglas, Jr. 1973. "Requiem for Large Scale Urban Development Models." *Journal of the American Institute of Planners*, 39:163–78.

Levy, Frank S.; Arnold J. Mettsner; and Aaron Wildavsky. 1974. *Urban Outcomes*. Berkeley: University of California Press.

Lineberry, Robert L. 1975. "Equality, Public Policy and Public Services." Paper presented at the 71st Annual Meeting of the American Political Science Association, San Francisco, Calif., September 2–5.

Lucas, Henry C. 1975. *Why Information Systems Fail*. New York: Columbia University Press.

Mladenka, Kenneth R. and Kim Quaile Hill. 1978. "The Distribution of Urban Police Services." *Journal of Politics*, 40(1):112–33.

Mowshowitz, Abbe. 1976. *The Conquest of Will*. Reading, Mass.: Addison-Wesley.

National Commission on Productivity. 1974. *Improving Police Productivity*. Washington, D.C.: National Commission on Productivity.

Ostrum, Elinor. 1975. "The Design of Institutional Arrangements and the Responsiveness of the Police." In Leroy N. Rieselback, ed., *People vs. Government*, pp. 274–364. Bloomington: Indiana University Press.

President's Commission on Law Enforcement and the Administration of Justice. 1967a. *The Challenge of Crime in a Free Society*. Washington, D.C.: U.S. Government Printing Office.

——. 1967b. *Task Force Report: Science and Technology*. Washington, D.C.: U.S. Government Printing Office.

Press, S. James. 1971. *Some Effects of an Increase in Police Manpower in 20th Precinct on New York City*. New York: New York Rand Institute.

Whisenand, Paul M. and Tug T. Tamaru. 1970. *Automated Police Information Systems*. New York: Wiley.

Wilson, James Q. 1970. *Varieties of Police Behavior*. New York: Anthenum.

——. 1975. *Thinking about Crime*. New York: Basic Books.

CHAPTER SEVEN
Management Control and the Automated Budget

THE EARLIEST perceptions about the computer's role in organizations focused on its potential for increasing the productivity of clerical operations. But beginning in the 1960s, the computer also came to be perceived as a tool for management control (Leavitt and Whisler 1958; Simon 1960, 1965). Along with the realization that the computer could potentially do more than replace clerks came the realization that it could potentially replace organizational control systems based on informal and filtered information.

Automated Budget Control

Although there are a number of organizational resources that might be computerized in the interest of managerial control (e.g., money, personnel, equipment, and inventories), budget control traditionally has been the chief instrument of monetary control and, indirectly, of other resource control as well (Anthony and Herzlinger 1975; Davis, Dempster, and Wildavsky 1966; Wamsley and Salamon 1975; Wildavsky 1974). Some budget-control automation has existed for some time in the largest cities, which traditionally experience chronic fiscal problems. However, it is the urban fiscal crisis of the 1970s that has provided a special impetus for budget-control automation (Danziger 1977; Lodal 1976). Cities already faced with overspending problems have found these problems exacerbated by declining revenues from local as well as federal and state sources, limited capacity of the city's tax base to absorb further increases in the tax rate, and unprecedented increases in city expenditures due to the energy crisis and inflation. These and other fiscal problems have meant that managing the cities' money resources has come to be perceived as second only to finding new revenue sources (Meltzner 1971; Scott

1972). The computer's capacity for assisting in budget and managerial control has come to be perceived as a major instrument in handling the current crisis. Consequently, cities are turning increasingly to automating or to revamping already automated budget control and related organizational tasks, such as general accounting and budget preparation. As a result, these automated systems have become increasingly complex. For example, cities have sought to integrate accounting of all revenues (from federal, state, local, and enterprise sources) and expenditures (by line item, department, project, program, and fund) into a single system that would produce monitoring reports needed for budget control (ARMS Task Force 1973; Lodal 1976; Sartoris 1977; Young 1968). The complexity of these systems makes the question of how computer-based budget control can be successfully implemented a central one for urban management.

Successful Implementation of Automated Budget Control

"Success" in automated budget control refers to the computer's impacts on costs, information, and control (Fig. 7.1). It has been expected that automation would improve *cost efficiency* in the central units, which prepare budget reports and monitor department expenditures, and to a lesser extent in the departments themselves. It also has been expected that automation would produce *information benefits*.

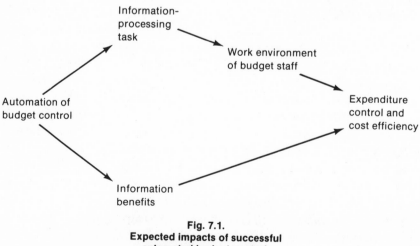

Fig. 7.1.
Expected impacts of successful
automated budget control.

Chief among these benefits would be increases in the accuracy, timeliness, frequency, and relevance of information supplied to top management and staff, and to the departments.

It has further been expected that automation would improve *expenditure control.* The improved information and reporting efficiency provided to central management would enable them to continuously monitor expenditures of the operating departments, quickly discern emerging financial problems that require correction, and promptly act to limit department spending, reallocate department funds, or allocate contingency funds. To the extent that similar information was supplied to department and division heads about their subunits, the computer would facilitate expenditure control several levels down the hierarchy. In this way, the operating units might even become self-controlling and reduce the need for central management oversight of expenditures (Danziger 1977; Lodal 1976).

This chapter focuses on budget control as illustrating a general class of managerial control tasks in organizations. It asks whether the automation of budget control improves cost efficiency and the quality and utilization of information for control, without leading to work impacts of a type that might nullify whatever benefits are achieved. It also asks whether the impacts of such automation are responsive to alternative management policies (technological development, structural arrangements, and systems design) and organizational contexts, or if they are determined by environmental variables.

The chapter (1) describes the multiple activities of budget control in local government, (2) examines the impacts of automation in performing budget control, (3) describes the patterns by which computer-based support for this task has been implemented in our cities, and (4) assesses alternative approaches to the implementation of computer-based systems for budget control. Based on these analyses, we conclude with a set of policy prescriptions about how best to implement computer-based systems to improve the budget-control function in local governments.

Automated Budget Control in Local Government

The executive budget is both a planning and a control tool in local government (Wildavsky 1965). Budget-making, which usually includes preparation and enactment of the budget, is a planning task by which financial resources are allocated among competing departmental needs (Fig. 7.2). Budget control, which usually includes reporting and monitoring of departmental expenditures, is a control task in which expenditures are monitored for their consistency with budget plans and, when variations occur, remedial actions are taken. However, because budget plans are themselves dynamic or changeable, budget control also affects budgetary replanning throughout the year (Schick 1964).

How do budgets control departmental behavior? From a behavioral standpoint, the budget represents a set of financial commitments for meeting departmental goals (Cyert and March 1963; Hrebenar 1973). Usually the goals and related commitments are arrived at by agreement of both top and department management, but sometimes they are imposed on a department by top management. Although occasionally they use rewards, top managers more frequently use sanctions for getting department managers to comply with the agreement. Since the attainment of department goals is difficult to measure, top managers tend to focus control on the equalization of budgets with expenditures (Stedry 1960). If expenditures exceed budgeted levels, this fact is called to the department head's attention. Generally, it is assumed that some valid change in operating conditions is behind every variation from the budget. Consequently, when deviations from budget plans arise, top managers seek an explanation for the deviations from the department managers closest to the operation in question, and thus department managers must hunt for causes, or at least reasons, for the deviations. Often these occasions are used by department managers to justify a

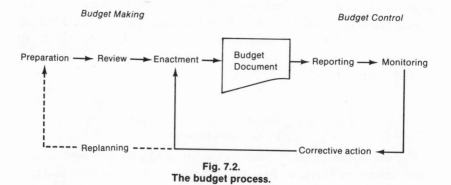

Fig. 7.2.
The budget process.

Activities	Central Unit	Departments
Budget reporting		
Purpose:	Timely, accurate, relevant, inexpensive reporting	Checking department records with central-unit records
Locus:	Central reporting unit in finance/controller	n.a.
Nature of reports:	Current balances for all departments and funds	Current balances for the department and divisions
Nature of computer capabilities potentially available:	Data storage and retrieval Record restructuring Continuous monitoring Exception reporting	Data storage
Budget monitoring		
Purpose:	Fiscal and managerial control across departments and within funds	Fiscal and management control within the department, across divisions and accounts
Locus:	Central budget-monitoring unit in finance/controller department or in independent department under chief executive	Department/division managers and administrative staff
Nature of information potentially available:	Current balance comparisons Exceptions, expenditure variations from budget Cost accounting Project accounting Expenditure/revenue gaps Uneven expenditure patterns	Same as central unit, but for department and divisions only

Fig. 7.3.
Budget-control activities.

budget change which, if granted by top management, will allow the department to compensate for the reported causes of trouble. Alternatively, department managers might demonstrate that the overspending is due to some uncontrollable factor (e.g., the impact of the energy crisis on expenditures for fuel), and it might be excused. But if inefficiency is suspected as the cause, internal auditors might investigate the case and recommend reprimands, promotion passover, or dismissal as sanctions.

Budget-Control Activities

Budget control, then, involves three interrelated activities: budget reporting, budget monitoring, and management action (Fig. 7.3). Budget reporting is the preparation and distribution of statistics on the relation between budgets and expenditures for a given period. It is performed by a central unit in the finance or controller department in nearly all the cities (Table 7.1). Budget monitoring is the examination of the current balance report for variances or differences between budgets and expenditures that warrant investigation. These may be differences in "levels" or in "rates" of expenditure or both. Monitoring is performed at both the central and the department level.[1] Centrally, it is performed by a budget-monitoring unit in the finance department, or in an independent budget office under the chief executive (Table 7.1). This reporting of statistics and monitoring of variances are not in themselves control. Instead, control occurs upon completion of management action, the third budget-control activity, which consists of the steps that any level of management takes to excuse, regulate, or limit department expenditures. The overall effectiveness of budget control is gauged by the degree to which actual expenditures approach, or are less than, budgets.

Budget control, then, is a critical managerial task in the administration phase of the budgetary process. Unlike the other phases of budget preparation and budget enactment, which involve intensive activity for a relatively short period of time, budget control is a continuous activity that peaks during the closing months and weeks of the fiscal year (Shadoan 1963). The chief instrument of budget control is the current-

Table 7.1
Location of Central-Budget-Control Activities[a]
(N = 40)

Location	Central-Budget Reporting		Central-Budget Monitoring	
	%	N	%	N
Controller/auditor department	30	12	12	5
Finance department	70	28	48	19
Independent budget office under chief executive	0	0	40	26

[a]Two cities do not centrally produce a balance report or centrally monitor department expenditures.

balance report, which is a periodic (usually monthly) accounting of budgets and expenditures, usually broken down by department and by line item of expense, although more elaborate breakdowns and data sometimes are reported. Ostensibly, the report is designed to serve multiple approaches to control and multiple levels of managerial control.

Approaches to Budgetary Control

The fiscal and managerial approaches to budget control highlight a major distinction in approaches to budget reporting, and to the accounting system on which the report is based. The fiscal approach emphasizes fiscal accountability and legal compliance with financial laws. Consequently, financial reports are "designed to show that all money went for designated public purposes, that operations were within the budget, and that all was done within the rules laid down" (Moak and Hillhouse 1975:331). The balance report therefore is used to account for all the money spent and to ensure that operations are within the budget.

The managerial approach emphasizes managerial control in accordance with certain standards (Stedry 1960). These standards may include quarterly allotments, monthly spending rates, work-load estimates, unit costs, and so forth. The balance report is used as an exception-reporting device to highlight deviations from the standards in order to control expenditures, and/or to evaluate whether budget estimates require revision because of unanticipated needs, rising costs, or other factors.

Levels of Budgetary Control

As these differences in approach to budget reporting suggest, different clients are potentially served by the different kinds of balance reports. Budget-reporting systems tend to vary in terms of whether they are primarily helpful to control of department expenditures by central management or by the departments themselves. Some budget-reporting systems are aimed primarily at producing detailed information on a weekly or daily basis for use by the finance office and central budget offices in the auditing department expenditures. The departments receive only monthly summaries and these usually are two weeks old by the time of receipt. Consequently, the summaries are only used by the departments for reconciling departmental bookkeeping systems and not for controlling expenditures.

Other budget-reporting systems produce summary and detailed information on a weekly basis and get that information out to the departments, as well as to central management, within a day or two after the close of the accounting period. Consequently, these summaries can assist departments in controlling their own expenditures and still serve central management.

Whether these budgeting systems actually do serve departmental or other management, of course, depends on whether they are used and how they are used. Some department officials consider the monitoring aspect of budgetary administration as an intrusion on their freedom to conduct the affairs of their departments or agencies within the overall framework of the appropriations made available. Therefore, municipal departments sometimes resist the implementation of balance-reporting systems or refuse to use them when installed. However, the greater the emphasis placed by central management on use of the balance report as a tool for managing the city, the greater the likelihood that the departments will also use the report (Stedry 1960; Hale and Douglass 1977).

The Impacts of Budget Automation

Cities adopt an automated budget system so that their financial information is more accessible as well as more up-to-date. In addition, cities expect to realize cost savings and to achieve better monitoring capacity over expenditures, as a result of the automated systems.[2] But are these hoped-for benefits realized?

Information Benefits

Both finance and operating-department personnel agree that automation has increased the frequency and timeliness of balance reports. Thirty-six percent of the automated cities produce balance reports daily for the finance department, while a majority of automated cities produce the balance report at least biweekly. In contrast, a majority of nonautomated cities produce the balance report only monthly or quarterly.

Automation also increased the frequency with which current-

Table 7.2
Frequency of Budget Reports
(N = 42)

Frequency with which budget reports are regularly available	Finance[a]				Operating Departments			
	Nonautomated		Automated		Nonautomated		Automated	
	%	N	%	N	%	N	%	N
Daily	0	0	36	13	0	0	17	6
Weekly	0	0	11	4	0	0	8	3
Biweekly	0	0	6	2	0	0	6	2
Monthly	50	3	47	17	50	3	69	25
Quarterly	17	1	0	0	17	1	0	0
None	33	2	0	0	33	2	0	0
Pearson's r	.57*				.52*			
Controlled for city size	.53*				.47*			

[a]The central budget reporting unit in the finance or comptroller department.
*P < .05.

balance reports were available to the operating departments. All automated cities send balance reports to the departments at least monthly, compared to only half of the nonautomated cities (Table 7.2).

While the frequency of budget reporting is important for effective budget monitoring, getting that information to the departments quickly can be even more critical. For example, in one city the balance report is produced and distributed weekly, but the information contained in each report is three weeks old. As the following exchange indicates, the benefits of automation might be dubious:

"You get the balance report weekly, don't you?"
"Sure, but for three weeks ago. The time lag is devastating. It's not satisfactory. Where we're making rapid encumbrances in order to use funds which are designated for completion of a certain [public works] project, or when we have lagged in ordering materials, it's not timely enough. And, at the end of the year, we often forfeit a certain amount of federal and state project funds because we don't know where we stand." (URBIS Case Report, Grand Rapids)

Table 7.3 shows that the timeliness of balance reports is generally improved by automation, despite our example. Forty-one percent of the automated cities get the reports to the operating departments within a week, but none of the nonautomated cities does so. Fifty-six percent of the automated cities get the balance reports to the departments within one to four weeks, whereas only one-third of the

Table 7.3
Timeliness of Budget Reports

Elapsed Time between Closing Date of an Accounting Period and Departmental Receipt of Current-Balance Report[a]	Kind of Automation			
	Nonautomated (N = 6)		Automated (N = 36)	
	%	N	%	N
Less than one day	0	0	11	4
One to three days	0	0	11	4
Four to seven days	0	0	19	7
One to two weeks	33	2	28	10
Two to four weeks	0	0	28	10
Four to six weeks	17	1	0	0
Over six weeks	0	0	0	0
No report of finer detail than the department	50	3	0	0

[a]Which is of finer detail than the department level.

Table 7.4
Special Requests for Current-Balance Information

| Requesting Agency | Average Number of Special Requests per Year[a] | | | |
| | Nonautomated | | Automated | |
	No.	N	No.	N
Finance [b]	90	4	505	35
Operating departments	10	6	22	35

| | Average Up-to-Dateness of Information Supplied in Response to Special Requests | | | |
| | Nonautomated | | Automated | |
	No. of Days	N	No. of Days	N
Finance[a]	5	3	8	31
Operating departments	11	5	6	29

[a]"No." is averge number of requests; N is number of cities.
[b]The central-budget reporting unit in the finance or comptroller department.

nonautomated cities do. The remaining nonautomated cities (67 percent) take over four weeks or simply do not produce a balance report with detail finer than the department level.

Yet, even with automation, budget reports usually are available to most departments only monthly and reach the departments about a week after the close of each reporting period. Therefore, departments frequently must make special requests for more current information, especially near the end of each reporting period. In principle, automation should increase the number of such requests that can be handled, as well as increase the currrency of the information, and decrease the time required to respond to special requests.

The automated cities clearly handle a larger number of special requests for current-balance information than the unautomated cities. The average total number of special requests during the year varies from 90 requests in unautomated cities to 505 in automated cities (Table 7.4). The average number of requests for a single department varies from 10 requests in unautomated cities to 22 in automated cities. It is unclear, however, whether automation improves either the currency or the timeliness of special-request information, because finance and operating-department personnel disagree over these two outcomes (Table 7.4 and Table 7.5).

Table 7.5

Timeliness of Response to Special Requests for Current-Balance Information

Average Time to Respond to a Special Request	In Finance[a] (N = 33)				In Operating Department (N = 31)			
	Nonautomated		Automated		Nonautomated		Automated	
	%	N	%	N	%	N	%	N
A few minutes	67	2	70	21	40	2	54	14
About an hour	33	1	13	4	20	1	30	8
A day	0	0	3	1	20	1	8	2
One to three days	0	0	10	3	20	1	4	1
Four days and over	0	0	3	1	0	0	4	1

[a]The central-budget reporting unit in the finance or comptroller's department.

Automation of the balance report also might be expected to affect the technical quality of information; that is, the accuracy and completeness of information. The responses we gathered in our site visits indicate that technical quality has improved. Finance personnel in 83 percent of the automated cities (35) and operating personnel in 74 percent of these cities, indicate that this is the case.

In summary, automation has produced information benefits. It has increased the frequency with which current-balance reports are produced, improved the technical quality of information, reduced the age of the information in the reports, and improved the timeliness with which they are made available to the operating departments. The following excerpt from our field notes illustrates the information benefits in one city:

Generally, there is a high level of satisfaction with the balance report. It is viewed as highly accurate, it is timely in that it generally appears within fifteen days of the close of the month, yet has both summary data and detailed data for those who desire it. It is somewhat capable of flagging areas where there is likely to be an expenditure problem and as a consequence of this and the forcefulness of the Finance Director, virtually no departments maintain parallel books. Rather, the departments rely on this report as their primary source of summary expenditure data. (URBIS Case Report, Stockton)

Automation has also increased the number of special requests that can be handled. However, automation's impact on the currency and timeliness of special-request information is ambiguous and, therefore, debatable.

Cost Payoffs

Cost efficiency refers to the impact of automation on staff numbers, staff time, and costs. Automation of the current balance report might be expected to produce staff and cost impacts in the finance department, which prepares the balance report; and in the operating departments, which use the report. Within the finance department, computing might reduce the number of people required to prepare the report, reduce staff time in searching for information, reduce errors that require staff time to detect and correct them, and reduce the time required to handle special requests. However, it might also require more skilled and expensive staff, new equipment, and more staff time in dealing with the new information possibilities offered by automation. Similarly, within the operating departments, staff-time savings might accrue to the administrative staff, particularly when the balance reports are accurately produced and available in a timely manner. This situation would facilitate checking department records against the balance report, and determining current balances for expenditure decisions. However, to the extent that the balance reports are untimely, difficult to use, and erroneous, they might also increase administrative-staff time and costs.

We have found that automation clearly does not increase staff in our cities. Basically, automation either has no effect on staff numbers, or it reduces them (Table 7.6). Finance personnel in 63 percent of the automated cities indicate that staff has decreased; 23 percent indicate no difference; and 14 percent indicate that staff has increased. Similarly, finance personnel in 46 percent of the cities indicate that costs have decreased; 18 percent indicate no difference; but 36 percent do indicate that costs have increased. One reason why costs might have increased is that some cities still maintain manual accounting records in addition to computerized records. Our field research indicates that dual records are likely to be kept by the operating departments, as the following field report indicates:

In principle, the accounting division is supposed to be *the* source of expenditure data in the city. In fact, however, the larger departments maintain their own accountants

Table 7.6
Staff and Cost Impacts of Automation on Preparation
of the Current-Balance Report

	In Finance[a]		In Operating Departments[b]	
	%	N	%	N
Staff impacts				
Staff has increased	14	5	12	4[a]
No difference	23	8	38	13
Staff has decreased	63	22	50	17
Cost impacts				
Cost has increased	36	12	6	2
No difference	18	6	56	19
Cost has decreased	46	15	38	13

[a]The central-budget reporting unit in the finance or comptroller's department.
[b]These responses refer to increases, decreases, or no differences in *staff time* rather than staff positions.

and use their own books for maintaining accurate and up to date expenditure data. That is, they have data which is available to the day rather than the bi-weekly data provided by the accounting office. They use the bi-weekly balance report provided by the accounting office to reconcile their books against the accounting division's.

When I asked whether work, staff or costs have been cut down the answers were often ambiguous. In part, department heads and accountants note that since they're working on two sets of books their work has gone up. But on the other hand, since they're reconciling their books with the city bi-weekly instead of simply once a year, their year-end work is cut down. (URBIS Case Report, Tulsa)

In some cities, dual records are kept in both finance and operating departments—for as long as several years after conversion to a new computerized system. Thus, costs would be increased.

Operating-department personnel see similar staff and cost savings as a result of computing. About 90 percent feel that computing either has made no difference or has reduced staff and costs.

This general correspondence of views between finance and operating-department personnel is an important indicator of the validity of the responses. While finance personnel might be predisposed to perceive benefits because they initiated automation, the department personnel would tend to be more critical in their assessment, since generally they neither initiate, nor participate in, the development of the automated system. In effect, department personnel might resent the intrusion of automation into their activities unless they truly found it helpful.

Expenditure-Control Payoffs: Fiscal and Managerial

A major intended impact from automation of the current-balance report is the improved ability of central management and the operating departments to exercise fiscal and managerial control over spending. The fundamental objective of fiscal control is to ensure that resources are expended on public goods and services for which revenues have been appropriated, and to prevent overexpenditure. The objective of managerial control is to enable central and department management to comprehend the pattern of spending for services quickly and fully, so that exceptions to budget plans can be recognized and evaluated, slack resources identified, and resource reallocations made.

Managerial officials indicate that automation has been helpful in assisting central management and the operating departments in controlling spending. For central management, the impacts have been particularly impressive (Table 7.7). Most cities indicate that the balance report has been "very helpful" in fiscal control—identifying accounts that have reached overspending levels, and identifying accounts with unspent funds. This is illustrated by the following excerpt from the URBIS fieldwork:

The Bureau of Accounting Operations uses these [current balance] reports to keep careful control in the sense of observing how much money has been spent and whether there is money available in a fund. The Bureau of the Budget uses these reports to estimate how the expenditure pattern of each department is going.

Although they still do their projections [of department spending to the end of the year] manually, the Bureau of the Budget people report that they could not have done these projections prior to automation. It gives them more capability to estimate earlier and more clearly which spending units are in trouble and to provide information and pressure to try and guide them out of their problems.

In the last fiscal year, five of the major departments spent substantially over their allocations. As a consequence of this problem, the Director of Finance this year has instituted a system of allocations which means that each of those five departments is allowed "X" dollars per month to spend and it is metered out over the 12 month period in order to control the expenditures more carefully. The decision to carefully monitor the five departments this year is facilitated to some extent by the automated systems. (URBIS Case Report, Baltimore)

In contrast, a majority of the cities indicate that the balance report is "not helpful" when it comes to providing more accurate information about expenditure patterns that are uneven throughout the fiscal year.

A more general indicator is whether the current-balance report is helpful for managerial control, and fully 82 percent of the cities indicate that it is helpful (Table 7.7). The fieldwork further indicates that the propensity of top management to emphasize and personally utilize the balance reports has a substantial effect on their perceived importance throughout the government. For example, in one city:

Underlying the use of this report, which is quite frequent by operating departments, is the fact that the current City Manager, one of the grand founders of the ICMA, is totally finance-oriented and his perspective of how to manage is to manage the budget. As a consequence, this document which he uses as his management document is, of course, most important to all operating personnel. (URBIS Case Report, Stockton)

Within the operating departments, the budget report also has been helpful in controlling expenditures but slightly less so than for central

Table 7.7
Impacts of Automation on Fiscal and Managerial Control

Kind of Control	In Central Management (N = 32)[a]						In Operating Departments (N = 33)					
	Not Helpful		Somewhat Helpful		Very Helpful		Not Helpful		Somewhat Helpful		Very Helpful	
	%	N	%	N	%	N	%	N	%	N	%	N
Fiscal Control												
Identifying accounts which have reached overspending level	3	1	15	5	81	26	21	7	27	9	52	17
Identifying accounts with unspent funds	6	2	15	5	78	26	15	5	27	9	58	19
Provided more accurate information about uneven expenditure patterns throughout the fiscal year	56	19	18	6	26	9	58	19	36	12	6	2
Managerial control												
Enhanced financial control over particular departments, sections, accounts, or programs	18	6	24	8	58	19	21	7	46	15	33	11

[a]The central-budget monitoring unit located in finance/controller department (60 percent of the cities) or in an independent budget office under the chief executive (40 percent of the cities).

management (Table 7.7). More than three-fourths of the cities indicate that the balance report is "somewhat helpful" or "very helpful" in identifying overspent and underspent accounts for fiscal control. And more than three-fourths of the cities indicate that the balance report has enhanced managerial control. But as with central management, operating-department personnel in a majority of the cities indicate that the balance report is "not helpful" in providing information about uneven expenditure patterns.

The extent to which automated budget monitoring is not helpful regarding uneven expenditure patterns might be due to the omission of certain capabilities in the automated systems, and to increases in the work of department administrative staff without compensating benefits. For example, our fieldwork indicates that few cities have built the capability to forecast uneven spending patterns into their automated budget-monitoring systems. Our fieldwork also indicates that while automated budget monitoring might include real capabilities for increased control of department expenditures, the paperwork burden connected with some systems prevents the administrative staff from using these capabilities; consequently, they would have to judge the systems as not helpful. One illustration of these burdens is provided by an early version of the automated finance system in Tulsa:

The automated financial system, called MACS I—an acronym for Municipal Administration and Control Subsystem, on the surface, seems to be a sophisticated computational device. The city reports label it an integrated MIS [Management Information System] and it is implemented on Honeywell's data base management system—IDS [Integrated Data Store]. It allows on-line up-dating as well as producing a variety of periodic reports such as the bi-weekly balance report. Despite the apparent sophistication of MACS I, the system has such severe deficiencies that it is resented by the finance department staff who use it, and is not used on a day to day basis by the staff in the larger departments.

It was simply designed as a copy of the manual system. When asked what he liked best about computers in preparing current balance reports, the head of the city's accounting department commented, "I don't know. We haven't gained too much." An accountant in his Department remarked on his questionnaire, "I hate it, I hate it, I hate it. I wouldn't give you 50¢ for it. It doesn't even provide as detailed information as when we had accounting machines."

Moreoever, for operational staff who provide various inputs into the accounting system (and therefore into the current balance report), MACS I is relatively cumbersome when compared with their earlier manual system. For example, consider purchase order processing. The computer was loaded when MACS I was put up, so to save space the vendor names weren't added to the system. As a consequence, vendor names have to be typed in after some of the computer-generated information is printed on the purchase orders. Moreover, one cannot write a warrant for more than one purchase order to the same company. That means that if ten different items are being purchased simultaneously from the same company, ten different warrants must be written, the same vendor name typed ten times on ten different warrants by a clerk, and the company mailed a rather thick packet of ten warrants from the city. These features of MACS I make a mockery of the use of IDS, the data base management system. If anything, IDS should make it easy to implement variable-length lists which would be the technical basis for allowing an arbitrary number of purchases to be listed on the same purchase order. (URBIS Case Report, Tulsa)

Expenditure-Control Payoffs:
Department Spending

Despite the apparent helpfulness of automated budget monitoring to municipal officials, one might still set the "bottom line" at whether department overspending is decreased and department underspending is increased as a result of automation. Table 7.8 shows that there is very

Table 7.8
Comparison of Overspending and Underspending in the Operating Departments[a]

	Nonautomated		Automated	
	No.	N	No.	N
Department overspending				
Mean number of departments that spent at least 5 percent more than allocated	3	6	3	35
Mean number of cases where computer aided identification of overspending	0	0	5	32
Mean number of cases where computer used to determine reallocation of funds	0	0	4	33
Department underspending				
Mean number of departments that spent less than 95 percent of what they were appropriated	2	5	9	34
Mean number of cases where computer aided identification of overspending	0	0	10	31
Mean number of cases where computer used to determine reallocation of funds	0	0	7	30
Overspending identification				
Mean number of days to identify overspending	15 days	6	11 days	31

[a]"No." is number of cases, and N is number of cities.

little, if any, difference in department overspending in unautomated and automated cities. This is true despite the use of computerized balance-report data to identify overspending and to determine the reallocation of funds in some automated cities.

On the surface, this finding suggests that automation is not in fact helpful to better money management in cities. However, department overspending can also be viewed as a measure of the fiscal problems many cities currently face, and thus budget automation might well be a response to the urban fiscal crisis. That is, the cities with fiscal problems might be using the technology to help them better report and monitor the fiscal problems precisely because they are in a fiscal crisis. For example, in one city:

It was noted that until a few years ago departments were relatively free to spend over their allocated amount. Now, as money has tightened, so has budget monitoring and this may explain the attention the top managers are placing on budget reports. The monitoring activity is done under a new Budget Office which was created by the new city manager two years ago. (URBIS Case Report, Hampton)

Moreover, the capability offered by data processing is viewed as directly related to the level of budget monitoring in the city:

The existence of the data processing capability is viewed as a sine qua non for the current level of monitoring. The weekly reports simply could not have been generated under the manual system and the monthly reports would have been much less timely. Consequently, to the extent there is stricter budget monitoring now, it is the function of both a policy decision and the existence of highly accurate, timely and useful automated balance reports. (URBIS Case Report, Hampton).

Further, while budget monitoring might help municipal officials to identify overspending more quickly, officials in some cities might be unable to reverse overspending patterns because of environmental factors. The influence of environment is particularly strong in the larger and eastern cities where uncontrollable environmental change (e.g., declining tax base), unanticipated cost increases (e.g., for gas and oil), and unexpected expenditures (e.g., for police and public works overtime) can have massive cumulative impacts.

Although automated budget monitoring has little effect on over-spending, it appears to increase department underspending. This is consistent with the earlier findings that automated budget monitoring was helpful to the departments in controlling spending. Whereas unautomated cities had an average of only two departments which underspent in 1976, the automated cities had an average of nine departments which underspent (Table 7.8). One explanation for the greater underspending is that the increased frequency and timeliness of the current-balance report in the automated cities focuses greater attention of department officials on staying within budgetary limits early on in the fiscal year. This is suggested by the greater frequency of special requests for current-balance information in the automated cities reported earlier (Table 7.4). It is also suggested somewhat by the fact that automated cities require only 11 days to identify over-spending, compared to 15 days for unautomated cities (Table 7.8). Automated budget monitoring also provides central management with the practical means for ensuring that most departments do stay within limits. Last-minute catch-up spending would be easily identified with automated systems, whereas it would be difficult with manual systems. Also, the automated balance report potentially facilitates enforcement of fiscal-crisis policies, such as "forced" salary savings and allocation of the costs of "overhead departments" (e.g., purchasing, finance) to the operating departments through simply changing operating-depart-ment balances across the board.

Expenditure Control and Decentralization

Finally, an unanticipated impact of automating the balance report is that information and control is decentralized to the department heads and their administrative staff, because the report can be widely distributed. With automation, the departments know what infor-mation finance has about them, and know just about as quickly as finance does, thereby increasing department control over subunits and over discussions with central management. This effect is contrary to the popular perception that automation inevitably centralizes infor-mation and control. In fact, it frequently centralizes and decentralizes simultaneously by centralizing some aspects and decentralizing others. The decentralizing effect can be seen by contrasting automated balance-report systems with manual ones. Prior to automation, all financial information was kept mostly in the finance department. Broad summary reports were provided to the departments on a monthly or quarterly basis, and these reports usually were several weeks to a month out of date by the time they reached the departments. This meant that department staff had to keep manual accounting records in order to determine actual current balances. Consequently, department administrative staff spent most of their time keeping independent records, trying to reconcile their records with those in finance, and determining current balances, rather than monitoring the pattern of expenditure.

Automation of the balance report increased the frequency and timeliness with which the report could be produced, thereby providing the operating departments with nearly the same information available to finance. This potentially increased the operating departments' ability to monitor and control their own expenditures and to fight over the need for additional funds earlier in the year. The foregoing data on spending patterns (Table 7.8) suggest that the automated balance report may have had precisely that effect.

To summarize, cities adopted an automated budget system so that their fiscal information would be more accessible, up-to-date, and accurate. They also hoped to realize cost savings and improved monitoring capacities. All these hoped-for benefits have been realized by most of our automated cities, although to varying degrees.

Implementation Strategies

Computing is used for budgetary control by most cities largely because budget and accounting applications were among the first computer applications. Despite the fact that budgeting and accounting automation is common, cities vary extensively in the ways they have implemented computing for budgetary control. These variations can be classified by whether they tend to follow a reform or post-reform approach to implementation, and they are considered here from three perspectives: technological development, structural arrangement, and socio-technical design. Generally, cities have heeded the post-reform approach to budgetary automation. That is, most tend to follow the strategies of appropriate technology, participatory management, and a human-relations approach to socio-technical design. Still, some cities have relatively advanced technology, such as on-line access to daily updated departmental accounts. Also, some cities have adopted quite centralized structural arrangements and approaches to socio-technical design, which clearly emphasize task efficiency over human relations. Here we describe the different implementation strategies that cities have adopted. In the next section, the impacts of these strategic differences are assessed.

Technological Development

As in other tasks, cities face a choice between two approaches to the technological development of budget control. Reformers advocate the use of advanced technology and advise finance departments to automate early, develop a large number of sophisticated applications, and encourage high levels of computer use. In contrast, the approach that most of our cities have taken is the post-reform approach involving appropriate technology. Advocates of this approach suggest that finance departments hold back on automation until there is a clear and demonstrated need, concentrate resources by developing a small number of basic applications, and automate existing procedures rather than introduce innovations into the applications. Such a strategy is expected to hold development to a rate consistent with maintaining enough stability in the technology to avoid the problems of continually learning new systems and procedures.

The appropriate-technology approach of most cities is somewhat surprising in that financial functions were the first to be automated in cities, and consequently the overall level of finance automation in cities is high when compared to other areas of city government. In fact, as of 1975, over 90 percent of American cities with populations over 50,000 had automated some financial function, and many had automated several functions. As might be expected, most of the 42 cities in our study have considerable financial automation (Table 7.9).

Consistent with the appropriate-technology strategy, however, cities have emphasized automation of a small number of basic functions rather than advanced ones. Among basic functions, 36 percent of the cities have automated general accounting, 71 percent have automated budget preparation, and 57 percent have automated budget monitoring (Table 7.9). In contrast, among advanced functions, only 36 percent of the cities have automated cost accounting, 38 percent have automated expenditure forecasting, and 21 percent have automated revenue forecasting. Most of these financial functions are automated in the conventional batch mode, rather than by advanced on-line

Table 7.9
Degree of Financial Automation
(in percent)

Financial Functions Automated	Operational	Batch	On-line
Basic functions			
General accounting	36	15	21
Budget preparation	71	57	14
Program budget preparation	43	33	10
Line item budgeting	48	34	14
Budget reporting and monitoring	57	31	26
Advanced functions			
Cost accounting	36	26	10
Expenditure forecasting	38	33	5
Revenue forecasting	21	19	2

processing. But the degree of on-line automation is greater for the basic finance functions than it is for the advanced ones (Table 7.9), again reflecting the greater attention of our cities to basic automation. Thus, while the degree of finance automation in the cities is moderately high, the functions automated are basic rather than advanced, and the sophistication of finance automation generally is low.

Automation of budget control in our cities follows the general strategy of appropriate technology in finance automation and is pervasive.[3] The current-balance report, which is the chief instrument of budget control, is computer-generated in 36 (86 percent) of the cities. Most of the systems are batch-oriented (25 cities, or 60 percent), although 11 cities (26 percent) have on-line balance report systems, with access for data storage, retrieval, or both.[4] Only one-fourth (28 percent) of the automated cities have on-line computing support for budget reporting, whereas three-fourths (72 percent) have batch computing.[5]

The cities' use of appropriate technology is further illustrated by the fact that most cities have chosen merely to automate existing accounting data, rather than to design systems that use the full capabilities of the computer for developing management information. The extent to which budget-reporting systems provide the capability to develop management information out of accounting-based data[6] depends on the extent to which they are designed to implement three critical features: record restructuring, exception reporting, and continuous monitoring.

With manual accounting systems, restructuring of basic accounting records from their usual "fund" structure to a "department" structure is a time-consuming task, which can be performed only periodically and then only in a limited fashion. Other structures such as "program" and "project" cannot be feasibly accommodated. The amount of detail that can be reported under this traditional structure also is limited. In contrast, computerization of accounting records, plus the addition of specified account codes, make it possible to reformat basic accounting data to produce a wide variety of reports, based upon fund, program, department, division, project, facility, or any other reasonable method of organizing the data. The record-restructuring ability of the computer provides the means for implementing "cross-walk" systems which, by the use of carefully specified account codes, restructure line-item accounting data organized by one category, such as fund, to another category, such as program or department (and vice versa).

This restructuring capability has considerable significance for the information needs of different managers. Top managers responsible for effective use of resources to accomplish specified goals have been attracted to program budgeting and other budgetary techniques, because these systems provide information about expenditure in terms of programs, plans, and objectives irrespective of the department(s) implementing the program. Others, such as department and agency heads, need allocation data based on their own organizational domains, rather than on program categories that might cross department boundaries. Finance personnel typically need budgetary data organized in terms of "fund" or source of monies. Still others, such as auditors of state and federal funds spent by the city, may require information organized to indicate the precise distribution of costs for a particular project, service, or facility supported by intergovernmental grant programs. Hence, the record-restructuring and cross-walking capabilities of computerized systems provide the means for satisfying these multiple needs for information from the same basic accounting data. To the extent that automated accounting systems are designed with these capabilities, their potential for supporting multiple management uses of the balance report is greatly enhanced. Only 9 of the 35 automated cities (25 percent) have designed this capability into their budget automation. Still, none of the cities without automation have this capability.

Computerization has also made it easier to implement exception-reporting capabilities in budget reporting. Some of these capabilities are relatively simple, such as the addition of special columns for such budgetary standards as "percent of allocation spent," "expenditure from start to date" (for multi-year projects), "cumulative expenditure to date this year/last year," and "expenditure this period this year/last year." Other capabilities actually monitor expenditure by projecting the implications of current spending trends over the entire fiscal year. When deviations from the projections occur, exception reports are then generated, identifying each account category that is projected to overspend or to underspend its budgetary allocation by a specified amount. This early identification of potential problems and opportunities in the relation between actual and authorized spending gives managers proactive, rather than reactive, control over spending. To the extent that these capabilities are provided in the reports to department management as well as to central management, control of spending is decentralized throughout the administration. Three-fourths (74 percent) of the automated cities have designed this capability in their budget systems, but about two-thirds (60 percent) of the nonautomated cities also report this capability. This suggests that in most of our cities computing has not been implemented to enrich capabilities for exception reporting.

Automation of the current-balance report also supports continuous monitoring by increasing the accuracy, frequency, and timeliness of budget and expenditure information. In this manner, department expenditures can be made with full recognition of cost trends, the monies currently available to the department, and overspending, or underspending, that might occur in the future. The more frequently the balance report is produced and the more quickly it is available, the greater is the likelihood that budget plans can be met. Yet, less than one-half of our automated cities (44 percent) have the capability of producing current-balance reports weekly or more often. None of the unautomated cities has this capability.

One reason for the low sophistication of budget automation in our cities might be that budget applications were among the earliest to be automated. Because of this, many applications were implemented before the common use of on-line computing, and before the recognition that the computer offers unique capabilities for budget control. But it might not be just the early adoption of budget applications that accounts for low sophistication, because at least one-third of the cities have developed or redeveloped budget reporting and monitoring since 1970. Of possibly greater importance is the fact that many managers fear that redevelopment of these applications will seriously disrupt both finance and the operating departments. Some observers believe that technological instability is endemic to the data-processing function, due to continuous advances in the technology and the penchant of data-processing managers for having the most modern and up-to-date technology. While our cities vary in the levels of technological instability they experience, overall they experience only moderate levels of instability, consistent with an appropriate-technology strategy.[7]

Appropriate technology is evidenced as well by the moderate utilization of automated budget reports. For example, in 56 percent of the cities, the central budget unit uses computerized reports weekly or daily, but in 44 percent, such reports are used monthly or even less often. Utilization by the operating departments is much less than that of the central unit. In only 3 percent of the cities do operating departments use computer reports daily or weekly; most (97 percent) use them monthly or less often (Table 7.10).

Yet it would be difficult for utilization to be much higher given that the current-balance report is not produced very frequently and is not very timely in most of our cities. In half the automated cities (20), the

Table 7.10
Percentage and Number of Cities Utilizing Computing
for Budget Control
(N = 36)

Amount of Use	Central Budget Unit[a]		Operating Departments[b]	
	%	N	%	N
Daily	14	5	0	0
Weekly	42	15	56	20
Monthly	42	15	3	1
Rarely	3	1	42	15

[a]Use mainly involves receiving reports based on computer data and/or requesting others to get information from a computerized file; in a few instances, it also involves personally operating a computer terminal to get information from a computer file.

[b]Use mainly involves receiving reports based on computer data, and in a few instances, requesting others to get information from a computerized file.

balance report is produced only monthly. But 13 cities do produce it daily, and another 6 cities produce it weekly or biweekly. The timeliness of balance reports is also poor. Timeliness is defined in terms of how much time elapses between the closing date of an accounting period and the departments' receipt of the balance report; the less the elapsed time, the more timely the report. Roughly one-third of the cities produce the balance report within a week; another third produce it within two weeks, and the rest within four to six weeks. Given this lack of timeliness, it should not be surprising that computer utilization for budget control is only moderate, even though many cities have automated the task.

In summary, our cities clearly have followed a post-reform appropriate-technology approach, rather than a reform advanced-technology approach, in their budget automation. In fact, budget automation appears more retarded than other financial automation in the cities. While most of our cities have automated budget applications, most of these were automated very early, operate in the batch mode, lack sophisticated design features, and produce current-balance reports with only moderately improved frequency and timeliness over manual systems. Consequently, utilization of computing is only moderate in the central budget unit and low in the departments.

Structural Arrangements

There are two strategies regarding structural arrangements for budget-control automation. The classical strategy suggests that one should leave the major system decisions to the finance director and the EDP unit. One should also charge for computing and not allow the finance department to have its own computer. In this way, centralized control is maintained and budget automation is integrated into the priorities and organizational constraints of the whole city. In contrast, the post-reform approach involving participatory structural arrangements suggests that one involve budget and accounting staff in system design, provide computing free, and give the finance department its own computer. In this way, budget automation is managed by those closest to the needs of this task, allowing for better design and smoother implementation. It appears that the cities have heeded the post-reform participatory message, although perhaps because of historical accident more than conscious policy choice.

Table 7.11
Centralization of Finance Computing

Degree of Centralization[a]	Percentage and Number of Cities Having Each Arrangement (N = 36)	
	%	N
On-line computing in finance	33	12
Batch computing in finance	11	4
On-line computing in an independent EDP department	20	7
Batch computing outside finance	36	13

[a]This categorization is from low to high centralization, with the most centralized arrangement being the most remote, physically and institutionally, from users in the finance department. To users in the operating departments, computing is always centralized because it is in the finance department.

Since cities historically began using computers for finance functions, the computer resource was initially located in the finance department. And when computing became centralized in an independent city department, many finance departments still retained preferred access to the computer through remote terminals because of their earlier connection. Our cities reflect this tradition of decentralized[8] computing for finance, with 44 percent locating it within the finance department and another 20 percent providing on-line access to computing resources located in an independent data-processing installation. Only 36 percent have totally centralized computing outside the finance department (Table 7.11). Clearly, then, participatory arrangements characterize this structural area.

Because computing is located in the finance department in nearly half of our cities, it is not surprising that involvement of finance personnel in system design is high (Table 7.12). Generally, the influence of finance officials and staff is greater than that of other officials in our 36 automated cities.[9] Top managers and middle managers in the finance department are involved in design of budgeting applications, either in a consultative capacity or as participants on the design team, in 86 percent or more of the cities (Table 7.12). In contrast, elected and appointed chief executives and their staff are involved in design in only 16 percent of the cities for the reporting aspects of budget applications, and in 27 percent for the monitoring aspects (Table 7.12). Thus, from the standpoint of finance personnel, who are the primary users of budget automation, system design has been highly participatory.

Table 7.12
User Involvement in Design of Budget Applications

Category of Officials	Budget Reporting—Percentage of Cities in Which Official Had:				Budget Monitoring—Percentage of Cities in Which Official Had:			
	N	No Role in Design	Consultant Role	Membership on Design Team	N	No Role in Design	Consultant Role	Membership on Design Team
Chief appointed official and staff	31	84	16	0	26	73	27	0
Chief elected official and staff	35	91	9	0	32	91	6	3
Department top managers[a,d]	35	14	40	46	33	12	46	42
Department computer specialists[b,d]	28	71	4	25	28	64	4	32
Department middle managers[c,d]	36	19	44	36	33	21	33	46
Central EDP unit	36	14	8	78	31	23	6	71
Outside service bureau or consultant	35	51	6	43	33	52	6	42

[a] Finance director or controller for budget reporting; budget director for budget monitoring.
[b] Specialists in the finance/controller's department for budget reporting; in the budget unit for budget monitoring.
[c] Chief accountant for budget reporting; budget analysts for budget monitoring.
[d] The user-involvement policy variables discussed later in the chapter are built by using the involvement of these three officials.

Participatory arrangements also are reflected in our cities' approaches toward charging for computer use. Computing is provided free to finance and budget units in 62 percent of the cities. A charge for computing services, based on actual use for budgeting monitoring and reporting, is employed by only 35 percent of the cities, with another 3 percent charging a flat fee for use.

Socio-technical Design

While computing is intended to increase the quality of budget reporting and monitoring, and the effectiveness of central and departmental budget staff in their job, it also is likely to alter the work environment of these analysts.[10] On the one hand, computing may be implemented with a reform emphasis on task efficiency, and as a by-product it might create additional demands and pressures on budget analysts, which could decrease their sense of accomplishment in their work. On the other hand, computing may be implemented with post-reform attention to human relations in system design so as to increase, or at least not decrease, the analysts' ability to work with and influence other people, particularly policymakers,[11] thereby increasing their sense of accomplishment and satisfaction in their work.

It seems that our cities have been sensitive to the work environments and have tended to follow a post-reform, human-relations approach. Table 7.13 indicates that the computer's impact on the central staff's work environment has been moderately positive. Although our respondents believe computing has increased time pressures and the number of things the central staff must do in their jobs, it also is perceived to have increased their opportunities to work with other people and to influence other people, and to have increased their sense of accomplishment. And, central staff do not believe that computing has increased work supervision.

The computer's impact on the department staff's work environment has been largely neutral. The department staff in a majority of the cities indicate that computing has increased their work demands but has not affected their time pressures, opportunities to work with other people, or the degree to which their work is supervised. However, where there has been an effect, the impact has been largely positive, following the same pattern as occurs among the central staff.

Budget-staff support for computing and for computing personnel

Table 7.13
Budget Staff's Perceptions of Changes in Work Environment
caused by Computers[a]
(N = 36)

Work Impacts	Central Staff:[b] Percent Indicating	Department Staff: Percent Indicating
Has computing changed the number of things you do?		
(0) Decreased	3	0
(50) Not affected	27	42
(100) Increased	70	58
Average score	(77)	(68)
Has computing changed time pressures on your job?		
(0) Decreased	8	14
(50) Not affected	56	66
(100) Increased	36	20
Average score	(60)	(51)
Has computing changed your sense of accomplishment?		
(0) Lowered	6	3
(50) Not affected	47	44
(100) Raised	47	53
Average score	(69)	(70)
Has computing changed your opportunities to work with people?		
(0) Decreased	6	0
(50) Not affected	44	69
(100) Increased	50	31
Average score	(71)	(62)
Has computing changed the degree your work is supervised?		
(0) Decreased	11	8
(50) Not affected	81	86
(100) Increased	8	6
Average score	(47)	(50)
Has computing changed your influence over the actions of others?		
(0) Less influence	0	0
(50) No change	42	72
(100) More influence	58	28
Average score	(71)	(63)

[a] Average scores are the mean of individual responses within each city, scored from 0 to 100. Each variable was trichotomized to represent the percentage of cities with scores less than 33.3, between 33.3 and 66.7, and greater than 66.7.
[b] Central staff includes those in the central budget-reporting unit and in the central budget-monitoring unit.

Table 7.14
Budget Staff's Attitudes toward Data Processing
(N = 36)

Categories and Items	Percentage of Cities in Which Central Staff Agree[a]	Average Score[b]	Percentage of Cities in Which Department Staff Agree	Average Score[b]
Support for computing				
I want to use computers and data processing more in doing my job	100	89	84	81
Within the next five years, computers will greatly improve the operations of this government	86	65	92	68
Within the next five years, computers will greatly improve the way my job is done	72	67	81	63
Views toward DP personnel technocractic image				
Data-processing personnel are more intrigued with what the computer can do than with solving the problems of my department	33	39	27	35
Data-processing staff confuse our conversations with their technical language	39	44	14	31
Data-processing staff are more interested in working on new computer uses rather than making improvements in ones we now use	47	48	24	33

[a] Central staff includes those in the central budget-reporting unit and in the central budget-monitoring unit.
[b] Average scores are the mean of individual responses within each city scored 0 to 100. Each variable was dichotomized to represent the percentage of cities with scores greater than 50, indicating agreement.

also suggests that computing has been implemented with a sensitivity to their needs and demands. Generally, both the central and departmental budget staff support computing and feel that computing will improve their jobs in the future (Table 7.14). Interestingly, the department staff are even more positive than the central staff about the future impacts of computing on their jobs and on the operations of the government, although both are very positive. Most budget staff further believe that computing personnel are interested in solving department problems, in communicating in the user's language, and in making improvements in operational computer applications.

At the same time, nearly one-half of the central staff feel that data-processing personnel are more interested in working on new computer uses than in making improvements in existing applications. And one-third of the central staff believe that data-processing personnel are more intrigued with what the computer can do than with solving departmental problems, and that they confuse conversations with technical jargon. Since the central staff are the primary people who interact with data-processing personnel during design and implementation of budget automation, this suggests that a considerable proportion of the cities experience problems with insensitivity of data-processing personnel during implementation of budget systems.

In summary, while the implementation of computing in most cities seems to have followed a post-reform, human-relations approach, and to have been sensitive to the work environment of central and department budget staff, there remains important variation in the attitudes and work environments of budget staff across cities. Such variation indicates that some cities' implementation efforts focus on a reform approach, maximizing the task efficiency of budget automation with minimal sensitivity to the human-relations impacts of its design.

Organizational Context

From an organzational-context perspective, the reformers argue that a professional administrative environment with rational management practices and reformed government structures is conducive to successful implementation. However, the post-reformers argue that a political administrative environment with partisan activity is just as conducive. Clearly, cities are moving toward the development of a more professional administrative context. Yet many cities, and many city practices, remain closer to a political administrative context; and the trend toward professionalism is certainly in a state of flux, given recent evidence that many legislators are losing faith in professional management reforms. In sum, the organizational context of our cities is varied and changing.

Assessment of Implementation Strategies

Thus far, the weight of the evidence is in the direction of positive payoffs with automated versus manual budget-control activities. Yet not all automated cities have attained positive benefits from EDP. Clearly, some automated cities perform better than others. Therefore, the focus of this section is on the extent to which choices of implementation policies affect optimization of computing's benefit as regards budget performance. Specifically, we ask, To what extent can the reform versus post-reform approach to implementation explain the variation in performance rates among automated sites?

To accomplish this, we focus only on those cities with automated budget control. For these automated sites, we first describe the pattern of relationships between measures of implementation policies and summary indices of cost efficiency and budget-control performance. Simple, zero-order correlations provide an initial description of these relationships between implementation policies and performance. However, to identify those policies which most clearly predict performance, a multiple stepwise regression analysis is used. The fact that there are different organizational levels of budget control has led us to perform a comparative analysis of the impact of implementation policies on performance between the central budget units and the departments, because implementation policy effects might differ between these two levels.[12]

The Performance Indices

A major set of outcomes from automated budget control includes information benefits, managerial control, fiscal control, and pinpointing of department overspending and department underspending.[13] Indicators for each of these outcomes were selected, and a summary measure of budget-control performance, the average score over all indicators, was then computed. Individual performance measures were constructed for both the central level and the department level.

Information benefits are measured by the degree to which officials perceive computing as providing more accurate, complete, and up-to-date information. Managerial control is measured by the degree to which EDP has been helpful in enhancement of financial control over particular departments, sections, accounts, or programs. Fiscal control is measured by the extent to which computing has been helpful in providing more accurate information about uneven expenditure patterns throughout the fiscal year. Department spending at the central level involves two measures—percentage of departments within the city that overspent by 5 percent and percentage of departments that neither over- nor underspent their allocated budgets. Department spending at the department level involves two measures, one of underspending and one of overspending. Underspending is the percentage of budget accounts within the department that are at least 10 percent under allocation, and overspending is the percentage of the budget accounts within the department that are at least 10 percent over allocation.

Each indicator was normalized, and an average standardized score for budget-control performance was computed for both the central level and the department level. These scores provide a measure of the relative success of automated budget-control performance within each city. A listing of the cities and their budget performance scores is shown in Table 7.15. The table underscores the value of separate anaylses at both levels of the budget-control process. High budget-control performance at the central level within a city does not necessarily mean high performance at the department level.

A second major outcome from budget automation has to do with cost and staff savings, an internal organizational benefit from automation. To assess it, we have developed a second measure separate from the performance index. We have kept this measure separate because it involves benefits to the central unit and department that are unrelated to controlling spending. Yet it is an important consideration in pursuing automated budget control. Thus, cost efficiency is measured by the degree to which officials have experienced reductions in costs and/or staff due to the use of computers.

Table 7.15
Budget Performance Index

Central Level	Z-Score	Department Level	Z-Score
Very high		Very high	
Spokane, Wash.	1.163	Portsmouth, Va.	1.099
Milwaukee, Wis.	.950	Montgomery, Ala.	.878
Costa Mesa, Calif.	.812	Sacramento, Calif.	.876
Little Rock, Ark.	.760		
		High	
High		Milwaukee, Wis.	.645
Grand Rapids, Mich.	.649	Chesapeake, Va.	.619
Las Vegas, Nev.	.618	Florissant, Mo.	.584
Kansas City, Mo.	.608	Warren, Mich.	.566
Sacramento, Calif.	.531	Stockton, Calif.	.513
Portsmouth, Va.	.457	Little Rock, Ark.	.512
Fort Lauderdale, Fla.	.406	Spokane, Wash.	.299
Burbank, Calif.	.370	Grand Rapids, Mich.	.238
Medium		Medium	
Hampton, Va.	.194	Tulsa, Okla.	.223
Riverside, Calif.	.150	Miami Beach, Fla.	.217
Lancaster, Pa.	.140	San Francisco, Calif.	.164
Long Beach, Calif.	.136	Oshkosh, Wis.	.163
Cleveland, Ohio	.120	Riverside, Calif.	.077
San Francisco, Calif.	.084	Lancaster, Pa.	.012
Miami Beach, Fla.	.075	Baltimore, Md.	−.012
Atlanta, Ga.	.062	New Orleans, La.	−.042
Lincoln, Nebr.	.039	Hampton, Va.	−.066
Chesapeake, Va.	−.134	Atlanta, Ga.	−.141
Tampa, Fla.	−.210	Louisville, Ky.	−.182
Philadelphia, Pa.	−.211	Fort Lauderdale, Fla.	−.212
		Philadelphia, Pa.	−.218
Low		Burbank, Calif.	−.235
Florissant, Mo.	−.292	St. Louis, Mo.	−.240
Montgomery, Ala.	−.334		
Stockton, Calif.	−.352	Low	
Louisville, Ky.	−.358	Cleveland, Ohio	−.287
Baltimore, Md.	−.484	Costa Mesa, Calif.	−.301
Seattle, Wash.	−.515	San Jose, Calif.	−.322
San Jose, Calif.	−.540	Kansas City, Mo.	−.336
St. Louis, Mo.	−.666	Seattle, Wash.	−.404
		Lincoln, Nebr.	−.632
Very Low		Tampa, Fla.	−.635
Warren, Mich.	−.826		
Oshkosh, Wis.	−.852	Very low	
Tulsa, Okla.	−1.079	Las Vegas, Nev.	−.797
Newton, Mass.	−1.321	Long Beach, Calif.	−.998
New Orleans, La.	−1.507		

The Independent Variables

The independent variables are divided into the three general categories of implementation policies—technological development, structural arrangements, and socio-technical design. In addition, organizational-context and community-environment characteristics are included in the analysis.

Technological development variables include degree of finance automation, degree of automation sophistication, the orientation of computing, the degree of routinization of computing and technological instability. Degree of finance automation is measured by the number of finance-related applications available to the central-budget level. It is further broken down into two variables—the number of finance applications that are batch-oriented and the number of finance applications that are on-line. The degree of automation sophistication is measured in three different ways. First, there is a dichotomous measure of the types of finance applications available—batch predominating or on-line predominating. Second, there is a measure of the number of on-line terminals located within the finance department. Finally, there is a composite measure of the level of technological sophistication of the hardware, software, and personnel within the computer installation. Routinization of finance automation is measured by the first year in which an operational finance application was available to the central-budget level. Routinization is thus operationalized in terms of the number of years that the budget unit has had access to automated finance applications. The earlier the application was available, the more routinized the automation is within the central-budget level. Orientation of computing is measured by the level of use of computing for budget control. This four-point scale ranges from rarely used to daily use. Finally, technological instability is a count of the number of technological changes that have occurred within the computer installation within the past year.

Structural variables include measures of user involvement, the degree of centralization of the computer installation, charging for computer time, and structural instability. Three measures of user involvement are included. We have distinguished between user involvement in the design of budget-reporting applications and budget-monitoring applications. Both measures involve the initial decision-making regarding design of finance applications. In addition, there is a measure of the degree of continuous user involvement in decisions within the computer installation. Centralization is measured by a single four-point scale with the highest value being assigned to installations located within the finance department and providing on-line terminal access and the lowest value assigned to installations located outside the finance department and providing only batch access. Charging is a measure of whether the finance-installation users must pay for computer time and memory or whether this time and memory are provided free to finance and central-budget-level users. Finally, structural instability is a count of the number of structural changes made within the computer installation during the past year.

Socio-technical design is represented by two variables—one measuring the level of job pressure experienced by users due to automation of budget-control activities; the other measuring the level of job satisfaction and job accomplishment experienced by users that is attributable to automated budget control.

The organizational-context indicators include both general, city-wide organizational characteristics and characteristics specific to the central-budget-level organization. Citywide, we have included a measure of the degree of slack financial resources available to the city government, the degree of partisan politics within the city, the degree of professional-management practices adopted by the city bureaucracy, and finally whether the city government is a reformed council-manager structure or a mayor-council form. At the central budget level, we have included both a measure of the budget-reporting efficiency, which is a composite factor score of the frequency and timeliness of the budget reports, and a measure of budget-monitoring efficiency, which is a composite factor score of the frequency and strictness of the budget-monitoring process at the central-unit level.

The general community environment is measured by the size of the city population in 1975 and the growth of the city's population between 1970 and 1975.

Findings

We present our analysis by describing the relationships between the implementation strategies and each performance measure separately. We also discuss the strategies most helpful in explaining the respective performance measures in budget control.

Table 7.16
Pearson Correlations between Cost and Implementation
Strategies and Environments

Implementation Policies and Environments	Performance Measures			
	Central Budget Unit Cost Efficiency		Department Cost Efficiency	
	r	N	r	N
Technological development				
Degree of automation				
Degree of finance automation	.33*	33	.43*	34
Batch automation	.00	33	.24	34
Sophistication of automation				
Batch or on-line predominating in finance automation	.39*	33	.17	34
Number of on-line terminals in finance	.30*	33	.32*	34
Sophistication of computing installation	.16	33	.08	34
Orientation of computing				
Utilization of computing for budget control	.14	33	.42*	34
Other technological arrangements				
Routinization of the technology	.02	31	−.06	32
Technological instability	−.03	33	−.08	34
Structural arrangements				
Centralization-decentralization				
Non-finance located EDP installation	−.30*	33	−.17	34
User involvement				
User involvement in design of budget reporting	.43*	33	.37*	34
User involvement in design of budget monitoring	.32*	33	−.17	34
User involvement in decisions of the computer installation	.22	32	.18	33
Other structural arrangements				
Charging for computer services	−.37*	32	−.02	33
Structural instability	−.50*	33	−.35*	34
Socio-technical design				
Job pressure due to computing	−.22	33	−.02	34
Job satisfaction due to computing	.20	33	−.35*	34
Organizational context				
Reformed government structure	.40*	33	.13	34
Level of partisanship	.05	33	.10	34
Degree of professional management practices	.09	33	−.06	34
Slack financial resources	.21	33	.05	34
Community environment				
Size of city	.11	33	.17	34
Growth of city, 1970-1975	.07	33	−.05	34

*$P < .05$.

Cost Efficiency

Overall, our analysis indicates that central-budget units with higher levels of performance in terms of cost efficiency tend to have participatory structural arrangements and advanced technology. Regression analysis indicates that central-budget units are likely to realize staff and cost savings when they work with a structurally stable computing installation that allows for high user involvement in designing budget applications and with one that provides free computing.

Advanced technology also is consistently related to cost efficiency (Table 7.16), although technological strategies are not as important as structural strategies. In general, on-line budget automation is preferable to batch automation. State-of-the-art advances in technology can be capitalized upon because technological instability, which occurs during periods of technological upgrading, does not affect the cost-savings from computing. Neither the organizational context nor the

Table 7.17
Correlations and Path Coefficients for Cost Efficiency,
C **(Dependent Variable)**

Independent Variable	Zero-Order Correlation	Path Coefficient	Variance Explained %
Central budget unit			
Structural instability: X_1	−.50	−.62	25
User involvement in design— budget monitoring: X_2	.32	.48	13
User involvement in design— installation level: X_3	.22	.42	18
Charging: X_4	−.37	−.30	9

$R = .80$ Variance explained = 65%
$C^* = 1.91 - .72X_1 + .02X_2 + .03X_3 - .01X_4$
        (.15)   (.01)   (.01)   (.00)

Department level			
Automation: X_1	.43	.38	19
Utilization: X_2	.42	.39	12
Job pressure: X_3	−.25	−.33	10

$R = .64$ Total Variance explained = 41%
$C^* = 1.86 + .16X_1 + .59X_2 - .28X_3$
        (.06)   (.22)   (.12)

*Regression coefficients unstandardized; standard errors in parentheses.

Table 7.18
Pearson Correlations between Budget Performance Index and
Implementation Strategies and Environments

	Central Level		Departmental Level	
	r	N	r	N
Technological development				
Degree of automation				
Number of finance automated applications	.38*	36	−.06	35
Number of batch finance applications	.04	36	−.23	35
Number of on-line finance applications	.38*	36	.21	35
Sophistication				
On-line applications predominating in finance automation	.27	36	.22	35
Number of on-line terminals in finance	.19	36	.08	35
Sophistication of computing installation	.14	36	−.07	35
Orientation of computing				
Utilization of computing for budget control	.05	36	.14	35
Other technological attributes				
Recency of finance automation	.05	34	.56*	33
Technological instability	−.12	36	−.23	35
Structural Arrangements				
User involvement				
User involvement in design of budget-reporting applications	.23	36	.12	35
User involvement in design of budget-monitoring applications	.14	36	.00	35
User involvement in decisions of the installation	.13	35	−.01	34
Centralization-decentralization				
Nonfinance located EDP installation	.12	36	.10	35
Socio-technical design				
Job pressure due to computing	.06	36	−.11	35
Job satisfaction due to computing	.55*	36	.43*	35
Organizational Context				
Reformed government structure	.51*	36	.06	35
Level of partisanship	−.37*	36	−.19	35
Degree of professional-management practices	.14	36	−.12	35
Slack financial resources	−.16	36	−.06	35
Community Environment				
Size of city, 1975	−.12	36	−.15	35
Growth of city, 1970–1975	.24	36	.08	35

*$P < .05$.

community environment is associated with cost efficiency in budget control.

Generally, the implementation policies that contribute to cost efficiency at the department level mirror those at the central-budget unit. However, the relative importance of these policies varies. At the department level, a combination of advanced technology and human-relations policies is far more important than the participatory structural arrangements for computing (Tables 7.17 and 7.18). Specifically, extensive automation (either batch or on-line), frequent utilization of computing, and a departmental working environment in which computing has not added to job pressure are the most important implementation strategies for realizing department staff and cost savings. Yet a participatory structural strategy is also conducive to cost savings at the department level. Consequently, a city can pursue the same set of implementation strategies and realize cost savings at the department level as well as in the central-budget unit.

Budget-Control Performance

The strategies conducive to effective budget control contrast with those conducive to cost efficiency. Structural arrangements are not major factors affecting budget-control performance. Instead, the socio-technical design of the applications supporting budget control is the key to success (Table 7.19).

In line with a post-reform approach, we find that at both central and department levels, the most successful socio-technical design strategy is human relations. Much of the variation in budget-control performance at the central level is attributable to a positive integration of automation into the budget-control process. Those units in which the personnel perceive the computer as intrusive and problem-generating are least likely to achieve success in budget control. Similar results are seen at the department level (Table 7.19).

What is striking from the regression analysis, however, is that the organizational context also has an independent and strong effect on budget-control performance. Specifically, a professional administrative environment, characterized by reformed government structure, is conducive to successful performance at the central budgeting level. And a political administrative environment, characterized by the level of partisan politics in the city, is not conducive to successful performance. Approximately one-quarter of performance variation is

Table 7.19
Correlations and Path Coefficients for Budget Performance,
P **(Dependent Variable)**

Independent Variable	Zero-Order Correlation	Path Coefficient	Variance Explained (%)
Central budget units			
Job satisfaction due to computing: X_1	.55	.54	30
Level of partisan government: X_2	-.37	-.35	16
Number of on-line terminals: X_3	.19	.43	13
Reformed government structure: X_4	.51	.33	8

$R = .82$ Total variance explained = 67%
$P^* = -.15 + .40X_1 - .01X_2 + .04X_3 + .41X_4$
       (.09)   (.002)   (.01)   (.16)

Department			
Routinization of the technology: X_1	.56	.51	31
Job satisfaction due to computing: X_2	.43	.36	13

$R = .67$ Total variance explained = 44%
$P^* = -3.58 + .05X_1 + .22X_2$
        (.04)   (.08)

*Regression coefficients unstandardized; standard errors in parentheses.

attributable to both these organizational characteristics (Table 7.19), although the most important constraint would be the level of partisan activity within the city. What seems to matter, then, is the level of political pressure and competition present within the city bureaucracy that might hinder successful budget control. In effect, the presence of partisan considerations can lessen a "businesslike" orientation to city government.

Successful budget-control performance is also related to the reform strategy of advanced technology (Table 7.19). This is clearly the case in terms of the kind of automated finance applications available. An on-line technology is consistently associated with high budget performance. While on-lineness is not as highly associated with department performance, it still contributes to the quality of budget-control performance. In fact, extensive batch automation works against good performance at the department level (Table 7.18).

In summary, the findings suggest that high budget performance is a function of a human-relations perspective, advanced technology, and professional administration. Structural arrangements and the community environment tend to be unimportant to budget control. In addition, while similarities are present between implementation policies and central-unit and department-level budget-control perfor-mance, the dissimilarities warrant further discussion.

In general, our analyses suggest that departmental control in the budget-control process is not a designed feature of current technolog-ical developments or at least not a well-designed one.[14] Instead, automated budget applications are designed to serve the central budget-reporting unit. The kinds of reports, report formats, and frequency of report production are geared primarily to the needs of the central budget-reporting unit and, to some extent, to the needs of the central budget-monitoring unit. They are not designed to serve the management needs of the departments. Consequently, while our analysis suggests enhancement of central-unit performance through automation, similar enhancement is not found in the departments except in recently automated sites, where departments see stark contrasts to previous unautomated systems. Yet the departments can benefit from automating the budget process. Thus an unintentional by-product of automation is increased ability at the department level for their own budget monitoring. However, implementation strategies that lead to improved budget performance for the central unit might not have a similar impact on the performance of the departments.

To summarize, both our cost-efficiency and budget-control findings suggest a mixture of reform and post-reform approaches to implemen-tation of computer technology for budget-control automation. The reform approach is suggested by the importance of advanced techno-logical features—such as on-line automation, extensive automation, and recent automation—to improved cost and control performance in central budget and the departments. But the post-reform approach is suggested by the importance of participatory structural stability and a human-relations strategy in socio-technical design to improved cost-efficiency performance in central-budget units and in the departments. The findings also indicate that reform or professional administrations characterized by low partisan activity and reformed government structure tend to achieve higher levels of performance. Thus the city's organizational context can be an important constraining force on the achievement of success in budget automation.

Policy Recommendations

The preceding analysis demonstrates the importance of maintaining a mix of implementation strategies and policies in automating budget control. Indicators of technology, structure, and socio-technical design intertwine in explaining success or failure in budget performance. Moreover, while the community environment has no effect on performance, organizational-context factors outside of the immediate control of managers (political structure, reform government, slack financial resources) impinge on the performance benefits from computing. Nonetheless, patterns of successful implementation strategies result from the analysis. Based on this analysis, the following policy proposals are suggested.

Technological Development

Advanced technology should be used by cities in the automation of budget control. Specifically, cities should proceed as follows.

1. *Automate.* The automation of budget control produces substantial benefits to the central-budget unit and, indirectly, to the departments. The benefits to the departments can be increased by structural strategies indicated below.

2. *Automate a large number of finance applications.* The degree of finance automation is consistently related to improved budget control, because basic finance automation—such as automation of general accounting, cost accounting, and program budgeting—must precede, or be done jointly with, the automation of budget control. These other applications pave the way, both technically and behaviorally, for automated budget control.

3. *Develop more sophisticated budget applications, especially on-line update and inquiry capabilities.* On-line processing provides more up-to-date and easily retrieved information for handling special requests for financial information from top management, the departments, and central budget, as well as from the finance department itself. In addition, on-line automation increases cost efficiency within the finance department. This result appears to be due to the greater ease of producing financial reports and the time saved in updating and searching for information.

4. *Develop a sophisticated computing installation.* On-line processing and advanced budget-control applications require sophisticated staff and advanced computer technology to support them. It is unrealistic to expect that an inexperienced staff can implement advanced finance and budget automation, or that a batch computer environment can adequately support such automation.

Structural Arrangements

Cities generally should use participatory structural arrangements for the implementation of budget control and similar kinds of information-processing tasks. Specifically, cities should do the following.

1. *Involve users in the design of finance and budget applications.* Cost efficiency, or reduction in costs and staff, is significantly improved by high user involvement in design. User involvement increases the probability that the applications will adequately take user needs into account, develops user understanding of the nature of the applications, and heightens the interest in and commitment to using them. Furthermore, since budget applications cross departmental and hierarchical boundaries and are intended for multiple use, it is important that all relevant users (central-budget staff, top-management staff, department staff, and finance staff) have significant input in design. Similar cross-departmental applications, such as purchasing and word-processing, probably would benefit also from high user involvement in design.

2. *Involve users in policy boards and other decision-making structures of the computer installation.* Cost efficiency also is improved by user involvement in the computer installation's decision-making. Unless users understand and accept the policies and technological advances made by the computer installation, their motivation and support will diminish and so will their efficiency in using the technology. Participation is important to developing and maintaining user commitment at all levels.

3. *Consider locating the computer installation inside the finance department.* Whether the computer installation is located within the finance department, or outside the department, makes little difference to budget performance, but cost efficiency is improved for finance and for the central-budget unit if the central budget unit is located within finance. However, maximizing the benefits to the finance department might not be the most important consideration in a city with multiple departments using the computer. We believe that an installation located outside finance might make considerable difference for nonfinance applications. When computing is located in an independent installation, other departments obtain considerably more benefits than they do when the computer is located in the finance department. From this broader perspective, we urge that an outside location be considered because of the tendency for finance installations toward

parochialism, even for automated systems (such as budget reporting and monitoring) that are intended to have organizationwide benefits.

4. *Change in the structural arrangements for computing should be limited.* Relocation, reorganization, consolidation, and decentralization of computing and change in computing management are highly disruptive to the computer installation and to the user departments. During periods of such structural change, positive budget outcomes will diminish greatly. This is not to argue that structural changes should never occur. Rather, they should be limited in extent and frequency. Also we emphasize that during structural changes the budget performance (and presumably performance in other application areas) will be decreased.

Socio-technical Design

Although we recommend the use of advanced technology, this strategy should proceed only in conjunction with a human-relations strategy for socio-technical design. The socio-technical design is important to realizing automation payoffs in budget performance. Throughout our analysis, it was clear that the perceptions and attitudes of the users of the technology are important because performance rates consistently vary in terms of staff attitudes, *independent* of technological sophistication or structural arrangements. We find that those central staffs which perceive themselves to be adversely affected by automation also receive little benefit from budget automation. Implementation strategies frequently neglect this important fact. Yet unless the nontechnical users are instructed in the personal impacts of automation and in the use of computerized applications, the full potentials of automated budget control will not be realized.

There has been little emphasis by local government policy-makers on including this area of concern when automating the budget. Instead, either the structure or the technological issues have been emphasized. Indeed, one finding from our analysis is important in this context. We find that staff support for computing is more negative in the automated budget units that utilize predominantly on-line applications ($r = -.33$). Given that our analysis indicates that an advanced technology might be beneficial to budget-performance activities and that a nonintegrative socio-technical environment is a hindrance to realizing automation benefits, we would argue for more concern in implementing strategies for adjusting personnel to automation.

Organizational Context

The organizational context within which budget control is performed places constraints on the optimal performance of computing. Our research indicates that the administrative structure of the city affects technological performance. Although we can only speculate on the reason for the relationship between administrative structure and budget performance, it appears that technology is importantly shaped by the organization that uses it. Reformed administrative structures and their attendant orientation to professional practices, managerial control, and nonpartisanship appear to provide the most congenial environment for the automated budget. On the one hand, this means that cities with professional administrative environments should consider budget automation as an integral part of administrative reform within the government, and can expect to achieve improved budget performance with automation. On the other hand, cities with political administrative environments need to recognize that the benefits from budget automation are likely to be less than might be achieved.

Summary

Automation of budget reporting and monitoring does result in more effective budget control both in central-budget units and in the operating departments, and further, it results in greater cost efficiency. But the strategies an agency chooses to follow in implementing an automated system affect the degree to which it receives improved performance payoffs. Earlier in this chapter, we argued that most local governments have chosen appropriate technology, participatory structure, and human-relations strategies for implementation of automated systems. In other words, they have basically chosen a post-reform approach to the management of information systems. However, our analysis indicates that a mixture of reform and post-reform approaches leads to more performance benefits. Specifically, the analysis indicates that management policies which promote advanced technology, participatory structural arrangements, and human-relations strategies in socio-technical design are the keys to improved performance.

But our analysis also indicates that these management policies can be importantly constrained by the organizational context. Cities with highly political administrations are less likely to achieve improved performance than cities with highly professional administrations. Apparently the level of political pressure and competition within the city government hinders successful implementation of budget automation. However, the community environment has no measurable effect on success.

Our analysis also indicates the importance of examining automation benefits from the standpoint of the multiple users of the system. Benefits to one group of users are not necessarily benefits to another group; in fact, they might be costs. Consequently, managers need to recognize these different payoffs and take them into account in their policies for the management of information systems. The mixture of policies recommended in this chapter was designed to do just that—to optimize the benefits to both central budget units and to the departments from budget automation.

NOTES

1. For simplicity, the central budget-reporting and central budget-monitoring units are referred to as the central budget unit(s), or central budget. These units include the finance and budget offices which have direct responsibility for budget control. They do not refer to central management offices such as the mayor, manager, or council offices.

2. These impacts can be assessed from various vantage points: from the perspectives of the finance department and the operating departments, and in some cases from the perspective of top management and elected officials.

3. The current-balance report is produced by a central unit in 40 cities of the 42-city study; 2 cities do not produce budget reports. Most often the budget report is produced by the controller or finance department.

4. The 42 cities have somewhat more budget automation than most American cities. In 1975, 50 percent of the cities over 50,000 in population had automated the budget report. Of these, 11 percent were on-line.

5. This is somewhat surprising, since the technical sophistication of finance automation and of finance computing installations appears considerable. For example, nearly two-fifths of the cities have on-line computing for some financial functions and 80 percent of the cities have EDP installations with medium-to-high technical sophistication. That is, the technological sophistication of budget automation appears relatively lower than some other finance automation. For example, many cities with on-line processing capabilities continue to use batch processing for budget monitoring and reporting.

6. The current-balance report is a periodic report of budgeted, expended, and encumbered amounts drawn off the general accounting system and variously summarized by department, fund, program, and line item. Because the current-balance report usually is automated as part of the automation of general accounting in the city, the quality of balance-report automation is dependent upon the quality of the automated accounting systems.

7. About one-fourth of the cities changed generation of machine, the level of programming language used, and the priorities of applications in development within the last year. Only 3 percent made a change of major equipment vendor. Most cities had only one such change; only five cities had two or more changes.

8. Decentralization refers to the degree to which computing resources are located in the departments which use these resources, rather than centralized within a department or installation outside the user department's span of control. If cities radically decentralized computing for the budget reporting and monitoring function, computing resources would be located in the finance department, since finance and budget (sometimes located in finance) are the primary users of budget applications. A lesser form of decentralization would give finance-department staff on-line access to these applications. Another definition of decentralization would examine the extent to which computing resources are decentralized to the departments as well as to finance. This was not examined, since only 4 cities have any form of direct departmental access to the automated systems, i.e., terminals in the user departments.

9. The budget reports generated by computer-based systems are intended to be utilized by the central finance staff, the central budget staff, the departments, and top management. The utility of these computer-generated reports to the different users depends considerably on the extent to which the computerized applications supporting budget reporting and monitoring are designed with a sensitivity to the various information needs of these users.

10. Budget staff includes budget analysts and accountants in the finance and budget office, and administrative assistants, accountants, and others who work with the budget.

11. Policy-makers themselves generally are not direct users of the budget reports. Although they receive these reports, policy-makers tend to pass them on to staff aides, who analyze the reports and communicate their implications to the policy-makers.

12. The fact that the central unit serves as a filter between the departments and the computer technology is a critical factor. Requests for budget information are sent to the central unit, not to the computer installation. The departments are neither directly involved in the means of obtaining the information, nor directly involved in the

implementation decisions for automating the budget. This indirect association by the department might be expected to result in different consequences for the department than for the central unit. For example, intended positive benefits within the central unit might not even filter down to the department. Given that implementation policies might have different consequences at each level of budgetary control, a comparative approach is necessary in relating implementation policies to central unit and department budget-control performance.

13. The selection of performance variables used in this analysis was guided by an attempt to sample adequately not only major budgetary activities, but also internal organizational benefits from automation. Several measures were dropped due to lack of variation in responses by the sample cities to certain benefits of computing. For example, the near-unanimity by the central units that computing was helpful in identifying overspent accounts led us to eliminate this measure of fiscal control from further analysis.

Whenever possible, comparable performance measures were used for both the central-budget units and the departments. All performance measures are operationally defined in the Appendix.

14. For a detailed analysis of the differences between the determinants of departmental versus central-budgeting control, see Kraemer, Dutton, and Northrop (1978: 8-72-8-77).

REFERENCES

Anthony, R. N. and R. Herzlinger. 1975. *Management Control in Nonprofit Organizations.* Homewood, Ill.: Richard D. Irwin.

Anton, T. J. 1966. *The Politics of State Expenditure in Illinois.* Urbana: University of Illinois Press.

ARMS Task Force. 1973. "ARMS Feasibility Study." Prepared for ARMS Steering Committee, County of San Diego, April (mimeographed).

Bassler, R. A. and N. L. Enger, eds. 1976. *Computer Systems and Public Administrators.* Alexandria, Va.: College Readings.

Bertone, T. L. 1971. "Legislative Control of Executive Expenditures in Maryland State Government." D.P.A. dissertation, George Washington University.

Cornog, G. Y. et al., eds. 1968. *EDP Systems in Public Management.* Chicago: Rand McNally.

Cyert, R. M. and J. G. March. 1963. *A Behavioral Theory of the Firm.* Englewood Cliffs, N.J.: Prentice-Hall.

Danziger, J. N. 1977. "Computer Technology and the Local Budgetary System." *Southern Review of Public Administration,* 1(3): 279-92.

Davis, O.; M. A. H. Dempster; and A. Wildavsky. 1966. "A Theory of the Budgetary Process." *American Political Science Review*, 60(3): 529–44.

Friedland, E. I. 1971. "Turbulence and Technology: Public Administration and the Role of Information-Processing Technology." In D. Waldo, ed., *Public Administration in Time of Turbulence*. Scranton: Chandler Publishing.

Graham, C. B. 1975. "Budgetary Change in South Carolina, 1945–1970." Ph.D. dissertation, University of South Carolina.

Hale, G. E. and S. R. Douglass. 1977. "The Politics of Budget Execution." *Administration and Society*, 9(3): 367–78.

Hearle, E. F. 1970. "Information Systems in State and Local Governments." *Annual Review of Information Science and Technology*, 5. Washington, DC: American Society for Information Science.

Hrebenar, R. J. 1973. "Washington State Budgeting: Roles, Expectations, Outcomes." Ph.D. dissertation, University of Washington.

Kraemer, K. L.; W. H. Dutton; and A. Northrop. 1978. *The Management of Urban Information Systems*, URBIS Final Report, Vol. 1. Springfield, Va.: National Technical Information Service.

Leavitt, H. J. and T. L. Whisler. 1958. "Management in the 1980's." *Harvard Business Review*, 36(6): 41–48.

Lodal, J. M. 1976. "Improving Local Government Information Systems." *Duke Law Journal*, 6(1): 1133–55.

Lonergan, G. J. 1977. "The Louisville Award." San Diego: Municipal Finance Officers Association.

Meltzner, Arnold J. 1971. *The Politics of City Revenue*. Berkeley: University of California Press.

Moak, L. L. and A. M. Hillhouse. 1975. *Local Government Finance*. Chicago: Municipal Finance Officers Association.

Sartoris, Inc. 1977. "ARMS: A Proven, Operating Financial Management System for Public Agencies." Charmichael, Calif.: Sartoris, Inc. (mimeographed).

Schick, A. 1964. "Control Patterns in Budget Execution." *Public Administration Review*, 24(2): 97–108.

Scott, C. 1972. *Forecasting Local Government Expenditure*. Washington, DC: Urban Institute.

Shadoan, A. T. 1963. *Preparation, Review, and Execution of the State Operating Budget*. Lexington: University of Kentucky, Bureau of Business Research.

Simon, H. A. 1960. "The Corporation: Will It Be Managed by Medicine?" In *Management and Corporations, 1985*. Tenth Anniversary Symposium, Graduate School of Industrial Administration, Carnegie Institute of Technology.

——. 1965. *The Shape of Automation*. New York: Harper and Row.

Stedry, A. C. 1960. *Budget Control and Cost Behavior*. Englewood Cliffs, N.J.: Prentice-Hall.

Turnbull, A. B. 1967. "Politics in the Budgetary Process: The Case of Georgia." Ph.D. dissertation, University of Virginia.

Wamsley, G. L. and L. M. Salamon. 1975. "Rethinking Budget Theory: Toward a New

Conceptualization." Paper presented at the annual meeting of the American Political Science Association.

Wildavsky, A. 1965. *Budgeting: A Comparative Theory of Budgetary Processes.* Boston: Little, Brown.

——. 1974. *The Politics of the Budgetary Process.* Boston: Little, Brown.

Young, M. A. 1968. "The ARMS System of San Diego County: A Management Evaluation." Master of Public Administration thesis, San Diego State University.

CHAPTER EIGHT

A Tool for Policy Analysis: Automated Databanks

THE URBANIZATION of America has brought increasing complexity to such urban problems as housing, public safety, education, and transportation, as well as to the problems of managing the expanded and interwoven bureaucracies that address these problems. Correspondingly, there has been a continuous push to improve the quality of information needed to understand and monitor urban communities and bureaucracies (Brewer 1974; Lineberry and Sharkansky 1978; Webber 1970). Many of these efforts center around the establishment of large "databanks" that utilize the vast storage and computational capacities of computers (Hearle and Mason 1963; Kraemer and King 1977). These databanks are aimed at pooling great stores of facts about a city's people, its real estate, its crime, its traffic, its economy, and its governmental operations.

Computer-based statistical and mapping programs have been developed which can utilize these large databanks to aggregate and analyze such community attributes as the condition of housing; the neighborhood distribution of government services; the differential value and assessment of properties; the government's current and anticipated revenues and expenditures; the performances of departments, programs, and individuals in the government; and the political sensitivities surrounding government plans and programs. These social, managerial, and political indicators can then be used as a guide to public officials in identifying problems, determining needs, developing programmatic remedies, and assessing political feasibility. Also, computer simulations and other computer models have been developed that use databanks to mimic the behavior of the city's people, its real estate markets, its overall economy, and its government operations. These analyses and models can be used to pretest the effects of various public actions, as a guide to public officials in deciding among alternative policies. Thus, computerized databanks are potentially a major tool for policy analysis in local government.[1]

Successful Databank Automation

The major rationale for automating databanks is to increase the quantity and quality of information available to policy-makers in order to increase their effective utilization of information for urban decision-making (Fig. 8.1). Such an effect is desired in order to increase the rationality and decrease the uncertainty, of local government policy. Yet the automation of databanks is also likely to affect the distribution of power within local governments by altering information flows. Such power shifts have policy implications by affecting the relative influence of different participants in the local policy-making process (Dutton and Kraemer 1977; Kling 1978c; Lawler and Rhode 1976). In addition, automated databanks are likely to affect the work environments of policy analysts by altering their information-processing tasks. These work-environment impacts are of direct relevance to job satisfaction, and of indirect relevance to the performance of policy analysts. Thus, the successful implementation of

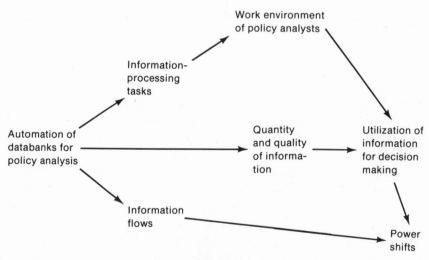

Fig. 8.1.
The expected impacts of automated databanks for policy analysis.

automated databanks concerns the degree to which computer-based databanks influence local government officials and the work environment of policy analysts.

This chapter explores the degree to which automated databanks have been successfully implemented so as to constitute a tool for policy analysis in local government. Implementation strategies are assessed by examining variations among local governments in the structural, technological, and systems-design strategies that have been followed in implementing computer-based databanks. These variations in the way that computer-based databanks have been implemented are then related to the effects of databanks on decision-making and on power shifts within local governments to determine the most successful mix of implementation strategies.

The chapter (1) describes the policy-analysis task in local government, (2) examines the impact of automation in performing local-government policy analyses, (3) shows the way in which computer-based support for this task has been developed; and (4) assesses the impacts of alternative approaches and strategies for the implementation of computer-based databanks for policy analysis. Based on these analyses, the chapter concludes with a set of policy prescriptions on how best to implement computer-based databanks to improve the policy-analysis function in local governments.

Policy Analysis in Local Government

Types of Policy Analysis

Policy analysis occurs in many different organizational contexts in local governments. However, these can be distinguished by three prototypical uses of the analysis: planning, management, and politics. These three uses of policy analysis are ideal types and may seldom occur in their pure form in the real world. Nevertheless they are useful for illustrating the varied decision-making contexts within which policy analyses are conducted (Table 8.1).

Planning analysis usually focuses on problems and issues in the development of the community (Altschuler 1965; Pack and Pack 1977). The problem may be to prepare the city's master plan, locate freeway routes, attract new industry and commerce, or develop a housing-assistance program. Planning analysis is future-decision ori-

Table 8.1
A Typology of Policy Analysis

Dimensions	Kind of Policy Analysis		
	Planning	*Management*	*Political*
Problem focus	Community development	Management of government facilities and services	Political need and viability
Illustration	Prepare master plan, locate freeway routes, attract new industry or commerce, develop housing program	Estimate city revenues, monitor departmental expenditures, control staff growth	Define community constituencies, determine need of various constituencies, identify implications of plans and programs for constituencies
Decision orientation	Future-decision oriented, long time scale, broad scope of considerations	Present-decision oriented, short time scale, narrow scope of considerations	Present-decision oriented, short time scale, broad scope of considerations
Decision-support data	Conditions and events in the community and its environment	Conditions and events in the departments and agencies which provide public services	Characteristics of constituent groups

ented, with a relatively long time scale and a broad scope of physical, social, and economic considerations (Dykman 1961). The analysis is aimed at clarifying the problem to be resolved, evaluating various environmental controls and public or private actions for handling the problem, and choosing among these actions for implementation. The data used in the analysis relate to conditions and events in the community and its larger environment.

In contrast, management analysis focuses on problems and issues in the management of government services and facilities. The problem may be to estimate city revenues, monitor departmental expenditures, control staff growth, or negotiate staff salaries (Quinn 1976). Management analysis is present-decision oriented, with a relatively short time scale and a narrow scope of considerations. The analysis is aimed at clarifying the problem to be resolved, evaluating various managerial controls and departmental actions for handling the problem, and choosing specific controls and actions for implementation. The data used in the analysis relate primarily to conditions and events within the departments and agencies that provide public services.

Political analysis focuses on problems of political need and feasibility. The problem may be to define different community constituencies, determine the needs and preferences of various constituencies, or identify the implications of specific community-development plans and government programs for various constituencies. Political analysis is present-decision oriented, with a relatively short time scale but with a potentially broad scope of relevant considerations. The analysis is aimed at clarifying the constituencies relevant to any particular decision or action, evaluating the implications of alternative plans and programs for their interests, and choosing which constituencies' interests will be satisfied. The data used in the analysis relate primarily to the characteristics of constituent groups and to the distribution of gains and losses among them.

Despite these differences in use and data, all three types of analysis are interrelated. The results of planning analysis frequently form the context for specific management analyses; the results of management analysis point to the need for new or additional planning analyses; political analysis indicates the implementation feasibility of planning and management recommendations. Consequently, any policy analysis is likely to involve all three types. Increasingly, too, all three types of analysis are likely to be performed by the same organizational unit. Most importantly, the intellectual processes underlying planning, management, and political analyses are essentially characteristics of all policy analyses (Kraemer 1973).

The Process of Analysis

Policy analysis, like other kinds of decision-making, is theoretically conceived as a rational process of intelligence, design, and choice (Simon 1960, 1961, 1965, 1971). Any complex analysis typically begins with a statement of the problem or issues requiring resolution. The problem may be to determine the city's eligibility for health, social service, housing, or other federal assistance; to prepare the city's public-works plan, housing-assistance plan, redevelopment plan or master plan; to locate freeway routes, parks, or community facilities; to determine the public-service needs of the elderly, the poor, or other interest groups; to deploy police, fire, and other emergency forces; or to control spending, staff growth, and municipal-services expansion.

Generally, the initial statement of the problem is vague and, therefore, a major intelligence task is to develop a better definition of the problem—usually a quantitative definition of current conditions requiring resolution or emerging opportunities warranting action (Pounds 1969). This may refer to the condition of housing, the vacancy rate among multiple-housing units, the current pattern of land use, the distribution of municipal services, the location of existing public facilities, the patterns of urban traffic, or the socioeconomic characteristics of the city's people. Alternatively, it may refer to the opportunities for business, industry, investment, jobs, and so forth.

Given that these conditions are distributed in geographical or social space, the policy analyst often must collect and aggregate information by areal units of the city or the government.[2] Depending on the nature of the problem, these areal units may be planning districts (census tracts), administrative service districts (fire zones, code-enforcement zones, police precincts, and so on), political districts, departmental boundaries, or several of these. Data are collected from special surveys, data archives, published sources, or from automated files maintained by the operating departments of the city. These data are then aggregated by the chosen unit of analysis (census tract, police precinct, political district, department) and analyzed to identify historical, current, and likely future patterns. The process of analysis is essentially one of comparisons—over time, across geographic areas, across department boundaries, and so forth. The aim is to discern significant differences and patterns that suggest a problem or condition to be solved, or an opportunity to be realized. Most frequently, the analysis involves identifying problems to move away from rather than future desired conditions to move toward (Braybrooke and Lindblom 1963; Lindblom 1968).

Having defined the problem, policy analysts usually will next design alternatives for solving the problem. This might involve defining alternative routes for freeway location; alternative locations for urban-renewal projects; alternative areas for housing-code enforcement or rehabilitation; target populations for social services; or alternative locations for parks, recreation facilities, fire stations or other public facilities. While design is largely a task of invention not based on data, it usually launches another search for information to support the invention of alternatives. For example, defining alternative freeway routes involves collecting and organizing information about the value of property, condition of structures, characteristics of the population, and physical barriers along possible routes. The purpose is to define alternative freeway locations that are feasible within a broad set of considerations.

Having defined the alternatives, the analyst's next step is to evalute them according to some criteria in order to facilitate choice among them. The criteria used to evaluate the alternatives usually relate to the considerations used to define them in the first place. For example, the freeway route with least cost for land acquisition, or the route least disruptive of existing social neighborhoods, or some combination of these considerations might be used. If least cost is the chosen criterion, then data about the value of property, costs of demolition or relocation of structures, costs of removal of physical barriers, and costs of relocating the current population must be calculated in order to compare the alternatives. This might lead to a search for information related to property values from the assessor's records, demolition costs from building records, relocation costs from urban-renewal records, and physical-barrier removal costs from public-works records. In evaluating such alternatives, the policy analysts also might analyze them for political feasibility. For example, alternative housing-assistance plans might be evaluated in terms of the populations affected, the existence of opposition and support groups in the areas affected, or the distribution of benefits among councilmanic districts. Alternative freeway locations might be evaluated against similar criteria.

Upon completion of the analysis, the analysts' results are organized, usually in written form, and presented to the policy-makers, who choose among the alternatives on the basis of the analysis and frequently other criteria outside the analysis. The relative importance of analysis to the final decision depends on the extent to which the analysis clearly points to a preferred alternative, the degree of controversy about the alternatives, the agreement about the criteria to be used in making a choice, and the extent to which political feasibility was considered in the initial analysis.

As the scope of policy analysis increases from a single site to an area of the city, to the city as a whole, so does the complexity of the analysis. As the complexity of considerations involved in the analysis increases (i.e., from purely physical planning criteria to concern with the socioeconomic impacts of physical plans, to concern with social planning), so does the variety and scope of information needed to analyze a problem. And this information usually must be related to common geographic and social units so that it can be compared. Frequently, too, the amount and variety of data involved require sophisticated computational capabilities to discern the underlying patterns, or simply to perform numerous data aggregations and reorganizations. Thus, analysts face enormous tasks of collecting, organizing, and manipulating data in the policy-analysis process. Automated databanks and related analytical applications are designed to facilitate these tasks and thereby extend the capabilities of policy analysts.

Automated Databanks

By the early 1960s, computers had been developed that were sophisticated enough to link information collected by a variety of government agencies within a functional area (e.g., all agencies involved in real estate or tax parcels) and usually within a single jurisdiction (e.g., city or county). The information stored in these databanks generally was in the form of a one-time statistical survey, audit, or summary on people, property, events, or money within the jurisdiction. The surveys were submitted by a variety of agencies, usually stored within a single agency (e.g., the Planning Department or Community Development Department), and made available on request to other agencies within the jurisdiction. The early databanks were expected to function as automated libraries. Agencies would turn to the databanks whenever they needed statistical information about people, places, or events within their jurisdiction, in order to prepare plans, comply with federal programs, obtain federal funds, or prepare special analyses and reports (Laudon 1974).

By the late 1960s, it was argued that the one-time surveys which formed the basis of most early databanks were inadequate to serve the continuing needs of municipal officials for information. It was also argued that much of the data needed for policy analysis already existed in, or could be collected as part of, routine government operations, such as property-tax assessment; the building, housing-occupancy, and business-license permit processes; public-utility operations and public record-keeping (vital statistics, public-health records, voter registration) (Kraemer, et al. 1974). Since cities had automated many government records, some cities devoted considerable effort to developing various kinds of operational databanks by merging data from the automated records of the government. These, in turn, could be combined with survey data (e.g., city sample surveys, neighborhood surveys, patron surveys, Dun and Bradstreet business surveys) and statistical data (e.g., those collected by state and federal agencies in such areas as population, employment, and income) to expand enormously the volume, kind, and currency of data contained in the databanks.

Kinds of Databanks

Two distinctive kinds of databanks evolved and were sometimes intermingled in cities: urban databanks and operational data systems. These databanks can be distinguished by whether they are primarily oriented toward data about the environment or about the day-to-day operations of the government (Table 8.2).

Urban databanks pool facts about people and their environment (e.g., a jurisdiction's demography and its economy). In turn, this new information is aggregated and analyzed to determine environmental

Table 8.2
A Typology of Computer-Based Systems for Policy Analysis[a]

Kind of System

Purpose		Urban Databanks[b]		Operational Data Systems[c]
Management	Uses:	Completing grant applications; preparing proposals; meeting inter-governmental reporting requirements.	Uses:	Monitoring the activities of individuals and the operations of departments; monitoring revenues and expenditures, equipment and supplies.
	Ex.:	U.S. Census of population; housing survey; land use inventory	Ex.:	Budget-monitoring systems; inventory-control systems; activity-reporting systems; accounting systems.
Planning	Uses:	Analyzing socioeconomic characteristics of populations, geographic areas, and political districts; forecasting demand.	Uses:	Allocating resources and manpower; scheduling activities; forecasting revenues & expenditures; forecasting cash flows; optimizing routes.
	Ex.:	Population, land use, traffic and economic inventory systems; urban-development models; fiscal-impact models.	Ex.:	Manpower-allocation models; emergency-vehicle dispatch models; routing models; revenue and expenditure-forecasting models.
Politics	Uses:	Legitimation of policy positions to clients; political assessment of development plans; analysis of political constituency; analysis of distribution of costs and benefits of government services.	Uses:	Handle client requests and complaints; document policy positions
	Ex.:	Social-indicator systems; planning models and analyses (above); political analyses.	Ex.:	Complaint-monitoring systems; collective-bargaining models; performance analyses.

[a] Adapted from Kraemer and Dutton (1979).
[b] Contain data about the population/clientele and their environment.
[c] Contain data about government personnel and operating departments.

conditions (e.g., social indicators of the welfare of citizens and the health of the economy). These analyses can be used as a guide for public officials in identifying problems, determining needs, developing programmatic remedies, and applying for outside assistance. In some instances, information also is being fed into simulation and other models that mimic the behavior of some aspect of the environment (e.g., population growth and economic development). These analyses and models can be used to pretest the effects of various public actions, which can then be used as a guide to public officials in deciding among alternative policies. Also, information about people (their demographic characteristics, likes and dislikes, and so on) can be used to assess the political feasibility of development and financial plans. As these examples illustrate, such databanks serve management, planning, and political purposes.

Operational data systems are the functionally oriented computer systems that serve the day-to-day operations of the government, and that contain data about government employees and departmental operations. This information is variously aggregated and analyzed to determine revenue and expenditure patterns; personnel vacancies, turnover, vacations, or sick leave; individual and departmental workloads; and operational indicators of performance. These analyses can be used by public officials in monitoring expenditures, identifying personnel problems, determining work assignments, and scheduling or rearranging departmental operations to improve performance. Sometimes, information is fed into computer models that imitate some operation of a department, such as handling emergency calls, dispatching vehicles, assigning personnel, or predicting cash flow. These analyses and models can be used to predict the effects of various alternative operational priorities and procedures. Also, individual and aggregated data from the operational systems can be used in support of particular policy positions, personnel actions, collective bargaining negotiations, or citizen requests and complaints. Consequently, operational data systems can serve management, planning, and political purposes, as do their databank counterparts.

The Impacts of Databank Automation

The automation of databanks is said to provide more up-to-date, comprehensive, and sophisticated information for use by policy analysts and decision-makers. While the evaluation of computing has centered on such informational benefits, automation also might bring power payoffs. To the extent that power effects are mentioned in the literature, there is debate over both the existence and the direction of power payoffs. There are many reasons given for believing that computing is apolitical and does not result in power shifts. For example, computer-based information is said to be unsophisticated, of low quality, often conflicting or irrelevant, and only one of many sources of information, which nevertheless is open to interpretation. In turn, it is thought that decision-makers would seldom develop or change their position primarily on the basis of computer reports and analyses (Kling 1974; Simon 1971; Westin 1972).

The opposing argument is that information is a political resource within organizations, much like status or positional authority, and is closely akin to expertise. Because computers can change the character of information flows within organizations, they might influence the relative decisional effectiveness of different actors, and therefore the relative influence of different interests in the governmental system (Downs 1967; Lawler and Rhode 1976). Furthermore, those who control the technology might shape its utilization so as to enhance their decision-making effectiveness and interests within the organization (Hoffman 1977). Thus computing is likely to entail power shifts—gains in one person's decision-making or personal effectiveness at the expense of another person's (Downs 1967; Dutton and Kraemer 1977; Kraemer and Dutton 1979).

In this section, we consider first whether or not automating databanks provides informational and decisional benefits. We then turn to the power payoffs of automated databanks; in sum, who gains or loses power: policy analysts, managers, mayors and/or city-council members?

Information Benefits

Computing is most likely to be a decisional aid to the degree that it provides "better" information. While the information benefits of computing are widely accepted in the literature, planners and management analysts do not necessarily agree that such informational improvements result (Table 8.3). For example, planners in only about one-half of the cities perceive informational improvements. Planners

Table 8.3
Policy Analysts' Perceptions of Computer's Information Benefits

Impacts	Planners[a]		Management Analysts[b]	
	Percentage Agreeing[c] (N = 38)	Average Score	Percentage Agreeing[c] (N = 40)	Average Score
Information improvements				
Computer makes new information available	47	52	25	42
Computer provides more up-to-date information than manual files	44	51	43	48
Computers make it easier to get information	68	59	45	48
Computers save time in looking for information	52	55	43	45
Lack-of-information problems				
Computers have increased the information that must be reviewed and analyzed	27	39	23	38
Computer data are less accurate than manual records	6	15	0	15
Computer data are difficult to change	12	36	15	36
Computer data take too long to get	15	36	8	30

[a]Planning analysts include planning staff and databank custodians.
[b]Management analysts include the staff of the chief administrative officer and the mayor.
[c]Percentage indicating "frequently true" and "nearly always true."

in 47 and 44 percent of the cities, respectively, feel that the computer makes new information available and provides more up-to-date information than manual files.

The fieldwork clearly indicates that the main reason for the frequent lack of information improvements for planning is the relatively low priority given computerized planning uses by top management. The following case report typifies the situation in most cities:

Top management is relatively unconcerned with computing as long as they get some basic reports (e.g., budget, current balances). They are relatively unconcerned with sophisticated planning analyses and therefore don't care that the Planning Department is having a great deal of trouble negotiating with the computing department over the development of sophisticated computer analyses. Computing tends to be viewed by top management, and by elected officials and department heads, as similar to the typing pool—a neutral technology designed to serve basically the task of doing what used to be done manually, but somewhat faster and more accurately. (URBIS Case Report, Kansas City)

In cases where the computer is viewed as potentially more of a political tool, support for planning applications often is no better. Here, elected officials and managers are concerned that planners will use computerized analyses to strengthen their advocacy of particular policy decisions. What the officials most frequently want is the data, without interpretation, policy implications, or policy recommendations. For example, consider the case of Philadelphia:

According to one of the deputy directors of the planning department, planning has to come out with good findings about the city. The department has to be extremely careful about what it says and most of its reports do not tend to be broadly interpretative, but only summarizations of tables that are fairly close to the data. Moreover, several files that could represent sensitive areas are not updated by the city as a result of high level policy decisions. For example, the building vacancy file has not been updated [for the planners' use] since 1974. According to one staff member, the city officials don't want to know that there are 20,000 vacancies (URBIS Case Report, Philadelphia)

Planners are more positive, though, about the greater ease of using computer-based information. For instance, planners in 68 percent of the cities feel that computers make it easier to get information, and in 52 percent of the cities they feel that computers save time in looking for information. In one city:

Computer analysis of databanks is seen as beneficial because the analyses can be done quicker, easier, and with more complete data and somewhat more accurate analysis. Also, the use of computers in analysis of operational data is seen as simply improving the ease, speed and timeliness of data. In fact, the operational performance impacts seem to be more important than are some of the indirect policy or administrative control impacts. (URBIS Case Report, Kansas City)

The management analysts basically agree with the planners' perceptions. There is one exception of importance; that is, analysts in only 25 percent of the cities feel that the computer makes new information available. Our fieldwork in the cities indicates that the analysts' perceptions in this regard are only partially correct, although much of the information they need is indeed not available, the analysts frequently are unaware of what information is available, or how it might be used. For example, in one city the field researchers reported:

Speaking with the analysts on the manager's staff who do most of the research for the manager [and indirectly for the council], they reported that they tend not to rely much on computer-based data partially because it doesn't exist. However, they also tend not to be acutely aware of what data is available or of the ways in which it might be used. (URBIS Case Report, Little Rock)

Planners and management analysts agree that there are few problems associated with computerized information. Specifically, one-fourth, or fewer, of the planners or management analysts feel that computing has increased the information that must be reviewed and analyzed in their jobs, or that the information is less accurate than manual records, more difficult to change, or takes too long to get.

Influence in Decision-Making

Given the lack of unanimity over the information improvements from automation, it is not surprising that urban databank reports are considered to have altered previous decisions or policies made by managers or planners in only about 40 percent of the cities (Table 8.4).

Table 8.4
Decision-Making Impacts of Urban Databanks

	Percentage of Cities Where Decisions Were Affected							
	Management		Planning		Mayor		Council	
	%	N	%	N	%	N	%	N
Urban databanks								
Developing programmatic recommendations that are acted upon	79	28	79	38	59	34	60	37
Altering previous decisions or policy (in exceptional cases)	43	30	42	40	28	36	33	39
Operational data systems								
Changed or affected decisions (in exceptional cases)	82	28	—[a]	—	62	29	54	33

[a]Planners were not asked this question.

And in only about 30 percent of the cities have these reports altered decisions made by the mayor or council. The fieldwork suggests several additional factors related to the low influence of databank information. One is that to the extent that data are employed in policy-making, their primary use is to provide justification and elaboration of policy positions that have already been developed, rather than to consider changes in established policy. A second factor is that political officials, in particular, often feel that they have their own sources of information and that these are "better" than those produced by planners and municipal analysts. For example, in one city:

> The mayor says he never uses data bank information because he already knows the city. For example, he doesn't need to know the demographic characteristics of his citizenry because he knows what it is from just being a political person in Burbank. On the other hand, the mayor conducts his own surveys when he wants to know where the people stand on a certain issue. He told me about one study that dealt with watering rights in an area [during the recent Southern California water shortage] in which he sent his son and a friend with questionnaires which they distributed to a number of houses; they collected them and the mayor used yes/no percentages to make his decision on how to vote for the water question. (URBIS Case Report, Burbank)

Yet, urban databanks are quite likely to be used by more cities for programmatic recommendations involving new decision situations. For example, consider the case of New Orleans:

> This is one of the instances where information generated from databanks or operational files was definitely influential in forming policy decisions. The use was focused on specific issues rather than any broad or pervasive use. It included things like realization of the proportion of structures in the central business district which were vacant, the number of jobs that would be lost in the warehouse district if a planned redevelopment project were to be undertaken, and the priorities of citizens in an area. Perhaps the most pervasive decision impact was the projection of revenues and expenditures over the next five years made by the economic analysis unit within the Office of Policy Planning and Analysis. These substantially altered perceptions about the amount of revenue available to the city and led to some reassessments of how urban development expenditures should be allocated over the coming years. (URBIS Case Report, New Orleans)

Nor is the New Orleans case unique; databanks are used in programmatic recommendations by managers and planners in about 80 percent of the cities and by elected officials in about 60 percent of the cities (Table 8.4). Interestingly, reports from operational data systems appear to be as influential in municipal decision-making, particularly by managers (82 percent), but also by mayors (62 percent) and city councils (54 percent) (Table 8.4).

This finding might reflect the differential use of databanks and operational systems made by managers, planners, mayors, and councils. To discern the uses made of databanks by these officials, respondents in each office were first asked whether managers, planners, mayors, and councils used urban databanks for each of the five tasks displayed in Table 8.5, and whether they used operational data

Table 8.5
Orientation of Urban Databanks

		Percentage of Use by:			
Kinds of Use	Levels of Use	Manager (N = 30)	Mayor (N = 37)	Council (N = 39)	Planners/ Analyst (N = 40)
Planning oriented					
Problem finding					
—lead to new	(1) Not used[a]	27	40	41	18
or clearer per-	(2) Exceptional use	63	49	46	60
ceptions of	(3) Generally used	10	11	13	22
community	Median[b]	(1.87)	(1.69)	(1.69)	(2.04)
problems					
Policy	(1) Not used	21	41	40	21
development	(2) Exceptional use	4	0	0	3
	(3) Generally used	75	59	60	76
	Median	(2.83)	(2.30)	(2.32)	(2.84)
Politically oriented					
Legitimize	(1) Not used	40	33	36	26
existing	(2) Exceptional use	43	33	51	38
problems	(3) Generally used	17	33	13	36
	Median	(1.73)	(1.00)	(1.78)	(2.13)
Gain publicity	(1) Not used	40	47	54	38
	(2) Exceptional use	50	50	38	50
	(3) Generally used	10	3	8	12
	Median	(1.70)	(1.56)	(1.43)	(1.75)
Determine the	(1) Not used	76	78	77	73
political ac-	(2) Exceptional use	17	22	18	22
ceptability	(3) Generally used	7	0	5	5
of actions	Median	(1.15)	(1.14)	(1.15)	(1.19)

[a]Percentage of cities where one or more databanks are automated, but not used in this way by role type.
[b]Scored: 1, not used; 2, exceptional use; 3, generally used.

systems for each of three tasks displayed in Table 8.6. We then asked for examples and evidence of this use. The totality of responses was used to categorize each official by whether computing was "not used," "used only in exceptional cases," or "generally used" (not just in isolated or nonspecific cases) for each task.

Tables 8.5 and 8.6 suggest that operational data might be more influential than urban databanks, because the former tend to be used in making "housekeeping" decisions rather than in decisions which involve more political or conflictual problems. Furthermore, operational data simply are more frequently available in the cities. Some of the operational uses of data, and political uses as well, are illustrated by the following report from the fieldwork in one city:

In discussing the uses of data with the Mayor, he observed that "the City needs computer statistics not to make decisions, but to make federal applications." Here he was referring to the use of population and housing data in support of the City's community development application. Elsewhere he referred to a special run of tax exempt properties in the city that was used for making the case for greater State aid to

Table 8.6
The Orientation of Operational Data Systems

		Percentage of Use by:		
Kinds of Use	Levels of Use	Manager (N = 27)	Mayor (N = 31)	Council (N = 34)
Management oriented				
Monitor and control	(1) Not used[a]	18	20	24
departments and	(2) Exceptional use	33	63	61
agencies	(3) General use	49	17	15
	Median[b]	(2.44)	(1.97)	(1.93)
Politically oriented				
Respond to citizen	(1) Not used	35	55	59
requests and	(2) Exceptional use	38	19	22
complaints	(3) General use	27	26	19
	Median	(1.90)	(1.41)	(1.34)
Document policy	(1) Not used	26	28	47
positions	(2) Exceptional use	30	36	36
	(3) General use	44	36	17
	Median	(2.31)	(2.09)	(1.58)

[a]Percentage of cities where operational data are automated, but not used by role type.
[b]Scored: 1, not used in this way; 2, exceptional use; 3, general use.

Albany in view of the large proportion (67 percent) of tax exempt properties [large proportion of State offices].

The mayor also cited an instance where he used DMV [Department of Motor Vehicles] data to identify the owner of a car parked outside city hall with the dash strewn with traffic tickets. He found out it was a person in the Traffic Court who was flagrantly violating even the "lax" traffic ticket enforcement of the city. The Mayor's concern in this instance was that if he let this person continue to violate the traffic laws, it could lead to political embarrassment.

Another example of the Mayor's use of data is more difficult to describe or even attribute to him, since he would not say much about it. But I learned through discussions with other people that the Mayor and Urban Renewal Director make frequent use of ward by ward computerized assessment lists which show property owners, assessed value, exemption status and tax status (e.g., paid, delinquent). They have reportedly been concentrating recently on looking at data for the wards covered by the City's rehabilitation program. Because many assessments are pegged where they were thirty years ago, a quick search of the computer lists will uncover "good buys." It will also uncover properties with high tax debts for which the Mayor might recommend a "compromise"—a settlement below that required to pay off a high tax debt—thereby making these properties "good buys." Thus, the Mayor has essentially "insider" information which he can make available to party faithful, gaining for them good property investments and gain for him future loyalty and support. "Investment information" is thus a potential political resource of the Mayor and one which he personally becomes closely involved with just as he personally decides on city contracts and patronage appointments. The computer clearly is useful here in a simple practical way. That is, it facilitates and speeds-up his search for good real estate investments just as it speeded up his search for the car owner with multiple traffic tickets. (URBIS Case Report, Albany)

In summary, urban databanks and operational data systems are somewhat influential in local government decision-making; and there are exceptional instances where they have been very influential. In turn, planners and management analysts have considerable influence on other municipal decision-makers in at least half of our cities. Equally important, automation appears related to the influence of urban databank reports. For example, planners in 86 percent of the cities with automated databanks indicate that reports and analyses have affected decisions, whereas planners in only 60 percent of the unautomated cities do so.

Power Payoffs

The influence of urban databanks on municipal decisions suggests that power shifts are likely to occur. However, our data indicate that the magnitude of power shifts is likely to be less than predicted in much of the literature. First, while each kind of official tends to use urban databanks, the overall use of databanks is low (Table 8.5 and Table 8.6). In only about 10 percent of the cities does any given kind of public official *generally* use urban databanks. In over 10 percent of the cities, for only two tasks—problem finding and problem legitimation—does any kind of official tend to generally use databanks. And in about half the cities, the officials use urban databanks only in exceptional cases. Databank uses are illustrated for the mayor and council from the fieldwork in Tampa. For example, the mayor

receives the city conditions report from the MDA [Metropolitan Development Agency] and reports from the Hillsborough Planning Commission and the Environmental Protection Agency. He believes they are useful in deriving a general understanding of conditions in the city and in determining priority items within the city budget. When elected to office he ran partly on increasing recreation programs. According to people within MDA, databanks did not change or alter his priority for recreation, but databanks were instrumental in determining his allocation of monies across recreation programs and areas of the city.

In this same respect, databanks have apparently been useful in determining the allocation of community block grant funds. Moreover, the Mayor put in nearly 35 hours of his time familiarizing himself with MDA data and analysis concerning the allocation of community block grant dollars. The Mayor wishes to apply the same method of analysis to consideration of spending from all sources rather than only on community block grant monies. (URBIS Case Report, Tampa)

The council, on the other hand, seems to be less appreciative of databanks and analyses based upon them:

One councilperson said that he does not feel that databanks alter the perceptions of city officials about problems or policies, but gives the council a little better feeling for the "objective" needs of the city. However, another said that she lacks any trust of computer-based data and computer operations in the city. She cited, as the basis for her distrust, an outside auditor's report that was very critical of the type of information being processed in Tampa, the coordination of information and its utilization. She was also critical of databank reports partly because she was critical of MDA. According to her, MDA has too narrow a view of the community. She said that MDA is still using model cities areas as priority target areas and she thought that the whole city should be considered in terms of allocating community development monies. She also thought that the timing of the reports made by MDA was inappropriate for they were presented too close to the time when the decisions had to be reached. They were then presented as pressing issues requiring immediate decision. Thus the MDA presentations and reports placed the council in a situation where they lacked the time to read reports or to think through the analyses. (URBIS Case Report, Tampa)

Second, each kind of official tends to use urban databanks in somewhat different ways, although there is no clear special function. Table 8.5 indicates that while managers are more likely to use databanks for planning purposes (problem finding, decision-making, and policy development), they are about as likely as are the elected officials to use urban databanks for political purposes (legitimizing their position, gaining publicity, and determining the political feasibility of different actions). Thus, while there is some specialization among roles in the purposes for which computing is used, no kind of official seems to have a clear monopoly over the use of computing in a specific area.

Third, there are more similarities than differences in use by role. Planners/analysts are the major users of databanks, given that their median level of use is highest on five of the six tasks. The planners/analysts are followed by the managers, then mayors and council. But the total difference among roles on any task is less than 20 percent, and most frequently is around 10 percent. This small difference in use among officials is an unexpected challenge to the belief that major power shifts result from automated databanks.

The relatively low use of urban databanks by public officials might be due to the fact that databanks play a minor role in urban decision-making, especially when compared to operational data systems. Operational data systems *are* used more extensively than urban databanks (Table 8.5 and Table 8.6). In more than three-fourths of the cities, operational systems are used for management, planning, and political purposes. Also, there are somewhat greater differences in use of operational data systems by role. The managers' use of operational systems clearly dominates when compared to the use made by elected officials. In about one-half of the cities, the managers make general use of operational data systems for monitoring subunits, making decisions, and documenting policy positions. The only use that ranks low for the managers is responding to citizen complaints. In contrast, mayors most often use operational data for documenting policy positions and monitoring subunits. Still, the overall use of operational data systems remains moderate. Thus, our general implications remain the same. Power shifts are quite possible, but not dramatic in their intensity.

Distribution of Power Payoffs

The direction of power shifts is also likely to be sensitive to the degree and kind of use made of computers by municipal officials. The relative frequency with which each kind of official tends to use computing implies a loose hierarchy of officials who are more likely to gain in decision-making effectiveness (Table 8.5 and Table 8.6). Planners/analysts tend to dominate the use of databanks, and managers tend to dominate the use of operational data systems. This suggests that managers and planners generally gain somewhat more decision-making effectiveness than elected mayors or councils. While the frequency of utilization suggests power shifts, a more direct measurement is available in the form of judgmental ratings made on the basis of extensive case-study observations within each site. Table 8.7 shows the degree to which each type of public official was judged to gain and lose influence as a result of computing in local government. These ratings support the existence of power shifts and the same loose hierarchy of gainers described above. Computing is judged to have had some effect on the relative influence of at least one official in about 80 percent of the cities. Where there is an effect, computing has tended to increase rather than decrease the influence of public officials. (While computing has decreased the influence of at least some officials in 27 percent of the cities, it has increased the influence of some officials in 54 percent of the cities.) By rank, those who tend to gain (and not lose) influence are the planners/analysts, the top managers and department heads, and the mayor and council.

Table 8.7
Percentage of Cities Where the Use of Computer-Based Data
Shifted Influence Among Officials[a]

	Effect on Official			
Official Affected	Decreased Influence	No Effect	Increased Influence	N
Databank custodians and planners	0	68	32	40
Manager, chief administrative officer, and staff	3	70	27	27
Departments	10	72	18	40
Mayor and staff	14	67	19	37
Council and staff	20	75	5	40

[a]Investigators' judgmental ratings based on all interviews.

However, these rankings do not reflect major differences. Planners/ analysts are not great beneficiaries of computing, for they tend to gain influence in only about 32 percent of the cities. Likewise, managers have gained influence in only about 27 percent of the cities, while department heads and mayors gained influence in nearly as many, 18 percent and 19 percent, respectively. Only the councils generally tend to have lost influence (in 20 percent of the cities) as a result of computing more often than they have gained influence (in 5 percent of the cities). Thus, no single official appears to be a general, substantial, and sole beneficiary of power shifts from computing in cities. The shifts that occur are mainly gains rather than losses in the influence of officials, and the gains appear to be shared among nearly all officials.

In summary, the automation of databanks does lead to improved information and is somewhat influential in decision-making. The extent to which such information has resulted in shifts in influence among city officials is small, without any official being a serious loser.

Implementation Strategies

Like our other tasks, the impacts of urban databanks and operational data systems might be greatly dependent on the kinds of automated data available, who conducts the analyses, and other implementation factors. The varied ways in which local governments generally, and our 42 cities in particular, have implemented both urban databanks and operational data systems for policy analysis can be classified by whether they primarily involve a reform or postreform approach to implementation. And again, they can be viewed from three perspectives: technological development, structural arrangement, and socio-technical design.

Technological Development

The reformers who introduced the notion of databanks into cities envisioned the development of unified data systems that integrated huge quantities of data from operational records and secondary sources (Hearle and Mason 1963; Hair 1965; Parker 1965; Haak and Bigger 1966). These unified databanks would consolidate the otherwise fragmented data and make them readily available for use, with the aid of sophisticated computer software, for data management, analysis, storage, and retrieval. The databanks would be oriented to management, planning, and even political uses, and could be used to produce numerous reports and analyses for wide distribution throughout city hall.

Our 42 cities generally have rejected this reform, advanced-technology approach in favor of a post-reform, appropriate-technology approach to databank development. In our 42 cities, urban databanks and operational data systems tend to be less extensive, less integrated, and less sophisticated than the idea promoted by the reformers. Each tends to have different uses and different degrees of use by analysts and decision-makers. And the databanks in our cities tend to have only moderate reporting capacity, limited distribution of reports, and limited acceptance by decision-makers. But our cities vary greatly and, consequently, at least some show a tendency towards a reform approach to automation.

Degree of Automation

The post-reform, appropriate-technology approach of our cities is illustrated by the fact that urban databanks and operational data

Table 8.8
Distribution of Urban Databanks among 42 Cities

Number of Urban Databanks	Percentage and Number of Cities Where Urban Databanks Are:									
	Manual or Automated		Only Manual[a]		Only Automated[a]		Only Archival[b]		Only Records-Based[b]	
	%	N	%	N	%	N	%	N	%	N
None	0	0	33	14	14	6	0	0	40	17
One	0	0	9	4	10	4	2	1	19	8
Two	2	1	21	9	19	8	12	5	26	11
Three	19	8	17	7	14	6	19	8	7	3
Four	12	5	7	3	10	4	21	9	5	2
Five	14	6	7	3	5	2	19	8	2	1
Six	14	6	2	1	7	3	14	6	0	0
Seven	12	5	2	1	5	2	10	4	0	0
Eight	26	11	0	0	17	7	2	1	0	0

[a]Cities were asked to describe up to eight most-used databanks in the city and whether these were manual or automated.

[b]Records-based databanks are derived from departmental records; for example, the creation of a land-use databank from the assessor's real-property records and the building department's permit records. Archival databanks are derived from periodic field surveys and secondary sources; for example, the creation of a housing databank from a field survey of housing conditions in urban-renewal areas of the city.

Table 8.9
Kinds of Urban Databanks and Illustrations of Data Content

Kind of Databank	Illustrations
Public safety	
Crime	Criminal-offense reports, crime statistics, demographic data
Fire Incidents	Fire-incident reports
General government	
Public Opinion	Needs-assessment surveys, senior-citizen's opinion, neighborhood surveys, shopping surveys
Miscellaneous	Community organizations, handicapped barriers, sign inventory, grantee performance, environmental pollution
Community development and public works	
Census	Population, school children, 1970 U.S. Census
Land Use and Property	Land-use surveys, property records, tax records, property-tax delinquencies, property sales
Housing	Housing stock, condition, occupancy, vacancy, and permits
R. L. Polk Data	Population, household, housing, vacancy, occupations, income, commercial data
Business Data	Dun and Bradstreet data, census of business, business licenses, business survey
Planning Data	Integrated files with population, housing, land use, economic and other data
Transportation	Origin and destination surveys, transit use, transit-user attitudes
Building	Building permits, structure-condition surveys
Redevelopment	Field surveys, property inventories, relocation records, redevelopment-area opinion surveys
Traffic and Parking	Traffic surveys, accident statistics, traffic-device inventories, parking surveys
Utility Structures	Inventory of utility structures and locations
Human resources	
Employment	Jobs, unemployment, income, occupational licenses
Social Services	Parks and recreation-use surveys, library-patrons survey, social-services surveys and client records, juvenile services, youth summer work
Health	Health statistics, vital statistics, public-health records

systems are not unified. Urban databanks are fragmented, largely because of the kinds of information they contain and the sources of that information. Nearly all cities have three or more urban databanks and 52 percent have six or more (Table 8.8).[3] Most of these are automated rather than manual databanks, but there is considerable variation among cities. Some 34 percent have 5 to 8 automated databanks, 53 percent have 1 to 4 databanks, and 14 percent have none. Most databanks are based on field surveys and secondary sources rather than on operational records. However, cities with more databanks tend to have more records-based databanks. The nature of these databanks also varies across cities (Table 8.9). Only population and land-use databanks are common among the cities.[4]

Operational data systems are even more fragmented than urban databanks, for they are primarily oriented around a single department's operations. We measured these systems by the extent of automation in each city. We inventoried the total number of automated applications, because all of these potentially can be oriented to supporting the informational needs for policy analysis. The average number of computer applications for all 42 cities is 64, with a range from none to 147; clearly, there is broad variation. One-third of the cities have less than 50 automated applications, about one-half of the cities have 50 to 100 applications, and about one-fifth of the cities have over 100 applications.

But the functional breadth of operational data systems is not very great, being concentrated mainly in finance, police, utilities, and general administrative functions (Kraemer, Dutton, and Matthews 1975). Consequently, the breadth of data available for policy analysis is not very large. Still, because the finance and general administrative applications tend to cross departmental boundaries, these automated applications might be of special use to top managers and their staff in evaluating departmental performance.

Sophistication of Automation

Technological sophistication varies across cities in both the sophistication of the local government computing installations and the sophistication of databank reports and analyses. Generally, our cities exhibit moderate technological sophistication, consistent with an appropriate-technology strategy. But some cities have highly sophisticated installations, with on-line applications, database-management software, large core memory capacities, and modern operating systems. And these sophisticated capabilities are expected to aid planning and management analysts in integrating and analyzing their large and fragmented databases. This expectation seems to be fulfilled; given that cities with more sophisticated data-processing installations tend to have more urban databanks and more operational data systems.[5]

Our cities also tend to have moderately sophisticated databank reports and analyses. And the more automated they are, the greater the sophistication of reports. The reports and analyses produced from urban databanks in the 42 cities were found to range from simple to highly sophisticated methods of analysis: from frequency analysis, map analysis, graphic analysis, and fixed-area geo-based analysis, to bivariate analysis, multivariate analysis, and multiple-area geo-based analysis (Table 8.10).[6] Nearly one-half of the automated cities produced reports involving one or more of the three most sophisticated kinds of analysis, whereas only 17 percent of the unautomated cities produced such reports. This difference between automated and unautomated sites is important, because while the first four methods of

Table 8.10
Sophistication of Urban-Databank Reports

| | Percentage and Number of Cities with Databanks | | | |
| | Nonautomated Databanks (N = 6) | | Automated Databanks (N = 35) | |
Sophistication of Reports and Analyses[a]	%	N	%	N
0. No reports	0	0	3	1
1. Marginal or frequency tables	0	0	3	1
2. Maps plus 1	33	2	3	1
3. Bar graphs, histograms, frequency polygons plus 1, 2	33	2	26	9
4. Fixed area geo-based analysis plus 1, 2, 3	17	1	17	6
5. Bivariate correlations or cross tabulations plus 1, 2, 3, 4	0	0	20	7
6. Multivariate correlation, regression, factor or cluster analysis plus 1, 2, 3, 4, 5	17	1	20	7
7. Variable area geo-based analysis plus 1, 2, 3, 4, 5, 6	0	0	9	3

[a]These features are listed in order from least to most sophisticated.

analysis can readily be performed manually, the last three nearly always require computer assistance.[7]

The Orientation of Databanks

The limited and differential uses of databanks for management and planning purposes conform more closely to appropriate rather than advanced technology. But the dominance of management and planning uses suggests a reform orientation toward supporting rational analysis and top-management decision-making. Urban databanks have been primarily oriented to serve management purposes and, to a lesser extent, planning and political purposes (Table 8.5 and Table 8.6). Among management purposes, a large percentage of cities use urban databanks for preparing grant proposals and applications for federal and state financial assistance. This tendency reflects the substantial interest of cities in revenue generation from outside sources as well as from the local community (Meltzner 1971). A somewhat smaller percentage of cities use urban databanks for fulfilling federal and state reporting requirements. Other frequent uses of urban databanks include traditional planning functions: community analysis aimed at developing new or clearer perceptions of community conditions and problems; needs assessment aimed at determining what groups of citizens or what neighborhoods are in need of plans and programs; community planning for land use, housing, transportation, and social services; and program planning for implementing physical-development and social-services plans. Urban planners in most cities use urban databanks for these purposes (Table 8.5). As might be expected, fewer cities report these planning uses of databanks by other officials, such as managers, mayors, and council. However, the general pattern of use among these officials is similar to, while lower than, that of the planners.

Cities' use of urban databanks for political purposes is considerably less common, but also more varied, than the planning uses. For example, the use of databanks by planners for legitimizing problems already perceived to exist, and for gaining publicity for particular programs and policies, is common to most of the cities. Other uses—such as determining the political feasibility of policies, plans, and programs—are common to urban planners in only about one-fourth of the cities (data not shown). This general pattern of use is similar for other municipal officials as well.

A high proportion of the 42 cities report use of operational data systems for management, planning, and political purposes by managers; and a smaller, but still considerable, proportion report such uses by mayors and council. Management uses of operational systems focus on monitoring and controlling the municipal departments and agencies in such areas as expenditure, personnel, affirmative action, and performance. Managers in 78 percent of the cities use operational systems for these purposes; mayors and council in two-thirds and one-half, respectively, of the cities use them for these purposes (Table 8.6).

Planning uses of operational systems focus on examination of existing policies and procedures, such as the definition of taxable real estate in the city or the desirability of local sales taxes. Managers in 82 percent of the cities use operational systems for this purpose; mayors and council in 62 percent and 55 percent, respectively, use them for this purpose (Table 8.6).

Political uses of operational systems focus on documenting policy positions and recommendations, and on responding to individual, or citizen group, complaints and requests. Fewer cities report such political uses, but at least one-third do so for mayor and council, and as many as 70 percent of the cities do so for managers (Table 8.6).

In summary, the orientation of databanks suggests that cities have followed a mixture of reform and post-reform approaches to implementation. The reform approach is suggested by the orientation of databanks toward rational decision-making by professional managers and planners. The post-reform approach is suggested by the limited and differential, rather than organizationwide, uses of databanks.

Reporting Capacity

In general, the moderate reporting capacities of our cities reflect their appropriate-technology strategy for technological development. But the cities vary considerably in their reporting capacity, with the more automated cities having greater capacity. One indication of this capacity is the number of reports generated from databanks.

Planners in the cities with automated urban databanks produced an average of 21 basic reports over the last five years, compared to 6 reports in the cities with no urban databank automation. These included reports about community conditions such as the characteristics of people or the condition of housing in different neighborhoods of the city, site-location studies and needs assessments, among others. Similarly, planners in the cities with automated urban databanks produce an average of 17 special analyses per month, compared to 4 analyses in cities with no urban databank automation. These analyses usually relate to questions surrounding specific neighborhoods, population groups, properties, or businesses in the community.

Consistent with an appropriate-technology strategy, the reporting capacity of automated operational data systems in our cities also is moderate, but varies with degree of automation. The number of regular reports and special analyses produced for managers, mayors, and council by management analysts varies among automated sites from none to 10 reports and requests during a month. On the average, our cities produce about 4 regular reports during a month on matters such as budget expenditures, personnel status, and department performance. On the average, they produce about 3 special analyses during a week on topics such as vendor performance and comparative salaries.

Report Distribution

As might be expected from the orientation of automated databanks in our cities, the distribution of reports is limited rather than organization-wide. A reform orientation is also reflected in the centralizing of information in the hands of the chief executive or the departments, rather than elected officials. The major recipients of reports and analyses produced from databanks are top managers, rather than mayors, council, or the departments. Managers are the most frequent recipients of basic reports from urban databanks (Table 8.11). For example, 50 percent of the cities indicate that managers receive basic reports several times a year or monthly, whereas 41, 34, and 31 percent of the cities indicate that mayors, council, and departments, respectively, receive basic reports this often. By contrast, the departments tend to be the most frequent recipients of special information and analyses from urban databanks. For example, 46 percent of the cities indicate that the departments receive special analyses monthly or more often, whereas 27, 24, and 15 percent of the cities indicate that managers, mayor, and council, respectively, receive special analyses this often.

The kind of information most frequently received from operational data systems tends to be current budgets, expenditure and revenue forecasts, and personnel status. The differential distribution of this

Table 8.11
Distribution of Information from Automated Urban Databanks

Kind of Information and Frequency of Distribution	Percentage of Cities Where Information from Automated Urban Databanks is Distributed to:							
	Manager (N = 30)		Mayor (N = 39)		Council (N = 41)		Departments (N = 42)	
	%	N	%	N	%	N	%	N
Basic reports								
Once a year or less	50	15	59	23	66	27	69	29
Several times a year	30	9	28	11	24	10	24	10
Monthly or more	20	6	13	5	10	4	7	3
Special analyses[a]								
Once a year or less	27	8	34	13	51	21	22	9
Several times a year	46	14	42	16	34	14	32	13
Monthly or more	27	8	24	9	15	6	46	19

[a]For Special analyses, the number of mayors = 39, and the number of departments = 41.

information among municipal officials is even more pronounced for operational data systems than for urban databanks (Table 8.12). For example, managers receive regular reports about current budgets in 90 percent of the cities, compared to 69 and 64 percent of the cities for mayors and council, respectively. This pattern of distribution is similar for other categories of information (Table 8.12). This dominance of information distribution toward managers implies that managers should be among the greatest users of information and the greatest beneficiaries of automated databanks.

Quality of Reports and Analyses

Despite the greater sophistication of planners' reports and analyses in cities with automated databanks, the perceived quality of the reports is high, regardless of whether the databanks are automated or unautomated. For example, planners in two-thirds of the cities with databank automation, and 83 percent of the cities without databank automation, replied that the reports generated from urban databanks were widely recognized by other municipal officials as accurate and of high quality. It is interesting to note, though, that the accuracy and quality of databank reports are of "some dispute" in 17 percent of the cities.

Interesting, too, is the fact that mayors and councils in cities with

Table 8.12

Distribution of Information from Automated Operational Data Systems

Kind of Operational Data	Cities Distributing Information from Regular Reports to:						Cities Distributing Information from Special Analyses to:					
	Manager (N = 29)		Mayor (N = 36)		Council (N = 39)		Manager (N = 26)		Mayor (N = 31)		Council (N = 34)	
	%	N	%	N	%	N	%	N	%	N	%	N
Current budget data	90	26	69	25	64	25	58	15	26	8	21	7
Expenditure, revenue forecasts	34	10	25	9	23	9	46	12	23	7	18	6
Purchasing information (vendor lists, etc.)	21	6	3	1	5	2	19	5	3	1	9	3
Inventory data	17	5	3	1	5	2	19	5	3	1	0	0
Current personnel data by classification, salary, etc.	66	19	14	5	8	3	73	19	39	12	29	10
Performance or output indicators, service data	40	11	19	7	15	6	27	7	16	5	12	4
Capital and other project status reports	31	9	11	4	10	4	27	7	16	5	12	4

Table 8.13
Perceived Accuracy, Validity, and Objectivity of Databank Reports

Kind of Official	Percentage of Cities in Which Official(s):	
	Have Little or No Confidence in the Accuracy and Validity of Analysis	View the Analyses as Somewhat or Quite Biased
Council and council staff (N = 40)	18	54
Mayor and staff (N = 37)	11	49
Manager and staff (N = 30)	17	24
Planners and analysts (N = 40)	3	25

databank automation tend to believe that the planners' reports are somewhat or quite biased, whereas mayors and council in unautomated cities tend to feel planners' reports are impartial.[8] Surprisingly, the planners themselves seem to agree with these judgments (Table 8.13). Overall, a significant proportion of city councils (18 percent), mayors (11 percent), and managers (17 percent) have little or no confidence in the accuracy and validity of databank analyses (Table 8.13). Even more crucial is the fact that decision-makers, especially mayors and councils, are suspicious of the biases reflected in the various analyses and reports generated by policy analysts. About half of the mayors and councils view these analyses as being at least somewhat biased, and about one-fourth of the managers and policy analysts share this view (Table 8.13).

Other Technological Attributes

From the preceding discussion, it is clear that the technology associated with automated databanks varies in many respects across the 42 cities, although, on balance, it seems to reflect the appropriate-technology strategy. In part, an appropriate-technology strategy is common because cities have been late adopters of databanks. The year of automation is considered important to the degree to which automated applications are routinized (made a part of standard operating procedures) in the adopting organizations. In this respect, cities vary greatly in the length of time they have had urban databanks and operational data systems. For example, the average city adopted computing in 1965 but the date of adoption ranges from as early as

1955 to as late as 1974.[9] But the adoption of databanks is obviously more recent, since the concept was first introduced in the early–mid-sixties, and databank automation normally lags behind operational automation. Thus, most cities necessarily have been late adopters of databanks.[10]

Structural Arrangements

The second perspective that can be taken in regard to implementation of databank automation is structural. The reform-oriented, classical-structure advocates argue that policy-analysis units should take a service bureau role, and that the analysts should be the dominant participants in analysis. Also, computing support for policy analysis should be provided from a single central installation, control of databanks should be centralized, data sharing among departments should be maximized, users should be charged for computer use, and computing arrangements should seldom be changed in order to maintain a clear division of responsibility. In contrast, the post-reform, participatory-structure advocates recommend that policy-analysis units take a broad interpretative role, and that the end users of policy analysis (top management) have a dominant role in analysis. Uniquely in the case of databanks, participatory advocates would agree with their classical counterparts over the issue of centralization. A centralized installation and centralized databanks allow for the most direct access and user control by top management. But participatory advocates believe that computing services should be provided free to encourage use, and computing arrangements should be kept flexible in order to maximize the alternatives available to users. Our cities have followed a mixed reform/post-reform strategy in their structural arrangements for databank automation.

The participatory approach of our cities is illustrated by their strategies for user involvement. While the cities have placed policy-analysis units in a service-bureau role, they have used the participatory strategy of allowing the analysts to be the most influential participants in the analysis process.

Policy-analysis units can be assigned (or can assume) a narrow service-bureau role or a broad interpretative role. The service-bureau role is to respond to user initiatives by providing only what is requested, with little or no interpretation of the product. As the chief executive or council requests such listings as personnel by salary, or councilmanic districts by number of people over 65 years of age, the analyst's main job is to get this information quickly and efficiently. The broader interpretative role requires both technical and political sophistication, as well as a substantial commitment to policy analysis. The interpretative role is to anticipate user needs, aid users in formulating requests, respond to requests with the most useful information (not just the requested information), and interpret the analysis to the user. This role requires sophistication to understand user needs and how to address them without creating community or organizational conflicts that would defeat the purposes of rational analysis.

Our cities clearly have chosen the service-bureau role for their policy-analysis units. More than half (54 percent) of the analysis units in our cities tend toward the service-bureau role, whereas only about one-third (36 percent) tend toward the interpretative role (Table 8.14). Another 10 percent are mixed.

Even though most policy-analysis units are oriented to the service-bureau role and government officials might therefore shape the analyses by participating in them, the influence of the technicians on the reports and analyses is both substantial and greater than the influence of other officials. In 90 percent of our cities, planners and management analysts have a major influence on designing and generating analyses (Table 8.15). The technicians tend to be necessary to generating the outputs of policy analysis; and as a consequence, they tend to have a major influence on these outputs. Departmental

Table 8.14
The Role of Policy-Analysis Units

Role of Policy-Analysis Unit[a]	Percentage of Cities	N
Service bureau: respond to letter of requests with little or no interpretation	25	10
Tend toward service bureau	29	12
Mixed	10	4
Tend toward analysis unit	23	9
Analysis unit: respond with interpretation of findings	13	5
Total	100	40

[a]Question: Does your office broadly interpret the findings of specific analysis, or do you respond to the letter of requests—not generally providing interpretation?

Table 8.15
User Participation in Databank Analyses
(in percent)

Participants[a]	Level of Participation (N = 40)		
	No Influence	Minor Influence	Major Influence
Planners and analysts	3	8	90
Departmental analysts	30	45	25
Chief appointed official and staff[b]	29	50	21
Mayor and staff	44	36	19
Council and staff	57	32	11

[a]Question: "Who participates in designing special analyses that are conducted and what kinds of reports are generated? Generally, how influential are each of the following groups and officials in determining what special analyses and kinds of reports are generated?"
[b]On this item, N = 28 cities with chief administrative officials.

analysts, also technicians, are influential in 70 percent of the cities, having a major influence in about one-fourth of the cities. The only top official who tends to be widely influential in databank analyses is the chief appointed official. This top bureaucratic influence is felt in about 70 percent of the cities, but is a major influence in only about 20 percent. Elected officials, especially the council, are the least involved and the least influential in policy analysis (Table 8.15).

The participatory approach of our cities is further illustrated by the fact that computing has been decentralized in relation to top officials, while relatively centralized in relation to the operating departments. If our cities had radically decentralized the databank function in cities, each department would have its own computer and automated databanks. Yet only one city (San Francisco) has placed a computer even in the planning department—the major user of databanks. And, in this case, the computer is a micro-processor run as a one-person operation. However, 27 percent of the cities have placed a computer installation within an independent department under the chief executive official.

Despite the centralization of computing equipment in most cities, control of databanks tends to be decentralized. Decentralization of databank control most often results from individual departments collecting and maintaining the databanks that serve their departments, rather than a single department, such as planning or EDP, being the custodian for all urban databanks. In this way, the control of databanks can be decentralized even though computing resources are relatively centralized in cities. On the average, databanks are located in three different municipal agencies. The number of agencies in which databanks are located ranges from the single agency to as many as eight agencies in at least one city. As might be expected with decentralized control of databanks, little data sharing goes on within our cities. Of 40 data-processing installations, 10 percent report that "no" automated files are shared by two or more city agencies or departments, 40 percent report "a few" files, 45 percent report "some," and only 5 percent report "many" shared files.

Other Structural Arrangements

Other structural implementation issues concern whether or not cities should charge for computer use, and whether or not cities should take a conservative stance toward reorganization of data-processing services to maintain structural stability. With respect to charging, most cities reflect the fact that computing is still in a developmental phase. To encourage development and use, most of our cities have taken a post-reform, participatory strategy and do not charge for the use of computing services and analysis of automated databanks. Free computing is provided to elected officials by 65 percent of the data-processing installations, to finance departments by 67 percent, and to planning departments by 64 percent of the installations. Cities also have taken a participatory perspective on structural instability, apparently accepting moderate levels of instability as part of the natural evolution of computing in the government.[11]

Socio-technical Design

While computing is intended to increase the quality of analysis and the effectiveness of policy analysts in their job, it also can alter the work environment of analysts and, to a lesser extent, of top policymakers. And this third perspective on implementation—socio-technical design—is also characterized by reform and post-reform approaches. Reformers suggest that computing be implemented with emphasis on task efficiency even if this creates additional demands and pressures on the analysts, thereby decreasing their sense of accomplishment in their work. Post-reformers suggest that computing be implemented with attention to human factors and in ways that increase the policy analysts' ability to work with and influence other people, particularly

Table 8.16
Policy Analysts' Perceptions of Changes in the Work Environment
Caused by Computers

Work Impacts	Planners: Percent Indicating (N = 34)	Management Analysts: Percent Indicating (N = 40)
Has computing changed the number of things you do?		
(0) Decreased	0	0
(50) Not affected	23	55
(100) Increased	77	45
Average score[a]	(69)	(69)
Has computing changed time pressures on your job?		
(0) Decreased	15	20
(50) Not affected	39	52
(100) Increased	46	28
Average score	(46)	(55)
Has computing changed your sense of accomplishment?		
(0) Lowered	3	0
(50) Not affected	23	55
(100) Raised	74	45
Average score	(72)	(69)
Has computing changed your opportunities to work with people?		
(0) Decreased	3	5
(50) Not affected	53	72
(100) Increased	44	23
Average score	(61)	(60)
Has computing changed the degree your work is supervised?		
(0) Decreased	20	5
(50) Not affected	68	95
(100) Increased	12	0
Average score	(52)	(47)
Has computing changed your influence over the actions of others?		
(0) Less influence	6	0
(50) No change	40	47
(100) More influence	54	53
Average score	(65)	(68)

[a]Average scores are the mean of individual responses within each city, scored from 0 to 100. Each variable was trichotomized to represent the percentage of cities with scores less than 33.3, between 33.3 and 66.7, and greater than 66.7.

policy-makers, thereby increasing the analysts' sense of accomplishment and satisfaction in their work. One means of assessing which strategy (task efficiency versus human relations) cities have followed in implementing automated databanks is to examine the responses of planners and management analysts to questions about the work environment, and the responses to top officials to questions about support for computing and their views of the computing staff.

Table 8.16 indicates that the computer's impact on the planners' work environment has been basically positive. Although computing has increased the number of things planners must do and the time pressures in their job, it also has increased their opportunities to work with other people, and to influence other people, and has increased their sense of accomplishment in their work. Here then, a task-efficiency perspective has been combined with a human-relations sensitivity.

In contrast, the computer's impact on the management analysts' work environment has been largely neutral. The management analysts in a majority of the cities indicate that computing has not affected their work demands, time pressures, opportunities to work with other people, the degree to which their work is supervised, or their sense of accomplishment. Still, where there has been an effect, the impact has been largely positive, following the same pattern as occurs among the urban planners.

Top-level support for computing and computing staff is likely to depend on the degree to which computing is implemented with a sensitivity to the needs and demands of top policy-makers—managers, mayors, and councils. Generally, top policy-makers support computing but differ widely on whether or not computing will improve *their* job (Table 8.17). Also, policy-makers in only one-fifth to one-third of the cities have a technocratic image of the computing staff (Table 8.17). Most city policy-makers believe their computing staffs are interested in solving department problems, communicating in the user's language, and making improvements in operational computer applications.

In general, the implementation of computing in most cities has followed a post-reform human-relations strategy. Implementation has been sensitive to the work environment of planners and management analysts, as well as to the needs and demands of policy-makers—the end users of automated databanks.

Table 8.17
Top Officials' Attitudes toward Data Processing

Categories and Items	Percentage of Cities in Which Top Officials Agree (N = 42)	Average Score[a]
Support for Computing		
I want to use computers and data processing more in doing my job	98	76
Within the next five years, computers will greatly improve the operations of this government	92	71
Within the next five years, computers will greatly improve the way my job is done	51	50
Views toward DP staff—Technocratic image		
Data-processing personnel are more intrigued with what the computer can do than with solving the problems of my department	28	38
Data-processing staff confuse our conversations with their technical language	38	41
Data-processing staff are more interested in working on new computer uses rather than making improvements in ones we now use	20	39

[a]Average scores are the mean of individual responses within each city, scored 0 to 100. Each variable was dichotomized to represent the percentage of cities with scores greater than 50, indicating agreement.

Assessment of Implementation Strategies

Automated databanks in local government are less extensive, unified, and sophisticated than the early promoters envisioned. Given this fact, however, the impacts of databanks are significant. In most cities with databanks, a small but appreciable number of decisions have been affected in the areas of management, planning, and politics. Furthermore, databanks have had a much greater effect in some cities than in others on the quality of information, the utilization of information for decision-making, and the distribution of power. Systematic variations in the way databanks were automated could explain the variations across cities in databank impacts. This section explores these variations in order to explain the relative success of the databank function in cities. This information is then used to derive prescriptive advice for local governments on the best strategies for implementing governmental databanks.

Our research strategy is to develop indicators of implementation variables which represent the technological, structural, and socio-technical approaches cities have used to implement databanks. In addition, we include indicators of the organizational context and the community environment of databank implementation. A correlational design is used to assess the statistical relationship between implementation variables and a variety of databank impacts. Multivariate regression techniques are used to select the variables most explanatory of the databank impacts among cities. Taken together, these correlations and regressions are used to derive policy advice on the most effective strategies for implementing automated databanks. Of course, the purposes for automating databanks may vary widely across organizations. Therefore, much of our prescriptive advice must be contingent on the agenda of those who are involved in the adoption and implementation of this technology.

The Dependent Variables

The major outcomes of databank use are the impacts of automation on policy-analysis performance, management-oriented computing, and power shifts. Policy-analysis performance is an index which indicates the degree to which automated databanks have affected the decisions of city officials. The index combines the individual scores for managers, planners, and politicians on indicators of the degree to which automated databanks have affected their decisions; that is, led to program recommendations, influenced their decisions, or changed previous decisions (see the Appendix for index).

The indicators were standardized so that city scores had a mean of zero and a standard deviation of one on each of the three indicators. The average score for a city on all three items is used as our policy-analysis performance index. Table 8.18 shows the distribution of automated databank sites on the index and illustrates three interesting features. First, the index scores are evenly and widely distributed. Second, the rankings show no clear tendency to reflect regional

Table 8.18
Automated Policy-Analysis Performance Index

City	Index Score	City	Index Score
Very High		**Medium** (*cont.*)	
Seattle, Wash.	1.67	Riverside, Calif.	−.10
Evansville, Ind.	1.42	San Jose, Calif.	−.10
New Orleans, La.	1.24	**Low**	
Philadelphia, Pa.	1.22	Las Vegas, Nev.	−.30
Cleveland, Ohio	1.05	Hampton, Va.	−.42
Little Rock, Ark.	1.05	Montgomery, Ala.	−.44
Portsmouth, Va.	.98	Newton, Mass.	−.59
Costa Mesa, Calif.	.87	Brockton, Mass.	−.62
High		Stockton, Calif.	−.68
San Francisco, Calif.	.68	**Very Low**	
Baltimore, Md.	.66	Albany, N.Y.	−.81
Burbank, Calif.	.62	Tulsa, Okla.	−.81
Grand Rapids, Mich.	.60	Miami Beach, Fla.	−.93
Long Beach, Calif.	.42	Warren, Mich.	−.94
Fort Lauderdale, Fla.	.42	Chesapeake, Va.	−1.00
Kansas City, Mo.	.40	Atlanta, Ga.	−1.00
Sacramento, Calif.	.32	St. Louis, Mo.	−1.17
		Florissant, Mo.	−1.26
Medium		Lincoln, Nebr.	−1.26
Oshkosh, Wis.	.23	Spokane, Wash.	−1.26
Louisville, Ky.	.23		
Milwaukee, Wis.	.20		
Lancaster, Pa.	.20	Mean	.03
Paterson, N.J.	.03	Standard Deviation	.83
Tampa, Fla.	−.03		

patterns. Third, the rankings show a tendency for larger cities to be at the high end of the index and smaller cities at the low end.

Management-oriented computing is an index which indicates the degree to which automated databanks serve management, planning, and political uses of information. The index combines the individual scores for managers, planners, and politicians on indicators of the degree to which automated databanks serve management, planning, and political uses. Management uses include satisfying federal, or state, reporting requirements; preparing grant proposals; and monitoring agency operations. Planning uses include assessing needs; identifying community problems; and planning social services, housing, transportation, and land use. Political uses include assessing political feasibility, buffering constituents, legitimizing policies, gaining publicity, and responding to constituent complaints (see the Appendix). The average score for a city on all three items is our management-oriented computing index.

The power-shift index is a judgmental rating scale of the degree to which computing has shifted greater influence to central management, elected officials, and technocrats (i.e., the skilled, professional analysts in the planning and operating departments.

The Independent Variables

The implementation variables fall into three broad categories: technology, structure, and design. The technology variables represent differences among cities in the characteristics of databank technology. Indicators of databank technology include: the degree of automation, measured by the number of operational applications and the number of automated urban databanks; the sophistication of databanks, measured by the sophistication of the city's data-processing instal-lations and the sophistication of databank reports; the orientation of databanks, measured by the degree to which computing is oriented to serve management, planning, and political needs; the reporting capacity of databank applications, measured by the number of regular computer-based reports and the number of databank reports; and other technological attributes, including the perceived validity of databank reports, the first year in which data systems were automated, and the degree of technological instability in the city. Technology variables are listed in Table 8.19 and are operationally defined in the Appendix.

The structural variables represent differences among cities in the organizational policies that govern the structural arrangements of computing. Indicators include the degree of user involvement in the design of automated databank analyses, including the involvement of managers, mayors, councils, departments, and analysts, as well as the role orientation of the planning-analysis unit. Centralization versus decentralization of computing and databanks is measured by whether or not computing has been centralized within a single data-processing installation under the chief executive, and by a count of the number of operating departments that maintain and analyze one or more urban databanks—the latter being an indication of the degree to which databanks are decentralized. Other structural arrangements include whether top officials and planners are charged for computing services, the degree to which city departments share data files, and the degree of structural instability in the data-processing function.

The socio-technical design variables represent the sensitivity of databank design to the work environment. The measurement of these variables differs from other information-processing tasks because the direct use of computing is a minor activity for the end users of databanks—top policy-makers and analysts. Therefore, we measure the sensitivity of databanks to the work environment through indicators of top-level support for computing and top-level views of the data-processing staff. The greater the degree to which top users are supportive of computing and data-processing staff (viewing them as nontechnocratic), the more likely it is that databanks were designed with a sensitivity to the information needs and task requirements of policy analysts.

Measures of the organizational context are slack resources, form of government, the use of professional management practices, and the degree of partisan activity in the local government. Measures of the community environment include population size and growth.

Findings

The findings can be described best by discussing the relationships between the implementation variables and each outcome variable, in turn. First, we assess the determinants of policy-analysis performance—the utilization of information for decision-making by management, planners, and elected officials. This analysis points out the importance of the orientation of computing to its impact on decision-making. Therefore, we assess the determinants of management, planning, and politically oriented computing before turning to the impact of computing on power shifts to bureaucrats, technocrats, and politicians.

Policy-Analysis Performance

Correlational analysis indicates that technology is the key explanator of policy-analysis performance in our cities, although structure, organizational context, and community environment also have minor influence on performance. Advanced technology in particular is related to performance (Table 8.19). Those cities with high payoff for policy analysis from automated databanks tend to have a large number of operational applications; more automated databanks; a sophisticated computer installation; more sophisticated databank reports; a large number of operational reports and databank analyses; and more management-oriented computing, which serves operational, planning, and political uses. Only two technology variables—the routinization of computing and the instability of computing—are unrelated to policy-analysis performance.

Participatory policies are somewhat related to performance (Table 8.19). Participatory policies of user involvement (particularly by analysts but also by city management) in design of databank analyses and decentralization of control over automated databanks are related to higher performance. And so is the participatory structural policy of centralization of computing in a single independent installation. These participatory policies seem to provide for involvement and control of databanks and analyses by the end users, thereby increasing the utility and effectiveness of specific analyses, while also providing, through a single central installation, sophisticated computing support, which can further increase the utility of analysis.

Other structural arrangements—such as interdepartmental data sharing, charging for computer use, and structural instability—are unrelated to policy-analysis performance. Socio-technical-design policies also are unrelated to performance (Table 8.19).

The organizational context, however, is somewhat related to policy-analysis performance (Table 8.19). Those cities with high payoffs from automated databanks tend to be cities with partisan politics and limited financial resources, but also with professional management practices. Because many of these cities are plagued with fiscal limitations, they might have embarked on databank automation to support policy analysis aimed at understanding community, social, and economic conditions, and at developing solutions to ameliorate their fiscal problems.

The community environment also is related to policy-analysis performance. Those cities with high payoffs tend to be larger and slow growing. It is therefore likely that the growth problems of larger cities have combined with the fiscal problems to create a strong push for databank automation to support policy analysis.

Table 8.19
Pearson Correlations between Implementation Policies and Policy-Analysis Performance and Management-Oriented Computing[a]

Implementation Policy	Policy Analysis Performance		Management-Oriented Computing	
	r	N	r	N
Technological development				
Degree of automation				
Number of operational applications	.29*	41	.33*	41
Number of automated databanks	.30*	41	.15	41
Sophistication				
Sophistication of installations	.24*	40	.29*	40
Sophistication of databank reports	.58*	40	.42*	40
Orientation				
Management-oriented computing	.70*	41		[a]
Management use	.43*	41		[a]
Planning use	.65*	41		[a]
Political use	.59*	41		[a]
Reporting capacity				
Number of regular operations reports	.28*	41	.16	41
Number of databank reports	.29*	41	.23	41
Routinization				
First year of automation	−.09	41	−.09	41
Instability				
Technological instability	.05	41	−.05	41
Structural arrangements				
User involvement				
Manager's involvement in design	.25	28	.41*	28
Mayor's involvement in design	.07	35	−.20	35
Council's involvement in design	−.05	37	−.10	37
Departmental involvement in design	.19	39	.19	39
Analyst involvement in design	.28*	39	.23	39
Analyst involvement in interpretation	.09	39	−.10	39
Centralization-decentralization				
Single independent installation	.33*	41	.24	41
Decentralization of control over databanks	.36*	41	.35*	41
Interdepartment data sharing	.02	41	.03	41
Charging				
Charging for computer use	.12	37	.06	37
Instability				
Structural instability	.20	41	.00	41
Socio-technical design				
Support for computing	−.21	41	−.04	41
Technocratic DP staff	.03	37	.20	37

Table 8.19 (continued)

Implementation Policy	Policy Analysis Performance		Management-Oriented Computing	
	r	N	r	N
Organizational context				
Slack financial resources	−.45*	41	−.22	41
Partisan politics	.20	41	−.04	41
Council-manager form	−.01	41	.19	41
Professional management practices	.44*	41	.57*	41
Community environment				
Total population 1975	.32*	41	.05	41
Population growth 1970–1975	−.29*	41	−.01	41

ªComponents of dependent variable.
*$P < .05$.

Table 8.20
Correlations and Path Coefficients for Policy-Analysis Performance,
P (Dependent Variable), and Management-Oriented Computing,
MOC (Dependent Variable)

Independent Variable	Zero-Order Correlation	Path Coefficient	Variance Explained (%)
Policy analysis performance			
Management-oriented computing: X_1	.70	.50	48
Sophistication of databank reports: X_2	.58	.32	10
Slack financial resources: X_3	−.45	−.28	8

$R = .81$ Total variance explained = 66%
$P^* = −.97 + 1.18X_1 + .16X_2 − .007X_3$
$\quad\quad\quad\ (.34)\quad\ (.07)\quad\ (.001)$

Management-oriented computing			
Professional management practices: X_1	.57	.50	33
Sophistication of databank reports: X_2	.42	.32	9

$R = .65$ Total variance explained = 42%
$MOC^* = .04 + .002X_1 + .07X_2$
$\quad\quad\quad\quad\ (.00)\quad\ (.03)$

*Regression coefficients are unstandardized; standard errors in parentheses.

In summary, advanced technology, participatory structures, the organizational context, and the community environment are determinants of the extent to which automated databanks affect urban decision-making. But are these variables independent of one another or highly interrelated? To assess the independent effects of these variables and the policies they represent, we performed the multiple regression analysis shown in Table 8.20. The analysis indicates that advanced technology is the dominant explanator of policy-analysis performance. Management-oriented computing alone explains nearly one-half (48 percent) of the variation in performance among cities; the sophistication of databank reports explains another 10 percent of the variation (Table 8.20). One feature of the organizational context—slack financial resources—is related to poor policy-analysis performance from automated databanks. It might not be slack financial resources per se, but the organizational context in which slack financial resources exist that leads to poor performance. For example, officials in cities with limited financial resources might be more likely to perceive a need to automate databanks and to use the policy analyses derived therefrom to shape their decisions. Officials in cities with slack resources might not feel these same pressures.

Management-Oriented Computing

Given that the orientation of computing to management, planning, and politics is the primary determinant of policy-analysis performance, it is necessary to understand better the factors which lead computing to serve these functions. The correlations in Table 8.19 show that technology continues to be a major influence, along with less potent environmental and structural influences. Cities with computing more oriented to management, planning, and political functions have the same pattern of advanced technology that is found in cities with high policy-analysis performance. They have a high degree of automation, sophisticated automation, and extensive reporting capacity. They also have a similar pattern of structural arrangements. Involvement of databank users, particularly top managers but also analysts and the departments, is positively related to management-oriented computing; involvement of elected officials is negatively, but not significantly, related. Greater decentralization of control over databanks also is positively and significantly related, whereas centralization of computing in a single independent installation again appears related but less influential.

The organizational context is significantly related to management-oriented computing, but the community environment is not. Professional management practices are the key organizational influence. This suggests that neither a reformed nor a partisan government is more conducive than the other to developing automated databanks which serve management, planning, and political uses. Professionalism could be characteristic of either form of government.

The independent contributions of advanced technology, classical and participatory structure, organizational context, and community environmental factors were estimated through stepwise multiple regression analysis (Table 8.20). The latter analysis further supports advanced technology and professionalism as major explanators of management-oriented computing. Professional management practices, a key indicator of reformism, explains one-third of the variation among cities. Sophistication of databank reports, a key indicator of advanced technology, explains an additional 9 percent of the variance. Neither structural policies nor design policies explain an important component of the remaining variation among cities (Table 8.20).

In other words, cities with automated databanks oriented to serving the information and decision needs of city officials tend to be professionally oriented and technologically advanced. Hence it is likely that the professional orientation leads city officials to demand automated databanks which serve a variety of functions, and also leads city officials to use these databanks, creating still greater demand. It is further likely that the advanced technology in these cities is both a response to, and a facilitator of, such demand.

Power Shifts

From the foregoing analyses, it is clear that advanced technology leads to automated databanks that serve multiple information and decision needs, and that are influential in affecting the decisions of city officials. However, Downs (1967) and others (Bell 1973; Ellul 1964; Laudon 1974; Lowi 1967, 1972) have expressed concern that high technology would shift greater power to a technocratic elite within the government. In particular, planners, analysts, and other staff groups who are technically educated and know how to use computer technology are expected to gain power from greater use of automated databanks by the government. These power shifts might, or might not, be at the expense of top managers and elected officials, but generally they are expected to result in lessened influence for these officials.

Technocratic power shifts do result from automated databanks, and the number of databanks explains 35 percent of the variance in our cities on power shifts.

$$\text{Number of automated databanks} \xrightarrow{\;r = .59\;} \text{Technocratic power shifts}$$

The greater the number of automated databanks, the greater the likelihood that power gains will be realized by planners, management analysts, and other technically oriented policy analysts in the city. Because the analysts tend to be most involved in the design of policy analyses, it is very likely that the analyses are designed with their assumptions, values, and rationality. Since these frequently bear little relation to those of top management or elected officials, it is not surprising that these officials fail to realize power gains. In fact, theory suggests they are likely to experience power losses to the technocratic elites, which are better able to rationalize their particular policy positions through analyses based on automated databanks. The greater the number of databanks, the greater the variety and sophistication of information and databank reports that can be marshaled for uses by the technocrats. To the extent that the information is compelling, and our earlier analysis indicated that information (policy analyses) based on automated databanks is somewhat influential in shaping city officials' decisions, the technocratic elites gain additional influence.

This relationship between databank automation and technocratic power shifts tends to support a technocratic model of the politics of computing in local government. The technocratic model suggests that computing, like most high technology, will be controlled by experts with specialized skills in the use of computing—technocrats. They will control the design, development, and use of technology, for only they understand its operation, potential, and limits.

But technocrats are only one of several kinds of officials who gain power from their use of automated databanks, which is a serious problem to the technocratic model. Generally, the technocratic model assumes that power shifts only to the technocrats. Consequently, the technocratic model fails to explain the fact that, in many cities, automated databanks and operational systems have shifted power to bureaucrats and politicians as well as technocrats (Table 8.7).

Therefore, we suggest a more comprehensive model of the politics of computing in local government, which we call "reinforcement politics." The reinforcement-politics model is developed in our earlier analyses of power shifts (Kraemer and Dutton 1979) and is also suggested in other research on computer impacts (Hoffman 1977). At the broadest level, this model suggests that computer-based systems tend to follow and reinforce the existing pattern of power relationships, whether that pattern be centralized in technocrats, bureaucrats, or politicians, or decentralized and fragmented. Computing reallocates power or influence by accentuating existing inequalities of influence. That is, computing seldom shifts power away from those who control governmental decision-making. In local government, the reinforcement-politics model suggests that computing will increase the decision-making effectiveness of managers in reform governments, mayors in strong-mayor governments, and departments and planners in governments with departmental autonomy.

The reinforcement-politics model provides a plausible explanation of why the nature of power shifts varies across cities (Table 8.7). It might be that computing tends to reinforce the influence of those officials in control, rather than to shift influence to a particular type of official. Because the influence structures of local governments vary, so might the nature of power shifts. In order to test the reinforcement hypothesis, we next explore the relationship between the structure of influence within a city and power shifts. If the reinforcement hypothesis is valid, then those in control should gain, and certainly not lose, power as a result of computing.

Table 8.21 describes the relationship between power shifts and several independent variables that tend to reflect the influence structures of local governments. Generally, power shifts tend to conform to the structure of influence within the city, thereby supporting the reinforcement-politics model (Table 8.21). In strong-mayor cities, computing tends to shift greater influence to the mayor,

Table 8.21
**Pearson Correlations between Selected Independent Variables and Power Shifts
to Managers, Mayors, Councils, Planner Analysts, and Departments[a]**

	Power Shifts to:[b]				
Independent Variables	Manager	Mayor	Council	Planner/ Analyst	Departments
Structure					
Strong-mayor city	-.22	.38	-.03	.12	-.13
Council-manager city	.22	-.37	.09	-.23	.05
Size and Complexity					
Total population	-.31	-.03	-.20	.39	.41
Government expenditures	-.26	-.15	.03	.29	.46

[a]Adapted from Kraemer and Dutton (1979:99).
[b]Marginals for these dependent variables are presented in Table 8.7.

while in council-manager cities, computing tends to shift influence to the manager. In larger cities with more complex and decentralized influence structures, automated databanks are most extensively developed ($r = .53$) and computing tends to shift power away from the top manager and toward the planners and the operating departments, which already are likely to enjoy more autonomy than their counterparts in smaller cities. And where mayors and councils are influential in computing decisions, managers are less likely to gain power as a result of computing.

Summary

Our findings tend to support a reform approach to the implementation of automated databanks. The reform approach is suggested by the importance of advanced technology and professionalism to policy-analysis performance. The degree, sophistication, and orientation of databank automation are especially powerful in shaping performance. And an organizational context characterized by professional management practices is importantly related to the orientation of automated databanks.

The approaches of cities toward socio-technical design appear to be unimportant to policy-analysis performance. This is probably because the way general computing support is implemented in the cities is less important than the way databanks are controlled and specific policy analyses are designed. Indeed the analysis lends minor support to a participatory structural arrangement involving decentralized databanks, user involvement in design of analyses, and centralization of the computer resource in a single independent installation.

When power-shift impacts are considered, one can make a better case for stressing participatory-structure policies—in particular, involving top managers, departments, and elected officials, as well as technocrats, in the design of databank analyses. Such participation might counterbalance the current dominance over the design of analyses by technocratic elites in the larger and most automated cities, and might give greater influence to the top managers and elected officials, who are accountable, in the end, for policy decisions based on databank analysis. And generally, more decentralized, participatory structures might facilitate the incorporation of a broader array of interests in the design, analysis, and interpretation of computer-based policy analyses. Currently, the process of reinforcement politics tends to exclude those interests not reflected in the status quo; that is, those interests that are not influential in the local decision-making process.

But it also presents an interesting dilemma. While formal accountability might be greater, policy analysis appears least effective when top managers and elected officials are involved in design. This might occur because many of these officials have already made up their minds—and the number of opinions to change is larger—or because some officials try to bias the analysis, refuse to accept unfavorable results, or otherwise politicize the analysis. In contrast, policy analysis is most effective when technocrats (planners, analysts) are involved in design. This probably is because the technocrats are perceived as a more independent, objective source, which produces quality analysis without serving any particular political interest. Their analyses are more influential because top officials' opinions are not solidified in advance and the number of opinions to be changed by the analysis is small.

Policy Recommendations

On the basis of the foregoing findings, it is possible to prescribe several implementation policies for databanks in support of policy analysis and similar information-processing tasks. Although automated databanks in our cities are less extensive and less sophisticated than anticipated, we recommend automation because the payoffs are significantly greater than from unautomated databanks. In addition, we recommend that cities generally follow the reform approach to databank automation. However, these same policies also are likely to enhance the influence of planners and analysts in the policy-making process—a side effect of increasing the rationality of that process.

Technological Development

In accord with the reform approach, cities should adopt the advanced-technology perspective and should proceed as follows.

1. *Automate.* Automation of urban databanks and operational databanks appears to have significant positive impact on quality, utilization, and effectiveness of information in decision-making. These performance payoffs are accompanied by improvements in the work environment of urban planners and, to a lesser extent, of management analysts.

2. *Automate a large number of databanks.* Computers can be used to automate operational databanks or urban databanks in support of one or more policy-analysis tasks: constituency analysis, needs assessment, urban planning, policy monitoring, municipal-services planning, and performance monitoring. Cities that have automated a large number of databanks tend to perform significantly better than cities that have automated a smaller number. Apparently, the automation of multiple databanks increases the total supply of data from which analysts and decision-makers can derive useful information. Possibly, the availability of large stores of data that can be manipulated rapidly and easily with the computer also increases their sensitivity to the potential uses of information and encourages them to use it.

3. *Develop sophisticated computer installations to support databank automation.* Advanced technology in the form of large computer-core capacities, modern operating systems, database management systems, and on-line storage and retrieval can greatly increase the computing power, storage capacity, file flexibility, and manipulation ease of databank files. The more powerful these support capabilities, the easier it is for analysts and decision-makers to digest the information they need for policy analysis from the databanks.

4. *Develop more sophisticated databank analyses and reports.* Cities that have automated sophisticated analysis and reporting capabilities (e.g., statistical analysis, graphic analysis, geo-based analysis) as part of databank automation perform significantly better

than cities without these features. Apparently, these features improve the objectivity, credibility, and richness of analyses and, consequently, their relative influence in urban policy-making.

5. *Develop automated databanks to serve multiple decision uses by multiple local officials.* The decision orientation of automated databanks is the greatest single explanator of performance. Databanks that serve management, planning, and political uses by a variety of analysts (urban planners, management analysts, budget analysts) and decision-makers (mayor, manager, council, department heads) have a significantly greater effect on decisions than databanks that serve few uses by a small group of decision-makers. Possibly, multiple use of the data in automated databanks by various officials creates greater collective understanding of the potential meanings, and reasonable interpretations for decision use. This might not only reduce conflict over the results of policy analyses, but also increase the area of decision agreement among policy-makers with competing interests. Consequently, analyses would be more influential in shaping decision outcomes.

6. *Develop the capability of producing many reports from automated databanks.* As might be expected from the foregoing recommendations, the number of reports also improves databank performance. It seems that a larger number of reports, especially when tailored to the decision needs of particular officials, have more utility than a single general-purpose report.

Structural Arrangements

Cities should follow participatory structural arrangements in databank automation.

1. *Centralize computing operations but decentralize control of databanks.* Relying on multiple sources of computing might appear to increase a city's flexibility. However, databank automation usually involves collecting data from several independent (automated and unautomated) sources, organizing it around common entities (people, property, money), and circulating it widely. Consequently, a centralized operation provides greater opportunity for exercising the coordination required to achieve uniform consolidation and wide circulation of the data. It also provides greater staff and technical capability to support databank analyses.

Even with a centralized installation and data consolidation, there will be multiple databanks in most cities, because more effective usage is served by decentralizing control in the hands of the owners or primary users. These people are most knowledgeable about the raw-data content and also about the continuously changing content which results from analysis. Consequently, they can make best use of the data and advise others in its use.

2. *Increase the involvement of all users in the design of databank analyses and reports.* Although only the involvement of analysts is significantly related to policy-analysis performance, we also recommend the involvement of top officials in design of databank analyses.[12] These officials are ultimately responsible for the outcomes of the analyses and the decisions based upon them, and top-official involvement should provide a counterbalance to potential excessive influence by the analysts. Analyst involvement is important too, of course, to ensure high-quality, objective results.

Socio-technical Design

Post-reformers have been concerned that databank automation might be extremely burdensome for analysts, top managers, and middle managers, who might be overloaded with information and information-processing tasks from computerization. Thus, postre-formers stress a human-relations orientation to design, where only the data relevant to prescribed and recurring decisions is automated, in order to reduce the workload, pressure, and change experienced by city officials and staff. Our findings do not support the post-reform concerns. City officials are basically positive in their evaluation of computing. Analysts perceive the work environment as either improved or not affected by databank automation. Differences among cities in their approach to socio-technical design have no appreciable affect on the officials' or the analysts' perceptions. Thus, the best approach to socio-technical design is to use advanced automation in support of extensive and sophisticated policy analyses.

Organizational Context

The organizational context within which automated databanks are used potentially places constraints on the optimal performance of computing. However, our research indicates that whether the organizational context is characterized by nonpartisan or partisan governmental structures is less important than whether it is characterized by professional management practices. Next to technological development, professional management practices are most importantly related to the orientation and performance of automated databanks. From a policy perspective, this suggests that all cities can improve the performance of automated databanks by increased emphasis on professionalism in the government.

Summary

Automation of databanks does result in more effective policy analysis. But the strategies that a city chooses to follow in implementing automated databanks affect the degree to which it receives improved performance. Early in the chapter, we argued that most cities have chosen a post-reform approach to implementation, consisting of appropriate technology, participatory structure, and a human-relations strategy in socio-technical design. Then we presented data indicating that a reform approach leads to more performance payoffs. Specifically, the analysis indicates that advanced technology and professional administration are the keys to improved performance. In addition, participatory strategies contribute to performance, but socio-technical design has no impact.

The data also indicate that databank automation shifts power to the policy analysts, primarily because they dominate the process of analysis. Consequently, we recommend greater involvement of top officials in design and implementation of analyses, because these officials are utlimately responsible for the outcomes of decisions based on analysis, and because their involvement will provide a counterbalance to the influence of analysts.

NOTES

1. Such policy analyses might include constituency analysis, needs assessment, urban planning, policy monitoring, municipal-services planning, or performance monitoring and evaluation.

2. While conditions tend to be temporally disaggregated also, most analyses of temporally disaggregated data are technically simple and routine within local governments. Therefore, we focus on geographically disaggregated data (Department of Civil Engineering, 1977).

3. Field investigators identified up to eight databanks in each city. In cities with more than eight databanks, the eight that were used most by planning and management analysts and decision makers were inventoried.

4. All cities have population databanks and 62 percent of the cities have these databanks automated. It is significant that the seven databanks common to at least one-fourth of the cities are all related to traditional physical-planning concerns of housing, land use, business, and transportation. In contrast, very few cities have databanks related to social-planning concerns of health, social welfare, employment, or crime. These databanks undoubtedly reflect the historical importance of various policy issues in the government, a recent interest in social indicators, and a dominant concern for physical development in the 42 cities.

5. This association is quite strong. The Pearson correlation between the index of the sophistication of data-processing installations in the city and the degree of urban data automation is .64, and the degree of automation of operational systems is .88.

6. These methods form a Guttman scale with a coefficient of reproducibility of .90. See the Appendix for construction of the scale.

7. Moreover, the difference in analytical power of these two analysis groupings is considerable. For example, *fixed-area* geo-based analysis severely limits the extent to which community conditions can be analyzed from multiple perspectives, from changing geographic boundaries, or in relation to entities that might split prearranged geographic units (e.g., analysis of freeway routes). *Multiple-area* geo-based analysis allows an infinite number of possibilities, to fit both different analytical categories and the needs of different users of geo-based information.

8. These perceptions of bias in computer-based reports and the dispute about such reports is surprising. The perceptions might be related to a tendency of public officials to regard sophisticated analyses with suspicion. The analyses may be overly complex, poorly presented, or poorly understood. However, it also is possible that the perceptions of public officials may be related to increased understanding about the bias underlying all analyses and that this perception is directly related to the sophistication of the analyses performed in different governments. In this sense, automated databanks may contribute to greater realization on the part of public officials and policy analysts of the sensitivity of their results to differing methods of analysis, and to differing geographic or social boundaries used in the analysis.

9. In general, the earliest adopters have a higher level of automation, both in terms of quantity of applications and level of sophistication. The Pearson correlation between the year of adoption and the number of automated applications is −.23.

10. The late adoption of databanks might also be related to the level of instability in computing technology and operations. Some observers believe that high levels of instability are endemic to the data-processing function because data-processing managers are constantly trying to keep up with the state-of-the-art of computing technology. While our cities vary significantly in the levels of technological instability

which they experience, overall they experience only moderate levels. Within the last year, 8 of our cities have changed major equipment vendor, 10 have changed the priorities of applications in development, and 9 have changed the level of programming language used. This moderate level of instability reflects the appropriate-technology strategy that our cities have taken in implementing their databank applications.

11. Over one-fifth of our cities have reorganized EDP during the past year, either changing the departmental location of computing (10 percent) or consolidating/dividing EDP installations (12 percent). Five percent have changed the physical location of the computer installation. And fully one-fifth have changed top EDP management within the past year. These structural changes further reflect the fact that computing is still in a developmental stage. They might have harmful consequences for successful use of databanks in policy analysis, because this information-processing task is complex and difficult to manage without the added burden created by disrupting support services such as computing.

12. Top official involvement is so negligible in most cities that we are unable to examine its impact empirically.

REFERENCES

Altshuler, Alan A. 1965. *The City Planning Process: A Political Analysis.* Ithaca: Cornell University Press.

Bell, Daniel. 1973. *The Coming of Post-Industrial Society.* New York: Basic Books.

Braybrooke, David and Charles E. Lindblom. 1963. *A Strategy for Decision.* New York: Free Press.

Brewer, Gary D. 1974. *Politicians, Bureaucrats and Consultants.* New York: Basic Books.

Department of Civil Engineering. 1977. *Regional Environmental Systems: An Assessment of RANN Projects.* Seattle: University of Washington.

Downs, Anthony. 1967. "A Realistic Look at the Final Payoffs from Urban Data Systems." *Public Administration Review*, 27(3):204–10.

Dutton, William H. and Kenneth L. Kraemer. 1977. "Technology and Urban Management: The Power Payoffs of Computing." *Administration and Society*, 9(3):305–40.

——. 1978. "Management Utilization of Computers in American Local Governments." *Communications of the ACM*, 21(3):206–18.

Dykman, John W. 1961. "Planning and Decision Theory." *Journal of the American Institute of Planners*, 27:335–43.

Ellul, J. 1964. *The Technological Society*. New York: Vintage.

Greenberger, Martin; Matthew A. Crenson; and Brian L. Crissey. 1976a. "Modeling and the Political Process." *Computers and Society*, 7(1):3–14.

———. 1976b. *Models in the Policy Process*. New York: Russell Sage Foundation.

Hair, Albert M., Jr. 1965. "EDP Offers Key to Information in City Hall." *Public Management*, 47:80–85.

Hearle, Edward F. R. and Raymond O. Mason. 1963. *A Data Processing System for State and Local Governments*. Englewood Cliffs, N.J.: Prentice-Hall.

Hoffman, Eric P. 1977. "Technology, Values and Political Power in the Soviet Union: Do Computers Matter?" In F. J. Fleron, Jr., ed., *Technology and Communist Culture: Socio-cultural Impact of Technology under Socialism*, pp. 397–436. New York: Praeger.

Kling, Rob. 1974. "Computers and Social Power." *Computers and Society*, 5(3): 6–11.

———. 1978a. "Automated Welfare Client Tracking and Service Integration: The Political Economy of Computing." *Communications of the ACM*, 21(6):424–93.

———. 1978b. "Information Systems in Policymaking: The Influences of Computer Technology and Organizational Arrangements." *Telecommunications Policy*, 2(1): 3–12.

———. 1978c. "Information Systems as Social Resources in Policymaking," *Proceedings of the 1978 ACM National Conference*. Washington, D.C.: Association for Computing Machinery.

Kraemer, Kenneth L. 1973. *Policy Analysis in Local Government*. Washington, D.C.: International City Management Association.

Kraemer, Kenneth L. and William H. Dutton. 1979. "The Interests Served by Technological Reform." *Administration and Society*, 11(1):80–106.

Kraemer, Kenneth L.; William H. Dutton; and Joseph R. Matthews. 1975. "Municipal Computers." *Urban Data Service Report*. Washington, D.C.: International City Management Association.

Kraemer, Kenneth L. and John L. King. 1977. *Computers and Local Government, Vol. 1*. New York: Praeger.

Kraemer, Kenneth L.; William H. Mitchel; Myron E. Weiner; and Oliver E. Dial. 1974. *Integrated Municipal Information Systems*. New York: Praeger.

Laudon, Kenneth C. 1974. *Computers and Bureaucratic Reform*. New York: Wiley.

Lawler, Edward E., III and John G. Rhode. 1976. *Information and Control in Organizations*. Pacific Palisades, Calif.: Goodyear.

Lee, Douglas. 1973. "Requiem for Large Scale Planning Models." *Journal of the American Institute of Planners*, 39(2):136–78.

Lindblom, Charles E. 1968. *The Policy-Making Process*. Englewood Cliffs, N.J.: Prentice-Hall.

Lineberry, Robert L. and Ira Sharkansky. 1978. *Urban Politics and Public Policy*. New York: Harper and Row.

Lowi, Theodore. 1967. "Machine Politics—Old and New." *Public Interest*, 9: 83–92.

———. 1972. "Government and Politics: Blurring of Sector Lines, Use of New Elites— from One Vantage Point," In *Information Technology: Some Critical Implications for Decision Makers*, pp. 131–48. New York: Conference Board.

Lucas, Henry C., Jr. 1975. *Why Information Systems Fail.* New York: Columbia University Press.

Meltzner, Arnold J. 1971. *The Politics of City Revenue.* Berkeley: University of California Press.

Pack, Howard and Janet R. Pack. 1977. "The Resurrection of the Urban Development Model." *Policy Analysis,* 3(3):407–27.

Parker, John K. 1965. "Operating a City Databank." *Public Automation,* 1.

Pounds, William F. 1969. "The Process of Problem Finding." *Industrial Management Review,* 11(1):1–19.

Quinn, Robert. 1976. "The Impacts of a Computerized Information System on the Integration and Coordination of Human Services." *Public Administration Review,* 36(2):166–74.

Simon, Herbert A. 1960. *The New Science of Management Decision.* New York: Harper and Row.

——. 1961. "Decision Making and Planning." In Harvey Perloff, ed., *Planning and the Urban Community,* pp. 188–92. Pittsburgh, Pa.: University of Pittsburgh Press.

——. 1971. "Designing Organizations for an Information-Rich World." In Martin Greenberger, ed., *Computers, Communications and the Public Interest.* Baltimore, Md.: Johns Hopkins University Press.

Webber, Melvin M. 1970. "The Politics of Information." In Norman K. Denzin, ed., *The Values of Social Science.* Chicago: Aldine Publishing.

Westin, Alan. 1972. "Information Technology and Public-Decision Making." In *Harvard University Program on Technology and Society: A Final Review,* pp. 59–67. Cambridge, Mass.: Harvard University.

Part Three

CHAPTER NINE
Successful Management Policies

THE PRECEDING chapters have provided an intensive analysis of information-processing tasks ranging from traffic-ticket processing to policy analysis. This chapter provides a broader focus on computing in local government by comparing findings across these information-processing tasks. These findings allow us to offer several practical recommendations for managers in organizations involved with the implementation of computer-based information systems. After presenting these recommendations, the chapter returns to the themes with which this study began, for our findings underline the degree to which the payoffs of technology-as-an-administrative-reform are contingent on both the politics and management of organizations.

Performance Outcomes

We have found that the primary impacts of computing sometimes are positive and in line with the predictions of early literature (Hoos 1960; Leavitt and Whisler 1958; Simon 1965). Our comparisons of automated operations demonstrate that computing has made better information available for planning and management decision-making, provided greater administrative control, and improved operational performance. Moreover, in four of our six information-processing tasks, automation accomplished its intended purpose (Table 9.1). For example, automated traffic-ticket processing and patrol-officer support improved the operational performance of clerks and patrol officers. Automated budget control accomplished its major objective of providing greater administrative control, while policy analysis made better information available for decision-making—actually influencing the decision-making process in local government.

Automation also has resulted in several unintended but positive impacts. Uniformly, computing has created a more positive work environment for users. And in the case of budget control, computing had several secondary benefits, including the provision of better information for decision-making and the improved operational performance of budgeting activities at both the department and central-management levels. In short, computing has sometimes accomplished its intended purposes and has served several positive secondary purposes as well.

We have also found, however, that computing can have negative impacts. First, computing has sometimes failed to accomplish its intended purposes, as in the case of two of our six-information-

Table 9.1
Intended and Unintended Performance Outcomes of Automation by Task

Information-Processing Tasks	Performance Outcomes of Automation	
	Intended	Unintended
Traffic-Ticket Processing (record-keeping)	Improved operational performance	Positive work environment
Detective Investigative Support (record searching)	Operational performance *not* improved by local automation	Positive work environment
Patrol Officer Support (record searching)	Improved operational performance	Positive work environment
Police Manpower Allocation (sophisticated analytics)	Neither decision-making nor operational performance improved	Positive work environment Bureaucratic power shifts
Budget Control (process control/printing)	Greater administrative control	Better decision-making Improved operational performance Positive work environment Bureaucratic power shifts
Policy Analysis (record restructuring)	Better decision-making	Positive work environment Bureaucratic power shifts

processing tasks. Local automation had only a marginal, and somewhat mixed, impact on the operational performance of detectives. Also, automated police manpower-allocation programs had a negligible effect on either decision-making or operational performance. Second, even in those cases where computing accomplished its intended purposes, performance has varied greatly among local governments.

Third, computing also has had secondary impacts which are sometimes negative, largely unintended, often unperceived, and significant because they concern the power relationships within the government. For instance, computing results in a variety of bureaucratic power shifts for decision-oriented applications such as police manpower allocation, budget control, and policy analysis. In each case, computing has tended to reinforce the existing patterns of influence in local government. Automated patrol allocation reinforced the influence of central managers in the police department in dealing with police district managers. Automated budget control reinforced the influence of central management in relation to departmental managers. Automated databanks for policy analysis reinforced the influence of professional managers in city-manager cities, or mayors in strong-mayor cities, and of department heads and technical staff in cities with highly decentralized and fragmented structures.

These findings indicate that the benefits of computing are more problematic than suggested by the promoters of computer technology. Computing sometimes fails to accomplish its intended purposes, and even in those cases where it succeeds, performance varies greatly. Finally, computing has political implications for relationships among local government officials. Given this pattern of impacts, it was especially important for our study to explore (1) which management policies might explain why some local governments have been more successful than others in achieving the intended benefits of computing, and (2) which management policies might influence the power relationships among local government officials.

Management Policies for
Successful Automation

Local government approaches to the management of computer technology are off-target. For the most part, local governments have heeded the advice of post-reform advocates over that of reform advocates. The management strategies for implementing automation in most local governments are characterized by appropriate technology, participatory management, human relations, and a mix of a professional and a political administrative context. Yet our research suggests that the most successful policy–technology mix combines aspects of the reform approach with the post-reform approach. Most importantly, local governments should carefully consider the merits of advanced technology and a professional administrative context for the implementation of computer-based information systems. Figure 9.1 organizes our comparative findings by showing successful policies in contrast with current policies for each information-processing task.

Technological Development

Technological development is an important perspective for understanding the success of implementation. In fact, technological development is associated with the performance of computing for nearly every information-processing task investigated. It might well be the *most* important perspective for understanding the performance of computing in traffic-ticket processing, detective and patrol support, and policy analysis. And technological development was found to affect clearly the performance of budget reporting and monitoring applications. Only for patrol manpower-allocation systems is the role of technological development unclear, owing to the minimal technological variation among police departments.

An advanced-technology strategy is uniformly linked to the success of implementation. In general, automation tends to show higher levels of performance for every information-processing task when compared to manual operations. And the better-performing automated sites tend to be those with the more advanced technological development. That is, higher performance is associated with high levels of automation, more sophisticated applications, more sophisticated personnel, higher levels of computer utilization, and greater routinization. In no case is such advanced technology associated with lower performance. Therefore Figure 9.1 shows advanced technology as the recommended approach to technological development for every IPT except patrol-allocation analysis. Even in this case, though, advanced technology is our tentative recommendation.

The success of advanced technology has a rather straightforward explanation. While many so-called advancements in computer technology are cosmetic, many also are incremental improvements that cumulatively create fundamental improvements in the value of computing to users. For example, the increased reliability and storage capacity of modern hardware is a major benefit to users. Also, on-line processing increases the speed and ease of access to computerized files, as well as increasing the accuracy and timeliness of data by permitting the immediate and continuous updating of files from various locations. In addition, direct personal access via terminals in user work areas often enhances the user orientation of automation. Moreover, recent technological advances—such as database management systems and generalized statistical software packages—facilitate more complex and flexible restructuring, reaggregation, analysis, and presentation of data in computer-based files. In short, many of the advancements in computer technology over the last two decades might be considered analogous to the advancement represented by moving from candles to an incandescent lamp, rather than simply increasing the intensity of a lamp.

However, the current approach of local governments toward technological development approximates appropriate technology more closely than it does advanced technology. While there are examples of leading-edge technological developments in nearly every local government function, the state-of-the-art in most local governments is far behind the leading edge. In fact, local-government computing is rather primitive in most application areas. Only in the areas of detective investigative support and patrol officer support have most local governments tended to take an advanced approach. Thus, only for these two IPTs are the current approaches of local governments on-target in relation to our policy recommendations (Figure 9.1).

Current trends do not point toward a bright future for cities. There continue to be advancements in the available computer hardware and software to support such tasks as detective investigative support, patrol allocation analysis, and budget control. But the widespread diffusion of the more advanced, as opposed to the more conventional technologies is unlikely. In fact, with the decline of federal funding from the Law Enforcement Assistance Administration, there is likely to be a slowdown in the adoption of advanced technology even for the police. Only in the area of budget control is the current fiscal crisis likely to spur interest in the wider adoption of technologically advanced applications, such as highly integrated financial-accounting systems.

Structural Arrangements

Structural arrangements shape the success of implementation for most information-processing tasks. Only in the case of patrol officer support and policy analysis do structural arrangements appear to be relatively unimportant to performance, but some indications point to a small role there too.

The most successful strategy in terms of structural arrangements appears to be highly contingent on the routineness of automated information processing. The classical-structure strategy is clearly beneficial for the implementation of traffic-ticket processing applications. In contrast, the participatory-structures strategy tends to be more beneficial for the implementation of detective and patrol officer support as well as patrol allocation, budget control, and policy analysis.

One interpretation of this discrepancy across tasks is that the appropriate structural arrangements are unique to each task to which computing is applied. An alternative interpretation is that there are particular classes of information-processing tasks for which classical or participatory strategies might be most appropriate. Our study supports this latter interpretation. Classical strategies are more appropriate for routine tasks, whereas participatory strategies appear most appropriate for nonroutine tasks. Traffic-ticket processing is representative of routine tasks. These are generally clerical record-keeping and calculating-printing tasks, which involve large volume, routine, and repetitive operations, performed according to standard operating procedures. Computing for such routine clerical tasks is not a support tool; rather, computing is the essential tool by which the task is performed. Computing plays a similar role in other routine operations, such as utility and tax billing, financial accounting, payroll processing, and regular reporting. Consequently, these also might benefit from a classical strategy for implementation of computing (Table 9.2).

Table 9.2
Tasks Illustrative of Variation in the Routiness of
Automated Information Processing

Routineness	*Illustrations*
High—strict standard operating procedures (SOPs), great repetition, consistent purposes for use	Traffic-ticket processing
Low—flexible SOPs, little repetition, changing purposes for use	Budget control Patrol officer support Detective investigative support Patrol manpower-allocation analysis Policy analysis

Budget control, manpower allocation, policy analysis, and investigative support illustrate nonroutine tasks. They are distinguished by their need for more flexible, less routine, and more individualistic computer support. Detectives must imaginatively use many data files to distill the most useful information from criminal leads that vary greatly from case to case. Likewise, budget analysts need the capability to examine expenditures from multiple perspectives—program, department, project, line item. Consequently, computing tends to be used as a support tool for these tasks—a tool which involves considerable discretion by the user. Budget analysts, manpower analysts, patrol officers and detectives need systems that are responsive to their needs and sensitive to the kinds of quantitative and qualitative information they need. In such nonroutine tasks, user involvement, decentralized control, and other participatory structural arrangements are likely to be more successful.[1]

Current structural arrangements of local governments are either a mixture of classical and participatory arrangements or in line with a participatory perspective. The only exception is the correct use of classical strategies in traffic-ticket processing. The common use of participatory strategies is understandable in light of the initial resistance of government personnel to the automation of operations important to their work. Participatory arrangements have traditionally been used to prevent staff resistance by alleviating the participants' fears about the possible impacts of computing and by gaining their support through involvement (Dutton and Kraemer 1978). Not only does the process of involvement develop support per se, but involvement also potentially increases the influence of government personnel over the design of computer applications and, consequently, increases the utility of the applications for them. While participatory strategies might ensure that systems are responsive to user needs, such strategies are unlikely to generate extensive change in the operations of user agencies. In fact, participatory arrangements are likely to have a braking effect on the extent of operational change attempted and, consequently, on the need for advanced technology to support it.

Current trends suggest that cities will continue to follow a participatory strategy. Trends toward participatory structures in the police function are becoming prevalent, especially in the larger cities where police computer installations are becoming common. The dynamics of organizational politics, which promote the fragmentation of local-government bureaucracy as well as computing operations, reinforces the adoption of participatory arrangements. Therefore, the structural arrangements associated with the implementation of most information-processing tasks are likely to be pressured toward the participation strategy, even if this strategy is not always beneficial, as in the case of routine tasks.

Socio-technical Design

Socio-technical design can be considered the least important perspective for understanding the success of implementation (Figure 9.1). However, for two tasks—detective support and budget control—socio-technical design had an important role in predicting the performance of computing operations. Furthermore, other analyses show socio-technical design to be especially important when considering the performance of computing at the *individual* rather than the task level (Kraemer, Danziger, and Dutton 1978). Thus, we do believe that the socio-technical-design perspective should be carefully considered during the implementation process.

When linked to the performance of computing operations, a human-relations strategy appears most successful. Interestingly, the two tasks—investigative support and budget control—in which human relations were found especially important are the two in which decision-makers are often the direct users of computing. In each of these tasks, the best human-relations strategy appears to be the design of systems which permit users to access easily information that is more accurate and timely. This is a difficult task in both police and finance information systems. Not only is the information difficult to keep timely and accurate, but the users of such information are likely to have a lower tolerance for error than many other users.

The current approach of cities toward socio-technical design more closely approaches human relations than task efficiency for every IPT investigated (Figure 9.1). Cities have generally implemented systems that are quite sensitive to the work environment of users. Thus, we find widespread support for computer operations and a general belief that computing improves the work environment of local-government personnel. Positive assessments are especially pronounced for those directly using the technology, such as traffic-ticket clerks, as compared with more indirect users of computing, such as top managers.

Current trends suggest continued adherence to a human-relations approach for many of the same reasons that cities will move toward participatory management. Yet as public concerns for productivity and economy gain ever-increasing significance, moves toward classical structures and task efficiency in design might become a concern of public officials who hope to build more confidence in public bureaucracies.[2]

Organizational Context

The organizational context is one of the least controllable perspectives but certainly an important one for understanding the success of implementation. Indeed, the organizational context is associated with the performance of computing in investigative support, budget control, and policy analysis, though not in traffic-ticket processing.

When the organizational context is associated with performance, a professional administration is almost uniformly more successful in the implementation of computing than is a more political administration. Given that computing was promoted early on as a tool of administrative reform (Laudon 1974; Dutton and Kraemer 1978), it is not surprising that the reformed and professionalized organization is normally more congenial to the implementation and use of computing.

However, patrol-allocation analysis represents an interesting exception. For this task, a political context appears to be associated with more successful performance. This might indicate that the political context is more congenial to the adoption and use of automation for manpower allocation. We believe that an alternative, and perhaps more plausible, interpretation is that a political context creates a greater need for the reallocation of manpower on the basis of rational (need for service), as opposed to political, criteria. And the use of automated patrol-allocation analyses is a means for professionals within the police department to overcome their political context, since it aids them in the documentation and legitimation of their allocation decisions. Thus, the introduction of automated patrol-allocation analysis within a political context will effect the greatest changes in allocations and performance.

Currently, the organizational context of most local governments is mixed. Most local governments have aspects of both professionalism and politics. The council-manager form of government has been widely adopted but is facing increased criticism as local politics becomes characterized more by conflict than by consensus. The development and adoption of professional management practices also is widespread and fashionable, as illustrated by the spread of planning, programming, and budgeting (PPB), zero-based budgeting (ZBB), and management by objectives (MBO) budgeting techniques. But here too there is a growing disenchantment with professional management. And most recently there is the less professional practice of resorting to the tax cut as the means for achieving economy and efficiency in government.

Thus, trends are in flux. There are currents toward both greater political administration and greater professional administration. Whichever direction is taken will affect the success of computing operations. And to the degree that the shift is toward the principles of politics as opposed to the principles of professionalism, the performance of local government computing operations is likely to suffer.

The Community Environment

Local government managers operate within an environment that is more or less outside of their short-run control. However, the community's environment is likely to shape and condition the performance of computing operations. At the extreme, critics of reform and post-reform efforts suggest that organizational performance is determined by the organization's community environment and that, as a consequence, the organization's reform efforts will be ineffective.

This does not seem to be the case. In general, management strategies for shaping the technology, structure, socio-technical design, and organizational context of computing operations are more important in explaining performance variations than is the community environment. Nonetheless, environmental variables are of some significance to several information-processing tasks. For example, cities without slack resources are somewhat more likely to experience higher levels of performance for policy analysis. However, we have found management strategies to be far more relevant than environmental variables to gaining an understanding of implementation success in local government automation.

Implementation Recommendations and Policies

Recommendations for Managers: Manage the Technology

Computers clearly can increase the effectiveness and efficiency of local government operations, but many cities have failed to realize such benefits from computing and also face new problems as a result of computerization. However, some cities are realizing the benefits because their top officials manage the technology well. Unfortunately, this is not the usual situation. Some officials fail to manage the technology, for they consider its problems to be inevitable, in the domain of technical experts, and probably outweighed by the benefits. Others abandon responsibility for the technology, for they consider the problems to be inevitable, unresolvable by top management or anyone else, and not outweighed by the benefits. Still other officials simply mismanage by excusing the technology and looking "elsewhere" for the source of problems with computing. They place such an abiding faith in the technology that they always look to people as the cause of problems and more technology as the solution (Dutton and Kraemer, 1979).

In contrast to these responses, this study suggests that managers should recognize problems as symptoms of a technology that is being poorly implemented for the given task. Thus, local government officials should concentrate their attention on the management of the technology. Many problems are resolvable; solutions are often in the domain of managers rather than technical experts, and the benefits are likely to outweigh the costs if properly managed.

There are two primary considerations in approaching the management of technologies like computing. One concerns the role that managers should play in the implementation process. The other concerns specific policies for implementation of the technology.

The Management Role

The management of computing and other high technologies cannot be left in the hands of the technical experts. While everyone in the organization necessarily has some role in the management of technology—in that his action or inaction affects its performance—the greatest role in the management of computing and other organization-wide technologies[3] devolves upon chief executives and the top managers within the various user departments and agencies.

If these managers neglect their role, the consequences are far-reaching and negative. So, if top managers are to implement computer automation successfully, they should consider the following actions.

1. *Take an active role in the management of the government's information systems.* Top managers must face the key decisions about their government's information systems. Managers can avoid these decisions by ignoring them or by delegating them to subordinates, but they cannot avoid the overall responsibility for the results of these decisions. When large expenditures for computer equipment produce few tangible results, top management is responsible. When the information practices of the government bureaucracy appear "out of control," top management is responsible. By taking responsibility for computerized information systems, top managers recognize who is ultimately responsible. More importantly, managers can decide which decisions will receive their attention, which will be personally decided, and which will be delegated to others.

2. *Clarify the purposes of the information systems and set priorities for the kinds of systems needed to assist the government.* The toughest policy issue for chief executives and department managers concerns the

allocation of resources to alternative kinds of information systems. Priority-setting should not be left to the computer experts, for their attention is focused on technical feasibility, and on the maintenance and enhancement of the data-processing function. Nor should these priorities be left only to the department users, for computing resources are scarce, while the appetite of users for computer applications can be insatiable. Top management should actively participate in the task and critically review the recommendations of the computer specialists and the department users.

3. *Once priorities are established and adoption decisions are made, concentrate on the important management decisions concerning the implementation process.* These decisions concern the best policies for the technological development, structural arrangement, socio-technical design, and organizational context of computing, to which we now turn.

Policies for the Management of Automated Information Systems

The preceding chapters demonstrate the importance of maintaining a mix of reform and post-reform strategies for the implementation of computerized information systems. Indicators of technology, structure, socio-technical design, and organizational context intertwine in explaining successful and unsuccessful performance. In addition, different reform and post-reform strategies explain the success of information-processing tasks. Furthermore, some factors outside the control of managers impinge on the performance of computing. Nonetheless, patterns of successful implementation are observable from the analysis and suggest strategies within each of the four decision areas.

Technological Development

The performance of computing is generally better in cities that have implemented more advanced technology. Cities should take the *advanced-technology strategy* when increased performance appears to be worth the dollar costs of increases in the level and sophistication of computing hardware, software, and personnel. Cities should do the following.

1. *Automate.* Automation generally provides information benefits,

increased efficiency and effectiveness, and new services. Furthermore, the performance payoffs are accompanied by improvements in the work environment of government personnel.

2. *Automate early.* The routinization of automated applications—the extent to which they have become an accepted, routine part of government operations—is often important to the performance of computing. The longer an application has been around, the more likely it is to have the "bugs" worked out of it and to be commonly used.

3. *Automate rapidly.* Given that technological development is associated with improved performance, and technological instability is not associated with performance, rapid development is likely to be more effective than a conservative "go slow" strategy.

4. *Automate a large proportion of the operations involved in the information-processing task.* The automation of a small segment of an information-processing task often improves only one part of an integrated and sequential process and, as a result, the total task is not appreciably affected. In fact, the automation of only small segments may create bottlenecks in manual operations. The comprehensiveness of automation within a task is important to achieving the full benefits.

5. *Develop sophisticated applications with on-line inquiry capabilities.* On-line processing provides easier access to more up-to-date information and improved performance for nearly every kind of information-processing task.

6. *Recruit experienced, sophisticated data-processing personnel.* Advanced technological development requires experienced and sophisticated staff. It is unrealistic to expect that an inexperienced and minimally trained staff can implement and support advanced automation. This recommendation might require that local governments repeatedly adjust the salaries of their local computing personnel to approximate those of equivalent positions in the private sector.

7. *Obtain sophisticated computing hardware.* Sophisticated on-line processing requires sophisticated computer hardware. The small, batch computer environment of most local governments cannot support advanced automation.

8. *Develop applications to serve multiple decision uses by multiple local officials.* Automated files can serve management, planning, and political uses by a variety of analysts (urban planners, management analysts, budget analysts) and decision-makers (mayor, council,

manager, department heads), as well as serve more immediate operational needs. For example, multiple reports, especially tailored to the decision needs of particular officials, have more utility than a single general-purpose report.

Structural Arrangements

The structural arrangements associated with higher levels of performance depend on the routineness or nonroutineness of the information-processing task that is automated. Therefore, our structural recommendations differ with the kind of user task being considered (Table 9.3).

Routine tasks like traffic-ticket processing are characterized by standard operating procedures, high repetitiveness, large processing volumes, and consistent purposes over time. The automation of such routine tasks should generally follow classical structural arrangements. For routine tasks, cities should proceed as follows.

1. *Centralize computing operations.* Relying on multiple sources of computing might appear to increase an agency's flexibility. But this is not the case for routine information-processing tasks. For routine tasks, it is more likely that the agency is highly dependent on each of the multiple sources for an integrated and sequential process, which increases the agency's difficulty in coordinating and processing information.

2. *Limit user involvement.* Routine information-processing tasks are normally conducted manually in a craft-shop work environment.

Table 9.3
Successful Structural Arrangements

Kind of Information-Processing Task	Illustrative Tasks	Successful Structural Arrangements
Type I. Routine	Traffic-ticket processing	Classical structures
Type II. Nonroutine	Budget control Patrol officer support Detective investigative support Patrol manpower allocation Policy analysis	Participatory structures

Therefore, the efficient automation of routine tasks might necessitate major changes in such standard operating procedures, such as moving toward a production-line work environment. In such a situation, the high involvement of users in design decisions might increase the difficulty of instituting innovations that threaten to change a familiar work environment. The simple emulation of manual operations might not use the potential of the technology and might not achieve the full benefits of automation.

Nonroutine tasks like detective investigation support are characterized by flexible operating procedures, many different and small-volume operations, and frequently changing purposes. The automation of such nonroutine tasks should follow the participatory structural arrangements for the implementation of computing, as follows.

1. *Decentralize computing.* The more direct and personal the involvement of users with the technology, the greater their ability to mold it to their specific and changing needs. Decentralized computer access, such as computer terminals in the users' work area, facilitates direct and personal involvement with the technology. Minicomputer technology creates the potential for many operating departments in large cities to have their own computer installations. Short of such extreme decentralization, the location of computing in an independent computing department—rather than, say, in the finance department— might make a considerable difference for the operating departments within the city.

2. *Involve users in the design of applications.* The more closely that users are involved in the design of nonroutine computer applications, the more likely that the applications will meet their needs, will be understood and accepted by the users, and will be utilized.

3. *Limit the involvement of nonusers in the design of nonroutine applications.* To the degree that nonusers of an application shape its design, the application is less likely to meet the needs of users.

4. *Establish policy boards and other interdepartmental decision-making structures.* When nonroutine tasks involve users from multiple operating departments, as in the cases of budget control and policy analysis, formal structures might be helpful in integrating and meeting the different needs of the diverse users of computer systems.

5. *Do not charge for computer use.* Nonroutine applications require an environment that permits flexible, imaginative, and experimental

uses of computing by a variety of users. The efficiency requirements imposed by strict charging policies are likely to depreciate greatly the value of computing for such nonroutine tasks.

Socio-technical Design

The performance benefits of computing are generally greater in cities that have implemented computing with a sensitivity to the work environment of users. Therefore, cities should adopt a human-relations strategy in the design of information systems, as follows.

1. *Pay attention to the impact of computing on the work environment of users.* The most economical approach to data entry and retrieval might not always be the best approach. For example, on-line access might be more costly, but it might greatly improve the attitudes of personnel toward the use of computing and generally improve the performance of computer operations.

2. *Provide training programs.* Many users' apprehensions are based on a lack of knowledge concerning the way computing will be used and the manner in which it will affect their jobs. Training programs might increase their understanding of these factors and ease the transition to automated operations.

Organizational Context

The performance of computing is generally higher in cities that have implemented computing within a more professional administrative context, especially in the case of nonroutine tasks.[4] Thus, in implementing computer applications, city officials should realize that the success of implementation is likely to be somewhat greater if the organization is oriented toward reformed and professional management practices.

Public Technology

The Automation of Productivity: Management Contingencies

Viewpoints on the role of public technology are often divided into two opposing camps. On the one side stand the administrative reformers and promoters of public technology, who advocate a technological solution to a nearly unlimited checklist of governmental problems.[5] On the other side stand the post-reformers and technology critics, who have pointed out both the limitations and dysfunctional spillovers of many technological "solutions."[6]

Our research indicates that advanced technology does produce benefits, but that their successful achievement is highly contingent on management policy. For example, the benefits and problems of computing vary widely among automated city operations. This variation is highly dependent on the approach different cities have taken toward the implementation of computing applications.

Thus, many debates over the wisdom of advanced technology might be overlooking the real issue of the best approach to managing technology. There are important management contingencies for the successful implementation of any given technological innovation. We have found that computing tends to pay off—to provide the intended benefits—*when properly managed*. And we have been able to prescribe management policies that are likely to improve the performance of computing for a variety of tasks. Of course, not every organization is able to follow our policy recommendations, in that some recommendations might be economically or politically infeasible for a particular city. In fact, most cities will not be able to afford advanced technology and to recruit the sophisticated personnel necessary to support advanced technology. And some highly political organizations cannot develop a more professional administrative context simply for better implementation of computer applications. In such cases, advanced technology is likely to be less warranted, even if the potential impacts of the technology are benign and attractive.

Consequently, in considering the wisdom of automation, managers should carefully weight the likelihood that they will be able to shape the implementation process—afford the technology, create the structures, shape the design, and alter the administrative context. Knowing the most appropriate mix of technology, structure, socio-technical design, and administrative context is an important step, but not sufficient in itself. This mix must be implementable.

The Automation of Bias: Political Contingencies

The debate over the wisdom of advanced technology also concerns the potential political impacts of high technologies like computing. The reformers and promoters of public technology normally overlook the political implications of technologies. The post-reformers and critics have pointed out the potential of new technologies to have dramatic political implications regarding who gains and who benefits as the technology of organizations changes. In the case of computing, it is suggested that development will shift greater control and influence to a growing computer elite—the computing experts. And it is feared that computer technology appears more suited to aiding the control functions of organizations than to aiding their service functions.

This study indicates that computing does have certain political implications. However, the political consequences of advanced technology are neither dramatic nor revolutionary. Computing has a marginal impact on the relative influence of people within an organization. For example, policy and management analysts do gain somewhat more influence over decisions in cities with extensive, and highly sophisticated, computerized applications in support of policy analysis. However, for the most part, computers do not dramatically alter power relationships among the people in organizations, nor do they dramatically alter the missions of organizations. Most often, computers tend to reinforce current power relationships and to improve the performance of existing operations. In doing so, computing is likely to support the status quo of local governments, rather than alter the existing structure of influence, or mission, of local governments.

Organizations are not neutral, however; they are biased toward serving some interests above others. We have found computing to be a highly malleable technology, which can be shaped to serve the interests of those who control the organization (Kraemer and Dutton 1979). Because of this, the social and political ends which computing serves are dependent on the bureaucratic politics of the organization. Computing is not a change agent. Rather, it tends to reinforce the existing biases of organizations. In this respect, the desirability of technological development is contingent on one's assessment of the biases of a particular organization.

Administrative Reform

The Reform of High Technology

Despite the potential value of computing in improving the efficiency and effectiveness of organizations, computing as implemented in

American cities raises several concerns, for computing can be a problem generator as well as a problem solver.

We have seen that computing can be poorly managed and become a problem generator in at least two important respects. First, the benefits of computing often fall short of expectations. That is, the very performance of high technology is a serious problem for local governments, calling for improved management policies. Second, the impacts of computing make it a political resource in the bureaucratic politics of organizations. That is, the adoption and use of high technologies can create a series of political issues and conflicts in the adopting organizations.

The argument of this study has been that the current approach of local governments toward the implementation of computing should be altered in two major respects. First, local governments should change their approach to the management of high technology. In the case of computing, local governments should:

1. Take a more *advanced* approach toward technological development.
2. Gear the *structural arrangements* for the management of computing to the routineness of the information-processing task.
3. Adopt a *human-relations* strategy toward socio-technical design.
4. Create a *professional administrative context* for the implementation of computing operations.

For the most part, local governments have tended to avoid advanced technology and a professional administrative context. The introduction of these management strategies might well improve the performance of computing and other high technologies in local government.

Second, local governments should change their approach to the politics of high technology. In the case of computing, local governments should:

1. Realize that computing will not have dramatic or revolutionary impacts on the operations and decision-making processes of the organization. It will reinforce existing structures.
2. Recognize that computing is a political resource in the bureaucratic politics of organizations. It will affect the interests of people inside and outside the organization.

For the most part, local governments have tended to view computing and policies for its management as either apolitical or politically charged. A better realization of the limited and predictable political nature of high technology might improve the ability of politicians, bureaucrats, technicians, and citizens to deal with the issues raised by technology, and with the policies designed to manage technology.

The Politics of Technological Reform

In conclusion, it is important to be aware of the practical politics that will confront those who attempt technological reform in local government. We have suggested an approach to the implementation of computing that might increase the likelihood of success. Although such an approach might be a technically rational approach to the management of high technology, it might not be a politically feasible approach. People are likely to resist management strategies that are not perceived as being in their interest, that alter the status quo, or that create uncertainty. Because management policies are likely to affect differentially the interests of people within the organization, and because there is likely to be uncertainty about these effects, policy innovations are almost inevitably resisted. Also, to many decision-makers the optimal performance of a technology might be far less important than other organizational goals, such as the degree of personal loyalty or interpersonal harmony within the organization. In such cases, the technically rational approach might not be the best one in light of the overall goals of the organization.

The implications of this study, however, go beyond any single local government and what it might do to improve its own situation. They extend to the prospects for improvement among local governments generally. Broadly, we have found that, when well-managed, computers have payoffs for local governments. "Well-managed" here means using advanced technology in a professional administrative context. However, most cities do not have advanced technology. Moreover, they have little prospect of obtaining it, because the investment required is large and cannot be marshaled in the midst of current tax limitations and inflation. And while most cities have been moving toward a professional administrative context, it is unclear to what extent this progress will continue, in view of current attacks on the professional management movement and in view of the rise of political management (e.g., county mayors). Consequently, it is very likely that most cities will not obtain the benefits from computer automation in the foreseeable future.

This situation presents a real dilemma for officials at all levels of government who are concerned about local-government computerized information systems. Ever since revenue sharing and the new federalism of the 1970s, it has been the federal government's policy to shy away from direct investment in local government computing and information-systems development. Yet, at the same time, the capabilities of local governments to make their own investments have been diminishing. Thus, if local officials cannot increase their investments and federal officials will not, there is little hope for changing the current state of computing and the current low level of benefits from the computer's application in most American local governments.

Notwithstanding these limitations, we have attempted to identify empirically the benefits of computing and prescribe the management policies that are most likely to improve the management of computing in those local governments which marshal the will and the resources required.

NOTES

1. Simon's (1960), Gorry and Morton's (1971), Ackoff's (1967), and Colton's (1978) distinctions between routine and nonroutine applications are a partial description of our findings.

2. Certainly, this is one thrust of President Carter's Civil Service reform proposals at the national level. See Frederick Thayer's (1978) critique of Carter's proposals.

3. Clearly, such technologies as the jet-axe (used by fire fighters to break through doors) are specific to particular functional departments and therefore somewhat less of a concern to central management.

4. An exception to this pattern is patrol manpower allocation.

5. The promotional arguments are represented by: Pendleton (1971), Gibson and Nolan (1974), and Federal Council for Science and Technology (1975).

6. The critics are represented by Argyris (1970a,b), Kling (1978), and Mowshowitz (1977).

REFERENCES

Ackoff, Russell. 1969. "Management Misinformation Systems." *Management Science,* 14(4): B147–57.

Argyris, Chris. 1970a. "Management Information Systems: The Challenge to Rationality and Emotionality." *Management Science,* 17(6): B275–92.

——. 1970b. "Resistance to Rational Management Systems." *Innovation,* 10: 28–35.

Colton, Kent W. 1978. *Police and Computer Technology: Use, Implementation and Impact.* Lexington, Mass.: Lexington Books.

Dutton, William H. and Kenneth L. Kraemer. 1978. "Determinants of Support for Computer-Based Information Systems." *Midwest Review of Public Administration,* 12(1): 19–40.

——. 1979. "Urban Technology, Executive Support and Computing." *Urban Interest,* 1(2): 35–42.

Federal Council for Science and Technology. 1975. *Automation Opportunities in the Service Sector.* Washington, D.C.: National Science Foundation.

Gibson, Cyrus F. and Richard L. Nolan. 1974. "Managing the Four Stages of EDP Growth." *Harvard Business Review,* 52(1): 76–88.

Gory, G. Anthony and Michael S. S. Morton. 1971. "A Framework for Management Information Systems." Sloan School Working Paper 458-70. Cambridge, Mass.: Massachusetts Institute of Technology, Sloan School of Management (mimeographed).

Hoos, Ida R. 1960. "When the Computer Takes Over the Office." *Harvard Business Review,* 38(4): 102–12.

Kling, Rob. 1978. "Automated Welfare Client Tracking and Service Integration: The Political Economy of Computing." *Communications of the ACM,* 21(6): 484–93.

Kraemer, Kenneth L.; James N. Danziger; and William H. Dutton. 1978. "Automated Information Systems and Urban Decision Making." *Urban Systems,* 3(4): 177–90.

Kraemer, Kenneth L. and William H. Dutton. 1979. "The Interests Served by Technological Reform: The Case of Computing." *Administration and Society,* 11(3): 80–106.

Kraemer, Kenneth L. and John Leslie King. 1976. *Computers, Power and Urban Management.* Sage Professional Papers in Administrative and Policy Studies, Vol. 3. Beverly Hills, Calif.: Sage Publications.

Leavitt, H. J. and T. L. Whisler. 1958. "Management in the 1980's." *Harvard Business Review,* 36(6): 41–48.

Laudon, Kenneth C. 1974. *Computers and Bureaucratic Reform.* New York: Wiley.

Mowshowitz, Abbe. 1977. "Computers and the Mechanization of Judgment." Technical Report 77-3, Department of Computer Science, University of British Columbia, Vancouver, B.C., Canada.

Pendleton, J. C. 1971. "Integrated Information Systems." *AFIPS Conferences Proceedings, 1971 Fall Joint Computer Conference*, Vol. 39, pp. 491–500. Montvale, N.J.: AFIPS Press.

Simon, Herbert A. 1965. *The Shape of Automation.* New York: Harper and Row.

Thayer, Frederick C. 1978. "The President's Management Reforms: Theory X Triumphant." *Public Administration Review*, 38(4): 309–14.

Appendix

Appendix Contents

Appendix

DEBORA DUNKLE, WILLIAM H. DUTTON,
KENNETH L. KRAEMER, AND
ALANA NORTHROP

I. Technology Variables

A. Common Variables

1. Sophistication of Installation

This index measures the degree of computer-installation sophistication in terms of hardware, software, and personnel capabilities. The index score is a factor score derived from a general factor analysis using communalities in the diagonal (SPSS: PA2). Separate factor analyses were performed for each department or agency (police, finance, traffic, and central management). In each case, a single factor solution using the criteria of a minimum eigenvalue -1.00 resulted. Given the large proportion of cities with single installations, the factor solutions are similar for the various departments. However, slight differences occurred, since some cities had multiple computing installations servicing different departments, and some cities were not automated across all departments considered. The results of the four factor analyses are shown in Table A.1. Below are descriptions of the various indicators of installation sophistication used in the factor analysis.

a. *Staff-sophistication index.* The staff sophistication of a given installation is measured by summing the number of persons on that staff who perform the following types of sophisticated analyses: teleprocessing, simulations, statistical analyses involving correlation and more advanced statistics, use of a database management language, geo-coded data, such as Dual Independent Map and Encoding (DIME) files, and computer graphics.

Table A.1
Level-of-Sophistication Factor Loadings

	Traffic	Police	Budget	MOC
Staff sophistication	.86	.88	.86	.88
Installation's total core	.70	.72	.68	.76
Sophistication of installation's mainframe and operating system	.83	.79	.79	.82
Total number of applications operational	.86	.79	.88	.86
Total number of on-line applications	.84	.82	.83	.82
Level of application development	.70	.67	.65	.70
Technique sophistication of staff	.70	.68	.67	.81
Level of database management	.80	.63	.73	.73
Level of data linkage	.65	.52	.68	.66
Percentage of variance explained	64	58	62	66

b. *Installation's total core.* This index represents the total storage capacity, measured in kilobytes, of core of all computers within the given installation. The higher the index value, the more core available within the installation.

c. *Sophistication of installation's mainframe hardware and operating system.* For each machine in an installation, both the mainframe computer and its operating system were assigned a value for level of sophistication. Values range from a low of 1 to a high of 5. The index is the sum of these two values for each machine/operating-system combination within the installation. The higher the index value, the more sophisticated the installation's machine/operating system.

d. *Total number of applications operational.* This index is the total number of operational applications within a given installation. The more applications, the higher the index value.

e. *Total number of on-line applications.* This index is the total number of applications within a given installation that are on-line. The more applications, the higher the index value.

f. *Level of application development.* Each application in the installation was classified as one of six "application types": record-keeping, record searching, record restructuring, process control, calculating/printing, or sophisticated analysis (Table 2.4). The Level of Application Development Index measures the breadth of application types; how many different *kinds* of applications there are in a given installation. The higher the index level, the more different application types within the installation.

g. *Technique sophistication of staff.* This index measures the extent to which sophisticated techniques are used by a given installation. Sophisticated techniques include: teleprocessing, simulations, statistical analyses involving correlation and more advanced statistics, use of a database management language, geo-coded data, such as DIME files, and computer graphics. The more technically sophisticated an installation, i.e., the more different types of sophisticated techniques that are used, the higher the index value.

h. *Level of database management.* This index indicates whether or not the installation has a database management system (DBMS), the values being 1 and 0, respectively.

i. *Level of data linkage.* This index is a measure of the level of data-linkage capabilities in a particular location. Two linkages were considered: (1) the capability of linking data coded on the basis of one geographic base, such as address, to other geographic bases, such as census tract or land parcel; and (2) the capability of using a standard identifier, such as social security numbers, for linking files on individuals in the community. The "easier" it is for the installation to link different databases together, the higher the index value.

2. Utilization of Computing

This index is a measure of the frequency with which personnel within the specific departments (i.e., police, budget, and traffic) use computing on the job. These variables are based on responses to a mailed-back questionnaire distributed to personnel within each city department. The respondents were asked to indicate the frequency with which, in doing their jobs, they (1) keypunch, code, or enter data on a computerized file; (2) personally use a computer terminal to get information from a computerized file; (3) request others (by phone, radio, or in person) to get information from a computerized file; and (4) receive reports that are based on computer data. The frequency of use for each of these activities was scored as: never; at least once a year; several times a year; a few times a month; a few times a week; and daily. The utilization of computing index is the highest mean level of frequency for at least one of the four activities within each department. Hence a score of 1 (rarely or never) was assigned when the highest average response of the personnel in the specific department was for "several times a year or less"; a score of 2 (monthly user) was assigned when the highest average response was "a few times a month" for at least one activity; a score of 3 (weekly user) was assigned if the highest average response was a few times a week for at least one activity; and a score of 4 (daily user) was assigned when the highest average response was "daily" for at least one of the four activities. A single utilization score was computed for each department investigated by aggregating the responses of the relevant personnel returning the questionnaire. In terms of traffic, the traffic clerks' responses were aggregated; for detectives, the detectives' responses were aggregated; for patrol officers, the patrol officers' responses were aggregated; and for patrol manpower allocation, the manpower-allocation staff analysts' responses were aggregated.

3. Degree of Technological Instability

This index measures the degree to which technological changes have occurred in the particular computer installation over the past year. Technological changes include: a change of major equipment vendors (switching from one to another); a change in generation of machine; a major change in priorities among systems that are in development; and a major change in kinds or level of programming language available (such as moving from RPG1 to RPG2). The more changes experienced by the installation over the past year, the higher the index value.

B. Traffic-Ticket-Processing Socio-technical Variables

1. Number of Automated Operations

This index is a count of the operations automated in the traffic ticket processing agency. The operations included were: (1) maintaining records of all citations; (2) searching records to answer inquiries from citizens; (3) searching for previous citations of person or vehicle; (4) determining, calculating proper bail and fines; (5) printing of delinquent notice(s); (6) printing arrest warrants; and (7) other operations not previously mentioned. The index is a count of the number of operations that are automated for parking, traffic, or both parking and traffic. The more operations that are automated, the higher the index value. Data used in this index were obtained from interviews with the director of the traffic division.

2. Number of Automated Parking Operations

This index is a subset of the Number of Automated Operations Index. The index consists of the number of operations automated for parking only. The higher the index value, the more automated parking operations there were.   •

3. Number of Automated Moving Operations

This index is a subset of the Number of Automated Operations Index. The index consists of the number of operations automated for moving (traffic) only. The higher the index value, the more automated moving (traffic) operations there were.

4. Number of Automated Applications

This index is a sum of the automated applications useful for traffic that are operational at the local computer installation. The applications include the following: a parking-ticket file, a traffic-accident file, and a traffic-violations file. The higher the index value, the more applications available at the computer installation. This information was obtained from interviews with the data-processing manager of the city computer installation providing service for the traffic-ticket processing agency.

5. Percentage of Computer-Generated Statistical Reports

This index is a count of the computer-generated statistical reports available from traffic-ticket operations. The type of statistical reports included were: (1) total number of traffic tickets; (2) total number of parking tickets; (3) proportion of traffic tickets paid; (4) proportion of parking tickets paid; (5) total revenue of traffic tickets issued or paid; (6) total revenue of parking tickets issued or paid; (7) traffic tickets by type of offense; (8) traffic tickets by location of offense; (9) traffic tickets by time of day; (10) traffic ticket cross-tabulations by type of offense, location, or time of day; (11) traffic tickets by issuing officer; (12) parking tickets by issuing officer; (13) summaries on delinquent tickets of individuals; and (14) other, not listed above. The more EDP reports generated, the higher the index value. Data for this index were obtained from interviews with a statistician in the traffic division.

6. Degree of Terminal Queries

This index measures the degree to which traffic personnel query computer files directly at a terminal. The scores range from 0, no queries; 1, some queries; 2, most queries; to 3, all queries. The higher the index value, the more computer terminal queries there were. This information was obtained from interviews with the supervisor and/or head of the traffic division.

7. Number of Applications On-Line at City Level

This index is a count of the number of automated applications useful for traffic that are on-line at the local computer installation. The applications included were: a parking-ticket file, a traffic-accident file, and a traffic-violations file. The higher the index value, the more on-line applications are available at the computer installation. This information was obtained from interviews with the data-processing manager of the city computer installation providing service for the traffic-ticket processing agency.

8. First Year of Automation

This variable is the year in which the first application useful for traffic processing became operational at the computer installation. The applications considered were: parking-ticket file, traffic-accident file, and traffic-violations file. The longer ago (in years) that the first application became operational, i.e., the more "routinized" traffic automation is, the lower the value of the variable. The data for this variable were obtained from interviews with the manager of the computer installation.

9. Ticket-Processing Errors Scale

This scale measures the number of traffic and parking ticket processing errors discovered by citizens within the past month. The measure is the second factor score derived from a general factor analysis (SPSS:PA2) with varimax rotation. The indicators include the number of moving and parking citations paid, and the number of errors in parking and moving violations processing. The results of the

Table A.2
Factor Loadings for Increased Payment Scale and Ticket
Processing Errors Scale

Items	Increased Payment Scale	Ticket-Processing Errors	h^2
EDP affected number of moving citations paid	.88	.15	.79
EDP affected number of parking citations paid	.71	.23	.55
Number of parking-violation processing errors	.14	.84	.72
Number of moving-violation processing errors	.22	.66	.49
Percentage of variance explained	55	26	

factor analysis are presented in Table A.2. The more processing errors discovered, the higher the scale value. The number of processing errors was obtained from the supervisor or head of each traffic-ticket processing agency.

C. Detective and Patrol Technology Variables

1. Amount of Automated Criminal Information

This index is a count of the number of kinds of computer-based information to which detectives (investigators) have access. The kinds of files include: field-interrogation reports, known offenders, intelligence compilations, person or crimes committed with particular MO, persons passing bad checks, check forgery, bad credit cards or other "worthless" documents, criminal history of individual, index to photograph of individual, fingerprints of individual, owner of stolen vehicle, stolen motor vehicles, owner of registered firearm, owner of stolen property, pawn file, persons pawning property, and traffic and parking violations files. No distinction is made as to whether these files are automated locally or nonlocally. The higher the index value, the more automated criminal information that is available. This information was obtained from interviews with an EDP specialist in the police department.

Table A.3
Centrality-of-Computing Factor Loadings

Items	Clearance	Case Load	Centrality	h^2
How many of your last 10 cleared cases would probably not have been cleared without the use of computer-based information?	.81	−.09	.03	.66
Consider the last 5 people in custody which you had a role in linking to uncleared cases. For how many of these 5 did the use of computerized information assist in making this link?	.73	.04	.40	.70
How many of your last 10 actively investigated cases would have been "unworkable" without the use of computer files?	.70	.15	.12	.53
Of your last 10 arrests how many probably would not have been made without the use of computerized information?	.53	.09	.05	.30
How many cases assigned to you did you actively investigate over the past month?	−.02	.95	−.01	.91
In the last month, how many cases did you clear?	.15	.93	.15	.91
About how many cases were assigned to you over the past month?	.04	.80	.20	.67
For how many of your last 10 cleared cases (either by arrest or investigation of people in custody) did the use of computerized information assist in the clearance?	.60	−.05	.73	.90
For how many of your last 10 arrests did the use of computerized information assist in the arrest?	.54	−.01	.71	.79
For how many of your last 10 actively investigated cases were computer files used in the investigation?	.47	.23	.65	.70
In the last month, how many arrests were you credited with?	.06	.11	.37	.16
For how many of your last 10 actively investigated cases were manual files (excluding the initial crime report) used in the investigation?	.08	−.02	−.13	.02
Percentage of variance explained	38	21	10	

2. Degree of Local Automation

This index is a count of the number of automated applications that are available at the local computer installation for use by detectives (investigators). The applications include: field-interrogation-report file, intelligence compilations, MO (criminal patterns file), known-offenders file, criminal-offense file, criminal-history file, arrest records, fingerprint file, alias-name file, UCR file, other crime-reporting systems, wants/warrants file, stolen-vehicles file, stolen-property file. The higher the index value, the more local automation exists. This information was obtained from interviews with the data-processing manager of the installation that provides service for the police.

3. Degree of Local Patrol Automation

This index is a count of the number of automated applications useful for patrol officers that are available at the local computer installation. The applications include: wants/warrants file, stolen-vehicles file, and stolen-property file. The higher the index value, the more local automation is available. This information was obtained from interviews with the data-processing manager of the installation that provides service for the police.

4. Centrality of Computing

This scale measures the degree to which computerized information has been useful and successful for detective investigation. The measure is a factor score from a general factor analysis (SPSS:PA2) using varimax rotation. Indicators of detective investigative support were used, and the "centrality of computing" scale is derived from the third factor shown in Table A.3. The list of indicators can be found in Table A.3. High scores on this scale are assigned to cities in which detectives use computing for a larger proportion of their cases, i.e., in cities where computing is more central to investigative activities of the department. The indicators were obtained from the self-administered questionnaire completed by detectives within each city.

5. Year of Detective Automation

This variable is the year in which the first application useful for detective investigation became operational at the computer installation. It is assumed that the longer (in years) the first application has been operational, the more "routinized" the detective automation is. The lower the value of the variable, the more routinized the application. The data for this variable were obtained from interviews with the data-processing manager of the computer installation.

6. Stage of Redesign

This variable measures the degree to which computer applications have been redesigned. Specifically, it is the proportion (1, none; 2, few; 3, about half; 4, most; 5, nearly all) of police applications that have gone through two or more revisions or reconceptualizations. The more applications redesigned, the higher the index value. This information was obtained from interviews with an EDP specialist in the police department.

7. Year of Patrol Automation

This variable is the year in which the first application useful for police patrol became operational at the computer installation. The applications included wants/warrants file, stolen-vehicles file, and stolen-property file. The longer (in years) since the first application became operational, i.e., the more "routinized" police patrol automation is thought to be, the lower the value of the variable. The data for this variable were obtained from interviews with the data-processing manager of the computer installation.

8. Errors

This scale measures the degree to which errors have resulted from the use of computerized information. The measure is a factor score from a general factor analysis (SPSS:PA2) using varimax rotation. Indicators of patrol officer support were used, and the "errors" scale is derived from the second factor shown in Table A.4. The indicators are listed in the table. High scores on this scale indicate that the patrol officers in the department believe that a relatively high number of patrol errors resulted from the use of computer-based information on wants and warrants and stolen vehicles. The information for these indicators was obtained from the self-administered questionnaire completed by patrol officers within each city.

Table A.4
Patrol-Errors Factor Loadings

Items	Patrol Hits	Patrol Errors	h^2
For how many of the last 20 persons on whom you have requested a search of wants and warrants did you discover an outstanding want or warrant?	.97	−.02	.95
For how many of the last 20 persons stopped by you for traffic violations (or other violations, suspicious behavior) did you request a search of outstanding wants and warrants?	.67	.04	.45
For how many of the last 20 stopped or inspected vehicles did you request a search of a stolen vehicles file?	.45	.14	.22
How many times during the last year has the use of computerized police files led you to arrest a person who should not have been arrested?	.01	.81	.66
How many times during the last month have you been dispatched to an incorrect location (for whatever reason)?	.06	.50	.26
How many times during the last year has the use of computerized files led you to detain a person who should not have been detained?	.24	.50	.31
To your knowledge, has incorrect or incomplete information on a computerized police file ever led you to release or not detain a person who should have been kept in custody or detained?	.33	.18	.14
Percentage of variance explained	34	22	

D. Patrol Manpower-Allocation Technology Variables

1. Number of Automated Applications

This index is the number of computer applications useful for patrol manpower allocation. The applications include: dispatching, LEMRAS, other manpower-allocation systems, and service data (type of call, location, time, response, etc.). As the index increases, the number of applications operational at the computer installation increases. Information for this index was obtained from interviews with the data-processing manager at the computer installation that provides service for patrol manpower allocation.

2. Specialized Computer Package

This single-item variable indicates whether the police department uses a computer program package to assist in patrol manpower allocation. It is scored as 0, no program used, and 1, a computer package program is used. This information was obtained from interviews with the supervisor and/or analyst(s) involved in allocation (deployment) policies.

3. Number of On-Line Applications

This index is the number of computer applications currently on-line that are particularly useful for manpower allocation. The on-line applications include: dispatching, LEMRAS, other manpower-allocation systems, and service data (type of call, location, time, response, etc.). As the index increases, the number of applications on-line at the computer installation increases. This information was obtained from interviews with the data-processing manager of the computer installation that provides service for patrol manpower allocation.

4. Variety of Automated Data

This index is a count of the kinds of automated information utilized by the department to determine police patrol allocation. The kinds of automated data included were: number of calls, response time, type of call, crime rate, traffic accidents and/or violations, clearance and/or arrest rate, property loss, crime projections, total population, population density, street miles, and other physical or social data. The more types of automated information that are used for patrol allocation, the higher the index value. Information for this index was obtained from interviews with the supervisor and/or analyst(s) involved in operationalizing allocation (deployment) policies.

5. Data Sophistication

This index measures the degree of sophistication of data used for patrol allocation. Staff members involved in operationalizing allocation (deployment) policies were asked (1) at what level the data are aggregated that are used to assist in patrol manpower allocation—entire city, district, precinct, patrols within precinct, or subdivisions of patrol areas, such as blocks; (2) whether the police service data and crime or traffic-incident data used are available by patrol shifts; (3) whether the police service data and/or crime or traffic-incident data used are available by time of day. A high score on this index indicates that the data used are aggregated to subdivision of patrol areas or blocks and are available by patrol shifts and by time of day.

6. Frequency of Allocation Analyses

This index measures the frequency with which the department analyzes service, crime, incident or arrest data to evaluate current allocation of patrols. The categories used are: 1, never in last 5 years; 2, one to two times in last 5 years; 3, almost yearly; 4, twice a year; 5, four times per year; and 6, monthly. The more frequently the department analyzes the data, the higher the index value. Information for this variable was obtained from interviews with the supervisor and analyst(s) involved in allocation policies.

7. Use of Computing for Policy Legitimation

This variable is the extent to which computing is used to provide legitimacy or support for desired or needed changes in allocation to other police or city officials. This measure was obtained from responses to an open-ended question about what the staff like most about the use of computers to aid in police manpower allocation. A high score on this measure indicates that at least two staff members spontaneously mentioned legitimacy as one of the factors they liked most about the use of computers; a low score indicates that legitimacy of decisions was not mentioned.

E. Budget-Control Technology Variables

1. Number of Finance Automated Applications

This variable is the number of computer applications currently operational that are particularly useful to budget reporting and budget monitoring. The applications include: general accounting, expenditure forecasting, revenue forecasting, budget preparation, program budget preparation, and program structure related to line-item budget monitoring. As the index increases, the number of applications operational at the computer installation increases. Information for this index was obtained from interviews with the data-processing manager at the computer installation that provides service for budget control activities.

2. Number of Batch Finance Applications

This index is a subset of the Number of Finance Automated Applications Index; it is a count of the number of applications that are in batch-mode. As the index increases, the number of applications that are batch-oriented at the computer installation increases.

3. Number of On-Line Finance Applications

This index is a subset of the Number of Finance Automated Applications Index; it is a count of the number of applications that are on-line. As the index increases, the number of applications that are on-line at the computer installation increases.

4. On-Line Applications Predominating in Finance Automation

This variable is a summary measure of whether the majority of finance applications are operational in batch-mode (score of 0) or on-line (score of 1). Hence, a score of 1 indicates that the finance applications are predominantly on-line.

5. Number of On-Line Terminals in Finance

This index is a count of the number of terminals, both CRT-type terminals and hard-copy (typewriter) terminals, that are in the finance department. The information for this variable was obtained from interviews with the data-processing manager at the computer installation.

6. Recency of Finance Automation

This variable is the year in which the first application (defined by the Number of Finance Applications Index) became operational at the computer installation. The longer (in years) since the first application became operational—that is, the more "routinized" finance auto-mation is—the lower the value of the variable. The data for this variable were obtained from interviews with the data-processing manager of the computer installation.

F. Policy-Analysis Technology Variables

1. Number of Operational Applications

This index is the total number of operational applications within the installation that provides the majority of service for policy analysis. The more applications there are, the higher the index value. Information for this index was obtained from interviews with the data-processing manager at the computer installation.

2. Number of Automated Databanks

This index is a count of the number of automated databanks located within the city. "Databanks" are defined as those in which (1) environmental data are contained; (2) the data are aggregated for analysis yielding statistical descriptions; (3) the data are intended for and/or receive multiple uses; (4) the data are only updated periodically (several months or longer); and (5) the data may be merged from several files. The more automated databanks the city has, the higher the index value. Information for this index was obtained from interviews with the data-processing manager of the computer installation; additional information came from databank custodians within the city.

3. Sophistication of Databank Reports

This index measures the level of sophistication of the analyses contained in reports to government officials. The index fulfills the requirements for a Guttman scale (C.R. = .90) with the following ordering of the kinds of analysis represented from "easiest" to "hardest": (1) marginal, or frequency tables; (2) maps; (3) bar graphs, histograms, frequency polygons; (4) geo-based analysis by fixed geographic area, e.g., census tract, district; (5) bivariate correlations or cross-tabulations; (6) multivariate correlation, regression, factor analysis, cluster analysis; and (7) geo-based analyses involving changing geographic areas (data clearly aggregated at multiple levels of analysis). A high score on this index indicates that the reports contain sophisticated analyses. This information was obtained from inspection of a sample of reports that were sent to government officials. The investigator indicated whether or not these types of analyses were present in the reports.

4. Management-Use Index

This index is a count of the number of management uses of computer-based reports and analyses. Management uses of computer-based reports and analyses include the following activities: (1) completing forms for federal or state reporting requirements; (2) grant proposals—preparing applications for federal or state financial assistance; and (3) improving ability to monitor and control department and agency operations. Questions regarding the first two uses were asked of managers, mayors, councils, and planners; and the third, of managers, mayors, and councils. The score is the sum of the number of uses of computer-based reports or analyses made by the manager, mayor, council, and planners in each city. The higher the index value, the more management use within the city.

5. Political-Use Index

This index is a count of the number of political uses of computer-based reports and analyses. Political uses include the following activities: (1) political assessment—to determine the extent to which plans and recommendations reflect a proper mix of interests involved—race, age, ethnic, neighborhood; (2) buffering constituents or interests—to show people with complaints how data support the decisions; (3) legitimation of problems already perceived to exist; (4) gaining publicity for particular programs or policies; (5) determining whether features of a given policy or decision will be politically acceptable; (6) providing documentation for policy recommendations or decisions; and (7) responding to individual or citizen-group requests or complaints. Questions on the first five uses were asked of managers (chief administrative officer), mayors, councils, and planners, and the last two of manager, mayor, and council. The score is the sum of the number of uses of computer-based reports or analyses made by the manager, mayor, council, and planners in each city. The higher the index value, the more that computing is politically oriented within the city.

6. Planning-Use Index

This index is a count of the number of planning uses of computer-based reports and analyses. Planning uses include the following: (1) needs assessment—determining what group of citizens or area is in need of various programs; (2) advance planning—planning for social services, transportation, land use, and housing; and (3) problem finding—leading to new or clearer perception of community problems. Questions on all three uses were asked of managers, mayors, councils, and planners. The score is the sum of the number of uses of computer-based reports or analyses made by the manager, mayor, council, and planners of each city. The higher the index value, the more computing is planning-oriented within the city.

7. Management-Oriented Computing

This index is a summary measure of the Management-Use Index, the Political-Use Index and the Planning-Use Index. Each index was dichotomized at the median into 0, low, and 1, high. The index is the mean score over the three separate indices. Hence, it represents the degree to which computer-based reports and analyses are used for decision-making by government officials. The higher the index value, the more that computing is used for various types of decision-making.

8. Number of Regular Operating Reports

This index is the total number of regular computer-based information—listings, exception reports, forecasts, regular reports, and so forth—that the chief appointed official (manager), the mayor, and/or council receive. The higher the index value, the more computer-based information that is regularly generated and sent to government officials. This information was obtained from interviews with the data-processing manager of the computer installation.

9. Number of Databank Reports

The index is the total number of basic reports, such as community or neighborhood profiles, that have been generated. The more reports generated, the higher the index value. This information was obtained from interviews with the custodians of the two databanks that have generated the most interest, most reports, or most special requests/ analyses within the city.

10. First Year of Automation

This variable is the year in which the first application became operational at the computer installation. The longer (in years) since the first application became operational—that is, the more "routinized" automation is in the city—the lower the value of the variable. The data for this variable were obtained from interviews with the data-processing manager of the computer installation.

II. Structure Variables

A. Common Variables

1. Installation User Involvement

This index measures the degree to which users of the relevant computer installation are involved in EDP decision-making within the installation. Data-processing managers in the installations within the city were asked to rate the frequency—1, never; 2, for less than half of the applications; 3, for more than half of the applications; or 4, for almost all applications—with which the users of the data-processing unit performed the following tasks: (a) performed systematic analysis of benefits and costs anticipated from a proposed computer application; (b) performed systematic analysis of benefits and costs derived from implemented computer applications; (c) worked as a member of a technical group in designing an application; (d) reviewed designs for a new application; (e) did the programming necessary for an application; (f) provided test data for an application; (g) formally evaluated applications they used; (h) signed-off, accepting an application; (i) participated in assigning priority to data-processing projects; and (j) initiated major changes of EDP applications, such as changing the flow of information, the input or output, and so on. The index is the average frequency with which users of the unit performed the set of tasks above. The more user involvement in installation decisions, the higher the value of the index.

2. Elected Officials' Control of Data-Processing-Related Decisions

This index indicates the degree of control over data-processing decisions that elected officials exert at the particular installation; the higher the index value, the more influence a particular group possesses. Data-processing managers were asked whether the local legislative body and mayor were influential or involved in the following installation-level decisions: (1) deciding whether or not a new set of computer applications will be adopted; (2) setting priorities for the development of new applications; (3) approving budget requests for major computer-equipment purchases; (4) approving requests for new peripheral equipment in user departments; (5) evaluating the services provided by the installation; and (6) approving major reorganizations, such as changing the departmental status or location of EDP or consolidating several independent EDP units. The index is the total number of the above decisions in which elected officials are involved.

3. Chief Administrative Official's Control of Data-Processing-Related Decisions

This index indicates how much control over data-processing decisions the chief appointed official exerts at the particular installation; the higher the index value, the more influence the official possesses. Data-processing managers were asked whether the chief appointed official was influential in decisions on the same six topics as in the preceding index. This index is the total number of the above six decisions in which the chief appointed official is involved.

4. User-Department-Heads' Control of Data-Processing-Related Decisions

This index indicates how much control the user department heads exert over data-processing decisions at the particular installation; the higher the index value, the more influence they possess. Data-processing managers were asked whether user department heads were influential in the same six decisions as in the preceding two indices. This index is the total number of the six decisions in which user department heads are involved.

5. Charging

This variable measures the basis on which the specific departments or agencies are charged by the installation for using computer time and memory. The kinds of charging are: 1, free; 2, flat fee; or 3, charged for actual amount of use. In cases of multiple installations within the city, the code chosen for the index value was the code for the installation in the city that actually services the specific department or agency. Note that within a specific installation, charging practices may vary for different departments or agencies. A high score indicates that the department or agency is charged for actual usage.

6. Degree of Interdepartmental Data Sharing

This variable measures the degree to which data in the particular installation are shared by two or more departments or agencies within the government that the installation services. The score values are: 1, no agencies, 2, a few agencies; 3, some agencies; and 4, many agencies. The higher the degree of sharing, the higher the value of the variable. Information for this variable was obtained from interviews with DP managers of the installations within the city.

7. Structural Instability

This index measures the degree to which there have been structural changes in the computer installation over the past year. Structural changes include: a change in top EDP management, a change in the physical location of the installation, a change in the departmental location or status within the city government, and a change in relationship between computer installations, such as consolidation or division of EDP installations or the establishment of new installations. The more changes experienced by the installation, the higher the index value. Information for this index was obtained from interviews with the DP managers of the installations within the city.

B. Traffic-Ticket-Processing Structural Variables

1. User Involvement in Design

This index measures the traffic agency's degree of participation in the design of computer applications to support traffic-ticket processing. Four department-level groups are considered: department top managers, computer specialist(s) in the department, middle management (supervisors in traffic division), and clerical personnel in the traffic division. Each group was given a score of: 0, no role in design; 1, consulted, not formally on design team; or 2, formally on design team. User involvement in design is the sum of these scores. The more involvement there was by all user groups within the traffic division, the higher the index value. Information for this index was obtained from interviews with the supervisor or head of the traffic division.

2. Multiple Computing Sources

This variable indicates whether the city has a single installation servicing all departments and agencies (score of 0) or has multiple installations servicing different departments and agencies (score of 1). A score of 1 is indicative of decentralization.

C. Detective and Patrol Investigative-Support Structural Variables

1. User Involvement in Design

This index measures the police department's degree of participation in the design of computer applications to support detective investigations. Four department-level groups are considered: department top managers (chief, commissioner), computer specialist(s) in the police department, middle management in police (captains, lieutenants), and detectives. Each group was assigned a score of: 0, no role in design; 1, consulted, not formally on design team; or 2, formally on design team. User involvement in design is the sum of these scores. The more involvement there was by all user groups within the department, the higher the index value. Information for this index was obtained from interviews with computer specialist(s), supervisors, and administrators within the police department.

2. Police Installation

This variable indicates whether the city has a computer installation specifically dedicated to police applications (score of 1) or does not (score of 0). A score of 1 is indicative of decentralization.

3. Decentralized Personal Computing

This variable measures the degree to which detectives personally key in queries at terminals at the normal work area, rather than relying on requests submitted to data-processing personnel within or outside the work area. The variable scores are: 0, no queries; 1, some queries; 2, most queries; and 3, all queries. The more decentralized the computing is, the higher the index value. The information for this variable was obtained from interviews with detectives in the department.

4. Multiple Sources of Computing

This index measures the degree to which automated applications (Amount of Automated Criminal Information Index) are available both locally and nonlocally. The higher the index value, the more applications that are available from multiple sources. This information was obtained from interviews with EDP specialist(s) within the police department.

5. Skilled Operator Available

This index measures the degree—0, none; 1, yes, on irregular basis, not always when needed; 2, yes, on a regular basis—to which detectives having access to terminals also have access to a skilled terminal operator to assist them and perform queries for them. The higher the value, the more frequently a skilled operator is available. The information for this variable was obtained from interviews with detectives in the department.

6. Technical Training Provided

This variable measures the degree to which the training of detectives in computer use is conducted by a person with experience as a detective. The possible scores are: 0, there is no training in computer use; 1, person(s) has no prior detective experience; 2, person(s) conducting training has related police-work experience, but not as a detective; 3, person(s) conducting training has prior detective experience. The higher the score, the more likely that technical training is done by a person(s) with police experience. This information was obtained from interviews with two lieutenants (supervisors) in each police department.

D. Patrol Manpower-Allocation Socio-technical Variables

1. User Involement in Adoption

This index measures the police department's degree of participation in past decisions on whether or not to adopt computer applications to support patrol officer allocation. Four department-level groups are considered: department top managers (chief, commissioners), computer specialist(s) in the department, middle management (captains, lieutenants), and patrol officers. Each group was assigned a score of: 0, no participation; 1, minor participant; or 2, major participant. User involvement in adoption is the sum of these scores. The more involvement there was by all user groups within the department, the higher the index value. This information was obtained from interviews with the supervisor and staff analysts involved in allocation policies within the police department.

2. User Involvement in Design

This index measures the police department's degree of participation in the design of computer applications to support patrol allocation. Four department-level groups are considered: department top managers (chiefs, commissioners) computer specialist(s) in the department, middle management (captains, lieutenants), and patrol officers. Each group was assigned a score of: 0, no role in design; 1, consulted but not formally on design team; or 2, formally on design team. User involvement in design is the sum of these scores. The more involvement there was by all user groups within the department, the higher the index value. This information was obtained from interviews with the supervisor and staff analysts involved in allocation policies within the police department.

3. Middle Management Involvement in Design

This variable measures the degree to which captains and lieutenants (middle management) participated in designing computer applications to support patrol officer allocation. It is scored in the same way as the preceding variable. This information was obtained from interviews with the supervisor and staff analysts involved in allocation policies within the police department.

4. Police Computer-Specialists Involvement in Design

This variable measures the degree to which police computer specialists participated in designing computer applications to support patrol officer allocation. It is scored in the same way as the two preceding variables. This information was obtained from interviews with the supervisor and staff analysts involved in allocation policies within the police department.

5. Police Installation

This variable indicates whether the city has a computer installation specifically dedicated to police applications (score of 1) or does not (score of 0). A score of 1 is indicative of decentralization.

6. Decentralized Peripherals

This index is a count of the number of terminals, both CRT terminals and remote time-sharing typewriter terminals located in the police department. The higher the index value, the greater the number of terminals within the department—that is, the greater the decentralization. This information was obtained from interviews with the manager of the computer installation that provides service to the police.

E. Budget-Control Structural Variables

1. User Involvement in Design of Budget-Reporting Applications

This index measures the degree to which groups within the department in charge of preparing the current-balance report participated in the design of computer applications for budget reporting. Three department-level groups are considered: department top managers in the budget reporting unit, computer specialist(s) in the department, and middle management in the budget-reporting unit. Each group was assigned a score of: 0, no role in design; 1, consulted, not formally on design team; or 2, formally on design team. The more involvement there was by all user groups within the department, the higher the index value. This information was obtained from interviews with the head or assistant head of the unit or department in charge of preparing the current-balance report.

2. User Involvement in Design of Budget-Monitoring Applications

This index measures the degree to which groups within the department in charge of budget monitoring participated in the design of computer applications for budget monitoring. Three department-level groups are considered: department top managers in the budget-monitoring unit, computer specialist(s) in the department, and middle management in the budget-monitoring unit. Each group was scored in the same way as for the preceding variable. The more involvement there was by all user groups within the department, the higher the index value. This information was obtained from interviews with the head or assistant head of the unit or department in charge of budget monitoring.

3. Non-Finance-Department–Located Installation

This index measures the degree to which computing is centralized (distant) from the finance department. Each city was classified in terms of the location of the computer installation vis-à-vis the finance department (located within or outside the department) and whether on-line terminals were provided by the computer installation. Finance departments were assigned scores according to whether the computer facility is located (1) within the department, with on-line terminals in the department; (2) within the department, providing only batch computing; (3) outside the department, with on-line terminals in the department; or (4) outside the department, providing only batch computing. The higher the scale value, the more centralized the computer facility is vis-à-vis the finance department. Information for this index was obtained from interviews with the data-processing manager of the computer installation.

F. Policy-Analysis Structural Variables

1. Manager's Involvement in Design

This index measures the degree of influence the chief administrative official and staff have in determining what special analyses and kinds of reports will be generated from databanks. The investigator rated the manager's influence—1, no influence; 2, minor influence; or 3, major influence—on the basis of interviews with the databank custodian(s) of the two databanks that have generated the most interest, most reports, or most special requests/analyses. The higher the index value, the more influence the chief administrative official and staff have.

2. Mayor's Involvement in Design

This index is the same as the Manager's Involvement in Design Index, but measures the chief elected official and staff influence.

3. Council's Involvement in Design

This index is the same as the Manager's Involvement in Design Index, but measures the council and staff influence.

4. Departmental Involvement in Design

This index is the same as the Manager's Involvement in Design Index, but measures the department head and staff influence.

5. Analyst Involvement in Design

This index is the same as the Manager's Involvement in Design Index, but measures the databank custodians' influence.

6. Analyst Involvement in Interpretation

This index measures the degree to which analysts (databank custodians) provide interpretations of the findings of specific analysis requests. The index is a five-point measure ranging from 1, respond to letter of requests, with little or no interpretation, act as a service bureau; to 5, respond with interpretation of findings. The higher the index value, the more interpretation provided by the analyst. This information was obtained from interviews with the custodians of the two databanks that have generated the most interest, most reports, or most special requests/analyses.

7. Single Independent Installation

This measure indicates whether the organizational arrangement of the computer installation is that of an independent data-processing department under the chief executive (score of 1) or is some other type of organizational arrangement (score of 0). A score of 1 is indicative of centralization. Information for this variable was obtained from interviews with the data-processing manager of the computer installation.

8. Decentralization of Control over Databanks

This index measures the degree to which databanks are dispersed (decentralized) within the local government. Specifically, the index is a count of the total number of different agencies within the local government that maintain databanks. The higher the value of the index, the more decentralized control there is over databanks. The information was obtained from interviews with the data-processing manager and city department heads.

III. Socio-technical Design

A. Common Variables

Similar measures of socio-technical design were developed for each information-processing task. Because the major concern was to measure staff perceptions of the work environment, the indices were constructed from responses to the self-administered questionnaires distributed to personnel within each department, division, or agency in which interviews were conducted. Specifically, for chapter 4, the responses of traffic clerks were used; for chapter 5, the responses of detectives and of patrol officers were used; for chapter 6, the responses of manpower-allocation staff analysts were used; for chapter 7, the responses of central-budget-unit staff analysts and accountants were used for the central-unit indices, and department administrative assistants and accountants within the planning and public-works departments were used for the department indices; for chapter 8, the responses of top elected and appointed officials and their staffs were used. Five measures were developed from these responses and then factor analyzed. Although similar measures were used, the factor configurations differed among role types; hence, each solution is described separately. Given that there were multiple respondents from each department and agency in each of the 42 cities, a single city score for each role type was obtained by aggregating the responses by city by relevant role to a mean score. For example, the responses of all detectives who returned the self-administered questionnaire in Baltimore were averaged to obtain a Baltimore detective response. All indices were computed from these aggregated mean scores. Descriptions of the indicators follow.

1. Support for Computing Scale

This scale measures the degree of generalized support for computers and technology in the local government job context. Three statements about computers were used for this scale; the items are listed in Table A.5 along with reliability coefficients. The response values for each item were: 0, disagree; 33, somewhat disagree; 66, somewhat agree; and 100, agree. The average city-level scores range from 0 to 100, and the scale value is the average response over the three items. Therefore, the more support there is for computing, the higher the score.

Table A.5
Reliability Coefficients and Item-Total Correlations for Support-for-Computing Scale and Negative Views of Data-Processors Scale

	Traffic Clerks	Detectives	Patrol Officers	Manpower Analysts	Central Budget Users	Department Budget Users	Top Official Users
Support for computing scale	.89[a]	.81	.83	.61	.75	.80	.74
"I want to use computers and data processing more in doing my job."	.60[b]	.51	.62	.28	.56	.51	.48
"Within the next five years, computers will greatly improve the way my job is done."	.65	.81	.70	.59	.68	.71	.66
"Within the next five years, computers will greatly improve the operations of this government."	.78	.74	.76	.47	.62	.76	.59
Negative views toward data-processors scale	.82	.67	.85	.61	.81	.81	.75
"Data processing personnel are more intrigued with what the computer can do than with solving the problems of my department."	.60	.46	.74	.36	.64	.72	.65
"Data processing staff confuse our conversations with their technical language."	.65	.58	.72	.47	.65	.56	.53
"Data processing staff are more interested in working with new computer uses rather than making improvements in ones we now use."	.78	.45	.74	.43	.71	.70	.56

[a]Reliability coefficient used in Cronbach's alpha.
[b]The item-total correlations are calculated by correlating the specific item with the total score of the remaining items in the scale.

2. Negative Views toward Data-Processors Scale

This scale measures the degree to which the respondents perceive data-processing personnel as insensitive to user task-related problems and requests. Three statements about data-processing personnel were used for this scale. The items are listed in Table A.5 along with reliability coefficients. The response values for each item are identical to the preceding index. The average city-level scores range from 0 to 100. The scale value is the average response over the three items. The more negative the views toward data processors, the higher the score.

3. Increased Job Pressure from Computing

This single-item variable measures the degree to which the respondent perceives computing as having increased time pressures in the job. The exact wording of the item is: "Has computing increased or decreased time pressures in your job?" The response values are: 0, decreased; 50, not affected; and 100, increased. The average city-level score ranges from 0 to 100. The higher the score, the more time pressures in the job due to computing.

4. Increased Sense of Accomplishment

This single-item variable measures the degree to which computing has created a sense of accomplishment within the work situation. The wording of the item is: "Has computing raised or lowered your sense of accomplishment in your work?" The response values are identical to the preceding index. The average city-level scores range from 0 to 100, with a higher score indicative of a raised sense of accomplishment.

5. Increased Job Variety

This single-item variable measures the degree to which the respondent perceives computing as having increased job variety. The wording of the item is: "Has computing increased or decreased the number of different things you do in your job?" The response values are identical to the preceding two indices. The aggregated city-level scores range from 0 to 100, with a higher score indicative of increased job variety.

Table A.8
Patrol Officers Socio-technical-Design Factor Loadings

Items	Job Pressure	Support for Computing	h²
Increased job pressure	.67	−.40	.60
Negative views toward data processors	.54	.17	.32
Increased sense of accomplishment	−.59	.20	.39
Support for computing	−.45	.81	.85
Increased job variety	−.01	−.07	.00
Percentage of variance explained	43	21	

3. Support for Computing Scale (Patrol Officer)

This scale measures the degree to which patrol officers strongly support computer technology in their job. The score is a factor score based on the second factor of a general factor analysis (SPSS: PA2) of a set of socio-technical-design variables using a varimax rotation solution. The factor loadings are shown in Table A.8. Descriptions of the variables used in the factor analysis are discussed in Section III.A. A high score on this scale represents a supportive attitude toward computing.

D. Patrol Manpower-Analysts Socio-technical Design Variables

1. Job-Enrichment Scale

This scale measures the degree to which manpower analysts tend to perceive computing as creating a sense of accomplishment accompanied by positive attitudes toward data processors. The score is a factor score derived from the first factor of a general factor analysis (SPSS: PA2) of a set of socio-technical-design variables using a varimax rotation solution. The factor loadings are shown in Table A.9. The descriptions of the variables used in the factor analysis are discussed in Section III.A. Manpower-allocation divisions within the police department with high scores perceive computing as beneficial to their work environment.

2. Job-Pressure Scale

This scale measures the degree to which computing is perceived to have increased both the number of things to do on the job and the time pressures within the work environment. The score is a factor score derived from the second factor of a general factor analysis (SPSS: PA2) of a set of socio-technical-design variables using a varimax rotation solution. The factor loadings are displayed in Table A.9. The descriptions of the variables used in the factor analysis are discussed in Section III.A. The higher the score, the more that computing is perceived to have increased job pressure.

3. District-Level Complaints

This scale measures the degree to which district commanders and supervisors complain about the number of patrol officers allocated to their areas. The principal investigators, after interviewing supervisory and staff analysts involved in allocation policies, assigned one of the following scores to each city: 1, none complain; 2, very few complain; 3, some complain; 4, many complain; 5, nearly all complain. The higher the score, the more widespread are complaints within the city (see Table 6.16).

E. Budget Socio-technical Design Variables

1. Job-Pressure Scale (Central Level)

This scale measures the degree to which central staff perceive computing as providing negative impacts on their work situation through increased job pressure and job variety. The score is a factor score based on the first factor of a general factor analysis (SPSS: PA2) of a set of socio-technical-design variables using a varimax rotation solution. The factor loadings are displayed in Table A.10. Descriptions

Table A.9
Patrol Manpower-Analysts Socio-technical-Design Factor Loadings

Items	Job Enrichment	Job Pressure	h^2
Increased sense of accomplishment	.71	.29	.59
Support for computing	.45	−.05	.20
Negative views toward data processors	−.84	−.03	.70
Increased job variety	.13	.99	.99
Increased job pressure	.00	.54	.29
Percentage of variance explained	41	29	

Table A.10
Central-Unit-Level-Budget-Users Socio-technical-Design
Factor Loadings

Items	Job Pressure	Job Satisfaction	h^2
Increased job pressure	.98	−.17	.99
Negative views toward data processors	.57	−.28	.40
Increased job variety	.56	.08	.32
Increased sense of accomplishment	−.05	.79	.63
Support for computing	−.09	.65	.44
Percentage of variance explained	43	28	

of the variables used in the factor analysis are discussed in Section III.A. The higher the score, the greater the job pressure perceived by central-budget-unit staff.

2. Job-Satisfaction Scale (Central Level)

This scale measures the degree to which central-budget staff perceive computing to have increased a sense of accomplishment in budget-control activities. The score is a factor score derived from the second factor of a general factor analysis (SPSS: PA2) of a set of socio-technical-design variables using a varimax rotation solution. The factor loadings are shown in Table A.10 and the descriptions of the variables used in the factor analysis are discussed in Section III.A. Cities scoring high on this scale have central-level staff who perceive computing as increasing their job satisfaction.

3. Job Pressure Scale (Department Level)

This scale measures the degree to which department-level staff perceive computing as providing negative impacts within the work situation through increased job pressure and job variety. The score is a factor score based on the first factor of a general factor analysis (SPSS: PA2) of a set of socio-technical-design variables using a varimax rotation solution. The factor loadings are displayed in Table A.11. Descriptions of the variables used in the factor analysis are discussed in Section III.A. The higher the city score, the more that job pressure is perceived by department-level staff.

4. Job-Satisfaction Scale (Department Level)

This scale measures the degree to which department-level users support computing and feel a higher sense of accomplishment in their work due to computing. The score is a factor score derived from the second factor of a general factor analysis (SPSS: PA2) of a set of socio-technical-design variables using a varimax rotation for the final solution. The factor loadings are displayed in Table A.11, and the descriptions of the variables used in the factor analysis are discussed in Section III.A. Cities scoring high on this scale are those where department-level staff have expressed job satisfaction due to computing.

F. Policy-Analysis Socio-technical Design Variables

1. Support for Computing Scale

This scale measures the degree to which chief elected and appointed officials and their staffs support computing in the local government context. The reader is referred to Section III.A.1, where this scale is described.

2. Technocratic DP Staff Scale

This scale measures the degree to which chief elected and appointed officials and their staffs perceive data processors as insensitive to the needs and requests of local government officials. The reader is referred to Section III.A.2 (the Negative Views toward Data-Processors Scale), where this scale is described.

Table A.11
Department-Level-Budget-Users Socio-technical-Design Factor Loadings

Items	Job Pressure	Job Satisfaction	h^2
Increased job variety	.94	.06	.89
Increased job pressure	.67	−.37	.58
Support for computing	−.07	.62	.38
Increased sense of accomplishment	.00	.50	.25
Negative views toward data processors	.24	−.55	.36
Percentage of variance explained	41	26	

IV. Environment

A. Common Variables

1. Total Population, 1975

The estimated population figure was obtained from the United States Census Bureau, *Current Population Reports: Population Estimates and Projections—Series P-25.*

2. Population Growth, 1970–1975

The data were obtained from the United States Census Bureau, *Current Population Reports: Population Estimates and Projections— Series P-25.* The percentage change was calculated from the difference in 1975 population less the 1970 population divided by the 1970 population. The higher the value of the index, the larger the population in the city in 1975 relative to its size in 1970.

3. Council-Manager Form

A city was given a score of 1 if the form of government was council-manager, and a score of 0 for any other form of government.

4. Slack Financial Resources

This index measures the degree to which there are slack budget resources within a given city. Slack resources include: (1) whether the city taxing levels have moderate to substantial expandability; (2) whether over the past three years the growth in revenues in the city is near to or above the rate of inflation; and (3) whether, after accounting for inflation, most categories of expenditure have increased in real spending per year by at least 1 percent over the past three years. A city was given a score of 33 for each indicator of slack resources that it demonstrated. The index is the sum of the three indicators, with scores ranging from 0 to 99. Information for this index was obtained from interviews with the head of the governmental unit responsible for budget monitoring. A high value indicates that the city has a large amount of slack resources; a low value indicates few slack resources.

5. Partisan Government

This index measures the degree to which political parties are influential in local politics. Three measures were combined: the extent of influence of the Democratic party in community politics (scored as:

1, not influential; 2, somewhat influential; 3, quite influential; and 4, extremely influential); the extent of influence of the Republican party in community politics (scored the same way); and the degree to which, on major local issues, Republican and Democratic officials form opposing groups (scored as: 1, never; 2, seldom; 3, occasionally; 4, most of the time). The information for these measures was obtained from interviews with the elected officials and/or mayors of the city. The higher the index value, the greater the partisan influence and activity within the community.

6. Professional Management-Practices Index

This index measures the degree to which the city has instituted professional management practices within the city government. Professional management practices include: (1) whether the departments and agencies have established written objectives for the programs and services they provide; (2) whether there are measures of performance in meeting the objectives of city programs; and (3) whether cost-accounting procedures have been implemented for estimating costs of major programs and activities. A score of 100 was given if in most of the departments and agencies a given practice was instituted, and a score of 50 if at least half of the departments and agencies instituted these practices. The index is the sum of the scores on each of the three indicators. City scores range from 0 to 300. Information for this index was obtained from interviews with elected officials or the managers and their staffs. The more professional the city bureaucracy, the higher the value of the index.

B. Traffic-Ticket-Processing Environment Variables

1. Number of Statistical Reports

This index is a count of the statistical reports generated either through computing or manually and available from traffic-ticket operations. The statistical reports included were: (1) total number of traffic tickets; (2) total number of parking tickets; (3) proportion of traffic tickets paid; (4) proportion of parking tickets paid; (5) total revenue of traffic tickets issued or paid; (6) total revenue of parking tickets issued or paid; (7) traffic tickets by type of offense; (8) traffic tickets by location of offense; (9) traffic tickets by time of day; (11) traffic tickets by issuing officer; (12) parking tickets by issuing officer; (13) summaries on delinquent tickets of individuals; and (14) other, not listed above. The more reports generated, the higher the index value. Data for this index were obtained from interviews with the statistician in the traffic division.

C. Detective, Patrol, Investigative-Support and Patrol Manpower-Allocation Environment Variables

1. Reported Crimes per 1,000 Population

This index is the ratio of the total number of reported Type I crimes to the size of the city population. The number of Type I crimes for 1975 was obtained from the Federal Bureau of Investigation. Size of the city is the estimated 1975 population obtained from the United States Census Bureau. As the index increases, the number of crimes reported per 1,000 population increases.

2. Officers per Crime

This index is the ratio of the total number of actual (rather than authorized) sworn officers in the police department for 1975 to the number of Type I crimes reported in 1975. The number of sworn officers was obtained from interviews within the records division of the police department; the number of reported Type I crimes in 1975 from the Federal Bureau of Investigation. As the index increases, the number of sworn officers per crime increases.

3. Number of Patrol Cars on Duty

This variable is the average number of patrol cars on duty over 24 hours for the entire city. This information was obtained from interviews with personnel in the dispatch unit of the police department. As the index increases, the number of patrol cars increases.

4. Centralized Allocation Decisions

This variable measures the extent to which the central-administration allocation decisions affect the way district commanders and supervisors allocate personnel within their operational command. Each city is scored as one of the following: 1, central allocation just sets general rules and distributes personnel among districts, whereas district commanders make specific day-to-day allocations; 2, central allocation sets specific allocation guidelines, but district commanders have full authority to alter them; 3, central allocation sets specific allocation guidelines, which district commanders rarely alter, and only in specific circumstances. This information was obtained from interviews with the Director of Field Operations and staff involved with allocation policies. The higher the score, the more centralized are allocation decisions.

V. Performance

A. Traffic-Ticket-Processing Performance Variables

1. Traffic-Ticket-Processing Performance Index

This index is a summary measure of traffic-ticket-processing performance. The following indicators were included: percentage of parking violations tickets paid, percentage of moving violations tickets paid, number of clerical personnel per 100,000 tickets issued, EDP cost savings, EDP staff savings, increased payment of tickets scale, and new services. Each of these indicators was standardized to a mean of 0 and a standard deviation of 1, and an average score over all seven indicators was computed for each city. The indicators are described below.

a. *Percentage of Parking Violations Tickets Paid.* Each traffic-ticket-processing agency provided the number of parking violations tickets issued and the number paid for the 1975 reporting year.

b. *Percentage of Moving Violations Tickets Paid.* The traffic ticket agency provided the number of moving violations tickets issued and the number paid for the 1975 reporting year.

c. *Number of Clerical Personnel per 100,000 Tickets Issued.* Each traffic-ticket-processing agency was asked to provide the total number of actual (rather than authorized) full-time clerical personnel in the traffic division (including data-entry clerks and keypunchers) for the 1975 reporting year. The number of tickets issued includes both moving and parking violations for the 1975 reporting year. This information also was obtained from the specific agency.

d. *New Services.* The supervisor and/or head of the agency was asked whether the use of computers and automated files in the department has led to any new services to citizens. The response categories are; 1, no; 2, yes.

e. *EDP Cost Savings.* Cost savings due to computers were assessed by the investigators during interviews with the supervisor and/or head of the traffic-ticket-processing agency. Specifically, they were asked whether "allowing for inflation and salary increases, has the use of computers and automated citations files in this department altered costs relative to work load?" The investigator assigned a score based on whether the agency personnel provided evidence that it increased costs (score of 1) or decreased costs (score of 5); or was based on an overall judgment without evidence of an increase (score of 2) or decrease (score of 4); or there had been no effect on costs (score of 3) due to automation. The higher the value of this variable, the greater the cost savings realized by the traffic processing agency.

f. EDP Staff Savings. Staff savings due to computers were assessed by the investigator during interviews with the supervisor and/or head of the traffic-ticket-processing agency. Specifically, they were asked, "When you consider the total staff involved in your operation, has the use of computer and automated citation files in this department altered the size of your staff relative to your working load?" The investigator assigned a score based on whether the agency personnel provided evidence that it increased staff (score of 1) or decreased staff (score of 5); or was based on an overall judgement without evidence of an increase (score of 2) or decrease (score of 4) of staff; or there had been no effect (score of 3) on staff due to automation. The higher the value of the variable, the greater the staff reduction realized by the traffic-ticket-processing agency.

g. Increased-Payment Scale. This scale measures the extent to which EDP has increased the number of moving and parking citations paid. The measure is a factor score derived from the first factor of a general factor analysis with varimax rotation (SPSS: PA2). The indicators used were the number of moving and parking citations paid and the number of parking- and moving-violations processing errors. The results of the factor analysis are presented in Table A.12. The EDP effects on moving and parking citations paid were assessed by the investigators during interviews with the supervisors and/or heads of the traffic-ticket-processing agency. The investigator rated whether the agency personnel provided evidence that it decreased (score of 1) or increased (score of 5) the number of fines paid; or was based on an overall judgment without evidence of increase (score of 4) or decrease (score of 2); or there had been no effect (score of 3) due to automation. Thus, each agency was assigned a score from 1 to 5 for moving and for parking citations paid.

Table A.12
Automated Traffic-Ticket Processing-Effectiveness
Factor Loadings

Items	Increased Payment	Increased Errors	h²
EDP effects on moving violations paid	.88	.15	.79
EDP effects on parking violations paid	.71	.23	.55
EDP effects on parking violations processing errors	.14	.84	.72
EDP effects on moving violations processing errors	.22	.66	.48
Percentage of variance explained	55	26	

B. Detective and Patrol Investigative-Support Performance Variables

1. Detective Investigation Performance Index

This index is a summary measure of detective investigation performance. The following indicators of performance were included: improved performance, clearance rate, computer-assisted clearances, and case load. Each of these indices was standardized to a mean of 0 and a standard deviation of 1, and an average score over all four indicators was computed for each city. The indicators are described below.

a. Clearance Rate. This index measures the degree of success in crime clearance. It is a factor score derived from a general factor analysis (SPSS: PA2) of three measures of clearances: (1) percentage of stolen property recovered in 1975 (source: interviews with staff within the records division); (2) total Type I crime-clearance rate for 1975 (source: FBI); and (3) percentage of improvement in clearances for all Type I crimes from 1971 to 1975 (source: FBI). A single-factor solution using the criterion of an eigenvalue greater than 1.00 resulted. The results of the factor analysis are shown in Table A.13. The higher the index value, the higher the crime-clearance rate within the city.

b. Improved-Performance Scale. This index measures the degree to which computing and computerized files have improved the performance of detectives. It is a factor score derived from a general factor analysis (SPSS: PA2) of four indicators of detective performance: (1) more workable cases; (2) more cleared cases; (3) improved quality of court cases; and (4) multiple case load. A single-factor solution using the criterion of an eigenvalue exceeding 1.00 resulted. These four

Table A.13
Clearance-Rate Factor Loadings

Items	Clearance Rate	h²
Percent improvement in clearance of Type I crimes from 1971–75	.64	.55
Total Type I crime-clearance rate, 1975	.46	.29
Percent stolen property recovered, 1975	.29	.08
Percentage of variance explained	47	

performance measures were developed from the responses by detectives and supervisors within the detective division to a series of questions. The wording of the questions is shown in Table A.14, along with the results of the factor analysis. After interviews with several detectives and the supervisor, the investigators rated the cities on improved performance for each item. The scores and their meaning are the following: 1, no detectives believe that computing improves performance; 2, few detectives believe it does; 3, most detectives believe it does; 4, all detectives believe it does. Hence, the higher the score, the more that computers and computerized files have improved the performance of detectives for these activities.

c. Computer-Assisted Clearances. This index is a measure of the degree to which automation has assisted detective investigative activities. It is a factor score derived from the first factor of a general factor analysis with varimax rotation (SPSS: PA2) of a selection of detective-investigative-suppport items. The data were obtained from the responses to a series of items on the self-administered questionnaire completed by detectives within each city. The multiple responses per city were averaged to obtain a city-level score; it is the average score that is used in the factor analysis. The selected items are shown in Table A.15, along with the results of the factor analysis. The higher the index value, the higher the proportion of cases in which computing allowed more cases to be worked and cleared within the detective unit.

d. Case Load. This index measures the number of cases assigned and cleared by detectives during the past month. It is a factor score derived from the second factor of a general factor analysis (SPSS: PA2) with varimax rotation of a selection of detective-investigative-support items. The data were obtained from the responses to a series of items on the self-administered questionnaire completed by detectives within each city. The multiple responses per city were averaged to obtain a city-level score; it is the average score that is used in the factor analysis. The selected items are shown in Table A.15, along with the results of the factor analysis. The higher the index value, the more cases that detectives worked on during the past month.

2. Patrol Performance Index

This index is a measure of the degree to which patrol officers have been successful in apprehensions while on patrol. The index is a factor score derived from the first factor of a general factor analysis (SPSS: PA2) with varimax rotation. The selected indicators were obtained from the responses to a series of items on the self-administered questionnaire completed by patrol officers within each city. The items are displayed in Table A.16, along with the results of the factor analysis. The multiple responses per city were averaged to obtain a city-level score; it is the average score that is used in the factor analysis. The factor scores were converted to z-scores in order to preserve comparability with the other performance measures.

C. Patrol Manpower-Allocation Performance Variables

1. Automated-Patrol-Allocation Performance Index

This index is a summary measure of patrol-allocation performance. The following indicators of performance were included in the index:

Table A.14
Improved-Performance Factor Loadings

Items	Improved Performance	h^2
Has the use of computers and automated police files by detectives led to more workable cases?	.84	.70
Has the use of computers and automated files by detectives led to more cleared cases?	.77	.59
Does the use of computers and automated police files improve the quality of court cases?	.66	.43
Does the use of computerized files allow detectives to work adequately on more cases than they otherwise would be able to work?	.60	.36
Percentage of variance explained	64	

Table A.15
Detective-Performance Factor Loadings

Items	Clearance	Case Load	Centrality	h^2
How many of your last 10 cleared cases would probably not have been cleared without the use of computer-based information	.81	−.09	.03	.66
Consider the last 5 people in custody which you had a role in linking to uncleared cases. For how many of these 5 did the use of computerized information assist in making this link?	.73	.04	.40	.70
How many of your last 10 actively investigated cases would have been "unworkable" without the use of computer files?	.70	.15	.12	.53
Of your last 10 arrests how many probably would not have been made without the use of computerized information?	.53	.09	.05	.30
How many cases assigned to you did you actively investigate over the past month?	−.02	.95	−.01	.91
In the last month, how many cases did you clear?	.15	.93	.15	.91
About how many cases were assigned to you over the past month?	.04	.80	.20	.67
For how many of your last 10 cleared cases (either by arrest or investigation of people in custody) did the use of computerized information assist in the clearance?	.60	−.05	.73	.90
For how many of your last 10 arrests did the use of computerized information assist in the arrest?	.54	−.01	.71	.79
For how many of your last 10 actively investigated cases were computer files used in the investigation?	.47	.23	.65	.70
In the last month, how many arrests were you credited with?	.06	.11	.37	.16
For how many of your last 10 actively investigated cases were manual files (excluding the initial crime report) used in the investigation?	.08	−.02	−.13	.02
Percentage of variance explained	38	21	10	

Table A.16
Patrol-Officer-Performance Factor Loadings

Items	Patrol Hits	Patrol Errors	h^2
For how many of the last 20 persons on whom you have requested a search of wants and warrants did you discover an outstanding want or warrant?	.97	−.02	.95
For how many of the last 20 persons stopped by you for traffic violations (or other violations, suspicious behavior) did you request a search of outstanding wants and warrants?	.67	.04	.45
For how many of the last 20 stopped or inspected vehicles did you request a search of a stolen-vehicles file?	.45	.14	.22
How many times during the last year has the use of computerized police files led you to arrest a person who should not have been arrested?	.01	.81	.66
How many times during the last month have you been dispatched to an incorrect location (for whatever reason)?	.06	.50	.26
How many times during the last year has the use of computerized files led you to detain a person who should not have been detained?	.24	.50	.31
To your knowledge, has incorrect or incomplete information on a computerized police file ever led you to release or not detain a person who should have been kept in custody or detained?	.33	.18	.14
Percentage of variance explained	34	22	

improved performance, time to arrival, and clearance rate. Each of these indices was standardized to a mean of 0 and a standard deviation of 1, and an average score over all three indicators was computed for each city. The indicators are described below.

a. Improved Performance. This variable measures the degree to which the use of computers to aid police manpower allocation has led to any improvements in performance, such as lessening response times or increasing arrest rates. After interviews with the director of field operations and staff members involved with allocation policies, the study investigators rated the city on improved performance. A score of 1 was assigned if there had been no improvement, a score of 2 if there had been improvement, but it was based on vague, impressionistic evidence, and a score of 3 if there was improvement in performance and this assessment was backed by specific evidence concerning these improvements. A high score, therefore, is associated with improved performance to the use of computers.

b. Time to Arrival. This index measures the response time from the dispatch of highest- and second-highest-priority calls for police service to the arrival of the police at the scene. The score is a factor score derived from the third factor of a principal factor analysis (SPSS: PA2) with varimax rotation of three factors. The set of items that was factor analyzed included average response times (call to dispatch and dispatch to arrival) and average delay of calls for first- and second-priority calls. The response times were obtained from the dispatch unit within the police department. The results of the factor analysis are shown in Table A.17. This index was reversed in the computations of the Automated-Patrol-Allocation Performance Index.

c. Clearance Rate. This index is a measure of the degree of success in crime clearance. It is a factor score derived from a general factor analysis (SPSS: PA2) of three measures of clearances: (1) percentage of

Table A.17
Dispatching-Performance Factor Loadings

	Response	Delay	Dispatch	h^2
Seconds from incoming call to dispatch for second-priority calls	.97	.03	.12	.96
Seconds from incoming call to dispatch for first-priority calls	.82	−.05	−.09	.69
Average number of first-priority calls per day delayed	.16	.97	−.04	.97
Average number of second-priority calls per day delayed	−.16	.51	.19	.33
Minutes from dispatch to arrival for first-priority calls	.02	.08	.85	.74
Minutes from dispatch to arrival for second-priority calls	−.01	.54	.51	.55
Percentage of variance explained	35	31	17	

stolen property recovered in 1975 (source: interviews with staff within the records division of the police department); (2) total Type I crime-clearance rate for 1975 (source: FBI); and (3) percentage of improvement in clearances for all Type I crimes from 1971 to 1975 (source: FBI). A single factor solution using the criterion of the eigenvalue greater than 1.00 resulted. The results of the factor analysis are shown in Table A.15. The higher the index value, the higher the crime-clearance rate within the city.

D. Budget-Control Performance Variables

1. Central-Budget-Unit Performance Index

This index is a summary measure of central-budget-unit performance. The following indicators of performance were included in the index: information benefits from computing; enhanced financial control; exception-reporting capability; department overspending; and department-controlled spending. Each of these indices was standardized to a mean of 0 and a standard deviation of 1, and an average score over all five indicators was computed for each city. The indicators are discussed below.

a. *Information Benefits from Computing Index.* This index measures the degree to which automation is perceived as having resulted in more timely and better information. The index is the average response to three items on the self-administered questionnaire completed by accountants and staff analysts in the central budget unit(s). The set of items is listed in Table A.18, along the measures of reliability. The response categories are: 0, almost never true; 33, sometimes true; 67, frequently true; 100, nearly always true. The multiple responses per city were averaged to obtain a city-level score; it is the average score that is used in computing the index. The higher the score, the more information benefits from computing that are perceived.

b. *Enhanced Financial Control.* This variable measures the degree to which computers have been helpful in enhancing financial control over particular departments, sections, accounts, or programs. The values of the variable are: 1, not helpful; 2, somewhat helpful; 3, very helpful. Investigators assigned a city score based on interviews with the head or assistant head of the unit or department responsible for budget monitoring. The higher the value, the more helpful that computers have been in enhancing financial control.

Table A.18
Reliability Coefficients and Item-Total Correlations for
Information-Benefits-from-Computing Index

	Central Level	Departmental Level
Information benefits from computing index	.82[a]	.87
The computer makes new information available to me which was not previously available	.45[b]	.68
The computer provides me with more up-to-date information than that available in manual files	.82	.78
Computers have made it easier for me to get the information I need.	.85	.83

[a] Reliability coefficient used in Cronbach's alpha.
[b] The item-total correlations are calculated by correlating the specific item with the total score of the remaining items in the scale.

c. Exception-Reporting Capability. This variable measures the degree to which computers have been helpful in providing more accurate information about uneven expenditure patterns throughout the fiscal year. The values of the variable again are: 1, not helpful; 2, somewhat helpful; 3, very helpful. Investigators assigned a city score based on interviews with the head or assistant head of the unit or department responsible for budget monitoring. The higher the value, the more helpful that computers have been in providing information about uneven expenditure patterns.

d. Department Overspending. This variable is the percentage of monitored city departments that have spent at least 5 percent more than was appropriated for them last year. The information was obtained from interviews with the head or assistant head of the unit or department responsible for budget monitoring. Specifically, the information provided was the number of departments that are monitored and the number that spent at least 5 percent more than had been appropriated. The higher the index value, the more that department overspending occurred within the city. This item was reversed in calculating the Central-Budget-Performance Index.

e. Department-Controlled Spending. This variable is the percentage of monitored city department that spent at least 95 percent but less than 105 percent of their appropriated budget for the past year. The information was obtained from interviews with the head or assistant head of the unit or department responsible for budget monitoring.

Specifically, the information provided was the number of departments that are monitored, the number that spent at least 5 percent more than appropriated, and the number of departments that spent less than 95 percent of what was appropriated for them last year. The higher the index value, the higher the percentage of controlled spending in departments within the city.

2. Department-Budget Performance Index

This index is a summary measure of department budget performance (specifically, in the public works and planning department). The following indicators of performance were included in the index: information benefits from computing, enhanced financial control, exception-reporting capability, department overspending, and department underspending. Each of these indicators was standardized to a mean of 0 and a standard deviation of 1, and an average score over all five indicators was computed for each city. The indicators are described below.

a. *Information-Benefits-from-Computing Index.* This index measures the degree to which automation is perceived as having resulted in more timely and better information. The index is the average response to three items on the self-administered questionnaire completed by accountants and administrative assistants in the departments of public works and planning. The set of items is listed in Table A.18, along with measures of reliability. The response categories are: 0, almost never true; 33, sometimes true; 67, frequently true; 100, nearly always true. The multiple responses per city were averaged to obtain a city-level score; it is the average score that is used in computing the total performance index. The higher the score, the more information benefits from computing that are perceived.

b. *Enhanced Financial Control.* This variable measures the degree to which computers have been helpful in enhancing financial control over particular sections or accounts or programs within the department. The values of the variable are: 1, not helpful; 2, somewhat helpful; 3, very helpful. Investigators assigned a city score based on interviews with staff in charge of budget monitoring for the planning and public works departments. These responses were aggregated to obtain a "department-level" score. The higher the value, the more helpful computers have been in enhancing financial control.

c. Exception-Reporting Capability. This variable measures the degree to which computers have been helpful in providing more accurate information about uneven expenditure patterns throughout the fiscal year. The values of the variable are: 1, not helpful; 2, somewhat helpful; 3, very helpful. Investigators assigned a city score based on interviews with staff in charge of budget monitoring for the planning and the public works departments. These responses were aggregated to obtain a "department-level" score. The higher the value, the more helpful computers have been in providing information about uneven expenditure patterns.

d. Department Underspending. This variable measures the percentage of the budget accounts in the department that were at least 10 percent under allocation. Investigators interviewed staff in charge of budget monitoring for the planning and the public works departments. Specifically, they were asked: "Last year, relative to allocations, what percent of the budget accounts in your department were at least 10 percent under allocation?" Responses were then aggregated to obtain a "department-level" score. The higher the value, the higher the percentage of department underspending.

e. Department Overspending. This variable measures the percentage of the budget accounts in the department that were at least 10 percent over allocation. Investigators interviewed staff in charge of budget monitoring for the planning and the public works departments. Specifically, they were asked: "Last year, relative to allocations, what percent of the budget accounts in your department were at least 10 percent over allocation?" Responses were then aggregated to obtain a "department-level" score. The higher the value, the higher the percentage of department overspending.

E. Policy-Analysis Performance Variables

1. Policy-Analysis Performance Index

This index is a summary measure of the degree to which automated databanks have affected the decisions of city officials. The following indicators were used: impacts on management decisions, impacts on elected officials' decisions, and impacts on planners' decisions. Each of these was standardized to a mean of 0 and a standard deviation of 1, and an average score over the three indicators was computed for each city. The indicators are discussed below.

a. Management-Decisions Impacts. This index measures the degree to which computer-based reports and analyses have altered the decisions of chief appointed officials. Three impact questions were asked of two persons in the chief appointed official's office who were knowledgeable about the use of databanks. First, "Have these reports and analyses provided such surprising or persuasive results that they altered previous decisions or policy?" The scoring was: 0, no; 1, yes, but vague or no cases cited; 2, yes, but in exceptional cases, or yes, generally. Second, "Have these reports and analyses ever led to programmatic recommendations? Have some of these recommendations been accepted and implemented?" The scoring was: 0, never led to recommendations; 1, yes, but none have been accepted; 2, yes, and some have been accepted. Third, "Has the use of this computer-based information changed or clearly affected decisions made by the chief appointed official?" The scoring was: 0, no; 1, yes, but no specific examples; 2, yes, and specific examples cited. These three scores were summed to produce a single measure of management-decisions impacts. The higher the city score, the more effect that computer-related information has had on management decision-making.

b. Elected-Officials'-Decisions Impacts. This index measures the degree to which computer-based reports and analyses have altered elected officials' decisions. Three impact questions were asked of two persons in the mayor's office who were knowledgeable about the use of databanks and two persons in the council's office who were knowledgeable about the use of databanks. First, "Have these reports and analyses provided such surprising or persuasive results that they altered previous decisions or policy?" The scores were: 0, no; 1, yes, but vague or no cases cited; 2, yes, but in exceptional cases, or yes, generally. Second, "Have these reports and analyses ever led to programmatic recommendations? Have some of these recommendations been accepted and implemented?" The scores were: 0, never led to recommendations; 1, yes, and some have been accepted. Third, "Has the use of this computer-based information changed or clearly affected decisions made by the mayor (council)?" The scores were: 0, no; 1, yes, but no specific examples; 2, yes, and specific examples cited. These three scores were summed to produce a single measure of impacts on elected officials' decisions. The higher the city score, the more effect that computer-related information has had on elected officials' decision-making.

c. Planners'-Decisions Impacts. This index measures the degree to which computer-based reports and analyses have altered planners' decisions. Two impact questions were asked of two persons in the planning department who were knowledgeable about the use of databanks. First, "Have these reports and analyses provided such surprising or persuasive results that they altered previous decisions or policy?" The scoring was; 0, no; 1, yes, but vague or no cases cited; 2, yes, but in exceptional cases, or yes, generally. Second, "Have these reports and analyses ever led to programmatic recommendations? Have some of these recommendations been accepted and implemented?" The scores were: 0, never led to recommendations; 1, yes, but none have been accepted; 2, yes, and some have been accepted. These two scores were summed to produce a single measure of planners' decision impacts. The higher the city score, the more effect computer-related information has had on planner decision-making.

Index